ENTANGLED PERFORMANCE HISTORIES

Entangled Performance Histories is the first book-length study that applies the concept of "entangled histories" as a new paradigm in the field of theater and performance historiography.

"Entangled histories" denotes the interconnectedness of multiple histories that cannot be addressed within national frameworks. The concept refers to interconnected pasts, in which historical processes of contact and exchange between performance cultures affected all involved. Presenting case studies from across the world—spanning Africa, the Arab-speaking world, Asia, the Americas and Europe—the book's contributors systematically expand, exemplify and examine the concept of "entangled histories," thus introducing various innovative concepts, theories and methodologies for investigating reciprocally consequential processes of interweaving performance cultures from the past. Bringing together examples of entanglements in theater and performance histories from a broad variety of geographical and historical backgrounds, the book's contributions build together a broad basis for a possible and necessary paradigmatic shift in the field of theater and performance historiography.

Ideal for researchers and students of history, theater, performance, drama and dance, this volume opens novel perspectives on the possibilities and challenges of investigating the entangled histories of theater and performance cultures on a global scale.

Erika Fischer-Lichte is Director of the International Research Center "Interweaving Performance Cultures" at Freie Universität Berlin.

Małgorzata Sugiera is a Full-time Professor at the Jagiellonian University in Cracow, Poland, and Head of the Department for Performativity Studies.

Torsten Jost is a Researcher and academic coordinator at the Cluster of Excellence Temporal Communities: Doing Literature in a Global Perspective at Freie Universität Berlin.

Holger Hartung is a theater and dance scholar from Berlin, who works at the Hanns Eisler School of Music, Berlin, where he oversees digital transformation.

Omid Soltani is a Researcher at the International Research Center "Interweaving Performance Cultures" of Freie Universität Berlin.

Routledge Advances in Theatre & Performance Studies

This series is our home for cutting-edge, upper-level scholarly studies and edited collections. Considering theatre and performance alongside topics such as religion, politics, gender, race, ecology, and the avant-garde, titles are characterized by dynamic interventions into established subjects and innovative studies on emerging topics.

Entangled Performance Histories
New Approaches to Theater Historiography
Erika Fischer-Lichte, Małgorzata Sugiera, Torsten Jost, Holger Hartung, and Omid Soltani

Rechoreographing Learning
Dance As a Way to Bridge the Mind-Body Divide in Education
Sandra Cerny Minton

Politics as Public Art
The Aesthetics of Political Organizing and Social Movements
Martin Zebracki and Zane McNeill

Lessons for Today from Shakespeare's Classroom
The Learning Benefits of Drama and Rhetoric in Schools
Robin Lithgow

Notelets of Filth
An *Emilia* Companion Reader
Laura Kressly, Aida Patient, and Kimberly A. Williams

Transcultural Theater
Günther Heeg

For more information about this series, please visit: https://www.routledge.com/Routledge-Advances-in-Theatre–Performance-Studies/book-series/RATPS

ENTANGLED PERFORMANCE HISTORIES

New Approaches to Theater Historiography

Erika Fischer-Lichte, Małgorzata Sugiera, Torsten Jost, Holger Hartung, and Omid Soltani

LONDON AND NEW YORK

First published 2023
by Routledge
4 Park Square, Milton Park, Abingdon, Oxon OX14 4RN

and by Routledge
605 Third Avenue, New York, NY 10158

Routledge is an imprint of the Taylor & Francis Group, an informa business

© 2023 selection and editorial matter, Erika Fischer-Lichte, Małgorzata Sugiera, Torsten Jost, Holger Hartung and Omid Soltani individual chapters, the contributors

The right of Erika Fischer-Lichte, Małgorzata Sugiera, Torsten Jost, Holger Hartung and Omid Soltani to be identified as the authors of the editorial material, and of the authors for their individual chapters, has been asserted in accordance with sections 77 and 78 of the Copyright, Designs and Patents Act 1988.

All rights reserved. No part of this book may be reprinted or reproduced or utilised in any form or by any electronic, mechanical, or other means, now known or hereafter invented, including photocopying and recording, or in any information storage or retrieval system, without permission in writing from the publishers.

Trademark notice: Product or corporate names may be trademarks or registered trademarks and are used only for identification and explanation without intent to infringe.

British Library Cataloguing-in-Publication Data
A catalogue record for this book is available from the British Library

Library of Congress Cataloging-in-Publication Data
Names: Fischer-Lichte, Erika, editor.
Title: Entangled performance histories : new approaches to theater historiography / [selected and edited by] Erika Fischer-Lichte [and four others].
Description: Abingdon, Oxon ; New York : Routledge, 2023. | Series: Routledge advances in theatre & performance | Includes bibliographical references and index. |
Identifiers: LCCN 2022036613 (print) | LCCN 2022036614 (ebook) | ISBN 9781032405186 (hardback) | ISBN 9781032405131 (paperback) | ISBN 9781003353461 (ebook)
Subjects: LCSH: Theater--Historiography. | Theater--Social aspects. | Globalization.
Classification: LCC PN2115 .E688 2023 (print) | LCC PN2115 (ebook) | DDC 792.09--dc23
LC record available at https://lccn.loc.gov/2022036613
LC ebook record available at https://lccn.loc.gov/2022036614

ISBN: 9781032405186 (hbk)
ISBN: 9781032405131 (pbk)
ISBN: 9781003353461 (ebk)

DOI: 10.4324/9781003353461

Typeset in Bembo
by KnowledgeWorks Global Ltd.

CONTENTS

List of Figures viii
List of Contributors ix
Acknowledgments xv

    Introduction: Entangled Performance Histories:
    New Approaches to Theater Historiography   1
    Erika Fischer-Lichte

PART I
Methodological Reflections   35

1 Interweaving Stories, Altering Discourses   37
    Małgorzata Sugiera

2 Writing Entangled Theater/Performance Histories
    in the Arab World   58
    Khalid Amine

PART II
Hidden Histories—Forgetting and Remembering   77

3 William Kentridge's *The Head & The Load:* Theatrical
    Collage and the Color of Memory   79
    Catherine M. Cole

4 Hijikata Tatsumi at the Osaka World Exposition's
  Pepsi Pavilion, 1970: Multiple Historiographies
  of a Lost Performance   106
  Stephen Barber

PART III
Entanglements between Drama, Theater and Colonial Historiographies   125

5 Disentangling Colonial Archives: The Combustible
  Affair of Ensuring/Insuring Theater Safety in Colonial
  Singapore   127
  meLê yamomo

6 The Thorny Entanglements of Theater and Colonial
  Historiography in the Netherlands: Anti-colonial
  Critique and Imperial Nostalgia in J. Slauerhoff's Play
  Jan Pieterszoon Coen (1931)   145
  Sruti Bala

PART IV
Emergence and Transformation of Genres   165

7 Reversibility as Historiographical Method: Japanese
  Theater and Its Doubles   167
  Carol Fisher Sorgenfrei

8 Plumbing the Past to Project into the Future:
  The Entangled Trajectories of Flamenco's Twenty-
  First-Century Avant-Garde   190
  Catherine Diamond

PART V
National Theater Histories—Entanglements and Disentanglements   211

9 The Interwoven Performance Culture of Algeria   213
  Marvin Carlson

10 Writing History as Disentanglement: Toward a
    Historiography of Modern Greek Theater   234
    Platon Mavromoustakos

    Coda: The Whirligig of Tech: Theater as Media
    Archaeology   258
    W. B. Worthen

Index   *278*

FIGURES

0.1	Okuni with cross, dressed as a samurai.	11
0.2	From Christoph Weiditz's *Trachtenbuch* (1523).	21
0.3	From Christoph Weiditz's *Trachtenbuch* (1523).	22
0.4	From Christoph Weiditz's *Trachtenbuch* (1523).	23
7.1	A dancing drummer wearing a Namahage costume, performing Namahage-Daiko in Akita Station (2010).	172
7.2	This image of a *nō* mask shows how the expression changes with the tilting of the head.	174
7.3	Angela Winkler, Benjamin Lillie in Karin Henkel's *Drei Schwestern* (*Three Sisters*), Deutsches Theater Berlin, 2018.	183

CONTRIBUTORS

Khalid Amine is a Senior Professor of Performance Studies, Faculty of Letters and Humanities at Abdelmalek Essaadi University, Tétouan, Morocco. He has been a Research Fellow at the International Research Center "Interweaving Performance Cultures" at Freie Universität Berlin, and is now a member of its Advisory Board. He is the winner of the 2007 Helsinki Prize of the International Federation for Theatre Research (IFTR). He was Friedrich Hölderlin Guest Professor at Goethe-University, Frankfurt/M., Germany (2017–18). Since 2007, he has been the Founding President of the International Centre for Performance Studies (ICPS) in Tangier, and the convener of its annual international conferences. He was a member of IFTR Ex-Com (2011–18), Head of Jury at the Arab Theatre Festival (6th Edition, Sharjah 2014) and Advisor at the Saudi National Theatre (2020–21). Among his published books are *Beyond Brecht* (1996), *Moroccan Theatre between East and West* (2000), *Fields of Silence in Moroccan Theatre* (2004), *Dramatic Art and the Myth of Origins* (2007), *Dancing on the Hyphen: Essays on Arab Theatre* (2019). Amine is co-author, with Distinguished Professor Marvin Carlson, of *The Theatres of Morocco, Algeria and Tunisia: Performance Traditions of the Maghreb* (2012); co-editor of *Performing Transformations* (2012), *The Art of Dialogue: East-West* (2014), *Intermediality, Performance and the Public Sphere* (2014), *Memory and Theatre* (2015), *Across Borders and Thresholds: Performing in Zones of Contact and Friction* (2020); and editor of *Arab Journal of Performance Studies* [AJPS] and contributing editor of *New Theatre Quarterly* [NTQ] (2021–23).

Sruti Bala is an Associate Professor in Theatre Studies at the University of Amsterdam. Her research interests are at the intersections of performance and politics, which have taken shape in specific research projects on nonviolent protest, participatory art, artistic activism, feminist and postcolonial/decolonial literary and cultural theories and translation. She currently coordinates a Dutch Research Council-funded research project on cultural practices of citizenship in the Dutch Caribbean. She is an active member of the collective International Solidarity for Academic Freedom in India (InSAF India). Her publications include *The Gestures of Participatory Art* (Manchester University Press, 2018); *International Performance Research Pedagogies: Towards an Unconditional Discipline?* (Palgrave Macmillan, 2017, co-ed. M. Gluhovic, H. Korsberg, K. Röttger); *Translation and Performance in an Era of Global Asymmetries*, special issue of *South African Theatre Journal* 32, no. 1 (2019, co-ed. M. Fleishman).

Stephen Barber was a Fellow of the International Research Center "Interweaving Performance Cultures" at Freie Universität Berlin (2012–15), and wrote the monograph *Performance Projections* (Reaktion/University of Chicago Press, 2016) during his time there; he returned for a further stay in 2019 for research for his monograph *The Projectionists: Eadweard Muybridge and the Future Projections of the Moving Image* (diaphanes/University of Chicago Press, 2020). He is a Professor of Art and Film History at the Kingston School of Art, Kingston University, London. He previously held research-based and professorial positions at the California Institute of the Arts in Los Angeles, University of Tokyo, Institut Mémoires de l'Édition Contemporaine in Paris/Caen and the Berlin University of the Arts. In 2022–23, he was a Fellow of the Hamburg Institute for Advanced Study (HIAS). He has received many awards and grants for his research and books, from such foundations as the Leverhulme Trust, Henkel Foundation, Japan Foundation, Sasakawa Foundation, Daiwa Foundation, Rockefeller Foundation and Getty Foundation.

Marvin Carlson is Sidney E. Cohn Professor of Theatre, Comparative Literature, and Middle Eastern Studies at the Graduate Center, City University of New York. He has received an honorary doctorate from the University of Athens, the ATHE Career Achievement Award, the ASTR Distinguished Scholarship Award, the George Jean Nathan Award for Dramatic Criticism, and the Calloway Prize. He is the founding editor of the journals *Western European Stages* (now *European Stages*) and *Arab Stages*, and the author of over 250 scholarly articles in the areas of theater history, theater theory and dramatic literature. He is the director of the Marvin Carlson Theatre Center at the Shanghai Theatre Academy. Among his books are *The Theatre of the French Revolution* (1966), *Goethe and the Weimar Theatre* (1978), *Theories of the Theatre* (1984), *Places of Performance* (1989), *Performance: A Critical Introduction* (1996), *The Haunted Stage* (2001), *Speaking in Tongues* (2006), *Theatre Is More Beautiful than War* (2009) and *The Theatres of Morocco, Algeria, and Tunisia* (2012, with K. Amine). His work has been translated into fifteen languages.

Catherine M. Cole is a Professor of Dance and English at the University of Washington, where she recently served as Divisional Dean of the Arts. Her most recent book *Performance and the Afterlives of Injustice* (2020) on dance and live art in contemporary South Africa and beyond received a 2021 Special Citation for the Dance Studies Association's de la Torre Bueno Prize. Her previous books include *Performing South Africa's Truth Commission: Stages of Transition* (2010), the coedited book *Africa After Gender?* (2007) and the monograph *Ghana's Concert Party Theatre* (2001), a finalist for African Studies Association's Herskovits Prize and ASTR's Barnard Hewitt book award. Cole has published dozens of articles as well as numerous chapters in edited volumes. Her disability dance theater piece *Five Foot Feat*, created in collaboration with Christopher Pilafian, toured North America in 2002–05. She has received the UCSB Distinguished Teaching Award, fellowships from the National Humanities Center Fellowship, Harvard Theatre Collection, and AAUW, and grants from the Mellon Foundation, Freie Universität Berlin, National Endowment for the Humanities, and the Fund for U.S. Artists.

Catherine Diamond is a Professor of Theatre and Environmental Literature at Soochow University, Taipei, Taiwan. She was a Fellow of the International Research Center "Interweaving Performance Cultures" at Freie Universität Berlin (2013–14). She is the author of *Communities of Imagination: Contemporary Southeast Asian Theatres* (2012) and numerous articles about theater and the environment. She is the director/playwright of the Kinnari Ecological Theatre Project, which produces culturally specific plays about environmental protection in the Southeast Asian region (http://www.kinnarieco-theatre.org). She is also the flamenco dancer/choreographer of *The Daughters of Bernarda Alba* (2008) and the *Red Shoes Tablao* (2016).

Erika Fischer-Lichte is Director of the International Research Center "Interweaving Performance Cultures" at Freie Universität Berlin. From 1973 to 1996, she was a Professor of Modern German Literature, Comparative Literature and Theater Studies at the universities of Frankfurt am Main, Bayreuth and Mainz. In 1996, she joined the faculty of the Theater and Performance Studies department at Freie Universität Berlin. Between 1995 and 1999, she served as President of the International Federation for Theatre Research. She is a member of the Academia Europaea, the Academy of Sciences, Göttingen, the Berlin-Brandenburg Academy of Sciences, the National Academy of Sciences Leopoldina in Halle and of the American Academy of Arts and Sciences. She has held Visiting Professorships in China, India, Japan, Russia, Norway, Brazil and the US. Her research interests and recent as well as forthcoming publications focus on the interweaving of performance cultures in the context of historical and contemporary forms of globalization;

transformative aesthetics; performances of ancient Greek tragedies since 1800 worldwide; and performance-related concepts in non-European languages. Recent monographs (in English) include *The Transformative Power of Performance: A New Aesthetics* (Routledge, 2008), *The Routledge Introduction to Theater and Performance Studies* (2014), *Dionysus Resurrected: Performances of Euripides' The Bacchae in a Globalizing World* (Wiley-Blackwell, 2014) and *Tragedy's Endurance: Performances of Greek Tragedies and Cultural Identity in Germany since 1800* (Oxford University Press, 2017).

Holger Hartung, a theater, and dance scholar from Berlin, wrote his dissertation on "Ruptures, Tears, Cracks as Performative Figures in Scenarios of Art and Theory." His publications include *Moving (Across) Borders: Performing Translation, Intervention, Participation* (2017, co-ed. G. Brandstetter) and *Movements of Interweaving: Dance and Corporeality in Times of Travel and Migration* (2018, co-ed. G. Brandstetter, G. Egert). Currently, he works at the Hanns Eisler School of Music, Berlin, where he is in charge of digital transformation.

Torsten Jost is a Researcher and academic coordinator at the Cluster of Excellence *Temporal Communities: Doing Literature in a Global Perspective* at Freie Universität Berlin. After receiving his PhD from Freie Universität Berlin in 2017, he joined the faculty of the university's Theater and Performance Studies Department, where he teaches courses in the bachelor's and master's degree program. In 2018, Jost was invited as a guest lecturer by the Shanghai Theater Academy, China. His dissertation, which was nominated for the Ernst-Reuter-Prize, was published by Wilhelm Fink Verlag under the title *Gertrude Stein: Nervosität und das Theater* (2019, *Gertrude Stein: Nervousness and the Theater*). Together with Erika Fischer-Lichte, he has coedited numerous books on theater and performance in German and English, including *The Politics of Interweaving Performance Cultures: Beyond Postcolonialism* (Routledge, 2014), *Theatrical Speech Acts: Performing Language: Politics, Translations, Embodiments* (Routledge, 2020) and *Dramaturgies of Interweaving: Engaging Audiences in an Entangled World* (Routledge, 2021).

Platon Mavromoustakos is a Professor at the Department of Theatre Studies, National and Kapodistrian University of Athens, Greece. He has collaborated with theater organizations in Greece, directed research projects and published and lectured in Greece and abroad on twentieth-century theater and stage directing, ancient drama in modern times, modern Greek drama, Italian Opera and French theater. Founding member of the European Network of Research and Documentation of Performances of Ancient Greek Drama (1997–2022). Fellow of the International Research Center "Interweaving Performance Cultures" at the Freie Universität Berlin (2017–18). Books in Greek: *Theatre in Greece 1940-2000: A Survey* (2005), *Outlines for Readings* (2006), *In Lieu* of Critique (2006), *Karolos Koun Performances* (2008), *Theatre of Piraeus* (2013). Editor (select.): Yannis Sideris, *History of Modern Greek Theatre 1794-1944*, (4 Vols. 1990–2008); (with G. Varzelioti) *Stage and Amphi-Theatre: Tribute to Spyros A. Evangelatos* (2018). In French: (with V. Broze, L. Couloubaritsis et al.) *Le Mythe d'Hélène* (2005); (with S. Felopoulou) *Relations France-Grèce: Le théâtre des années 1960 à nos jours* (2017).

Omid Soltani is a Researcher at the International Research Center "Interweaving Performance Cultures" of Freie Universität Berlin. He recently coauthored, with Susan Arndt, the article "Dream★Hoping into FutureS: Black Women in the Harlem Renaissance and Afrofuturism" for *Angelaki: Journal of the Theoretical Humanities* (Routledge, 2022).

Carol Fisher Sorgenfrei is a Professor Emerita of Theatre at the University of California, Los Angeles (UCLA), where she formerly served as Vice Chair for Graduate Programs, Head of Critical Studies and Head of Playwriting. An authority on postwar Japanese and cross-cultural performance, she is also an award-winning playwright, director and translator of modern Japanese plays. Her seventeen original plays include *Medea: A Noh Cycle Based on the Greek Myth*, the commedia dell'arte-kyōgen fusion *The Impostor*, and *The Dybbuk: Between Two Worlds*, a Japanese-Israeli fusion co-created with director Zvika Serper. She is the author of *Unspeakable Acts: The Avant-Garde Theatre of Terayama Shūji and Postwar Japan* (University of Hawai'i Press, 2005) and coauthor of *Theatre Histories: An Introduction* (Routledge, 2010). She has presented over 100 papers and keynotes throughout the world and has published numerous articles in books and journals. She is the editor of the *Association for Asian Performance Newsletter* and Associate Editor of *Asian Theatre Journal*.

Małgorzata Sugiera is a Full-time Professor at the Jagiellonian University in Cracow, Poland, and Head of the Department for Performativity Studies. She was a Research Fellow of the Alexander von Humboldt Foundation, DAAD, Institut für die Wissenschaften vom Menschen in Vienna, the American Andrew Mellon Foundation, and the International Research Center "Interweaving Performance Cultures" at the Freie Universität Berlin. Her research concentrates on performativity theories, speculative and decolonial studies, particularly in the context of the history of science. She has published twelve single-authored books, the most recent of which are *Nieludzie: Donosy ze sztucznych natur* (2015, *Non-humans: Reports from Nonnatural Natures*) and, together with Mateusz Borowski, *Sztuczne natury: Performanse technonauki i sztuki* (2017, *Artificial Natures: Performances of Technoscience and Arts*). She has coedited several books in English and German, most recently *Crisis and Communitas: Performative Concepts of Commonality in Arts and Politics* (Routledge, 2023). She translates scholarly books and theater plays from English, German and French. She carries out the three-year international research project *Epidemics and Communities in Critical Theories, Artistic Practices and Speculative Fabulations of the Last Decades* funded by the National Science Centre (NCN).

W. B. Worthen is the Alice Brady Pels Professor in the Arts, Chair of the Department of Theatre at Barnard College, Columbia University, and Co-Chair of the PhD Program in Theatre at Columbia. His work ranges across the history and theory of modern performance, modern drama and contemporary Shakespeare performance. He is the author of six books, including *Print and the Poetics of Modern Drama* (2005), *Drama: Between Poetry and Performance* (2010) and *Shakespeare Performance Studies* (2014), written as a Fellow of the International Research Center "Interweaving Performance Cultures," and *Shakespeare, Technicity, Theatre* (2020). He is the editor or coeditor of several influential critical anthologies as well as of widely used collections of drama; he is the former editor of the *Theatre Journal* and *Modern Drama* and currently serves on the advisory board of *Global Shakespeares*.

meLê yamomo is an Assistant Professor of Theatre, Performance, and Sound Studies at the University of Amsterdam, the author of *Sounding Modernities: Theatre and Music in Manila and the Asia Pacific, 1869–1946* (Palgrave Macmillan, 2018), and project leader and principal investigator of the projects *Sonic Entanglements* and *Decolonizing Southeast Asian Sound Archives* (*DeCoSEAS*). meLê is a resident artist at Theater Ballhaus Naunynstrasse, where his creations *Echoing Europe*, *sonus*, and *Forces of Overtones* are in repertoire. meLê also curates the Decolonial Frequences Festival and hosts the *Sonic Entanglements* podcast. In his works as artist-scholar, meLê engages the topics of sonic migrations, queer aesthetics and post/de-colonial acoustemologies.

ACKNOWLEDGMENTS

We would like to thank the German Federal Ministry of Education and Research (BMBF) as well as the Freie Universität Berlin for supporting the International Research Center "Interweaving Performance Cultures." Without their backing, this book could not have been completed. Our special thanks go to all the contributors: we are deeply grateful for their inspiring research, their enthusiasm to engage in stimulating discussions and their trust and reliability. We would also like to express our gratitude to Christel Weiler, the Center's senior advisor, who gave thoughtful and incisive input throughout the process of this book's creation. Furthermore, we would like to thank Claudia Daseking, the Center's financial and operations manager, for her tireless assistance. Florian Thamer supported this publication with his technical expertise, which we truly appreciate. Thanks are also due to the Center's student assistants Naomi Boyce, Antonija Cvitic, Christina Handke and Clara Molau for their diligent editorial work. They facilitated the process of preparing the book's manuscript significantly. Last and certainly not least, we wish to thank Milos Kosic and Saskya Iris Jain, not only for their excellent proofreading but their unfaltering support and advice.

INTRODUCTION: ENTANGLED PERFORMANCE HISTORIES

New Approaches to Theater Historiography

Erika Fischer-Lichte

The last decade saw the publication of a substantial number of books devoted to problems and methodologies of theater and performance historiography (see, for instance, Bial and Magelssen; Canning and Postlewait; Wiles and Dymkowski; Bank and Kobialka; Cochrane and Robinson; Davis and Marx[1]). They cover a wide spectrum of approaches discussed and applied in the last two decades and, in many cases, set new standards, opening up novel perspectives for future research in the field. It is therefore all the more surprising that the term "entangled history" seems to be completely absent in these publications. It does not even appear in any of the indexes, even though it has been widely discussed in the field of historical studies since the beginning of the century.

The term "entangled history" is the English translation of the French term *histoire croisée* that was coined by the historians Michael Werner and Bénédicte Zimmermann[2] to denote the interconnected history of Germany and France, which cannot be sufficiently dealt with in the respective frameworks of French or German national history alone. As the historian Jürgen Kocka explains, the concept is applied when dealing with processes of "mutual influences," of "reciprocal or asymmetric perceptions" or when investigating "entangled processes of constituting one another [...] the history of both sides is taken as one instead of being considered as two units of comparison."[3]

The concept also aims to avoid the pitfalls of such terms as "influence" or even "reception." Both suggest that there is a difference in the outcome for the parties involved in processes and practices of exchange. While "influence" usually describes the impact one party had on another, unless it is explicitly stated that it was a mutual effect, "reception" considers the consequences of one party "receiving" something without leaving a trace on the party from which it was "received." In contrast, the term "entangled history" emphasizes that *all* parties involved in processes of exchange were recognizably transformed, even if in different ways and with different consequences. "Entanglement" suggests there was an imprint on *all* parties involved. Entangled history refers to an interconnected past, whereby all parties were affected by historical processes of contact and exchange—even if they occurred in highly asymmetrical power relations.

The term "entangled history" therefore seems quite apt when we discuss processes of interweaving performance cultures from the past: whenever these processes of interweaving had consequences for all parties involved, they brought forth what a historian today might describe and investigate as "entangled history." Although the two concepts of "entangled history" and "interweaving" seem closely related, they are by no means interchangeable. While the concept of "entangled history" denotes a specific genre and methodology of historiographical writing (as explained above), the concept of "interweaving"—in our case, "interweaving performance cultures"—focusses on the historical practices and processes themselves. Relating "interweaving" to the concept of "entanglement," one might explain the first as the practices and processes that brought about or led to an entanglement or, on the contrary, that aimed at or brought about its dissolution (what Carol Fisher Sorgenfrei has described as a "strategic unweaving"[4]). Histories exploring cases of interweaving between performance cultures focus on specific practices and processes as they unfold—the focus here lies on their very processuality. The concept of "interweaving" therefore specifically highlights (the interweaving of) concrete activities, actors, agents, forces, power dynamics, materialities, technologies, etc., which together have contributed to the dissimilar but always interlinked transformations that should be described, explored and theorized via an "entangled history." Furthermore, the concept of "interweaving" does not aim to embrace a culture (or multiple cultures) as a single unit. Rather, it directs the attention to concrete activities and processes of interweaving advanced by particular actors, agents, technologies, materialities, forces, etc., who or which have constitutively contributed to bringing about today's plurality of *diverse* but nevertheless *interlinked* performance cultures.

While many histories of interweaving focus on exchanges between two performance cultures, interweaving can also take place as a multilateral process—a frequent phenomenon since the beginning of the twentieth century at the latest. Histories of interweaving performance cultures thus generally do not center so much on the *results* of a process of interweaving (the "entanglement" itself) but more concretely on the processes and practices of interweaving themselves, in their very processuality and intersecting multiplicity.

Such processes of interweaving performance cultures by no means describe a new phenomenon that emerged in the twentieth century. Rather, they can be identified as historical phenomena going back hundreds of years or even a millennium—a point that is often overlooked.

In fact, neither do these processes begin with the twentieth century, when realistic-psychological theater was introduced to Japan and China, and directors in several European countries experimented with devices taken from various Asian performing art forms. Nor were they exclusively the result of colonialism, which forced various theater and performance genres developed in Europe onto the colonized people, who then developed new and highly diverse forms by incorporating elements from European theater and performance genres into their own traditional performances.

Processes of interweaving performance cultures have a long history. For instance, Korean and Chinese performing art forms were introduced to Japan during the Nara period (640–794 AD). Performers from these regions were invited to the Nara court to teach young Japanese their art, while Japanese performers traveled to the courts of Silla and Tang to learn from the Korean and Chinese masters. The masked pantomime *gigaku* and the cosmic court dance and music *bugaku* in Japan evolved from these encounters.

> According to *The Chronicles of Japan* (Nihon shoki a.k.a Nihongi) gigaku was introduced in 612 AD by Mimashi from the ancient Korean Kingdom Paekche, who taught in Nara. Gigaku was staged for the "eye-opening ceremony" of the Great Buddha in the Tōdaiji Temple in 752 AD and other, religious events.[5]

Some gigaku pieces were comic or erotic, conceived with the intention of attracting people to the temples. In contrast, bugaku is a highly dignified dance accompanied by music. In the seventh century, dance and music were common in the three Korean kingdoms. In Japan, they were paired with Chinese and Vietnamese music. Bugaku is particularly interesting in this respect, since its pieces adhered to a three-section structure called jo-ha-kyū, which later became one of the leading concepts in *nō*: "*Jo* (prelude) is usually in free rhythm with a slow tempo, *ha* (breach) a metrical rhythm with moderate tempo, and *kyū* (quick) a metrical rhythm with rapid tempo."[6]

As the concept of *jo-ha-kyū* indicates, the structure and dramaturgy of the bugaku ceremony followed a system that highlights dichotomies such as bright/dark, strong/weak, male/female, grounded in the *yin/yang* principle.

> A Chinese-music dancer appears from the left (east) side, dances in the center of the yard and exits, followed by a Korean-music dancer who mirrors the actions from the right side (west). This series of alternating dances continues for hours, interpreted as symbolizing the rotation of sun and moon, or day and night. While the two opposites never merge into one, their circulation brings balance to the universe.[7]

According to Terauchi Naoko, bugaku "boasts a continuous history of over 1,300 years of history. It has received governmental support since being instituted as the *Gagakuryō* in 701 AD."[8] Even today, some temples and shrines in Osaka and Nara present a number of bugaku dances by amateurs. Japanese culture at that time was quite open to "imports" from neighboring Buddhist cultures. In this respect, the history of bugaku can be regarded as an example of a performance culture that calls for an entangled performance history. Yet Terauchi does not elaborate whether the stay of the Japanese artists at the Chinese and Korean courts or that of the Chinese and Korean masters at Nara also resulted in—short-term or even long-term—changes in Korean and Chinese performing arts. Since this question has not yet been investigated (to my knowledge), we should call this (still one-sided) historical narrative a "history of interweaving performance cultures" but not (yet) an "entangled history."

The same applies to German theater and performance histories. Professional German theater, in the various German lands, developed from similar processes of interweaving performance cultures (which have not yet been thoroughly explored as "entangled histories"). In the second half of the sixteenth century—that is, before the development of professional theater in Germany—it was mainly Italian commedia dell'arte troupes and English comedians who performed in the German lands.

Some of the first documented commedia dell'arte performances in the German lands were staged as part of the wedding of Crown Prince Wilhelm of Bavaria and Princess Renée of Lorraine celebrated in Munich in 1568. Conceived by Orlando di Lasso, the performances consisted of comic interactions between Pantalone—played by Orlando di Lasso—and his servant Zanni.[9] That same year, commedia dell'arte actors—presumably members of the already famous troupe of the *Comici Gelosi*—performed before the Emperor in Linz. Latest by 1574, their troupe staged regular performances at the Court in Vienna. Particularly, the southern German states witnessed a number of performances by Italian troupes in the first decades of the seventeenth century. In Prague, for instance, the *Comici Fedeli*, headed by the famous Lelio player Giovanni Battista Andreini, were part of the court festivities held in honor of Ferdinand II and his wife Eleonora of Mantua in 1624. The commedia troupes were the first to have female parts played by women.

In the German countries, the commedia dell'arte troupes performed mostly, if not exclusively, at courts. They were able to accommodate the specificities of each court that hosted them and to adapt their material to the preferences of its spectators, on whose favor they depended. Since the performances mainly consisted of ready-made components, these could be adjusted depending on the situation at hand.[10] It was therefore easy to follow the performance, even if some of the spectators might not have understood the Italian language.

Such performances can be labeled "interwoven" in the sense that their process largely relied on the response of the spectators hailing—in their majority—from a different culture than the Italian actors.' The performance resulted from the encounter of the Italian performers and the German courtly spectators, whom they had to please. It came into being through the process of their encounter and not via a presentation of a fixed "product"—to which, as a matter of fact, the spectators could also respond, without, however, being able to fundamentally influence or even change it.

A rather different situation was created by the English companies. The first troupe that entered the continent was Lord Leicester's Men. In 1585, they performed first in Denmark and then at the court in Dresden for ten months. Among its members was William Kempe (who died in 1603), for whom Shakespeare had written numerous clown roles. In 1592, the troupes of Robert Brown, John Bradstreet, Thomas Sackville and Richard Jones followed Lord Leicester's Men to Europe. As documented in their passports, they intended to travel via the Netherlands to the German countries. One troupe followed the next until the outbreak of the Thirty Years' War in 1618.

In the beginning, the English performers used their mother tongue on stage. However, there is evidence that they switched to the German language already in 1605. Following the order of their princely patrons such as the Count Moritz of Hessen-Kassel (rule 1592–1627) and Duke Heinrich Julius of Braunschweig-Wolfenbüttel (rule 1589–1613), they trained young courtiers as well as incorporated other German members into their troupes, mostly students and journeymen, while the head of the troupe remained an Englishman. The repertoire of the English troupes consisted of the most popular Elizabethan plays. Crowd-pulling plays included Thomas Kyd's *Spanish Tragedy*, Christopher Marlowe's *Doctor Faustus and Jew of Malta* as well as William Shakespeare's *Titus Andronicus, Merchant of Venice, Romeo and Juliet, King Lear, Othello* and *Julius Caesar*. They were adapted to create a focus on the scenes which the audiences enjoyed the most. These were English plays translated into German, tweaked and performed in a way that appealed to the German audiences.

Such performances form part of or, better, constitute an English-German history of interweaving performance cultures. They presented English plays not only in their German translation but also in a modified form that accommodated the preferences, interests, tastes and emotions of the audiences. There are no documents informing us whether the success of the performances was due to their novelty and distinct "foreignness" that triggered a sense of wonder, surprise and intimacy with a world heretofore unknown. All we have is an account by an English traveler, Fynes Moryson, who was present at a performance still performed in English, which nonetheless enthused the German spectators: "[...] the Germans, not understanding a worde they sayde, both men and women flocked wonderfully to see their gestures and Actions."[11] This appears to confirm the impression that the performances of the English players were received as a kind of "exotic" spectacle.

That is to say, the performances came about out of a process of negotiation, whereby the actors found out what impressed or pleased their audiences most, and the spectators in turn contributed with their responses that were perceived by the actors as well as by other spectators. Since the actors were able to adjust their actions to these responses, the performances came into being out of an encounter between the English—or Italian—actors and the German spectators. No doubt, these were processes of interweaving performance cultures, from which German theater history developed.

Still, we can identify cases from the sixteenth century in which entanglements did in fact take place between cultures that had no prior contact with each other or indeed any knowledge of the other's existence. These encounters led to changes in the theater and performance traditions of both parties.

In 1524, a group of Franciscan monks arrived in "New Spain"/Mexico that had just been conquered by the Spanish. And in 1549, members of the Jesuit Order set foot on Kagoshima (Kyūshū Island). In both cases, these arrivals marked the beginning of an evangelization campaign that made ample use of performances.

In my discussion of these two evangelization campaigns, I take recourse to sources that in both cases were written by friars in charge of the respective campaign. In the Japanese case, these are the *litterae annuae*, the annual letters, which the missionaries sent to the Order in Rome in order to keep it informed about their progress. A collection of these letters was published in 1598 in Evora, Portugal.[12] Regarding Mexico, these are the writings by Diego Durán (1579–1581), Bartolomé de Las Casas (1528ff.), Toribio de Motolinía (1541) and Bernardino de Sahagún (1555–1577).[13] That is to say, the sources all present the point of view of the European monks. This has to be kept in mind for the following discussion.

Unlike the situation in the Spanish colony, which will be discussed later, the missionaries in Japan did not come in alongside a military invasion and conquest. They had to find ways beyond force to achieve their goal of evangelization. That is to say, they encouraged the Japanese Christians to adapt their performances to Japanese culture—that is, to the Japanese language and the people's tastes and preferences.

The performances of sacred plays took place on the occasion of important Christian holidays, such as Christmas, Good Friday, Easter and Pentecost. Similar to the mystery or sacred plays performed all over Europe in medieval times and partly still in the sixteenth and seventeenth centuries, the Japanese performances derived their stories from the Bible, featuring not only the events from the holy days—such as Jesus's birth and life until his death and resurrection—but also stories from the Old Testament, such as Adam and

Eve's expulsion from Paradise, Sodom and Gomorrah, the captivity of the children of Israel, and others.

However, the plays were not performed in Latin or a modern European language but in Japanese and used scenic devices that were invented by the Japanese Christians. One of the *Letters* (Funai, 8 October 1561) states,

> Some twenty days before Christmas, the Priest spoke to two or three Christians and asked that they stage some sort of play on Christmas Eve, so that all might rejoice in the Lord; and speaking thus, he left them no direction as to what he wanted them to do, placing the matter instead in their hands. And so it was that when Christmas Eve came, they came up with a great many inventions based upon the knowledge of the Holy Scriptures, with which they hoped to please the Lord. They first presented the fall of Adam and the hope of redemption, for which purpose they placed an apple tree with golden apples in the middle of the church, and showed Lucifer deceiving Eve beneath it. And this with motets sung in Japanese, and though it was indeed a festive day, there was neither great nor small who did not weep at the sight.
>
> And after the fall of man, an angel cast both of them from Paradise, which was also cause for much weeping and wailing. [...] And then there appeared an angel to comfort them and give them hope that in the end, both would be redeemed, whereupon both Adam and Eve departed singing, no longer with tears of grief but with happiness, and left the audience with much joy.[14]

Not only is it remarkable that the priest encouraged the Japanese Christians to choose what kind of play to stage on the occasion of Christmas Eve and how to do it, but it is rather striking that even the motets were sung in Japanese, so that the Japanese congregation could fully grasp what the motets were about, evoking a strong emotional effect in all present. The use of the Japanese language was the most important factor in letting the spectators receive the performance in the vein of *tua res agitur* (it concerns you), which was in fact the aim of sacred plays wherever they were performed.

The drive to adapt the Christian faith to the Japanese culture went even further. As another letter suggests, it was generally up to the Japanese Christians to invent the scenic devices. One letter describes the celebration of Easter in Funai in 1562:

> On Easter Day, during the procession of the Resurrection, some of the events in the Holy Scriptures were presented, namely, the flight of the children of Israel out of Egypt. For this purpose, there was no lack of ingenious devices created to form a Red Sea in front of our church,

which parted to allow the Israelites to pass and closed back in on itself when Pharaoh and his army tried to cross.[15]

By allowing the Japanese devotees to stake their own claims in these performances, they had the possibility to perform in ways that not only suited them best in terms of affirming their belief that the Christian religion was compatible with their own culture, but these plays also proved to be highly attractive for non-Christians.

It is often emphasized that in those years, the Japanese were generally open to the new, no matter if it was imported or invented at home. On festive occasions, those who could afford it would pride themselves in dressing up in the European fashion and adopt from the foreigners whatever suited their own purposes. Since the Japanese converts were the ones responsible for the performances of the sacred plays, they staged them in ways that met their compatriots' expectations of such an extraordinary event.

The fūryū became a mass movement in the second half of the sixteenth century. It was a performance genre that combined dances, the exposition of magnificent objects or even mechanical curiosities with performances of sketches in the context of festivals, pageants and processions. It was a genre that incorporated different elements, new and old ones.[16]

What was a common practice in the fūryū seems to also have been successfully applied to the performance of sacred plays. On the one hand, this meant the introduction of exciting new technical devices, such as the opening and closing of the Red Sea. On the other, the performances imbibed existing elements developed in other performance genres. In a letter by Father Melchior de Figueiredo sent from Bungo, on 27 September 1567, we learn the following about the celebration of Christmas in 1566:

> To this festival came many of the Christians from the surrounding villages with their wives and children. During the festival, always on the night of Christ's birth, we always stage a representation of several passages from the Scriptures in the middle of the church, using people to act out what took place. These passages are such as the fall of Adam, the sacrifice of Abraham, the story of Lot, and the great flood and Noah's ark, to which were added this year the story of Joseph and his brothers and his father Jacob, up to the point of their entry into Egypt. In these representations the Japanese are accustomed to using actors for the main scenes, and what appears to be most convenient for them is to have the actors speak in their own tongue. As for the lines belonging to the chronicler or evangelist, several people instructed for such a purpose sing these outside in a chorus, thus introducing some bit of doctrine to help the Christians understand the story and its message. And as these are admirable mysteries of our Holy Faith, and are so new to this amicable

people, and are presented in *such a fashion that has been adapted to their own ways*, there are many who come to this festival, not only Christians, but their many kindly relatives as well, who attend to ask for intercession in secret. And were it not held inside, to this celebration would come every last person, as it gives them all much pleasure, which would be good, in part, if it were so, such that all around, everyone would receive notice of something so important taking place for the salvation of the soul.[17]

Just as in the fūryū, new and old elements are interwoven here too, in that new stories are told by taking recourse to "old devices." Moreover, a device taken from nō is introduced—the chorus singing the lines of the evangelist. This way, aided by the use of the local language, the whole manner in which the story was performed became increasingly Japanese. In fact, the performances, born from the desire to present and transmit as their own the "new stories" on which their novel belief was based, generated processes of interweaving performance cultures. To become a Christian and live as one here meant absorbing this new belief—and anything related to it—into their own culture.

Although the expulsion of the Jesuits was decreed in 1587 and Christians were even crucified in 1596, there is sufficient evidence that performances of sacred plays continued into the first years of the new century. In Nagasaki, for instance, Christmas Day 1599 was celebrated in a square before the Collegio with performances of several plays by the local Christian community. On the day of the Assumption of the Virgin Mary in 1602, the most noble citizens performed several plays in Japanese, written by the Japanese, in the Church as well as in the square before it. There were firework displays, and we also have reports of an opulent procession along the festively decorated streets, led by the bishop carrying the monstrance, on the occasion of Corpus Christi Day 1605. Altars were erected in many places. The procession featured two richly embellished festive wagons and many musicians with instruments. There was even a stage on which two Japanese boys performed dances—one dressed as a European and dancing in a European style, while the other wore Japanese attire and performed a Japanese dance.[18] Another example is the procession held in Arima for Corpus Christi Day 1611, which was accompanied by music and several dances performed by young noblemen and the sons of ruling princes.[19] Performances of sacred plays thus continued even during the period when a new theater form, namely *kabuki*, came into being.

The name "kabuki" is already quite telling, and most researchers agree on its etymology. As Kamachi Mitsuru explains, "the word 'kabuki' comes from the verb 'kabuku,' which means 'to slant,' to be 'oblique,' 'to deviate from the normal path.'" Accordingly, a "kabukimono" is to be seen as "a deviant, a non-conformist in a society that, after more than a century of civil war, was suddenly being organized into a stable and fixed form of class system."[20]

A new era did indeed begin in 1603, when Tokugawa Ieyasu (1543–1616) seized power and was given the title *shōgun* (supreme commander). He transferred the administrative center from Kyoto to Edo (Tokyo), with Kyoto serving only as the seat of the emperor. A significant social shift went hand in hand with this new political development, leading to the rise of a middle class, with a prominent position allotted to the merchant class.

It was within this context that the new performance genre of kabuki emerged. It was founded by a woman named Izumo no Okuni, a former shrine maiden in Kyoto (1578–1613), who began performing on the dry riverbed of the Shijōgawara (Fourth Street Dry Riverbed) of the Kamo River at Kitano Shrine in 1603. The few pictures of Okuni show her wearing a rosary, which could be either Christian or Buddhist (*juzu*), with a cross attached to it (see Figure 0.1). The question arises then as to whether Okuni was a Christian and whether she had even witnessed performances of mystery plays during her time in Kyoto. On Palm Sunday, Maundy Thursday and Christmas Day of the year 1596, the Franciscan Church held processions performing Jesus's arrival in Jerusalem, the erection of a tomb with the Most Holy Place and a Nativity play.

There is a debate among Japanese scholars about whether Okuni wore the cross because this was the latest fashion or because she herself had converted. In order to substantiate the latter thesis, much emphasis is placed on Okuni's relationship with Nagoya Sanzō, who had served a Christian lord, and who therefore presumably also adopted the Christian faith. He is described as an attractive example of a *kabukimono*. Kamachi suggests that "Okuni's impersonation of a dandy could well have been based on his image."[21]

Kamachi goes on to argue that the mystery plays had been so successful with the Japanese audiences because they were exotic and spectacular to them, which is what the people yearned for. As discussed above, these plays not only included elements of nō but also of popular dance forms such as *kagura*, bon'odori and *kōwakamai*; they also used the Japanese *biwa* (lute) alongside the European organ, mixing traditional Japanese tunes such as *imayō* with those of Gregorian chants. This blend satisfied the yearning and enthusiasm for the "novel," which was characteristic of the Japanese upper and middle class of the time. Kamachi comes to the following conclusion regarding the new performance genre of kabuki:

> What Kabuki shared with the Jesuit theater was this tendency to become a melting pot for all kinds of performing arts, in order to attract and please a large, mixed audience. They also shared a talent for the invention of theater machinery. It has been pointed out that the same mechanism was employed to create the illusion of a huge running river onstage both in Kabuki and the Jesuit plays in later years. The famous revolving stage of Kabuki also had its counterpart in the Jesuit theater.[22]

FIGURE 0.1 Okuni with cross, dressed as a samurai.

Source: Art Collection 3/Alamy Stock Photo.

In this regard, both kabuki in its early stages and the sacred plays that were designed and performed by the Japanese Christians could be described as products of interweaving performance cultures. This process unfolded without being forced on the performers; it was a development that suited the

Japanese at that time and was therefore carried out according to their own tastes and preferences.

As in the case of gigaku and bugaku in the years that followed, especially after Japan closed its border to Europeans for more than 200 years, the fact that kabuki developed out of processes of interweaving with the foreign was forgotten or even intentionally denied, since it grew to become the most popular Japanese performing art form. Over the centuries, it exploited its potential "to swallow all that came within its reach, absorbing and giving out the exuberant energy of the common people." In this regard, it must indeed "be acknowledged as 'uniquely Japanese theater,'"[23] even if this very potential allowed it to embrace all that was at hand at its inception (as did the fūryū), including the developments around the mystery plays.

Such processes of interweaving in Japan were followed by concomitant processes on European stages. According to the theater historian Thomas Immoos, data for about 650 performances on Japanese themes could be found in the German-speaking countries and in the old Habsburg Empire, in which the Jesuits administered about 50 colleges.[24] A rather large number of these plays belong to the genre of the so-called martyr plays.

As already mentioned, the expulsion of the Jesuits was decreed in 1587, and in October 1596, 26 Christians were crucified. The decree was renewed several times. In its aftermath, many Jesuits and Japanese Christians were forced to leave the country. Those who remained were persecuted. Between 1619 and 1622, Christians were burned, decapitated and even thrown into the "hell" of the hot springs of the volcanic Mount Unzen (Kyushu).

The persecution of the Christians in Japan immediately became the topic of many plays written by Jesuits and performed in Europe on the stages of their schools and colleges. The so-called martyr plays were particularly popular in terms of strengthening the Catholic faith of these young noblemen. As early as 1607, a play was performed in Graz titled *De Japoniorum martyris* (On the Martyrs of the Japanese.) The Japanese martyrs were presented onstage as shining examples of believers prepared to defend their faith, thus calling on the young European spectators to emulate them. Interestingly, the Japanese rulers who forced their subjects to renounce their Christian faith were not generally presented as cruel monsters. One of the rare extant plays, *Happy Constancy in Faith, or Titus the Nobleman of Japan, tempted in vain by Tayndono King of Bungo to test the faith of Christ*, even has a "happy ending." Its "argument" runs as follows:

> Titus, a noble Gentleman more illustrious for his Christian courage, then [sic] parentage: was solicited by the King of Bungo, to desert his religion by severall, most artificious infernal plots, all which he sleighted and dashed with his invincible courage, and generous Christian resolution, whereat the King amazed, restored him to his liberty, wife and

children, and granted him the freedom of his Religion, with all his lands and possessions of which before he was bereaved as traitor to the Crowne.²⁵

Not only the persecuted Christians—Titus and his family—are presented as exemplary, but even their persecutor, finally, is revealed as gracious, just and deeply impressed by Titus's constancy.

The play seems to have been quite popular in Jesuit school theaters. It was performed in several versions. We know of performances in Munich (1622), Neuburg/Donau (1623), Augsburg (1629), Rottweil (1656), Eichstädt (1657), Augsburg (1712) and Freising (1715). Other versions were performed in the Southern Netherlands, for instance, in Mechelen (1623), Brussels (1663), Antwerp (1663), Ghent (1672) and Bergues (1729). It is a rather telling example of the many plays that featured Japanese Christians as exemplary, as martyrs constant in their faith and prepared to die for it. They served as models for the spectators—the young noblemen and their families who had gathered at the graduation ceremonies at which these performances took place.²⁶

However, the Jesuits were not the only ones to stage plays that propagated martyrdom for the Christian faith. The Spanish author Lope de Vega, who was even at odds with the Jesuits, also wrote a play on the subject: *Los primeros mártires de Japón* (The First Martyrs of Japan) (ca. 1621). It featured the Dominican mendicant Alonso Navarette and the Augustinian Hernando de San José Ayala, who had volunteered as martyrs and were decapitated on June 1, 1617, in Ōmura, a prefecture of Nagasaki. Moreover, it features the conversion of a young couple who "will populate Japan and reign under the paradigm of Christianity in political alliance with Spain."²⁷

Such processes of interweaving of Japanese and European performance cultures happened in both parts of the world—in Japan and in Europe. Since it was a long and historically reciprocal process, we can describe it as an "entangled history." Neither were the Jesuits in Japan in a position to force the new faith and resulting performance genres on the Japanese, nor did the Jesuits—or Lope de Vega—in Europe portray the Japanese condescendingly—quite the contrary. The Japanese martyrs were presented as role models for the European youth, appealing to them to defend and even die for the Christian faith.

This must be emphasized because it marks the difference between the evangelization campaign in Japan and in "New Spain"/Mexico. While the Jesuits in Japan had no power, especially no military power to back up the conversion process, and instead had to rely on the stories of the Bible and their own powers of persuasion, the situation in the "New World" was very different. The evangelization campaign there was carried out in the context of a military conquest and occupation.

In 1519, Hernán Cortés and his soldiers landed on the shores of Mesoamerica. Two years later, in 1521, together with his local allies, among them, most prominently, the Tlaxcalteca, he conquered the Aztec Empire and completely destroyed its capital Tenochtitlan. It was a huge city, comprising approximately 300,000 inhabitants at the time.

The victory of Cortés and his allies is rather surprising, considering the military power of the Aztecs. It is to be assumed that, at least partially, it was due to the behavior and actions of their ruler Moctezuma II. As Bernardino de Sahagún reports in his *Historia general de las cosas de la Nueva España* (1558–1560), it might well be that Moctezuma mistook the men on horsebacks—horses being unknown in Mesoamerica—for the companions of the god Quetzalcoátl and Cortés himself as the god. Cortés's arrival in 1519 coincided with the year of the god's sign *I REED*, which was to mark the return of the god. Following the Aztec calendar, this could happen every 52 years—that is, in the years 1415, 1467, 1519 and 1571. As the Aztecs told Sahagún, who had arrived in Mexico in 1529, a disastrous omen—an enormous fire that was visible across the sky—appeared ten years before the Spaniards arrived. The flame was seen at midnight in the east and continued to rage until sunrise. Other omens followed, leading Moctezuma to believe that the god Quetzalcoátl, in whose place he reigned, had returned and wanted to have his power reinstated.[28] He therefore sent a deputy to Cortés to ritually gift him the insignia of the god. Sahagún describes the response of the Spaniards as follows:

> And when they had given it (the gifts) to them, the Spaniards laughed heartily, immensely pleased, like monkeys they grasped at the gold, their whole heart, as it were, was set on it […]. For they thirst after it, they desire it, they seek the gold like pigs.[29]

There was little resistance when the Spaniards and their allies invaded, attacked and destroyed Tenochtitlan and took Moctezuma as their prisoner. He died shortly thereafter.

In the spring of 1524, Franciscan friars arrived in Tenochtitlan. Meanwhile, the city had been partially rebuilt in the Spanish style. A church had been erected on one side of the huge plaza where the main temple had stood. The Franciscans—twelve in number to emulate the apostles—had been brought over to embark on an evangelization campaign among the Indigenous population. Cortés greeted them in a special manner: "Accompanied by most of his soldiers and a large procession of Indian leaders, Cortés knelt and kissed each friar's hands. His soldiers did the same and the Indians followed suit."[30] This was Cortés's strategy to convince the Indigenous peoples of the high status of the mendicants.

One if not the most important means of the Franciscans—and some years later also of the Dominicans and Augustinians—were performances. There was a long and comprehensive tradition of ritual performances practiced by the Aztecs and other Indigenous peoples in Mesoamerica. In his *Historia de las*

Indias, Fray Diego Durán (1537–1588) describes some of the traditional ritual performances, most of which ended with a sacrifice, such as for the annual festival for Quetzalcoátl. A healthy and good-looking slave was bought 40 days before this festival, the most important one in the Aztec calendar. First, he was bathed and then

> they dressed him exactly as the idol was dressed, placing the crown and the bird's beak upon his head, giving him the mantle, the jewel, the stockings and gold earrings, the loincloth, buckler and scythe that pertained to the idol.
> This man was the living representation of the idol for those forty days. He was served and worshipped like the idol, and his own guard and many other people accompanied him every day [...]. And hearing him approach singing, the women and children emerged from their houses to greet him and offer him many things fit for a god [...].
> When the day arrived which, as we had said, was midnight on the third of February, after having done homage to him with music and incense, the slave was taken and sacrificed. At the appointed hour his heart was offered to the moon and he was then thrown in front of the idol, in whose presence they killed him, letting the body fall down the steps.[31]

The subsequent evangelization campaign could not make use of such ritual elements as human sacrifice, although it was prominent as a subject in performances such as *El sacrificio de Abraham* or *El sacrificio de Isaac* (in Tlaxcala, 1539). However, the plays were performed in Nahuatl, and the performances clearly drew inspiration from the traditional performances as regards the construction of the space, the decisive role of dance, songs and musical instruments, and the use of flowers and living animals, to name just the most obvious elements. Moreover, the evangelical performances "retained and developed [...] the spectacular and transformational aspects of ritual performance, wedding them to Christian theological and political concerns."[32]

The Franciscan Pedro de Gante, one of the first missionaries in Mexico, was convinced that the process of evangelization had to build on the existing culture, even while eliminating those elements that were deemed counterproductive, such as human sacrifice. When he suggested stories of the Bible to the Mexica as subjects for their performances, he supported that they enacted them by taking recourse to their traditional performances, even if he contributed some elements to them himself:

> By the grace of God, I began to understand them and to see how they must be won, I noted that in their worship of their gods, they were always singing and dancing before them. Always, before a victim was

sacrificed to the idol, they sang and danced before the image. Seeing this and that all their songs were addressed to the gods, I composed very solemn songs regarding the law of God and the faith, how God became man in order to free humanity. [...] Likewise, I gave them certain patterns to paint on their shawls for the dances as they were accustomed to do, according to the dances and songs which they sang. Thus they were dressed, gaily, or in mourning, or for victory.

Then when Christmas time drew near, I invited every one from a radius of twenty leagues to come to the festival of the Nativity of our Redeemer. So many came that the *patio* would not hold them all, and they sang, the very night of Nativity, "Today is born the Redeemer."[33]

While the Jesuits in Japan left it to the Japanese Christians to decide what episodes from the Bible to perform and how, the Franciscans contributed to the performances of the Mexica by changing some of the constitutive elements, such as the songs and the patterns of the shawls. They refrained from "directing" the performances but instead let the Mexica do it according to their own traditions.

The performances, staged by the baptized Indigenous people for various Christian holidays interwove different performance cultures. Motolinía described the performance of *Fall of Our First Parents*, which took place in Tlaxcala on the Wednesday following Easter in 1539, by emphasizing the luxuriance of the Garden of Eden displaying the particular qualities of pre-colonial performance traditions. There were many trees and flowers, some natural and others "made of feathers and gold." In their midst, birds and other animals led their life. Particularly prominent were the parrots, "whose chattering and screeching was so loud that it sometimes disturbed the play. Among the animals were even wild cats, albeit tethered. [...] Once Eve was careless during a performance and, as if trained, the beast went away. This was before the sin," as a friar explained who had been present, adding that "had it occurred after the sin, she would not have been so lucky." Besides the living animals, there were also "artificial animals, all well simulated, with boys inside them." An artificial lion pretended to tear to pieces and devour a real deer.

After Adam and Eve had tried the forbidden fruit, "God entered with great majesty, accompanied by many angels" and banished them both. They were transferred to a second stage by six angels singing in polyphonic harmony. "This stage play was presented by the Indians in their native language, so that many of them were deeply moved and shed tears, especially when Adam was banished from paradise and placed in the world."[34]

Evidently, the response of the spectators in "New Spain" was very similar to that of the Japanese spectators more than twenty years later, as is reported in one of the *Letters*: "And after the fall of man an angel cast both of them from Paradise, which was ... cause for much weeping and wailing" (see page 7). Even if we follow Diana Taylor's assessment, that "the native spectators (formerly participants) were not so much grieving the loss of Paradise" than "the loss of their own world,"[35] it can be concluded that the loss of Paradise as such seemed to have been experienced as a crucial event, a point of no return.

That same year at the Corpus Christi festivities in Tlaxcala, four plays were performed, the first being *The Conquest of Jerusalem*—which will be discussed later—and the last one, *The Sacrifice of Abraham* (or *The Sacrifice of Isaac*). Regarding the latter, a particular traditional feast for Tlaloc, the god of rain and water, is of great importance. For two children were sacrificed:

> Once a year, when the corn was a hand's breadth high, in the villages where there were high officials who called their houses palaces, a boy and a girl of three or four years old were sacrificed: these were not slaves, but children of the lords, and this sacrifice was made on a mountain, in worship of an idol which they said was the god of water and which gave them rain, and when there was a scarcity of water they asked for it from this idol.[36]

As Sahagún reports, this was a sacrifice that stirred strong emotions among the people. They cried as they watched the children proceed towards their death. And it was taken as a good sign when the children, too, shed tears.[37]

We can therefore assume that the story of Isaac's sacrifice reminded actors and spectators alike of the traditional—now forbidden—ritual on the occasion of the feast for Tlaloc, especially since in the play Isaac was approximately the same age as the children sacrificed for Tlaloc in the ritual. A preserved script of a later play on this subject refers to a feast in honor of Isaac—presumably "in celebration of Isaac's weaning, since Sarah refers twice to her breast milk."[38] Among the Nahuas, the weaning "took place during the third year, sometimes even later."[39] There is good reason to assume that the Nahua actors and spectators linked the supposed sacrifice of Isaac to the ritual for Tlaloc, also because this ritual took place on mountaintops surrounded by clouds,[40] as was the case with the supposed sacrifice of Isaac on Mount Moriah.

Keeping in mind these parallels between the ritual sacrifice for Tlaloc and the topic of Isaac's sacrifice, the astonishment, even wonder of the Nahua audience regarding God's interference at the final, decisive moment, is understandable: Isaac is blindfolded and Abraham has already drawn his knife in order to cut out Isaac's heart when the angel appears and reassures Abraham of God's love as a result of his total obedience, telling him to sacrifice a lamb instead of his son. Sources report that this sacrifice was not part of the performance but postponed until sometime after. No blood flowed. Instead, the angel told the audience that God's intervention was extraordinary and close to a miracle, and warned them to obey God's commandments:

> The didactic exemplariness of *El Sacrificio de Isaac* dangerously splits God's unique, tremendous, perhaps most controversial request in the scriptures into an iterable, duplicable one. Thus the Christian God […] becomes a hybrid. Unlike its Judeo-Christian versions, the God of *El sacrificio de Isaac* becomes partially Nahuatized, because he so resembles the violent, frightening, demanding pre-Hispanic deities to whom all had also to be offered constantly and unhesitantly in order to keep cosmic time alive […]. The attentive Nahua audience may have read then in the didactic *auto* of *El sacrificio de Isaac* that the difference between the new colonial deity and their own was that […] the material final ritual act of giving death sometimes might not be necessary to placate the former, feed it, and/or obtain its protection.[41]

Via the performances of the biblical stories, the colonizers undoubtedly wanted to spread their faith and the ethics derived from it among the Nahua. The Nahua, however, not only used the means and elements constitutive of their own, pre-colonial traditions in the performance. They did it in a way that connected it to their traditions. The performances came into being by a process of interweaving the Spanish/colonial and their own traditional cultures. While the colonizers seemed to find in them their own stories performed, the Nahua actors and spectators could relate them to their own traditions. In this sense, the performances were ambiguous. Both parties, the colonizers and the colonized, were able to experience the performance in the sense of *tua res agitur*.

Such an ambiguity could even turn into open criticism and a reversal of roles, as it happened in the first play of the Corpus Christi festivities in Tlaxcala in 1539, *The Conquest of Jerusalem*. As Las Casas states regarding the autos in Tlaxcala—such as *The Fall of our First Parents*, *The Sacrifice of Isaac* and *The Conquest of Jerusalem*—"all those who took charge of the play" were Nahuas.[42]

We can therefore assume that *The Conquest of Jerusalem* featured a reversal of roles between the colonizers and the colonized who once had been their allies. As Motolinía wrote, "the Great Sultan of Babylon and Tetrarch [tlatoani] of Jerusalem"—that is, the leader of the army of the infidels and the villain of the piece, "was the Marquis del Valle, Hernando Cortés," and the Turkish captain "was … Pedro de Alvarado."[43] Of course, neither Cortés nor Alvarado themselves appeared in the performance. Alvarado was in Honduras at the time and Cortés was lame from a wound. Both roles were played by Nahuas. This points to a "hidden transcript" in *The Conquest of Jerusalem*. One strand of it

> therefore, seems to have celebrated past resistance and enacted a form of theatrical vengeance [...]. Conceding the claims of Christianity to Jerusalem, the Tlaxcalteca appear to have asked: "If the Turks have no right to hold Jerusalem, by what right do the Spanish now hold Mexico?" From the perspective of a Tlaxcalteca Christian, the liberation of Jerusalem from illicit Turkish occupation and the liberation of Mexico from illicit Spanish occupation may not have seemed so different. It is striking, too, that whereas the European army is consistently identified as "the Spaniards," the Indian army is designated "the Christians." [...] If, as the play insisted, God helps Christian armies, the identity of the true Christians was a matter of real significance.[44]

It seems not too far-fetched to conclude that this performance not only used traditional means, as performances with biblical subjects did, but that it was also meant to identify the Nahua as the true Christians and the Spanish leaders Cortés and Alvarado as infidels.

In this case, the resistance toward the Spanish leaders as enacted in the performance was straightforward, albeit not too daring, for Cortés and the Spanish viceroy of Mexico, Antonio de Mendoza, were at odds with each other at the time. Still, such an assault on the conqueror—and former ally—who had subsumed the Nahua cities and their inhabitants into the Spanish empire, was an act of resistance—and not a "hidden" one. The process of interweaving performance cultures in *The Conquest of Jerusalem* displayed not only an aesthetic and religious but also a political dimension, claiming the right of resistance against the colonizers. Particularly striking in this context is the surrender of the Sultan/Cortés. It was done to

> an army, played in large part by Tlaxcalteca "lords and chiefs" and [he] declared himself and his troops to be their "natural vassals." The Tlaxcalteca nobles, proud of their own social standing and confident of their nation's inherent superiority over others, appropriated their conquerors' [...] ideology and reversed its Eurocentric application.[45]

We can conclude that, in the context of colonization, the performances as products of the evangelization campaign not only served the purpose to strengthen the Catholic faith in the conquered Nahua, as the political leaders and the monks had hoped. Since the performances incorporated elements from the Nahua's own traditional performances and even enabled an openly negative picture of the conquerors to be sketched in them, these performances can also be regarded as acts of criticism of and open resistance towards the colonizers.

Such processes of interweaving Mexica and Spanish/European performance cultures took place not only in the New World but in Spain/Europe as well. As Lynn Brooks states,

> There was constant population exchange and travel between the New World, Africa, and Spain, including the transporting of "savages" and "Indians" back home for show, where their costumes and dances were the cause of wonder and interest. The love of novelty, which Spanish theater of this period demonstrated, made these imports prime sources from which to appropriate innovations in themes, movements, rhythms, and costumes [...]. In this way, the dance compositions, presented at court, in the theater, and in public festivals,[46]

quite often drew heavily on Mesoamerican traditions, be it dances such as the *danza de los matachines* or the Mexica ballgame. On the other hand, there is good reason to assume that there were also "mutual influences," such as those that linked the mock battles of *moros y cristianos* in Mexico to their Spanish counterparts.[47]

When Cortés traveled to Spain in 1528, he was accompanied by a large delegation of Aztecs. It might have been up to seventy people—seven high-ranking nobles, including three sons of Moctezuma and the ruling son of Cortés's Tlaxcalan ally Maxixcatzin, and fifteen lesser nobles. In addition, there were seventeen men important enough to be named and given gifts. They were all baptized and had adopted Christian names.

> The principals may well have accompanied Cortés because they expected Charles to grant them rights, privileges, and lands, for Charles had granted *encomiendas* to two young Aztec nobles who had visited just three years prior. [...] Even without such a grant they would have recognized the political importance of visiting the emperor, a distinction that would serve them well once they returned to New Spain. One son of Moctezuma returned with a Spanish wife; records also reveal that another son was later granted the title of grandee of Spain with the key of a gentleman, a coat of arms and a royal pension.[48]

The delegation also included approximately thirty unnamed "entertainers—jugglers, dwarfs, ballplayers, prestidigitators and dancers. Most were from Mexico City [i.e., Tenochtitlan] but others came from Tlaxcala, Texcoco, Culhuacán and Cempoala."[49] Their dances and their ballgames were particularly popular. They stayed at the royal court from midsummer 1528 to April 1529. At the same time, the German artist Christoph Weiditz was also present at the court. It seems that he was quite impressed by the Mexican delegation. In any case, he regarded them as fascinating subjects for his drawings made

Introduction: Entangled Performance Histories **21**

for a European public. Among his depictions were a warrior in a feathered shirt, two playing a game with stones, two ballplayers and an antipodist, or foot juggler, lying on his back and spinning a wooden beam with his feet (see Figures 0.2–0.4). The latter seem to have enjoyed particular popularity. They performed even before Pope Clement VII in April 1529. Weiditz included the drawings in his *Trachtenbuch*,[50] which are often considered reliable sources regarding the look and attire of the Aztec delegation. However, as Boone has argued, this is quite unlikely: "The male figures have lip plugs and ear ornaments which Aztec men did wear, but they also have jewels in their cheek, in the side of their noses and in the center of their forehead, which Mesoamericans did not."[51] While these drawings must not be seen as "reliable documents," they do tell us what the artist—and most likely his contemporary Europeans—imagined about these "newly discovered people."

"New Spain" inspired not only Spanish festivals and popular entertainment but also theater. Dramatists began to refer to subjects from the New World from the second half of the sixteenth century onward, among them Lope de Vega, Tirso de Molina (the only one who had visited "New Spain") and Calderón de la Barca, but also lesser-known authors such as Gaspar Aguilar, Ricardo de Turia, Fernando de Zárate and Gaspar de Ávila. Despite the great differences between them—and their plays—they all address and deal with the problem of how to justify the *conquista*. Two arguments recur here: on the one hand, it is established that people who act in a morally reprehensible manner are inevitably of a low social standing, and, on the other, from a Catholic point

FIGURE 0.2 From Christoph Weiditz's *Trachtenbuch* (1523).

Source: Germanisches Nationalmuseum, photo by Monika Runge.

22 Erika Fischer-Lichte

FIGURE 0.3 From Christoph Weiditz's *Trachtenbuch* (1523).

Source: Germanisches Nationalmuseum, photo by Monika Runge.

of view, Christianization is a great aim, pursued by people of a high social status, who are impeccable in every respect.[52]

The *leyenda negra* (black legend) is not refuted in these plays. It states that the Spanish conquerors, greedy for silver and gold, subjugated and exploited the inhabitants of America with brutal violence. However, this accusation is presented alongside the argument that Christianization is the highest goal, to

FIGURE 0.4 From Christoph Weiditz's *Trachtenbuch* (1523).

Source: Germanisches Nationalmuseum, photo by Monika Runge.

be achieved without fail and through any means. This argument remained prominent in Spain, as Protestants were splitting up the German countries, ruled by Emperor Charles V, thus threatening the Catholic faith. Yet the performances in Spain clearly downplayed and whitewashed the brutality, exploitation, oppression and crimes done to the Indigenous population of the "New World."

Due to the fact that the situation of the colonized Mesoamerican Nahuatl-speaking Christians and that of their Spanish colonizers was, in fact, very different, there is good reason to assume that there might have been "mutual mis-constructions of the other" which

> became institutionalized in a manner that perpetuated the cultural differences while promoting an illusion of sameness. Each side imagined the other to be more similar to itself than it actually was, and assumed that ideas that were in fact quite different, bore analogous meaning in both cultures [...]. These mutual misunderstandings allow conqueror and conquered to co-exist within a single hierarchical order [...]. This ongoing gap between cultures of conqueror and colonized may be a common characteristic of colonial situations.[53]

Both cases discussed above are examples of entangled theater/performance histories—in the first case, between Japanese and European performance cultures, and in the latter, between Mexica and Spanish ones. However, these entanglements came into being under completely different conditions. In the first case, both parties acted according to their own interests and perspectives. The European Jesuits undertook the Christianization campaign in order to "save the souls" of the Japanese. The Japanese Christians found the Christian religion appealing. The performances they organized, arranged and staged were their own expressions of their new belief. Thus, on the one hand, they could take recourse to their own traditions in creating their performances. On the other hand, their performances seemed an appropriate springboard for developing new performance genres, maybe even kabuki.

The persecution of the Christians began when a new ruler decided that the Christian belief was "un-Japanese" and therefore not to be tolerated. It was this persecution and the heroic defense of their Christian belief, including their readiness to be tortured and killed for it, which made a suitable subject for the widespread Jesuit school theaters attended by noble pupils and their families.

While plays such as *Constancy in Faith, or Titus the Nobleman of Japan* were performed on the stages of the Jesuit schools in Europe well into the eighteenth century, any possible link between kabuki and the Christian plays, for example, was denied and ultimately forgotten in Japan during the 200 years of their isolation. Until the country opened its borders, such an entangled performance history never existed in the historical records.

In Mexico, by contrast, the outcomes and results of the entangled theater and performance history remain very much alive and continue until today. As Harris has shown, for instance, the mock battle between *moros y cristianos* (Moors and Christians), which came into being in Spain in the thirteenth/fourteenth century, became popular in Mexico in the aftermath of the *conquista* and remains popular to this day.[54] In this context, Diana Taylor's idea of "the so-called ephemeral *repertoire* of embodied practice/knowledge (i.e., spoken language, dance, sports, ritual)"[55] is of great importance. It is this repertoire that allows for the emergence and continuation of traditions as "embodied practice/knowledge." This repertoire not only "keeps" but also "transforms choreographies of meaning."[56] It allows for the transmission of performance genres such as the mock battle *moros y cristianos* that came into being hundreds of years ago.

As Taylor states, it cannot be proven—and it is indeed quite unlikely—that these mock battles performed today are choreographed in exactly the same way as those of the Mexica in the sixteenth century. Still, they form part of a living tradition because of the working of the *repertoire*. It allows for a particular continuity of a performance history that began as an entangled history.

When applied to theater and performance history, the concept of entangled history enables us to expose so-called national theater histories as at least partly entangled histories or, in any case, as springing from reciprocally consequential processes of interweaving performance cultures. It raises the question of whether it makes any sense at all to prioritize the paradigms of national theater history from today's point of view. European theater history is replete with examples of traveling troupes that performed in many countries—such as the commedia dell'arte troupes—and left their imprint. Plays were translated and performed in various parts of Europe. Dancers and singers circulated on the stages of different courts and countries. In this respect, we could regard European theater history as deeply entangled—in any case, as a history of interweaving performance cultures.

In fact, histories of interweaving performance cultures—or of intercultural performances—are frequently *not* written as entangled histories. Rather, the consequences of processes of interweaving are usually seen in a rather one-sided light. Brecht's recourse to Japanese theater or the introduction of spoken drama—in particular Ibsen's—on Japanese stages in conjunction with a realistic acting style, for instance, is discussed mostly from the perspective of the "recipient" culture. Yet *both* ought to be analyzed in terms of their relationship to each other and as "entangled histories."

These two examples alone make it evident that the coming into being of an entanglement does not provide any clear idea about the different but corresponding processes of interweaving performance cultures that contribute to it. It may therefore not come as a surprise that each of the following chapters in this volume deals with particular examples of processes of interweaving, which in some instances suggest the possibility of an entangled theater and performance history.

Part I, with contributions by Małgorzata Sugiera and Khalid Amine, presents further methodological reflections on investigating "entangled histories." In her chapter, Sugiera revisits and reconceptualizes practices, discursive forms and representational models that specialize in interweaving histories of different scales while working across geographical and temporal landscapes. Amine argues that the performance cultures of the Arab world have always been at the crossroads of diverse performance traditions and calls for a liberation of theater and performance historiography from the confines of the coloniality of knowledge/power.

Contributions to Part II explore methods for uncovering hidden entangled histories and contemplate processes of forgetting and remembering. Catherine M. Cole critically analyzes South African artist William Kentridge's work with historical fragments through the collage technique. And Stephen Barber rediscovers an almost forgotten performance by Hijikata Tatsumi (1928–1986) and asks how such a "lost" performance might become a starting point for multiple historiographies.

Part III examines entanglements between theater, drama and colonial historiographies: meLê yamomo takes a critical look at theaters as they appear in colonial archives in Singapore, and Sruti Bala develops avenues for feminist and decolonial historiographies by examining a 1931 play by the Dutch writer J. Slauerhoff (1898–1936).

Part IV revolves around the emergence and transformation of new genres through processes of interweaving: Carol Fisher Sorgenfrei examines entanglements with perceived "outsiders" in Japanese performing arts, asking why so many key innovators and artists of all eras were members of "outsider" groups, including (at various times) foreigners, females, Christians, the blind or disabled, apparently supernatural beings, the lower classes, and even inanimate objects. Catherine Diamond examines flamenco as an avant-garde art form that is entangled in various historical movements and actively engages with iconoclasts of the past, thereby resurrecting its roots in protest.

Part V reflects movements of entanglement and disentanglement in processes of constructing national theater histories. Marvin Carlson considers the interwoven performance cultures of Algeria. Platon Mavromoustakos looks at the historiography of modern Greek theater as a form of disentanglement.

In the book's Coda, W. B. Worthen considers contemporary performances that explore the entangled intermedial histories of theater through remediation, typically through an interaction between theater and digitally sourced media, taking the Wooster Group *Hamlet* (2007) as an index.

In sum, the contributions to the present volume seek to open up novel perspectives on the possibilities and challenges of investigating entangled histories *of* as well as *through* theater and performance. Introducing diverse concepts, theories and methodological approaches, the book's chapters consider different forms and dynamics of historical (dis)entanglement between theater and performance cultures on a global scale.

Notes

1 Henry Bial and Scott Magelssen, eds., *Theater Historiography: Critical Interventions* (Ann Arbor, MI: University of Michigan Press, 2010). Charlotte M. Canning and Thomas Postlewait, eds., *Representing the Past: Essays in Performance Historiography* (Iowa City, IA: University of Iowa Press, 2010). David Wiles and Christine Dymkowski, eds., *The Cambridge Companion to Theatre History* (Cambridge: Cambridge University Press, 2012). Rosemarie K. Bank and Michal Kobialka, eds., *Theatre/Performance Historiography: Time, Space, Matter* (New York, NY: Palgrave Macmillan, 2015). Claire Cochrane and Jo Robinson, eds., *Theatre History and Historiography: Ethics, Evidence and Truth* (London: Palgrave Macmillan, 2016). Claire Cochrane and Jo Robinson, eds., *The Methuen Drama Handbook of Theatre History and Historiography* (London: Bloomsbury, 2019). Tracy C. Davis and Peter W. Marx, eds., *The Routledge Companion to Theatre and Performance Historiography* (London and New York, NY: Routledge, 2021).
2 Michael Werner and Bénédicte Zimmermann, "Beyond Comparison: *Histoire Croisée* and the Challenge of Reflexivity," *History and Theory* 45, no. 1 (2006): 30–50.
3 Jürgen Kocka, "Comparison and Beyond," *History and Theory* 42, no. 1 (2003): 41–42.

4 See Carol Fisher Sorgenfrei, "Strategic Unweaving: Itō Michio and the Diasporic Dancing Body," in *The Politics of Interweaving Performance Cultures: Beyond Postcolonialism*, ed. Erika Fischer-Lichte, Torsten Jost and Saskya Iris Jain (London and New York, NY: Routledge, 2014), 201–22.
5 Terauchi Naoko, "Ancient and Early Medieval Performing Arts," in *A History of Japanese Theatre*, ed. Jonah Salz (Cambridge: Cambridge University Press, 2016), 5.
6 Ibid., 7.
7 Ibid., 8.
8 Ibid.
9 See Massimo Troiano, *Die Münchner Fürstenhochzeit von 1568*, ed. Horst Leuchtmann (München: Katzbichler, 1980).
10 See Stefan Hulfeld, "Notebooks, Prologues and Scenarios," in *Commedia dell'Arte in Context*, ed. Christopher Balme, Piermario Vescovo and Daniele Vianello (Cambridge: Cambridge University Press, 2018), 46–55.
11 Jerzy Limon, *Gentlemen of a Company: English Players in Central and Eastern Europe 1590–1660* (Cambridge: Cambridge University Press, 1985), 5.
12 *Cartasque os padres e irmãos da Companhia de Iesus escreverão dos Reynos de Iapão & China aos da mesma Companhia da India & Europa desdo anno de 1549, ate o de 1580*, 2 vols. (Evora: Manuel de Lyra, 1598; Tokyo: Tenri Central Library, 1972). In his book *Die Entstehung des Kabuki* (*The Genesis of Kabuki*), which in our context is of the greatest importance, Thomas Leims quotes extensively from these letters with regard to the performances which the Jesuits organized from 1552 onwards and refers to other relevant sources for the period between 1581 and 1611. He relates the performances to performance genres that were common in Japan at that time (unfortunately, to this day, Leims's book has not been translated into English or Japanese, although it includes such unprecedentedly rich archival material). In my following remarks, I rely quite heavily on Leims's book.
13 See Diego Durán, *Historia de las Indias de Nueva España y Islas de Tierra Firme*, ed. Jose F. Ramirez (1579–1581; Mexico: Impr. de J. M. Andrade y F. Escalante, 1867–1880); Bartolomé de Las Casas, *Historia de las Indias*, ed. El Marques de la Fuensante del valle, 5 vols. (Madrid: Impr. de M. Ginesta, 1876); Bartolomé de Las Casas, *Apologética Historia Sumaria*, ed. Edmundo O'Gorman, 2 vols. (1909; México: Universidad Nacional Autónoma de México, Instituto de Investigaciones Históricas, 1967); Toribio de Motolinía, *Historia de los Indios de la Nueva España*, vol. 1 of *Colección de Documentos para la historia de México*, ed. Joaquin Garcia Icazbacela (1541; Mexico: 1868), 1–250; and Bernardino de Sahagún, *Aus der Welt der Azteken: Die Chronik des Fray Bernardino de Sahagún*, trans. Leonhard Schultze Jena, Eduard Seler and Sabine Dedenbach-Salazar-Sáenz (Frankfurt am Main: Insel Verlag, 1989); Bernardino de Sahagún, *Historia general de las cosas de la Nueva España*, ed. Alfredo López Austin and Josefine García Quintana, 2 vols. (1558–1560; Madrid: Alianza, 1988).
14 Javier Rubiera, "Christian Sacred Plays and Nō Style," in *Faraway Settings: Spanish and Chinese Theatres of the 16th and 17th Centuries*, ed. Juan Pablo Gil-Osle and Frederick A. De Armas (Madrid: Iberoamericana; Frankfurt am Main: Vervuert, 2019), 217.
15 Ibid., 218.
16 Thomas Leims, *Die Entstehung des Kabuki: Transkulturation Europa–Japan im 16. und 17. Jahrhundert* (Leiden: E. J. Brill, 1990), 170.
17 Rubiera, "Christian Sacred Plays and Nō Style," 222, italics added.
18 Leims, *Die Entstehung des Kabuki*, 287.
19 Jesús López-Gay, "La Liturgia en la Misión del Japón del Siglo XVI," in *Studia Missionalia edita a Facultate missiologica in Pont. Universitate Gregoriana. Documenta et Opera 4* (Rome: Libreria dell'Università Gregoriana, 1970), 174.

20 Kamachi Mitsuru, "East Meets West: Japanese Theater in the Time of Shakespeare," *Shakespeare Studies* 32 (2004): 24.
21 Ibid., 26.
22 Ibid., 29.
23 Ibid., 30.
24 See Thomas Immoos, "Japanische Helden des europäischen Barocktheaters," in *Maske und Kothurn: Internationale Beiträge zur Theaterwissenschaft* 27, no. 1 (1981): 36–56.
25 Takenaka Masahiro, "Jesuit Plays on Japan in the Baroque Age," in *Mission und Theater: Japan und China auf den Bühnen der Gesellschaft Jesu*, ed. Adrian Hsia and Ruprecht Wimmer (Regensburg: Schnell + Steiner, 2005), 389.
26 See Goran Proot and Johan Verberckmoes, "Japonica in the Jesuit Drama of the Southern Netherlands," *Bulletin of Portuguese Japanese Studies* 5 (2002): 27–47.
27 Claudia Mesa Higuera, "Depicting Japan: Lope de Vega and *Los Primeros Mártires del Japón*," in *Faraway Settings: Spanish and Chinese Theatres of the 16th and 17th Centuries*, ed. Juan Pablo Gil-Osle and Frederick A. de Armas (Madrid: Iberoamericana; Frankfurt am Main: Vervuert, 2019), 246.
28 Bernardino de Sahagún, *Aus der Welt der Azteken: Die Chronik des Fray Bernardino de Sahagún*, trans. Leonhard Schultze Jena, Eduard Seler and Sabine Dedenbach-Salazar-Sáenz (Frankfurt am Main: Insel Verlag, 1989), 234–36.
29 Ibid., 257.
30 Adam Versényi, *Theatre in Latin America: Religion, Politics, and Culture from Cortés to the 1980s* (Cambridge: Cambridge University Press, 1993), 1.
31 Ibid., 9–10.
32 Ibid., 11.
33 Charles S. Braden, *Religious Aspects of the Conquest of Mexico* (New York, NY: AMS Press, 1966), 155.
34 Toribio de Motolinía, *History of the Indians of New Spain*, ed. and trans. Francis Borgia Steck (Washington, DC: Academy of American Franciscan History, 1951), 156–59, quoted in Max Harris, *Aztecs, Moors, and Christians: Festivals of Reconquest in Mexico and Spain* (Austin, TX: University of Texas Press, 2000), 133.
35 Diana Taylor, "Scenes of Cognition: Performance and Conquest," *Theatre Journal* 56, no. 3 (2004): 369–70.
36 Toribio de Motolinía, quoted in Viviana Diaz-Balsera, "A Judeo-Christian Tlaloc or a Nahua Yahweh? Domination, Hybridity and Continuity in the Nahua Evangelization Theater," *Colonial Latin American Review* 10, no. 2 (2001): 215.
37 Sahagún, *Aus der Welt der Azteken*, 105–6.
38 Diaz-Balsera, "A Judeo-Christian Tlaloc or a Nahua Yahweh?," 212. See also Fernando Horcasitas, *El teatro náhuatl: Épocas novohispana y moderna* (México: Universidad Nacional Autónoma de México, 1974), 209.
39 Diaz-Balsera, "A Judeo-Christian Tlaloc or a Nahua Yahweh?," 212. See also George C. Vaillant, *The Aztecs of Mexico* (Harmondsworth: Penguin Books, 1951), 116; and Inga Clendinnen, *Aztecs: An Interpretation* (Cambridge: Cambridge University Press, 1991), 155, 188–92.
40 Burr Cartwright Brundage, *The Fifth Sun: Aztec Gods, Aztec World* (Austin, TX: University of Texas, 1979), 70–71.
41 Diaz-Balsera, "A Judeo-Christian Tlaloc or a Nahua Yahweh?," 218, 222.
42 Las Casas, *Apologética Historia Sumaria*, 133.
43 Motolinía, *History of the Indians*, 156, 159.
44 Harris, *Aztecs, Moors, and Christians*, 139.
45 Ibid., 144.
46 Lynn Matluk Brooks, *The Dances of the Processions of Seville in Spain's Golden Age* (Kassel: Reichenberger, 1988), 187.

47 See María Soledad Carrasco Urgoiti, "Aspectos Folclóricos y Literarios de la Fiesta de Moros y Cristianos en España," *PMLA (Journal of the Modern Language Association of America)* 78, no. 5 (1963): 481; and *El Moro Retador y el Moro Amigo: Estudios Sobre Fiestas y Comedias de Moros y Cristianos* (Granada: Universidad de Granada, 1996), 39.
48 Elizabeth H. Boone, "Seeking Indianness: Christoph Weiditz, the Aztecs, and Feathered Amerindians," *Colonial Latin American Review* 26, no. 1 (2017): 47.
49 Harris, *Aztecs, Moors, and Christians*, 176.
50 Christoph Weiditz, *Das Trachtenbuch des Christoph Weiditz von seinen Reisen nach Spanien (1529) und den Niederlanden (1521–32)*, commentary by José Luis Casado Soto and Carlos Soler d'Hyver de las Deses (Valencia: Ediciones Grial, 2001).
51 Boone, "Seeking Indianness," 46.
52 Christopher F. Laferl, "Amerika im spanischen Barocktheater," in *Federschmuck und Kaiserkrone: Das barocke Amerikabild in den habsburgischen Ländern*, ed. Friedrich B. Polleroß, Andrea Sommer-Mathis and Christopher F. Laferl (Vienna: Bundesministerium für Wissenschaft und Forschung, 1992).
53 Louise M. Burkhart, *Holy Wednesday: A Nahua Drama from Early Colonial Mexico* (Philadelphia, PA: University of Pennsylvania Press, 1996), 41.
54 Harris, *Aztecs, Moors, and Christians*, 38.
55 Diana Taylor, *The Archive and the Repertoire* (Durham, NC: Duke University Press, 2003), 19.
56 Ibid., 20.

Bibliography

Bank, Rosemarie K. "A-foot in Time: Temporality in the Space of a Moment in Theatre History." In *The Methuen Drama Handbook of Theatre History and Historiography*, edited by Claire Cochrane and Jo Robinson, 56–66. London: Bloomsbury, 2020.

Bank, Rosemarie K., and Michal Kobialka, eds. *Theatre/Performance Historiography: Time, Space, Matter*. New York, NY: Palgrave Macmillan, 2015.

Bial, Henry, and Scott Magelssen, eds. *Theater Historiography: Critical Interventions*. Ann Arbor, MI: University of Michigan Press, 2010.

Boone, Elizabeth H. "Seeking Indianness: Christoph Weiditz, the Aztecs, and Feathered Amerindians." *Colonial Latin American Review* 26, no. 1 (2017): 39–61.

Braden, Charles S. *Religious Aspects of the Conquest of Mexico*. New York, NY: AMS Press, 1966.

Brooks, Lynn Matluk. *The Dances of the Processions of Seville in Spain's Golden Age*. Kassel: Reichenberger, 1988.

Brundage, Burr Cartwright. *The Fifth Sun: Aztec Gods, Aztec World*. Austin, TX: University of Texas, 1979.

Burkhart, Louise M. *Holy Wednesday: A Nahua Drama from Early Colonial Mexico*. Philadelphia, PA: University of Pennsylvania Press, 1996.

Cabranes-Grant, Leo. *From Scenarios to Networks: Performing the Intercultural in Colonial Mexico*. Evanston, IL: Northwestern University Press, 2016. https://doi.org/10.2307/j.ctv4cbhcz.

Canning, Charlotte M., and Thomas Postlewait, eds. *Representing the Past: Essays in Performance Historiography*. Iowa City, IA: University of Iowa Press, 2010.

Carrasco Urgoiti, María Soledad. "Aspectos Folclóricos y Literarios de la Fiesta de Moros y Cristianos en España." *PMLA (Journal of the Modern Language Association of America)* 78, no. 5 (1963): 476–91.

Carrasco Urgoiti, María Soledad. *El Moro Retador y el Moro Amigo: Estudios Sobre Fiestas y Comedias de Moros y Cristianos*. Granada: Universidad de Granada, 1996.

Clendinnen, Inga. *Aztecs: An Interpretation*. Cambridge: Cambridge University Press, 1991.

Cline, Howard F. "Hernando Cortés and the Aztec Indians in Spain." *The Quarterly Journal of the Library of Congress* 26, no. 2 (1969): 70–90.

Cochrane, Claire, and Jo Robinson, eds. *The Methuen Drama Handbook of Theatre History and Historiography*. London: Bloomsbury, 2019.

Cochrane, Claire, and Jo Robinson, eds. *Theatre History and Historiography: Ethics, Evidence and Truth*. London: Palgrave Macmillan, 2016.

Corona, Carmen. "El auto La conquista de Jerusalén: Hernán Cortés y la transgression de la figura." In *El teatro franciscano en la Nueva España: Fuentes y ensayos para el estudio del teatro de evangelización en el siglo XVI*, edited by María Sten, 291–97. Mexico: Universidad Nacional Autonóma de México, 2000.

Davis, Tracy C., and Peter W. Marx, eds. *The Routledge Companion to Theatre and Performance Historiography*. London and New York, NY: Routledge, 2021.

Diaz-Balsera, Viviana. "A Judeo-Christian Tlaloc or a Nahua Yahweh? Domination, Hybridity and Continuity in the Nahua Evangelization Theater." *Colonial Latin American Review* 10, no. 2 (2001): 209–27.

Diaz-Balsera, Viviana. *The Pyramid under the Cross: Franciscan Discourses of Evangelization and the Nahua Christian Subject in Sixteenth-Century Mexico*. Tucson, AZ: The University of Arizona Press, 2005.

Drábek, Pavel. "'Why, sir, are there other heauens in other countries?' The English Comedy as a Transnational Style." In *Transnational Connections in Early Modern Theatre*, edited by M. A. Katritzky and Pavel Drábek, 139–61. Manchester: Manchester University Press, 2019.

Durán, Diego. *Historia de las Indias de Nueva España y Islas de Tierra Firme*. 1579–1581. Edited by Jose F. Ramirez. Mexico: Impr. de J. M. Andrade y F. Escalante, 1867–1880.

Garcidueñas, José Rojas. "El Teatro De Evangelización." In *El teatro franciscano en la Nueva España: Fuentes y ensayos para el estudio del teatro de evangelización en el siglo XVI*, edited by María Sten, 65–74. Mexico: Universidad Nacional Autonóma de México, 2000.

Harris, Max. *Aztecs, Moors, and Christians: Festivals of Reconquest in Mexico and Spain*. Austin, TX: University of Texas Press, 2000.

Horcasitas, Fernando. "Los principios del drama náhuatl en México." In *El teatro franciscano en la Nueva España: Fuentes y ensayos para el estudio del teatro de evangelización en el siglo XVI*, edited by María Sten, 131–39. Mexico: Universidad Nacional Autonóma de México, 2000.

Horcasitas, Fernando. *El teatro náhuatl: Épocas novohispana y moderna*. México: Universidad Nacional Autónoma de México, 1974.

Hulfeld, Stefan. "Notebooks, Prologues and Scenarios." In *Commedia dell'Arte in Context*, edited by Christopher Balme, Piermario Vescovo and Daniele Vianello, 46–55. Cambridge: Cambridge University Press, 2018.

Immoos, Thomas. "Japanische Helden des europäischen Barocktheaters" ["Japanese Heroes in European Baroque Theater"]. *Maske und Kothurn: Internationale Beiträge zur Theaterwissenschaft* 27, no. 1 (1981): 36–56.

Kamachi Mitsuru. "East Meets West: Japanese Theater in the Time of Shakespeare." *Shakespeare Studies* 32 (2004): 23–35.

Kocka, Jürgen. "Comparison and Beyond." *History and Theory* 42, no. 1 (2003): 39–44.

Laferl, Christopher F. "Amerika im spanischen Barocktheater" ["America in Spanish Baroque Theater"]. In *Federschmuck und Kaiserkrone: Das barocke Amerikabild in den habsburgischen Ländern*, edited by Friedrich B. Polleroß, Andrea Sommer-Mathis and Christopher F. Laferl, 161–84. Vienna: Bundesministerium für Wissenschaft und Forschung, 1992.

Las Casas, Bartolomé de. *Apologética Historia Sumaria*. 1909. Edited by Edmundo O'Gorman. 2 vols. México: Universidad Nacional Autónoma de México, Instituto de Investigaciones Históricas, 1967.

Las Casas, Bartolomé de. *Historia de las Indias*. Edited by El Marques de la Fuensante del valle. 5 vols. Madrid: Impr. de M. Ginesta, 1876.

Las Casas, Bartolomé de. *History of the Indies*. Edited and translated by Andrée Collard. New York, NY: Harper & Row, 1971.

Leims, Thomas. *Die Entstehung des Kabuki: Transkulturation Europa–Japan im 16. und 17. Jahrhundert [The Genesis of Kabuki: Transculturation Europe–Japan in 16th and 17th Centuries]*. Leiden: E. J. Brill, 1990.

Limon, Jerzy. *Gentlemen of a Company: English Players in Central and Eastern Europe 1590–1660*. Cambridge: Cambridge University Press, 1985.

López-Gay, Jesús. "La Liturgia en la Misión del Japón del Siglo XVI." In *Studia Missionalia Edita a Facultate Missiologica in Pont. Universitate Gregoriana. Documenta et Opera 4*. Rome: Libreria dell'Università Gregoriana, 1970.

Mesa Higuera, Claudia. "Depicting Japan: Lope de Vega and *Los Primeros Mártires del Japón*." In *Faraway Settings: Spanish and Chinese Theatres of the 16th and 17th Centuries*, edited by Juan Pablo Gil-Osle and Frederick A. de Armas, 225–48. Madrid: Iberoamericana; Frankfurt am Main: Vervuert, 2019.

Motolinía, Toribio de. *Historia de los Indios de la Nueva España*. 1541. Vol. 1 of *Colección de Documentos para la historia de México*, edited by Joaquin Garcia Icazbacela, 1–250. Mexico: 1868.

Motolinía, Toribio de. *History of the Indians of New Spain*. Edited and translated by Francis Borgia Steck. Washington, DC: Academy of American Franciscan History, 1951.

Pagden, Anthony. *The Fall of Natural Man: The American Indian and the Origins of Comparative Ethnology*. Cambridge: Cambridge University Press, 1982.

Partida Tayzan, Armando. "El sacrificio de Isaac." In *El teatro franciscano en la Nueva España: Fuentes y ensayos para el estudio del teatro de evangelización en el siglo XVI*, edited by María Sten, 205–80. Mexico: Universidad Nacional Autonóma de México, 2000.

Portilla, Miguel León. "Teatro Náhuatl Prehispánico." In *El teatro franciscano en la Nueva España: Fuentes y ensayos para el estudio del teatro de evangelización en el siglo XVI*, edited by María Sten, 39–61. Mexico: Universidad Nacional Autonóma de México, 2000.

Potter, Robert. "Abraham Y El Sacrificio Humano." In *El teatro franciscano en la Nueva España: Fuentes y ensayos para el estudio del teatro de evangelización en el siglo XVI*, edited by María Sten, 219–26. Mexico: Universidad Nacional Autonóma de México, 2000.

Proot, Goran, and Johan Verberckmoes. "Japonica in the Jesuit Drama of the Southern Netherlands." *Bulletin of Portuguese Japanese Studies* 5 (2002): 27–47.

Ricard, Robert. *The Spiritual Conquest of Mexico*. Translated by Lesley Byrd Simpson. Berkeley and Los Angeles, CA: University of California Press, 1966.

Rinke, Stefan, Federico Navarrete and Nino Vallen, eds. *Der Codex Mendoza: Das Meisterwerk aztekisch-spanischer Buchkultur* [The Codex Mendoza: The Masterpiece of Aztec-Spanish Book Culture]. Darmstadt: Wissenschaftliche Buchgesellschaft.

Rubiera, Javier. "Christian Sacred Plays and Nō Style." In *Faraway Settings: Spanish and Chinese Theatres of the 16th and 17th Centuries*, edited by Juan Pablo Gil-Osle and Frederick A. De Armas, 209–24. Madrid: Iberoamericana; Frankfurt am Main: Vervuert, 2019.

Sahagún, Bernardino de. *Aus der Welt der Azteken: Die Chronik des Fray Bernardino de Sahagún* [From the Aztec World: The Chronicle of Fray Bernardino de Sahagún]. Translated by Leonhard Schultze Jena, Eduard Seler and Sabine Dedenbach-Salazar-Sáenz. Frankfurt am Main: Insel Verlag, 1989.

Sahagún, Bernardino de. *Historia general de las cosas de la Nueva España*. 1558–1560. Edited by Alfredo López Austin and Josefine García Quintana. 2 vols. Madrid: Alianza, 1988.

Sommer-Mathis, Andrea. "Amerika im Fest und auf der Bühne im 16. und 17. Jahrhundert" ["America in Festivals and on the Stages of the 16th and 17th Centuries"]. In *Federschmuck und Kaiserkrone: Das barocke Amerikabild in den habsburgischen Ländern*, edited by Friedrich B. Polleroß, Andrea Sommer-Mathis and Christopher F. Laferl, 161–84. Vienna: Bundesministerium für Wissenschaft und Forschung, 1992.

Sorgenfrei, Carol Fisher. "Strategic Unweaving: Itō Michio and the Diasporic Dancing Body." In *The Politics of Interweaving Performance Cultures: Beyond Postcolonialism*, edited by Erika Fischer-Lichte, Torsten Jost and Saskya Iris Jain, 201–22. London and New York, NY: Routledge, 2014.

Sten, María, ed. *El teatro franciscano en la Nueva España: Fuentes y ensayos para el estudio del teatro de evangelización en el siglo XVI*. Mexico: Universidad Nacional Autonóma de México, 2000.

Sten, María. "Sincretismo Del Teatro Evangelizante." In *El teatro franciscano en la Nueva España: Fuentes y ensayos para el estudio del teatro de evangelización en el siglo XVI*, edited by María Sten, 141–49. Mexico: Universidad Nacional Autonóma de México, 2000.

Takenaka Masahiro. "Jesuit Plays on Japan in the Baroque Age." In *Mission und Theater: Japan und China auf den Bühnen der Gesellschaft Jesu*, edited by Adrian Hsia and Ruprecht Wimmer, 379–410. Regensburg: Schnell + Steiner, 2005.

Taylor, Diana. "Scenes of Cognition: Performance and Conquest." *Theatre Journal* 56, no. 3 (2004): 353–72.

Taylor, Diana. *The Archive and the Repertoire*. Durham, NC: Duke University Press, 2003.

Terauchi Naoko. "Ancient and Early Medieval Performing Arts." In *A History of Japanese Theatre*, edited by Jonah Salz, 4–19. Cambridge: Cambridge University Press, 2016.

Troiano, Massimo. *Die Münchner Fürstenhochzeit von 1568* [The Munich Princely Wedding of 1568]. Edited by Horst Leuchtmann. München: Katzbichler, 1980.

Vaillant, George C. *The Aztecs of Mexico*. Harmondsworth: Penguin Books, 1951.

Versényi, Adam. *Theatre in Latin America: Religion, Politics, and Culture from Cortés to the 1980s*. Cambridge: Cambridge University Press, 1993.

Weiditz, Christoph. *Das Trachtenbuch des Christoph Weiditz von seinen Reisen nach Spanien (1529) und den Niederlanden (1521–32)* [*The Costume Book of Christoph Weiditz from his Travels to Spain (1529) and the Netherlands (1521–32)*]. Commentary by José Luis Casado Soto and Carlos Soler d'Hyver de las Deses. Valencia: Ediciones Grial, 2001.

Werner, Michael, and Bénédicte Zimmermann. "Beyond Comparison: *Histoire Croisée* and the Challenge of Reflexivity." *History and Theory* 45, no. 1 (2006): 30–50.

Wiles, David, and Christine Dymkowski, eds. *The Cambridge Companion to Theatre History*. Cambridge: Cambridge University Press, 2012.

Ybarra, Patricia A. *Performing Conquest. Five Centuries of Theater, History, and Identity in Tlaxcala, Mexico*. Ann Arbor, MI: The University of Michigan Press, 2009.

PART I
Methodological Reflections

1
INTERWEAVING STORIES, ALTERING DISCOURSES

Małgorzata Sugiera

For a Nonhistorical History

Today, Sande Cohen is admittedly not alone among professional historians with his bold yet controversial claim formulated more than a decade ago in his *History Out of Joint* that historiography is one of many failed discursive projects of modernity, largely irrelevant to our individual and collective acts of identification with and judgment about the past.[1] The question whether there is something inherent in the past which could guarantee that academic history offers a privileged descriptive and/or explanatory perspective on a no longer accessible "reality" has already been much debated, at least since the publication of Hayden White's *Metahistory* in the early 1970s.[2] After issues of how meaning and narrative are linguistically and rhetorically constructed, another important matter was raised: What justifies the discipline's oppressive truth claims and its institutionalized epistemological superiority to all other forms of past-talk? Yet, as Alun Munslow argued in the late 1990s, the past as history is only one of many practices of imagining and experiencing pastness, although it is still deemed to be epistemologically superior.[3] Quite recently, various emerging and often politically charged counter-practices beyond the borders of academic history's professional codes have resulted in a kind of ethical turn in history theory that could be illustrated, for instance, by a few themed issues of leading history journals such as *History and Theory* and *Rethinking History*.[4] As a result, the dominant ways of managing, understanding and representing temporality were contested, while other preferred narratives of the past came into prominence in the last decades. Also, long forgotten past possibilities or choices have been successfully revealed as still having a latent yet decisive impact on our present and, therefore, could be employed as tactical, ethical and affective resources for political resistance.

All recent turns and heated debates in the theory of history, which I could only cursorily mention here, can also be discerned in other disciplines in the humanities that explore either their own disciplinary past or descriptively and explanatorily follow historical changes of their objects, as is the case, for instance, in theater, literature or art. Staying within their own boundaries, each purports to explain its rationale in terms of its relations to a posited past. Here, the past is also still subjected to history's controlling disciplinary gaze, and many forms and ways of constituting pastness have recently been recognized as factually inaccurate—that is, "unreliable"—accounts of past events. However, many critical historians believe that the various attempts to revisit and reconceptualize conventional practices, discursive forms and representational models of their discipline, which have already had a visible impact on other disciplines, are probably futile. Claire Norton and Mark Donnelly, historians at St Mary's University in London, in their *Liberating Histories* come to this conclusion: "It might well be that institutionalised history as a discourse currently conceptualised and practiced lacks the flexibility to reinvent itself."[5] Their aim has been to explore history's relations with other ways of conceiving and communicating about the past, although they are perfectly aware that some of these ways will not be approved by their colleagues and the larger public as epistemological equivalents of factually accurate and, thus, "true" historical knowledge.

What seems to be of particular interest in my context is that, among "genuinely bold and politically imaginative uses of the past—the kind that might define new political communities, or stake out new subject positions,"[6] Norton and Donnelly privilege various artworks of mixed media and genres that intertwine archeological and ethnographic research methods with "critical fabulation," as Saidiya Hartman would have it.[7] As they explain, "[w]hile historians have a tendency to simplify the multiple meanings that make an event or action intelligible in a single, explanatory narrative, artists have a greater freedom to complicate, multiply and intertwine possible explanation."[8] In other words, not only are artists better positioned to change our view on and of the (or a) past, as the authors of *Liberating Histories* argue, but artists also offer refined means of looking otherwise at hegemonic practices of professional historians and provide new articulations to challenge or question them.

What is more, the slippage between the historical and the fictional on which Norton and Donnelly elaborate when analyzing various examples of performative documentary fictions should help (a) problematize the reductive binaries of fact and fiction, true and false, real and imaginary, and (b) conceptualize the past as a proper space of experience that could be used in our ethical deliberations on today's issues. In this way, as they posit, we can (and should) subvert the long-established dominance of the singular, linear and progressive notion of historical time—with the past behind us and the future ahead of us—the more so because the notion of historical time is so closely connected with the modern idea of the West being the theological end point of a single evolutionary process of human civilizational development.

The recent nostalgic romanticization and glamorization of the imperial past—which has strongly influenced the political strategies of many European countries, with the United Kingdom as the best-known example—has demonstrated that historians have not altogether dispensed with the discipline's old narratives and categories. In her recent book *Time's Monster*, which reflects upon how the discipline of history has figured in the making of our world, Priya Satia argues that it is mainly discernible in "the wider culture, in which a vast industry of popular history remains captive to the old great-man mode of narrating the past and inspiring action in the present."[9] That is why I would like to focus on artistic practices that offer new forms of "nonhistorical" writing, especially those that multiply and entangle spaces and opportunities for an undertaking that layers the past, the present and the future together in productive, nonlinear ways. Artistic practices of this kind can work across temporal and geographical landscapes in order to performatively create such time-space entanglements that are able to reveal—and materialize in cognitively and affectively effective forms—similarities and epistemic connections that otherwise would be impossible to constitute and/or suggest. Working in such a way, artists can also remind their audiences that the very word "history" comes from the Greek *istoría*, which means "to inquire"—a verb, not a noun. Thus, it should resume its original function as a verb once again, especially today when we have become increasingly aware of the complex entanglement of the environment and human history, of the "deep history" that connects the scale of human time with geological and astronomical timelines.

In order to corroborate this claim, in what follows, I take a closer look at two examples of recent artistic projects that attempt to inquire and, in so doing, denaturalize the Western conception of historical time as empty and universal, demonstrating the performativity of the boundaries between the past, the present and the future—once they become contemporaneous and entangled. Therefore, both these examples are characterized by reference to Elizabeth Povinelli's concept of "ancestral catastrophe," elaborated on in her *Between Gaia and Ground*. Ancestral catastrophe is radically different from a "thing-event" such as the coming catastrophe of climatic, environmental and social collapse. The coming catastrophe "is often read as [a] specific sort of event, a future event that will constitute a new and dramatic beginning, a radical death and a radical rebirth [...] as the potential end of one kind of human and natural history."[10] By contrast, as Povinelli underlines, ancestral catastrophes do not operate in the same temporality: they "are past and present; they keep arriving out of the ground of colonialism and racism rather than emerging over the horizon of liberal progress."[11] It is exactly this kind of complex temporality that takes center stage in the artistic projects I have chosen.

The first of my examples is a series of ethnofictional happenings conceived for three spaces within the Museo Nacional Centro de Arte Reina Sofía, namely *Of Lunatics, or Those Lacking Sanity* by the Bogota-based artistic laboratory Mapa Teatro, which I saw in Madrid in November 2018. The second one is, by contrast, a short film entitled *Afronauts* by Frances Bodomo, an African-American artist and filmmaker born in Ghana, educated in Norway and living in New York. The 14-minute short premiered at the Sundance Film Festival in 2014 and was subsequently presented at the Berlinale and several other festivals and exhibitions. I watched it as part of an exhibition called "Fly me to the Moon" in the Kunsthaus Zürich in April 2019, commemorating the 50th anniversary of the moon landing. Although quite different in their choice of topics, artistic forms and materiality, both these artworks draw on and recontextualize a network of past events, stories rather than histories, each in its own way collapsing the linear (historical) time. Thus, they offer entanglements of different temporal, geographical and onto-epistemological landscapes in order to reveal the injustices of the colonial past that are latently still part of our now. In so doing, they both critically approach the dominant representational practices of the performing arts, demonstratively refusing to embody and speak on behalf of absent others or to be simply anti-hegemonic. Also, with the same aim in view, they recalibrate and redeploy their available discursive capacities, counting on what could be named the participants' emergent understanding (since the projects have no clearly formulated message) as a conditional source of speculative imaginings of a future to come. In other words, they summon or even conjure a possible past—trying to open it toward a possible future instead of representing the past from an "objectifying" distance characteristic of history as an academic discipline—and openly calling attention to what is politically imperative for our time of late liberalism rather than empirically grounded in archival material. Therefore, they are still communicating about the (or a) past but, at the same time, go far beyond historiography as a "nomos" of the Western modernity, its failed discursive project, as Cohen has it.

Entangling Timescapes

In the second chapter of his *Provincializing Europe*, Dipesh Chakrabarty revisited Marx's writings on capital and its development in order to "rework the relationship between postcolonial thinking and the intellectual legacies of post-Enlightenment rationalism, humanism, and historicism."[12] Seeking to pluralize history, Chakrabarty found out that in the posthumously collected and published volumes of *Theories of Surplus Value*, Marx posited two types of history—History 1 and History 2—intimately entangled and mutually constitutive. What he named History 1 is the past posited by capital itself as its precondition. It forms the backbone of the usual narratives of transition to the capitalist mode of production, whereas History 2 provides a framework for all that does not participate in capital's own life-process. Since he assessed Marx's ideas about History 2 as rather underdeveloped, quite distant from a program of writing histories in postcolonial times, Chakrabarty suggested: "History 2 is better thought of as a category charged with the function of constantly interrupting the totalizing thrusts of History 1."[13] History 2, sometimes written by Chakrabarty also in plural as History 2s, is meant to be alternative to the analytical narratives of capital and should function as a ground for claiming historical difference of all these histories that do not partake in hegemonic History 1—"*affective* narratives of human belonging."[14] Significantly, the author of *Provincializing Europe*, while trying to get beyond Eurocentric history, still sought to theorize a subaltern historiography, not even trying, as a matter of fact, to question the very basis of the Western paradigm of gathering and ordering historical knowledge. At that time, he was simply not aware of the importance of that which has been more and more hotly debated in the field of Black feminism's philosophy of history in the last decade. Unfortunately, I have no place here to properly address the issue in all its complexity.[15] Hence, I will limit myself to referring to one of the most inspiring books in the field, Alys Eve Weinbaum's *Afterlife of Reproductive Slavery*.[16] She develops an epistemic argument about the afterlife of a racialization thought system and analyzes in depth a large plethora of idioms from various knowledge practices and media, including history, theory, literary fiction and films. Her argument corresponds particularly well with my first example, a series of three installations of Mapa Teatro's *Of Lunatics*, which in today's perspective entangles King Charles III's colonial Spain and the New Kingdom of Granada (present-day Colombia) at the time of the gold rush in the Americas in the second half of the seventeenth century, the very moment of the invention of racialization, and the beginning of globalized capitalist exploitation.

To put it straightforwardly, nowadays we may hardly speak about a subaltern historiography written in the way a professional historian might prefer, given the paucity of supporting evidence and the sparsity of historical archives that could provide objective, transparent representation of pasts which could fit within the overarching account of capital's development. Such an argument makes perfect sense, if we recall that the authorized history was part and parcel of the ideological framework of colonization and oppression—it was a hegemonic fictional construction. As a result, although both types of past-talk are intimately entangled and mutually constitutive, History 2s can by no means follow the same epistemological practices, discursive forms and representational models as History 1. While correcting the dominant historiography, postcolonial and decolonial historians have to take recourse to conditional or subjunctive tenses, and imagine what would have happened through directing attention to what was silenced, edited out, marginalized and, in consequence, made invisible. Therefore, they focus on historical entanglement, epistemic endurance, echoes and hauntings, imaginatively mobilizing various resources, deemed as unhistorical by the mainstream of their scholarly discipline. Thus, facing this lack of documented evidence, and incapable of establishing the so-called facts, subaltern histories cannot be empirically sanctioned. While wanting to counterbalance the shortage of archival resources, they have to be predicated on what is affective and felt as historically right, on the politically imperative, and actively constituted pastness as a subjunctive fiction rather than an objective reality, reconstructed on facts only, driven by rational logic and, in turn, realistically represented. Does what I have just written presuppose that subaltern histories, because of their epistemic condition of possibility, will always remain subaltern, alternative or counterfactual stories, epistemologically subordinated to the "proper" history, History 1?

Mapa Teatro's *Of Lunatics* offers a kind of solution to this problem since it does not entangle a factually accurate, historical account of past events as documented in colonial archives (History 1) with a "critical fabulation" of roughly the same events in conditional modes as potentially experienced by colonized Amerindians (History 2s, or rather empirically ungrounded stories). Looking recently at Mapa Teatro's former artistic projects in the broader context of a long legacy of decolonial practices in Latin America, Kati Röttger convincingly analyzes them as what she calls a "dramaturgy of decolonisation," which she defines as "a practice of decontextualising and recontextualising. This takes up the intertwined threads of references to recompose them again and again into reshuffled images, layered like an archaeological site where the colonial wounds have been covered."[17] This time, however, Mapa Teatro performed two epistemically equal and openly fictionalized stories, called "ethnofictions" by the creators, not only entangled and co-constituted but also significantly shaped by their relationship to the history and architecture of the museum building in which *Of Lunatics* was performed in the capital of once imperial Spain. That is how Mapa Teatro's ethnofictional practice, based on site-specific research, in a different way influenced the sometimes contradictory threads of History 1 and History 2s (in this case, forgotten or ignored stories) entangled by the collective creation method. The different way of entanglement in turn significantly changed the dramaturgy of decolonization identified by Röttger in the previous and more theatrical works of this group. *Of Lunatics* could hardly be referred to as "an archaeological site" whose layers would be removed one after another during a performance to uncover the colonial wounds. The specificity of the museum's architecture and its visitors' behavior made the artists focus on how a geopolitical past, a present knowledge and a bodily experience of the here and now are marked by colonial difference and problematized in interaction with both the actual installation space and the audience moving on its own through the space.

The Sabatini Building is a part of Madrid's Museo Reina Sofía. Until 1968 it served, however, as the main building of the Hospital General y de la Pasión, founded in the sixteenth century. Shortly after it was established, it became an infirmary for the convalescent and the insane. The building's basement was the place for "lunatics and the unsound of mind,"[18] as they were called at that time. To guarantee the hospital's maintenance, King Ferdinand VI decreed that all alms granted by the royal family or resources from Spanish colonies were to be donated to the hospital. From 1749 onward, vast quantities of gold coins and objects destined for the asylum arrived from the Americas. But it is not the only link between the Sabatini Building and erstwhile Spanish colonies in South America. One of the persons pronounced insane and kept in the vaults of the hospital, whose traces were found in the hospital archives, was Don Ángel Díaz Castellanos, a mineralogist and engineer of King Charles III, sent to the New Kingdom of Granada (present-day Colombia) on a special mission. Its aim was to support the establishment of the Royal Mining Company and to boost gold production by introducing new technologies of mining to make the extraction of gold ore considerably cheaper. After several years of visiting different mines across the region, while staying in Marmato, an area where people of Quimbaya lived, known for its sophisticated gold metalwork techniques, the royal mineralogist started to show first signs of mental illness and, for that reason, was forced to return to Madrid. There, he was diagnosed with *auriferous delirium* and confined to the hospital, where he died a few years later. Both his life story, closely entangled with the colonization of the Americas, and the history of the Sabatini Building stirred the interest of Mapa Teatro, when the group was invited to take part in "Fissures," a program organized by the Museo Reina Sofía in 2018.

Mapa Teatro was cofounded in 1984 by Heidi, Rolf and Elizabeth Abderhalden Cortés, siblings and multidisciplinary artists, with roots in the Colombian Andes and the Swiss Alps. After an initial period of artistic experimentation in Paris, Heidi and Rolf relocated Mapa Teatro to Bogota, the capital of Colombia. Their careers still branched across the Atlantic, however, and their aim remained to cross geographical, linguistic and disciplinary boundaries in order to create friction which produces a form of "thought-creation" in collaboration with artists, thinkers and local people from many countries. They insist that their collective is not a theater group but rather a "laboratory" of artists who experiment with mixed media, using absent and present human bodies to explore actual global issues from local perspectives. More often than not, the bodies they intend to activate are the bodies of museum or gallery visitors, compelled through spatial arrangements into taking the responsibility for giving meaning not only to what they see around but also to how they position themselves within the installations. Significantly, Mapa Teatro's cofounders call themselves "cartographer-anthropophagists," clearly referring to the *Anthropophagic Manifesto*, an essay written in poetic prose and published in 1928 by Oswald de Andrade (1890–1954), a poet and key figure in the cultural movement of Brazilian modernism. In his manifesto, Andrade posited that the greatest strength of Brazilian culture is exactly that which is regarded as its weakness: its history of "cannibalizing" other cultures. More recently, cannibalism as an alleged tribal rite of the people of Tupi became a way for Brazil to assert itself against European post-colonial (or neocolonial) domination as a fully original form of onto-epistemology.[19] Small wonder therefore that the Abderhalden Cortéses took interest in the story of the king's mineralogist, his diagnosed *auriferous delirium* which he developed while inspecting gold mines in South America, and his subsequent enforced stay in the basement of what today is Museo Reina Sofía in Madrid. What they decided to do was to bring his delirious visions of gold production in Spanish colonies into life and confront museum visitors with these visions in exactly these places where most probably the king's mineralogist had them—in the vaults, the staircase that leads to them and on the first floor of the Sabatini Building.

The visitor enters Mapa Teatro's installation through two rooms on the first floor. Besides some information about the project, the first well-lit room exhibits archival traces—facsimiles of chosen pages of the rules of procedure in royal hospitals, and of medical treatises on mental illnesses from the early nineteenth century, as well as maps of colonial South America and the New Kingdom of Granada from the same period. The second room is kept in deep darkness. The only spotlight is directed on a rather small, gold statue of a Quimbaya chief which—because of the way it is exhibited—emanates a strong power of attraction, an almost delirious "pull." Then, the visitor is supposed to go down, into the vaults, using a flight of old, stone stairs. Here, she can see a few narrow railways, trolleys for transporting gold ore, black-and-white images projected on thick, raw walls and sounds of working miners. A particularly impressive image which realistically depicts a group of miners pushing a trolley full of ore with all their might is projected on a PVC strip-curtain. However, the illusion of seeing a real-life scene is rather fleeting, because the workers, obviously, do not get through the curtain, which opens to allow the trolley to glide further on the rails. Only images—this time, in color—of people and pack animals in a mountain landscape are to be seen in the spiral staircase in the tower, leading three floors up. When the visitor laboriously climbs the stone stairs, a metal bucket rushes down every now and again, announced by a piercing sound, or is slowly pulled up on a rope. Still nobody but the museum visitors is present at Mapa Teatro's *Of Lunatics*.

Thus, only images, sounds and pieces of machinery have been employed to bring to life the gold miners' work of that time. Nobody represents the miners themselves, which actually makes the visitor's experience a kind of dream or phantasmagoria of distant times and geographic places, to which she has already been referred in a more distanced and objectified "scientific" way in the two rooms of the first floor. All this has at least one particular effect: when the visitor moves through the complex space, the installation could be said to materialize a mechanism that produced the colonial image of the Other, a process decisive for the individual and collective identity of the Moderns. This image of the colonial Other is clearly represented as delirious, but for many people of that time, it was the only one with which they could have a direct contact. However, it is not the whole truth about *Of Lunatics*, for Mapa Teatro did not limit their work to archival research. The group also established a temporary community of collaborators with the Marmato mining town in Caldas, Colombia. What is significant is that the Marmato mine had begun to be exploited long before the Spaniards colonized the Americas. It has been productive until today due to the strength of the local people who resisted control by various state factions and fended off the invasion of mining multinationals. Only after having experienced the place and stories of its inhabitants did Mapa Teatro decide to collapse time and space, the past and the present, by connecting the gold mine of Marmato to the hospital and present-day museum, and the king's mineralogist-lunatic to today's miners of the same region in the experience of each and every visitor, marked differently by colonial difference, here and now. In so doing, the group created a largely unacknowledged historical entanglement of European colonialism with its invention of racialization and the globalized capitalist exploitation of our time; the entanglement that Povinelli calls "the carbon imaginary of late liberalism."[20] Simultaneously, by skillfully immersing the visitor's body in the materiality of the installation without impersonating the absent other, the artists invited the visitor to change her definition of racialization. As Alexander Weheliye points out, racialization could rightly be understood "not as a biological or cultural descriptor but as a conglomerate of sociopolitical relations that discipline humanity into full humans, not-quite-humans, and nonhumans."[21] Mapa Teatro's *Of Lunatics* did exactly this; it materialized various, situated forms of such racism in order to reveal epistemic entanglements between different but similarly violent facets of modernity that we have inherited and that still live as a latent yet impactful thought system. A ghostly presence of this episteme haunts the series of happenings—Mapa Teatro's "ethnofictions"—in three spaces within Museo Reina Sofía and provides the very center around which the series coheres.

Therefore, the way the Abderhalden Cortéses make use of the reconstructed story of Don Ángel Díaz Castellanos's life should not be treated as metaphoric; it is rather symptomatic in the sense elaborated by Norton and Donnelly. In their *Liberating Histories* they explain,

> [t]he symptomatic cannot and should not be reduced to a symbol or allegory; it is not a micro-history trying to reflect a larger history. It is a way of appropriating history, producing a counter-narrative to dominant forms of representation, a way of narrating a subversive, unofficial history.[22]

However, producing a counter-narrative of entanglement to dominant forms of representation may not be enough to create liberating histories, as Weinbaum insists when commenting on Du Bois's *Black Reconstruction* and his refutation of five decades of "scandalous white historiography." "If history is to be set to work in the service of a more liberated future," she posits, "historical narrative must be keyed to the moment of its production."[23] Yet, Black feminism is not alone in using such historical narratives as its primary methodological and political insight. In a sense, Mapa Teatro has cannibalized the historical narrative in order to make it its own methodological approach in the name of a future yet to come in *Of Lunatics*.

Naming the Discourse

There are at least two crucial historical events of the twentieth century, the Second World War and the moon landing, which have brought forth a large variety of alternative, virtual and counterfactual narratives in different media and distinctive genres—pseudo-documentary, docufiction, mockumentary, docudrama, docucomedy and many others. In the context of my argument here, the moon landing is more interesting, not only because of the 50th anniversary of the first manned mission on the moon on 20 July 1969, which was much spoken about once again and celebrated in 2019. As Mateusz Borowski demonstrated in his recent article "Counterfactual Histories of Moon Landing,"[24] among well-known counterfactual narratives about space flight, there are not only Antoine Bardou-Jacquet's comedy *Moonwalkers* (2015), which follows many conspiracy theories showing the moon landing as a hoax, a carefully staged studio recording, and Aleksey Fedorchenko's mockumentary *First on the Moon* (2005), which mockdocuments a successful Soviet landing on the moon already in 1938, an event which would obviously have robbed the United States of glory. There are also such narratives that could be rightly identified as counter-hegemonic as, for instance, Margot Lee Shetterly's book *Hidden Figures* (2016) and the cinematic biographical drama of the same title which premiered in the same year. Both recount the life-stories of three major African-American female mathematicians who worked for NASA in the 1960s and were not only plain "computers"—that is, women who did manual computation for white male NASA engineers—but played a crucial part in the early attempts of space flight, which ultimately led to the moon landing in 1969. In so doing, both versions of *Hidden Figures*—each in a different way and, obviously, not without stirring controversies—counter a significant omission in the history of space flight, which, from the outset, was conceived as an undertaking that celebrated the White Anglo-Saxon Protestant culture. Confronted with scant sources, the author of *Hidden Figures* could not provide, as many postcolonial historians did, a properly evidenced historical account and had to rely primarily on unreliable testimonies of witnesses and her own imagination. However, I would like to focus here on two similar but less known counter-hegemonic narratives of space exploration in order to prepare a more relevant background for my second example—Nuotama Frances Bodomo's short film *Afronauts*.

The first one is a project, *The Lebanese Rocket Society: A Tribute to Dreamers* (2011–2013), which combines archival material with supplementing fictions in a documentary film and series of installations including performance, photography and textiles. The project resulted from Joana Hadjithomas and Khalil Lamia Joreige's research on the long-forgotten part of Lebanese past and its involvement with the space race and rocket research. The aim of this research was mainly an event from the early 1960s, when a group of students which named itself the Lebanese Rocket Society constructed and launched more than 10 rockets destined for space study and exploration. These launches made the front pages of the country's major newspapers, and even one of the rockets was pictured on a postage stamp celebrating the 21st anniversary of Lebanese independence in 1964. Unfortunately, three years later, because of the Arab defeat by Israel, the space program was terminated, and despite the interest it enjoyed in the 1960s, the story of the Lebanese Rocket Society is largely absent from history and collective memory today. Hadjithomas and Joreige decided to return to this topic, with the intention to capture a moment in which a different future was possible and to use "the past to create a space in which a future of possibilities and dreams becomes available,"[25] as Norton and Donnelly comment.

While *The Lebanese Rocket Society* directs our attention to a space adventure that—although nearly inconceivable today—still belongs to the domain of historical facts, Larissa Sansour's *Space Exodus* (2009), part of her sci-fi film trilogy, imagines, without any supporting evidence, a past in which the first Palestinian astronaut, played by Sansour herself, went into space. The artist clearly refers to the American moon landing by faithfully reconstructing the well-known scene of planting a national flag on the moon, yet in this case, it is the Palestinian national flag and the Palestinian astronaut making "one small step for man," to cite Neil Armstrong's famous declaration. The stakes involved in this change are discussed by Claire Norton in her article "The Counter/Actual: Art and Strategies of Anti-Colonial Resistance," in which she quotes a critic who emphasizes that, in this film, the moon becomes "a land without people for a people increasingly without land."[26] This counter/actual function, as Norton calls it, of Sansour's film is often additionally highlighted when it is presented in museums and galleries. For it is accompanied by the installation of small vinyl sculptures of tiny "Palestinauts" scattered around the gallery space, recalling the de-territorialization of Palestinians. In other words, the fictional event presented in *Space Exodus* derives its plausibility from the original scenario of the moon landing, even though the gender of the astronaut stepping on the lunar surface and the colors of the flag are different from the original scenario. In so doing, it paradoxically and simultaneously counters and confirms the hegemonic narration. This aspect of Sansour's project highlights the main, more or less evident, weakness of many counterfactual stories that are usually generic and depend on the institutional version of the past. The best example of that is the cinematic version of the already mentioned *Hidden Figures*, deservedly accused by many critics of "history whitewashing."[27] Therefore, the film I have chosen for a more detailed analysis in this section of my chapter addresses this weakness, showing not so much how to avoid the trap but rather to unearth its mechanism and demonstrate its workings. Although the title of Bodomo's project may suggest that her eponymous Afronauts have inherent similarities with Sansour's Palestinauts, the film is a skillful entanglement of the factual and the fictional. For Bodomo's 14-minute film is based on a story that is both true and quite incredible.[28]

At the height of the Cold War, while the United States and the Soviet Union were in a frantic space race to be the first on the moon and shortly after Zambia gained independence in 1964, a Second World War veteran and primary school science teacher, Edward Makuka Nkoloso, decided to finally fulfill his ambitious dreams of space travel while creating his private space program as a kind of nation-building project in Zambia. Fully independently, and without any kind of governmental support, he established the Zambia National Academy of Science, Space Research, and Philosophy in an old farmhouse, a few kilometers outside of Lusaka, where a dozen would-be astronauts began to study and train. To financially support his undertaking, Nkoloso applied for a large grant from the UNESCO, which unfortunately never came through. He scheduled a crew flight to the moon way ahead of the Soviets and the Americans. Subsequently, he thought about sending a rocket to Mars because his complex program included also the establishment of a Ministry of Christianity there, as he declared in a 1964 newspaper op-ed titled "We're going to Mars!" At the same time, he apparently had no intention of imposing the religion with violence on the inhabitants of the planet.[29] The first space crew which he hoped to launch in order to conquer the moon consisted of a 17-year-old girl named Matha Mwamba and two cats. To prepare them for the flight, Nkoloso used to place all three in a huge oil barrel, which he rolled down from steep hills or spun around a tree. The resourceful science teacher trained Matha for weightlessness, for instance, by cutting the rope of a swing at its highest point. At the same time, he constructed, step-by-step, a space rocket out of copper and aluminum scrap. Instead of a highly expensive cosmodrome, he envisioned a much cheaper ordinary catapult as sufficient to launch the rocket.

Because the venturesome plan of sending Zambians to the moon before the United States and the Soviet Union never came to fruition and has been rather sparsely documented, we know nothing about what happened next, despite all efforts of reconstruction by a Polish journalist, Bartek Sabela, who spent several months in Zambia in the fall of 2015 and the spring of 2016, researching archives and interviewing people, including Nkoloso's son.[30] As he found out, supposedly Matha became pregnant and was taken away by her parents. But after almost half a century and several years before Sabela went to Zambia, the unbelievable story captured the attention of the Spanish artist and photographer Cristina de Middel, who, in 2012, edited and published a booklet entitled *Afronauts*, in which she told a fictional story about Matha and the two cats, documenting it with made-up evidence and surreal photographs. Although Bodomo's project bears the same title as Middel's artistic booklet and fictionalizes the same story of Matha's preparations to be launched into space, the filmmaker decided to film it in black and white. What is more, the New Jersey landscape, where the film was shot, is by no means harsh and monumental like the lunar landscape, nor does it look surreal in any way. That being said, there are still more crucial differences between both artistic projects.

The story of the Zambian science teacher exemplifies a quite common thesis that a country which only recently gained independence has to take part in the race to the outer space in order to prove itself in the eyes of world powers and be given its rightful place in today's international community. In his article, Namwali Serpell, who analyzed press coverage of Nkoloso's undertaking, emphasizes that the teacher made it clear that racial issues were also at stake in the space race. The science teacher was certain that "[o]ur posterity, the Black scientists, will continue to explore the celestial infinity until we control the whole of outer space."[31] Mindful of often the deeply hidden or underrated nature of our social affective investments, which we make into imagined national (racial) communities in order to enhance our individual identity, Ghassan Hage, a Lebanese-Australian anthropologist, posits in his *Alter-Politics* that we should differentiate between an "identification with" and an "identification through." As he explains, "To identify *with* a nation keeps the nation at a certain distance from oneself, making it more an 'object' of identification. To identify *through* is a far more intense kind of identification that does not allow for any separation."[32] What is more,

> [t]his allows all the individuals who identify with the collective to see "its capacities and qualities" as theirs. The nationalist as an individual might be a technological nullity but they are still capable of saying, "We've sent a rocket to Mars." [...] Power here is through the acquisition of potentials: it is not that the nationalist who is uneducated becomes educated by merely identifying with a nation of educated people. Rather, the uneducated acquire power by thinking that they have *the potential* to be educated even if they are not.[33]

Nothing confirms Hage's argument about "affective nationalism" better than the history of the space race as an important part of the Cold War and its less acknowledged national repercussions, like the Zambian intended rocket launch in the 1960s.

The affective nationalist aspect was clearly visible in the aforementioned exhibition "Fly me to the Moon" in Zurich in 2019, especially in the part that gathered cultural artifacts from the Cold War period. As I assume, it was for this reason that Bodomo's *Afronauts* attracted my attention. What is worth highlighting in this context is that, at the outset, the artist wanted to demonstrate nothing in her short film but the Zambian project of moon landing as a proper way of proving the merit of an independent nation. After all, while doing research for the short film, she explicitly declared, "I am extremely excited to tell an underdog story from the perspective of exiles and outsiders, the people who most need the promises of the space race. The people whose stories are lost or silenced to an iconic mainstream history that documents fact."[34] As this quote demonstrates, Bodomo thought about exploring an alternative version of contemporary West-centered history or, even more, of a modern-day myth. That is why she decided that Matha's most probably fatal space adventure shown in the last sequence of her film should start on the same day in July 1969 as the Apollo 11 mission which lastingly affected our collective imagination. Coming back to Sansour's *Space Exodus* mentioned above, one important difference should be noticed: Bodomo does not show an alternative story as Sansour did; she sets them side by side, one illuminating the other.

Had Bodomo shot this film as originally planned, it would surely have come into existence as an artwork similar to other anti-hegemonic narrations with which I have started this section. She made a different decision, however. Nothing makes it more evident than her unfulfilled plan to adapt *Afronauts* into a full-length feature, in which she wanted to show how Matha consciously takes part in a suicidal mission. For Bodomo, this last scene would have been a kind of open political declaration. In an interview she explained,

> [i]t's a very painful thing to realize that you've lost a certain history, and I think that, because of that, people go into these neo-colonial missions—re-creating a certain violence. I thought that as it plays out in Matha's character, that cycle is going to be broken in the film.[35]

She said that in January 2016, but I think that we could read the short film *Afronauts* as already a successful attempt at breaking such a cycle of violence, an explicit gesture of blocking both mainstream and anti-hegemonic stories of the moon landing, of reflecting and refracting them at the same time. For Bodomo gave the role of Matha to the African-American model Diandra Forrest, who is albino. The model's white hair and fair complexion combined with African facial features clearly both connote the types of space race narrative and, simultaneously, negate them, in the same way that the stories about the American and the Zambian moon landing on the same day in July 1969 do when juxtaposed side by side. What is of particular interest here is that while the bodily absence of performers—contrary to main theatrical conventions—has made the "live" experience of Mapa Teatro's installation possible, it is the bodily presence of Forrest on which the cognitive and affective impact of Bodomo's film is predicated. In other words, both in a sense refrain from realistically representing the Other and denaturalize their medium of theater and film, respectively, in order to put their consciously ambiguous message across. Therefore, following Hage's argument, Bodomo's film could be recognized as a successful attempt at replacing "identification through," typical of both kinds of narrative about the moon landing, by "identification with," which imposes an equal critical distance onto those narratives. This allows the viewer to recognize not only the mechanism of affective identification but also the residual and emergent formations of national discourses: the hegemonic and the counter-hegemonic.

In her *History in the Discursive Condition*, Elizabeth Deeds Ermarth analyzes the role of artists in what she aptly calls "naming the discourse." What she means by this is that artists know how to "skillfully re-deploy their available discursive capacities in ways that open an interval between what the discursive system conventionally does and what it is capable of and could do."[36] No doubt, *Afronauts* is a case of such a redeployment of available discursive capacities of both the hegemonic version of the moon landing narrative and its counter-hegemonic version, and it was most often read by critics in this manner. But in view of my interpretation given above, and especially the last quotation of the artist's declaration of her intention to break the cycle of a neo-colonial violence, I would like to specify that she is using the capacities of the space race discourse to search for alternative modes of thinking and experiencing otherness. She demonstrates that hegemonic discourses could be not only critically countered but also critically altered in order to capture the possibilities of new modes of existence.

Performing the (or a) Past

In *The Afterlife of Reproductive Slavery*, while writing about the slave episteme and its largely unacknowledged afterlife in today's biocapitalism, which depends on the prior history of slave breeding as an epistemic condition of possibility, Weinbaum introduces the concept of persuasive sublation. She defines it as "the seemingly paradoxical movement by which ways of being in the world (Hegel) and systems of power such as feudalism or capitalism (Marx) are simultaneously *negated* and *preserved* by historical forces that transform the status quo by transcending it over time."[37] By no means does Weinbaum suggest that other systems of thought are not sublated—negated and preserved—in the neoliberalism of today. What I intended to demonstrate here were two further cases of sublation, revealed by the artistic projects I have analyzed, focusing on what has been retrieved from the past and activated in the present, and how. Thus, I have analyzed two examples of projects that should be qualified as performative rather than theatrical. It does not mean that theater artists have not offered refined means of looking otherwise at the hegemonic practices of professional historians and that they have not provided new articulations to challenge or question them. However, the performative projects discussed here approached the hegemonic practices in such a way that allows for reaching further conclusions that may help us reflect on how to write theater history(ies). It is my contention that theater studies as an already well-established discipline would need a kind of provincialization, as Chakrabarty would have it. First of all, it could become more open toward other disciplines and their methodological approaches, in particular when designing new ways of narrating pastness by entangling factions and fictions as well as mainstream discourses and speculative fabulations of different sorts in order to more deeply decolonize theater studies, and theater history in particular. In conclusion, therefore, I would like to formulate two such teachings that could help us adequately entangle (still visibly national) theater histories and alter what is still named theater historiography.

Firstly, the lesson to be learned from Mapa Teatro's *Of Lunatics* primarily concerns a much-needed move away from the understanding of situated knowledge as a story narrated from a well-defined, individual, embodied and embedded auctorial point of view. It is high time we changed the personal "I" of the history writer to the no less personal "eye" of the reader, which does not necessarily have to exclude other senses channeled via sight. For this reason, I would rather speak of a participant who takes an active part in entangling stories and other kinds of heterogeneous material provided within a given frame/site. For instance, with regard to taking advantage of the possibilities offered by digital technology, one can mention Anna Tsing and her research group at the Aarhus University creating the website *Feral Atlas*.[38] It allows the visitor to move freely around, reading about various—sometimes even contradictory—approaches to the issue of the Anthropocene, watching short videos, and zooming in and out various maps designed by Indigenous artists. In addition, the visitor is invited to ask the fundamental question of "how things hold"[39] while looking not only for causal relations but also for various sorts of temporary and contingent knots and coordinates, especially when they produce a new capacity or emergence. An example taken from *Feral Atlas* could thus challenge the linearity of narration typical of theater historiography, offering a more spatial arrangement that, in turn, would highlight the directionality and differentials of power that make some narratives seem more empirically grounded and truthful than others. Both encourage the active participation of the reader/viewer/visitor, in the same manner that Mapa Teatro's *Of Lunatics* does.

Secondly, the lesson to be learned from Frances Bodomo's *Afronauts* is that it is not enough to try to alter hegemonic discourses by providing counter-narratives, marginalized or forgotten facts, and critical fabulations. Also, it is not enough to cognitively and affectively engage the reader/viewer/visitor, making her—at least partially—response-able for entangling stories right there and then. What becomes increasingly important is to demonstrate that she is likewise ethically and epistemologically response-able for all that has been left untangled, just as Bodomo does while trying to break the cycle of a neo-colonial violence by "naming the discourse" in her *Afronauts*. Eva Haifa Giraud rightly points out in her *What Comes after Entanglement?* that it is not only all kinds of networked local strategies of political and social action that are vital.[40] An equally significant role is played by all kinds of exclusion and extant structural inequality, many of which have already been naturalized but still define the agency of various parties involved in social struggles and possessing uneven powers. The same, as I posit, remains valid when applied to academic disciplines, theater historiography included.

That is why it is so important to realize that there are consequences of employing the concept of sublation, of putting the lack of compartmentalization in our understanding of time—past, present and future—on display. It is not only the case that from the perspective of sublation, the (historical or set in conditional mode) past proleptically impacts the present, allowing for the perception of an entanglement of epistemic connections across different temporal and geographical landscapes that would otherwise be unavailable. Also, current political, economic, social and many other practices continuously and analeptically reshape our understanding of what happened or would have happened. Both movements create a world—tactically and strategically negated by the majority of professional historians—in which the local and the global past, present and future are perpetually interwoven into an ever-changing, dynamic entanglement. We should carefully consider the various modalities, especially contemporary affective modalities, through which we could collectively reproduce all three arbitrarily separated temporalities, both our own (national/global) and that of others (racialized/local). That is why I can only agree with Norton and Donnelly that the first step should be to liberate histories and, in so doing, to liberate our individual and collective imagination of the linearity and focus on national theater histories, inherent in traditional historiography, in order to demonstrate an original performativity of the past-present-future and local-global relationships. Many contemporary artists, including those whose works I have presented here, teach us how to do it effectively, by skillfully interweaving stories and altering discourses.

Notes

1 Sande Cohen, "Figuring Forth the Historian Today: On Images and Goals," in *History Out of Joint: Essays on the Use and Abuse of History* (Baltimore, MD: The Johns Hopkins University Press, 2006), 103–25.
2 Hayden White, *Metahistory: The Historical Imagination in Nineteenth-Century Europe* (Baltimore, MD: The Johns Hopkins University Press, 1973).
3 Alun Munslow, *Deconstructing History* (London and New York, NY: Routledge, 1997).
4 See "Historians and Ethics," ed. Brian Fey, special issue, *History and Theory: Studies in the Philosophy of History* 43, no. 4 (2004); "Politics and History," ed. Dennis Dworkin, special issue, *Rethinking History* 13, no. 4 (2009); and "Historical Justice," ed. Klaus Neumann, special issue, *Rethinking History* 18, no. 2 (2014).
5 Claire Norton and Mark Donnelly, *Liberating Histories* (London and New York, NY: Routledge, 2019), 188.
6 Ibid., 10.
7 Saidiya Hartman, "Venus in Two Acts," *Small Axe* 12, no. 2 (2008): 11.
8 Norton and Donnelly, *Liberating Histories*, 186.
9 Priya Satia, *Time's Monster: How History Makes History* (Cambridge, MA: The Belknap Press, 2020), 273.
10 Elizabeth A. Povinelli, *Between Gaia and Ground: Four Axioms of Existence and the Ancestral Catastrophe of Late Liberalism* (Durham, NC: Duke University Press, 2021), 2.
11 Ibid., 3.
12 Dipesh Chakrabarty, "The Two Histories of Capital," in *Provincializing Europe: Postcolonial Thought and Historical Difference* (Princeton, NJ and Oxford: Princeton University Press, 2000), 47.
13 Ibid., 66.
14 Ibid., 71, italics in the original.
15 There are many of works worth of reading in these fields. However, I name only a few books (in alphabetic order) which have been important for my studies: Saidiya Hartman, *Lose Your Mother: A Journey along the Atlantic Slave Route* (New York, NY: Farrar, Straus and Giroux, 2007); Lisa Lowe, *The Intimacies of Four Continents* (Durham, NC: Duke University Press, 2015); Christina Sharpe, *In the Wake: On Blackness and Being* (Durham, NC: Duke University Press, 2016); Stephanie E. Smallwood, *Saltwater Slavery: A Middle Passage from Africa to American Diaspora* (Cambridge, MA: Harvard University Press, 2007); Alexander G. Weheliye, *Habeas Viscus: Racializing Assemblages, Biopolitics, and Black Feminist Theories of the Human* (Durham, NC: Duke University Press, 2014).
16 Alys Eve Weinbaum, *The Afterlife of Reproductive Slavery: Biocapitalism and Black Feminism's Philosophy of History* (Durham, NC: Duke University Press, 2019).
17 Kati Röttger, "Mapa Teatro: Dramaturgies of Decolonisation," *European Journal of Theatre and Performance*, no. 3 (2021): 209.
18 Cited in a leaflet accompanying Mapa Teatro's *Of Lunatics, or Those Lacking Sanity* (Madrid: Museo Nacional Centro de Arte Reina Sofía, 2018), n.p.
19 Eduardo Viveiros de Castro, *Cannibal Metaphysics: For a Post-Structural Anthropology*, trans. and ed. Peter Skafish (Minneapolis, MN: Univocal Publishing, 2014). In the 1990s, Viveiros de Castro wrote as well on cannibalism as an alleged tribal rite of people of Tupi, grounding his finding on official documents and private letters from the archives of the Society of Jesus; see Viveiros de Castro, *The Inconstancy of the Indian Soul: The Encounter of Catholics and Cannibals in 16th-Century Brazil*, trans. Gregory Duff Morton (Chicago, IL: Prickly Paradigm Press, 2011).
20 See Elizabeth A. Povinelli, *Geontologies: A Requiem to Late Liberalism* (Durham, NC: Duke University Press, 2016).

21 Weheliye, *Habeas Viscus*, 3.
22 Norton and Donnelly, *Liberating Histories*, 177.
23 Weinbaum, *Afterlife of Reproductive Slavery*, 71.
24 Mateusz Borowski, "Counterfactual Histories of Moon Landing," *Art History & Criticism*, no. 14 (2018): 16–27.
25 Norton and Donnelly, *Liberating Histories*, 178.
26 Claire Norton, "The Counter/Actual: Art and Strategies of Anti-Colonial Resistance," *Art History & Criticism*, no. 14 (2018): 30.
27 For more information on that, see Borowski, "Counterfactual Histories," 23–25.
28 Derica Shields, "Frances Bodomo's 'Afronauts': What Became of the Zambian Space Program?" *okayafrika*, 14 May 2013, https://www.okayafrica.com/african-film-director-frances-bodomo-afronauts-zambia-space-race/; Namwali Serpell, "The Zambian 'Afronaut' Who Wanted to Join the Space Race," *New Yorker*, 11 March 2017, https://www.newyorker.com/culture/culture-desk/the-zambian-afronaut-who-wanted-to-join-the-space-race.
29 Edward Makuka Nkoloso, "We're going to Mars! With a Spacegirl, Two Cats and a Missionary," see *BootnAll* (blog), accessed 24 May 2022, http://blogs.bootsnall.com/theglobaltrip/updates/DSC00988marsprogramV.shtml.
30 See Bartek Sabela, *Afronauci: Z Zambii na księżyc* (Wołowiec: Czarne, 2017).
31 Nkoloso, quoted in Serpell, "The Zambian 'Afronaut.'"
32 Ghassan Hage, "On Ethnography and Political Emotions: Hating Israel in the Field," in *Alter-Politics: Critical Anthropology and the Radical Imagination* (Melbourne: Melbourne University Publishing, 2015), 109.
33 Ibid., 103, italics in the original.
34 Frances Bodomo, "Afronauts," *Kickstarter*, last modified 16 July 2019, https://www.kickstarter.com/projects/1036306318/afronauts.
35 Frances Bodomo, "The Afronauts," interview by Adwoa Afful, *The Awl*, 29 January 2016, https://www.theawl.com/2016/01/the-afronauts/.
36 Elizabeth Deeds Ermarth, *History in the Discursive Condition: Reconsidering the Tools of Thought* (London and New York: Routledge, 2011), 122.
37 Weinbaum, *Afterlife of Reproductive Slavery*, 10–11, italics in the original.
38 See https://feralatlas.org/.
39 This question is formulated already in the title of the article written by Elaine Gan and Anna Tsing. Although it addresses the question of how to study a specific kind of Japanese village forest, the proposed method seems to apply to the main issue of this chapter. See Elaine Gan and Anna Tsing, "How Things Hold: A Diagram of Coordination in a Satoyama Forest," *Social Analysis* 62, no. 4 (2018): 102–45.
40 See Eva Haifa Giraud, *What Comes after Entanglement? Activism, Anthropocentrism, and the Ethics of Exclusion* (Durham, NC: Duke University Press, 2019).

Bibliography

Bodomo, Frances. "Afronauts." *Kickstarter*. Last modified 16 July 2019. https://www.kickstarter.com/projects/1036306318/afronauts.

———. "The Afronauts." Interview by Adwoa Afful. *The Awl*, 29 January 2016. https://www.theawl.com/2016/01/the-afronauts/.

Borowski, Mateusz. "Counterfactual Histories of Moon Landing." *Art History & Criticism*, no. 14 (2018): 16–27.

Chakrabarty, Dipesh. "The Two Histories of Capital." In *Provincializing Europe: Postcolonial Thought and Historical Difference*, 47–71. Princeton, NJ and Oxford: Princeton University Press, 2000.

Cohen, Sande. "Figuring Forth the Historian Today: On Images and Goals." In *History Out of Joint: Essays on the Use and Abuse of History*, 103–25. Baltimore, MD: The Johns Hopkins University Press, 2006.

Deeds Ermarth, Elizabeth. *History in the Discursive Condition: Reconsidering the Tools of Thought*. London and New York, NY: Routledge, 2011.

Dworkin, Dennis, ed. "Politics and History." Special issue, *Rethinking History* 13, no. 4 (2009).

Fey, Brian, ed. "Historians and Ethics." Special issue, *History and Theory: Studies in the Philosophy of History* 43, no. 4 (2004).

Gan, Elaine, and Anna Tsing. "How Things Hold: A Diagram of Coordination in a Satoyama Forest." *Social Analysis* 62, no. 4 (2018): 102–45.

Giraud, Eva Haifa. *What Comes after Entanglement? Activism, Anthropocentrism, and the Ethics of Exclusion*. Durham, NC: Duke University Press, 2019.

Hage, Ghassan. "On Ethnography and Political Emotions: Hating Israel in the Field." In *Alter-Politics: Critical Anthropology and the Radical Imagination*, 91–119. Melbourne: Melbourne University Publishing, 2015.

Hartman, Saidiya. "Venus in Two Acts." *Small Axe* 12, no. 2 (2008): 1–14.

———. *Lose Your Mother: A Journey along the Atlantic Slave Route*. New York, NY: Farrar, Straus and Giroux, 2007.

Lowe, Lisa. *The Intimacies of Four Continents*. Durham, NC: Duke University Press, 2015.

Munslow, Alun. *Deconstructing History*. London and New York, NY: Routledge, 1997.

Neumann, Klaus, ed. "Historical Justice." Special issue, *Rethinking History* 18, no. 2 (2014).

Nkoloso, Edward Makuka. "We're going to Mars! With a Spacegirl, Two Cats and a Missionary." See *BootnAll* (blog), accessed 24 May 2022. http://blogs.bootsnall.com/theglobaltrip/updates/DSC00988marsprogramV.shtml.

Norton, Claire. "The Counter/Actual: Art and Strategies of Anti-Colonial Resistance." *Art History & Criticism*, no. 14 (2018): 28–39.

———, and Mark Donnelly. *Liberating Histories*. London and New York, NY: Routledge, 2019.

Povinelli, Elizabeth A. *Between Gaia and Ground: Four Axioms of Existence and the Ancestral Catastrophe of Late Liberalism*. Durham, NC: Duke University Press, 2021.

———. *Geontologies: A Requiem to Late Liberalism*. Durham, NC: Duke University Press, 2016.

Röttger, Kati. "Mapa Teatro: Dramaturgies of Decolonisation." *European Journal of Theatre and Performance*, no. 3 (2021): 166–213.

Sabela Bartek. *Afronauci. Z Zambii na księżyc [Afronauts: From Zambia to the Moon]*. Wołowiec: Czarne, 2017.

Satia, Priya. *Time's Monster: How History Makes History*. Cambridge, MA: The Belknap Press, 2020.

Serpell, Namwali. "The Zambian 'Afronaut' Who Wanted to Join the Space Race." *New Yorker*, 11 March 2017. https://www.newyorker.com/culture/culture-desk/the-zambian-afronaut-who-wanted-to-join-the-space-race.

Sharpe, Christina. *In the Wake: On Blackness and Being*. Durham, NC: Duke University Press, 2016.

Shetterly, Margot Lee. *Hidden Figures: The American Dream and the Untold Story of the Black Women Mathematicians Who Helped Win the Space Race*. New York, NY: William Morrow, 2016.

Shields, Derica. "Frances Bodomo's 'Afronauts': What Became of the Zambian Space Program?" *okayafrika*, 14 May 2013. https://www.okayafrica.com/african-film-director-frances-bodomo-afronauts-zambia-space-race/.

Smallwood, Stephanie E. *Saltwater Slavery: A Middle Passage from Africa to American Diaspora*. Cambridge, MA: Harvard University Press, 2007.

Viveiros de Castro, Eduardo. *Cannibal Metaphysics: For a Post-Structural Anthropology*. Translated and edited by Peter Skafish. Minneapolis, MN: Univocal Publishing, 2014.

———. *The Inconstancy of the Indian Soul: The Encounter of Catholics and Cannibals in 16th-Century Brazil*. Translated by Gregory Duff Morton. Chicago, IL: Prickly Paradigm Press, 2011.

Weheliye, Alexander G. *Habeas Viscus: Racializing Assemblages, Biopolitics, and Black Feminist Theories of the Human*. Durham, NC: Duke University Press, 2014.

Weinbaum, Alys Eve. *The Afterlife of Reproductive Slavery: Biocapitalism and Black Feminism's Philosophy of History*. Durham, NC: Duke University Press, 2019.

White, Hayden. *Metahistory: The Historical Imagination in Nineteenth-Century Europe*. Baltimore, MD: The Johns Hopkins University Press, 1973.

2
WRITING ENTANGLED THEATER/ PERFORMANCE HISTORIES IN THE ARAB WORLD

Khalid Amine

Theaters have never been stable grounds but, rather, fields of intersecting transitional realities, crossroads of diverse cultures, and nodes of translation and dialogue. Theatrical performances have always overflowed their locations, for theaters were and still continue to be interstitial spaces made by collaborations, meeting places of moving bodies, and entrepôts of diasporas and performance cultures. All performative locations are somehow contaminated and crisscrossed by various encounters past and present. World theater is made up of so many different cultural and historical influences. "Zones of cultural friction," according to Anna L. Tsing, are "zones of awkward engagement" co-produced within intersections she calls "friction": "the awkward, unequal, unstable, and creative qualities of interconnection across difference."[1]

For more than a decade, the International Research Center "Interweaving Performance Cultures" (IRC) has spawned an uprooted lexicon of mind crossing borders, highlighting zones of contact and friction, performative mobility, as well as sites of entanglements between coloniality and decoloniality, domination and resistance. The Center itself has become a contact zone, a site of constructive exchange and dialogue, from which new collaborative artistic/research trajectories have emerged as experiments in rewriting entangled theater/performance histories.

The IRC's partnership with the International Conference of *Performing Tangier*, Morocco,[2] and by extension, the Arab world, rests upon three major premises: (1) the possibility of achieving a democratic interweaving across worldwide performance cultures; (2) a collaborative rethinking of the intercultural paradigm and its configuration of the "other on the outside," a rethinking founded on reciprocity as both vision and negotiation of power/ knowledge; (3) last but not least, an invitation to practice a "double critique"

DOI: 10.4324/9781003353461-4

(Khatibi) as a rhyzomatic way of saying and doing whereby East and West come to terms with their age-old Manichaeism and finally recognize their permanent interweaving and zones of contact and friction within specific historic contexts. Since its inception in 2008, the IRC has sponsored and supported this forum, enabling it to contribute to the production and global circulation of knowledge about Arab theater and performance.

In line with Erika Fischer-Lichte's inspiring interweaving project, I believe that performance cultures absorb material vestiges, remnants, echoes, remains and tattoos of a silent history of entanglements that is quite literally inaccessible until subjected to an archaeology and a process of transcription or translation. Even the contemporary historical period of the "postcolony"[3] contains different temporalities (traditional, modern and postmodern), as if past epochs could persist relatively unchanged into the present. The interweaving performance cultures research project reevaluates that very landscape and invites the weavers to highlight the multiple crossroads and palimpsests of contact and friction. Beyond the dogmatism of polarization, the ecology of interweaving performance cultures builds bridges between self and other, seeking alternative ways of living theater/performance, rhyzomatic thinking about performance cultures, and new modes of re-writing theater historiography with a particular focus on "the historical practices and processes themselves."[4]

My modest contribution to the debate highlights Moroccan sociologist Abdelkébir Khatibi's *An-Naqdu al-Muzdawij* (*Double Critique*)[5] as a form of decolonial deconstruction that goes beyond the dogmatism of polarization. It is an invitation to redeem postcolonial performance history from its interminable oppositional thinking "by shifting the postcolonial subject's fixation on the Other/West to an inward interrogation of his political and ideological self-colonization and self-victimization."[6] The postcolonial turn in the Arab world and elsewhere requires an evaluation of all different "Occidents" and "Orients" that have produced most Arabs as postcolonial subjects. Postcoloniality needs to be reconceptualized anew as a historical period during which ex-colonized countries can conjure up entangled histories in order to imagine possibilities for the future.

The interweaving performance cultures debate in the Arab world today—and broadly in the "post-colony" or the "Global South"[7]—challenges us with pending questions and problematics: What is the task of Arabic performance research in an era of globalization and coloniality of power? What are the affordable options of rewriting theater histories within these processes of entanglement? How far are our local theater/performance histories affected/inflicted by what Walter D. Mignolo calls "global designs"? Mignolo argues, "Silenced societies are, of course, societies in which talking and writing take place but which are not heard in the planetary production of knowledge managed from the local histories and local languages of the 'silencing' (e.g., developed) societies."[8] How then can we engage "in epistemological disciplinary disobedience and bring to the fore the existential experience of dwelling in the border?"⁹ The present undertaking will be around these lines of questioning, with a particular focus on dancing over slashes: West/East, and border thinking/double critique as forms of interweaving. The slash is often used to link and delink alternatives or words denoting or describing a dual (or multiple) function or nature. It connects and disconnects, unites and separates consents and contests. The slash, in this case, connects and at the same time instigates contest with regard not only to language but also to identity politics. In Mignolo's terms, the slash is the "space of border thinking."¹⁰ In our case, the slash also implies a fundamental interference between two different languages and modalities and allows the dancer to tap into the "epistemic potential" of new ways of inhabiting the world through language.

Delinking Theater/Performance Historiography

> [Africa] is no historical part of the World; it has no movement or development to exhibit.¹¹
>
> —G. W. F. Hegel, *The Philosophy of History*

In the 1830s, the German Philosopher Georg Wilhelm Friedrich Hegel (1770–1831) was a voice of authority. His remarks about Africa have not only revealed an arrogant breadth of ignorance about the history of an entire continent, but, and most importantly, they have also contributed to the foundations of European imperialism ever since the mid-nineteenth century.

Historiography has been central to epistemic coloniality since the neoclassical period. Europe has ever been the silent referent in world theater and performance histories (con)fusing the local/universal. Theater and performance historiography is among the powerful means of coloniality of knowledge/power. For Aníbal Quijano (1928–2018), coloniality is interconnected with race, labor and knowledge:

> [It] is still the most general form of domination in the world today, once colonialism as an explicit political order was destroyed. It doesn't exhaust, obviously, the conditions nor the modes of exploitation and domination between peoples. But it hasn't ceased to be, for 500 years, their main framework. The colonial relations of previous periods probably did not produce the same consequences, and, above all, they were not the corner stone of any global power.¹²

Upon rising demands for further global democratizing theater and performance historiography, as an academic discipline, new modes of writing theater/performance history from below have emerged with an earnest desire for inclusion and revision. International theater/performance research has long studied the world before undergoing its revolution from inside. Now, key edited books are being published by international scholars highlighting localized approaches to studying, contesting and rewriting dominant performance paradigms and histories. Among these, we can mention *Contesting Performance: Global Sites of Research* (2010), *The Theatres of Morocco, Algeria and Tunisia: Performance Traditions of the Maghreb* (2012), *The Politics of Interweaving Performance Cultures: Beyond Postcolonialism* (2014), *The Methuen Drama Handbook of Theatre History and Historiography* (2020). By reflecting the diversity of the world's theater/performance experiences, theater historiography has become one of the many spaces of struggle and entanglement which cogently lay bare the colonial epistemic violence.

But the task of decolonial scholarship is further complicated while revisiting the massive body of world theater/performance histories. Non-Western performance cultures are hardly visible in the "universal narrative of capital—History 1,"[13] typically edited out, and if ever mentioned as local histories, it is often on the borderlines between absence and presence. "History 1" is part of the global designs that, as Mignolo once put it, "also hide the local history from which they themselves emanate and are presented as if they were a natural unfolding of history."[14] However, the provincialization of Eurocentric theater/performance scholarship can only be achieved by recovering the irreducible plurality and age-old interweaving between European local theater/performance traditions with other non-European theater/performance histories, cultures and traditions. The question that poses or perhaps imposes itself is how to retrieve or rather bring to the fore such repressed histories of entanglement and articulate subaltern positions in their name without falling into the essentialist creed of "wild difference," "deviant nationalism," or worse, as Dipesh Chakrabarty puts it, "the sin of sins, nostalgia."[15] This primordial question still constitutes one of the most fundamental difficulties facing postcolonial theater and performance historians and critics today.

The Napoleonic military expedition to Egypt and Syria (1798–1801) constitutes a significant historical moment. It has ever since marked the beginning of a conflicting interplay in the Arab world between modernity and coloniality as its darker side.[16] The "Molierization" of Arab stages and the desire of the Arabs to appropriate Western models of theater production came as an effect of this interplay. Napoleon's[17] introduction of theater was aimed to serve two main objectives: 1) as a means of entertainment for the soldiers, and 2) as an agency aimed at changing people's traditions and implementing the French civilizing mission.

The Arabs' appropriation of Western models of theater making came as a consequence of their inceptive submission to the French metropolitan cultural norms. Such a submission marks the beginning of various forms of degradation, chief of which is the redefinition of performance/theater according to

Western standards. The colonial enterprise has, indeed, brought about divided loyalties manifested in two mystifying discursive practices that look different but share a slot of essentialism as a major source of epistemic violence. The first practice sees Western theater as a supreme universal model opposed to its local counterpart that is so often reduced into local performance traditions and pre-theatrical forms. In fact, this position also reproduces the same Eurocentric eclipse, if not exclusion, of other peoples' performance traditions. The Palestinian-Lebanese critic Mohamed Youssef Najm (1925–2009) made the above abyssal exclusion of theater in Arabic culture an undeniable reality:

> Theater in its precise meaning is a new art form that was introduced into our civilization as part of modern renaissance following the French campaign on Egypt. And if we want to speak about theater proper, we have to discard other forms of popular entertainment that might be imbued with theatrical similarities, yet they are radically different. Therefore, we need a clear-cut definition of theater, which distinguishes it from other popular performances such as *Khayāl Al-Zill* (shadow play), *Al-Qarakuz* (puppet show), and the works of itinerant entertainers and popular poets. These forms of entertainment are not part of theater, even if they contain some of its formal characteristics.[18]

In this context, the European local theatrical traditions have been considered as universal models that should be imitated and reproduced to the detriment of other local traditions. Otherwise put, there is no other theatrical practice but the one that developed in ancient Greece only to be reappropriated by many parts of Europe some 20 centuries later and then handed down to Arabs.

As to the second practice, the age-old Arab performances, such as *al-Ḥalqa* and *al-Ḥakawāti*, have been idealized as pure theatrical forms. The aforesaid discourse is a manifestation of Pan-Arab nationalism in its adherence to traditional Arab heritage and a unified sense of Arab identity. The Egyptian literary critic Ali Al-Rai (1920–1999) stands out as the most prominent advocate of traditional performance cultures. Al-Rai's life-long project consists of searching for authentic roots/routes of Arab theater: "We can say—with much trust—that the Arabs and all Muslims in general had known different forms of theater and theatrical activity for centuries before mid-nineteen century."[19] Drawing on local vernacular performance traditions, Al-Rai brought evidence of the practice of Khayāl Al-Zill during the rule of the seventh Abbasid caliph Abdallāh ibn Hārūn al-Rashīd, known by his caliphal name of Al-Mamūn (813–833). Al-Rai came to the conclusion that "we have to root a real Arab identity for our theater. We need to stop looking at theater as a dramatic literature beforehand. We need to consider our theater as an extension into the present day for artistic and performing traditions deeply rooted in our history, yet burdened with disrespect and contempt."[20]

Though Mohamed Youssef Najm and Ali Al-Rai represent polar opposites, in practice, Arabic theater lies more in a grey area between those two extremes. The introduction of Western theatrical traditions in the Arab world took place precisely during the colonial period. The first negotiations of Western/Greek dramas represent the phase of duplicating the Western model, though they can be considered double enunciations outspoken by the colonized in order to subvert the surveying model of the colonizing Other. The result is not a return to any illusive authentic state desired by Al-Rai nor a full enactment of the Western model as advocated by Youssef Najm, but a creation of what Homi Bhabha calls the "'in-between' space, that innovates and interrupts the performance of the present. The 'past–present' becomes part of necessity, not the nostalgia, of living."[21] It is precisely this interstitial perspective that makes critique an urgent call for transcending the polarities of East/West within a global environment. From 1847 until the mid-1960s, Arabic theater/performance could not escape the Western telos as manifested in the European apparatuses of playwriting and theater/performance-making.[22] Dramatic texts were ranging from translations and adaptations of Molière and Shakespeare, and embryonic forms of Arabization were attempted—mostly coming from the Middle East, as it was far ahead in assimilating Western theater and performance traditions. Meanwhile, the Arabization of foreign texts (texts written, or rather rewritten, with recourse to a European text) was a common practice. Thus, these were native appropriations of an alien medium, though they strove to mirror an inner self, for in borrowing the Western model, "the shape of lives and the shape of narratives" changed in the process. This period was characterized by native collaboration through various excesses of self-annihilation and the othering of the self. Consequently, the Western text becomes the model of all writing. Here, again, coloniality found its way in structuring and refashioning dramatic writing in the Arab world.

The fiction, invoked by the great narrative of Eurocentric historiography in order to assert itself as a founding presence, became reality through various strategies of containment, appropriation and dissemination. Such historiographic interventions, despite their positivistic claim of objectivity, were framed within what Mignolo calls "the colonial matrix of power" (coloniality in short).[23] In the context of the Arab world, the religion of Islam has often been inaccurately portrayed by hegemonic theater/performance historiography as a largely negative force against theatrical activity in the MENA region (Middle East and North Africa). Such misleading scholarship has been sustained by Westerners and Arabs beginning with Jacob Landau (1958) and continuing through John Gassner and Edward Quinn (1969), Peter J. Chelkowski (1979), and M. M. Badawi (1988), among others.[24]

When Oscar Brockett and Franklin Hildy's *History of the Theatre* first appeared in 1968, it immediately established itself as the model for world theater history, and it still retains its aura of authority in the field today. Islam, they claimed, was in large part responsible for the absence of theater in Arabo-Islamic contexts: "[Islam] forbade artists to make images of living things because Allah was said to be the only creator of life [...] the prohibition extended to the theatre, and consequently in those areas where Islam became dominant, advanced [i.e. European] theatrical forms were stifled."[25]

This stigmatizing generalization, though inaccurate, is still widely accepted. This view of the incompatibility of Islam with European concepts of theater and performance is by no means restricted to Western scholars; one can find many Arab writers on theater/performance taking a similar position. The problem is often traced back to the Arabs' first encounter with the Greek heritage through Syriac translations. This took place during the golden age of the Abbasid dynasty (the second century of Islam). Mohammed Al-Khozai, for example, argues that by "this time, Arabic poetry was maturing; and because of the new monotheistic faith, it was unlikely that Arab scholars would turn to what they considered a pagan art form."[26] At this time, Islam was still struggling to make space among other religions that preceded it. Moreover, Greek drama's celebration of simulacra and conflict constituted a real danger to the newly established monotheistic Arabo-Islamic structure, as well as to the social and political orders. Mohammed Aziza (b. 1940) concludes that "it was impossible for drama to originate in a traditional Arabo-Islamic environment."[27] The prohibition of *taswir* (lit. image) in Islam has always been subject to different interpretations and legislations. Thus, Islam's presumed opposition to totemism was by no means a permanent orthodoxy, nor should it be taken as implying a generally accepted condemnation of theater and performance. The Baghdad-school miniatures stand as exemplary instances for the strengthening of the arts, including performing arts. The miniatures are still conspicuous in the extant scripts of *maqamat*.

The Postcolonial Turn and Double Resistance

With the postcolonial turn, new modes of writing theater/performance history from the below have emerged with an earnest need for inclusion that is often coupled with a desire for subversion. We are constantly reminded of Frantz Fanon's conclusion in *The Wretched of the Earth* (1963), where he repudiated the degraded "European form" and called for something different: "Come, then, comrades, the European game has finally ended; we must find something different. We today can do everything, so long as we do not imitate Europe [...]. For Europe, for ourselves, and for humanity, comrades, we must turn over a new leaf, we must work out new concepts, and try to set afoot a new man."[28]

Fanon's reliance on theoretical Marxism, however, soon undermined his oppositional thinking. "Salvation," Mignolo reminds us, "cannot come from the same epistemology that created the need for salvation."[29] Unlike Fanon, Chakrabarty ends up proclaiming "an anticolonial spirit of gratitude": "provincializing Europe cannot ever be a project of shunning European thought. For at the end of European imperialism, European thought is a gift to us all. We can talk of provincializing it only in an anticolonial spirit of gratitude."[30] Such spirit attracts our attention to an ambiguous compromise that is complicit with the radical West in its critique of Eurocentric underpinnings of consumerist modernity, along with the coloniality of power as manifested in the hegemonic world theater/performance history. Obviously, "third-world historians feel a need to refer to works in European history; historians of Europe do not feel any need to reciprocate."[31] Chakrabarty's attempt to interrupt the totalizing thrust of History 1 is immediately caught in a double bind and was soon problematized by Rustom Bharucha in the margins of his seminal essay "Foreign Asia/Foreign Shakespeare" (2004), in which he argues that Chakrabarty's "historicist debt to Europe had overpowered his critique of Eurocentricity, so much so that [...] Chakravarty [sic] ends up 'provincializing Bengal'"[32] rather than Europe.

This is precisely where Abdelkébir Khatibi's concept of double critique is effective in problematizing the very notion of the binary opposition of West/East: Khatibi's call is similar to Fanon's, but his strategy deconstructs rather than reverses the dualistic theory. He confronts two local histories and narratives beyond the language of Manicheism. By casting the West as the Other, Fanon runs the risk of homogenizing the multifold West into one single entity. Perhaps it is a tactical move on Fanon's part in an effort to counter what he sees as Europe's lack of differentiation of "silent societies" she commonly categorizes as "Third-World," "under-developed" or "developing." Khatibi's line of questioning, on the other hand, disrupts all sorts of hierarchical definitions of Self/Other and East/West. It is essentially a border-thinking critique that weaves philosophical lines of influence belonging to both East and West only to emerge as a dance over hyphens and slashes within liminal spaces. In this context, Mignolo also highlights the epistemological potential of Khatibi's double critique as a form of border thinking[33], "since to be critical of both, of Western and Islamic fundamentalism, implies to think from both traditions and, at the same time, from neither of them."[34] Equally, "non-Western local histories (and knowledges) cannot be constituted without entanglements with Western local history."[35] Double critique brings deconstruction to bear on the tasks of delinking and decolonizing the colonial matrix of power, to use Mignolo's terms. Khatibi's "decolonizing version works in between French and Arabic: that is, 'an other thinking' is thinking in language, in between two languages and their historical relations in the modern world system and the coloniality of power."[36] He injects deconstructive critique to Arabo-Islamic modalities of writing and thought; at the same time, he initiated a yawning gap in the French language (he writes with) and where Arabic and Berber can be heard as they are already underwritten within the spatial confrontation between mother languages and French.

Khatibi's call for a *"pensée-autre"* (an other thinking) is a third path toward decoloniality, a double subversion that strives to elude "wild difference."[37] This pensée-autre is a way of rethinking difference and sameness without recourse to essentialist absolutes and "isms"; it is an "epistemic resistance" and spatial confrontation of all closed systems. An other thinking requires a radical rupture to "escape its own theological and theocratic foundations which characterize the ideology of Islam and of all monotheism."[38] Meanwhile, it claims to stand on a different ground than both the East and the West; "for we want to uproot Western knowledge from its central place within ourselves, to decenter ourselves with respect to this center, to this origin claimed by the West."[39] As Mignolo explains,

> The epistemological potential of border thinking, of "an other thinking," has the possibility of overcoming the limitation of territorial thinking (e.g., the monotopic epistemology of modernity), whose victory was possible because of its power in the subalternization of knowledge located outside the parameters of modern conceptions of reason and rationality.[40]

The transgressive effects of such a critique as a subaltern form of decolonizing deconstruction are already apparent in its transformation rather than passive borrowing from the radical West.

Double critique also calls for rethinking the Maghreb, the home country, and considering it for what it currently is: a container of multiple identities, a sedimental layering of cultures past and present, in permanent flux between moments of conviviality and tragic sublimity. The Maghreb has long been at the crossroads of civilizations, a point of intersection for various encounters, coveted by different powers, notably Phoenicians, Romans, Vandals, Spaniards, Portuguese, the English, the Arabs and the Turks. Double critique is a decolonizing archeology that leads to an examination of the binary concepts of East and West, Occident and Orient, and the philosophical, metaphysical and theological traditions propagated in each domain. This double-edged critique encompasses a deconstruction of critical discourses on theater/performance that used to speak in the name of the Arab world but was informed by a deeply rooted Eurocentrism. In the meantime, the second critique is a reflection on the "politics of nostalgia" and how the Arabs view their performance cultures. Double critique is an effect of a plural genealogy wherein one stages his/her confrontation of Self and Other, East and West. Khatibi often referred to himself as a "professional foreigner." The question, here, is very much related to the location of exile in any attempt to restore the postcolonial subject to his/her humanity. "A double critique," as Mignolo puts it, "becomes at this intersection a border thinking, since to be critical of both, of Western and Islamic fundamentalism, implies to think from both traditions and, at the same time, from neither of them. This border thinking and double critique are the necessary conditions for 'an other thinking.'"[41]

Who Is Afraid of Interweaving in the Arab World Today?

> [H]e who fears and is afraid is captive to the mood in which he finds himself. Striving to rescue himself from this particular thing,
> he becomes unsure of everything else and completely "loses his head."[42]
> —Martin Heidegger, "What Is Metaphysics?"

At this point, it is important to address the question of fear of interweaving in the Arab world today. Fear reflects an intense moment of fragility within a person or a culture. It involves something that is impending; thus it expresses uncertainty and legitimizes speculations. True that fear might help to reestablish a sense of community and group identification in the face of the external threat. However, the venture of making one Arab nation has always been fraught with violent pursuits. Our evaluation of essentialist paths such as "Pan-Arabism," followed by the first generation after independence, and still pursued by many scholars and artists today as inevitable failures leads us to revive a pensée-autre, a critical dynamic that challenges Western hegemony and the deeply rooted onto-theology of Arabo-Islamic discourse on identity and difference.

In the seventh edition of the Arab Theatre Festival in 2015 (which is now the most prestigious festival in the Arab world organized by the Arab Theatre Institute of Sharjah), I was asked to convene an international conference under the title "Interweaving Performance Cultures: The North-South Dialogue" in Rabat, the capital of Morocco. The conference provided a timely intervention into the fields of performance/theater studies. The participants offered provocative arguments for rethinking the scholarly assessment of how diverse performative cultures interact, how they are interwoven, and how they are dependent upon each other. The relation between North and South within the realm of performance exchange was at the heart of the discussions. The conference invited international case studies to explore the politics of globalization, looking at new paternalistic forms of exchange between North and South and the new diversities emerging from it. The authors explored the inextricability of the aesthetic and the political, whereby aesthetics cannot be perceived as opposite to the political; rather, the aesthetic *is* the political.

In the same conference, Abu Al-Kacem El-Gour from Sudan was chosen by the Arab Theatre Institute to present a synthesis of the debate. Instead, his closing statement, under the title "The Structure of European Hegemony," voiced many of the attitudes and opinions articulated by Pan-Arabists, Pan-Islamists, and Pan-Africanists. Abu Al-Kacem El-Gour declared,

> The unequivocal fact is that the West will not let us alone, or at least will not tolerate our differences with it within the framework of any project supporting diversity management. Every time these raids take new forms and different characters; colonization is a raid, post-colonization is an incursion, the end of history a raid, and the theory of necessity in international law is another open-air raid.[43]

Abu Al-Kacem El-Gour's (and many others') attitudes are based on an idea that the world is divided into two axes: the infidel West and the oppressed Muslim/Arab/African world.

In the middle of the tenth edition of the same festival held in Tunis in 2018, Yousif Aydabi (a poet, playwright, film critic and adviser of the Arab Theatre Institute) addressed the participants in a letter critiquing the East-West dynamics and inviting all to retrieve the authentic Arab voice that has been lost in the endless quest for a true Arab tradition. An edited version of the same letter is published at the official site of the Arab Theatre Institute based in Sharjah (UAE). Aydabi's call is worth mentioning in the present context:

> The question that (im)poses itself is as follows: How can our souls, selves and bodies be subjected to a different Eurocentrism? Let every soul in the Arab world contemplate the essence of its being/existence and how it is theatrically disclosed. What will accrue out of this search is that what is ours is not what the other has. So, let us improve that which is ours, taking into account our specificities instead of imitating the Other, who may be bewitched by that which comes as no surprise to us. Take heed of the Japanese, the Chinese, the Indian, the African, each of whom has gone with their own doctrine to the extent that European theaters have borrowed from them in fortifying the human theatrical fabric. Why wait for theatrical forms and formulas when we could turn ourselves from old to new magicians whose art no other can keep up with but the makers of the Italian commedia dell'arte. O theater people, should we continue to be followers of a bygone myth?![44]

Again, Aydabi's call strongly echoes Fanon's closing remarks in *The Wretched of the Earth*: "For Europe, for ourselves, and for humanity, comrades, we must turn over a new leaf, we must work out new concepts, and try to set afoot a new man."[45] However, the Arab world is made up of many cultural and historical entanglements, and one cannot simply turn one's back on any of them. Cultures absorb material vestiges, remnants, echoes, remains and tattoos of a silent history that is quite literally inaccessible until subjected to an archaeology and a process of transcription or translation. The method of "double critique" reevaluates that very landscape and highlights the multiple crossroads and palimpsests of interweaving and underlying processes of writing under erasure. Moroccan theater, as an exemplary instance of Arab theater, exists in a liminal space between East and West. It is located in a zone replete with contact and friction between Western theatrical traditions and the Arabo-Amazegh performance cultures. The interweaving processes of such a theater are evident in the way popular performance behavior rooted in performance spaces such as *al-Ḥalqa* (the circle) has been transposed from public squares and marketplaces like Marrackesh's *Jemaa el-Fna*[46] into modern theater buildings.[47]

Concluding Remarks

The growing tendency toward the interweaving of theater cultures since the dawn of the twentieth century, according to Fischer-Lichte, has led neither to the "Westernisation" nor the homogenization of non-Western theater cultures and discourses. Instead, it has created new standards of diversity.[48] Today, the decolonial practice is already apparent in many contemporary Arab theater projects. The new dramaturgies of the Arab Spring are offshoots of such a creative tension rather than imitative Westernized projects. They have developed at the intersections between European modernism and postmodernism and postcolonial denials, or manifest decoloniality (if we wish to put it in Mignolo's terms). Are there any parallels between the consequent failure of avant-garde art in the West in the historical post-1968 moment and the emergence of Arab avant-garde aesthetics after the historical defeat of Gamal Abdel Nasser in 1967? The 1968 moment was also informed by an alarming decolonial discourse held by the Western left as well as the rising tide of postcolonial discourse. The so-called Arab Spring of 2011 has, indeed, intensified or rather radicalized the previous Arab avant-garde critique of modernist regimes of theatrical representation, reinjecting more "worldliness, or 'historical actuality,' 'figuration,' and 'narrative' into modernist 'formalist' self-reflexivity,"[49] If the retrieval of traditional performance cultures lies at the heart of the Arab avant-garde of the late 1960s, the present aesthetics of narrative performance are way beyond that.

Many current performances in the Arab world and also in diaspora, allow an erasure of the age-old binarism. Works from the countries of the so-called Arab Spring have become "contaminated" by displaced reenactments, narrativization and postdramatic styles. Theater/performance in the Arab world was from the start trapped in an ambiguous compromise and confronted with the necessity of interpolating between different paradigms. Yet, Arab theaters are also hybrid narratives that articulate and explore cultural interactions and revisions of power relations across countries and cultures. Arab artists rewrite and perform the "us and them" dialectic and try to offer a distinctive view of the self/other interrelationship through intersectionality and dancing over hyphens. Artists such as Rabih Mroué and Sidi Larbi Cherkaoui are more visible in the grand festivals and biennials in a period of megalopolises such as Paris, Brussels, Amsterdam, and post-Wall Berlin, which exemplifies the increasing significance of global cities. In a period also shaped by migratory conditions, it is also apparent that artists of "color" are no longer making traditional art to reflect the local culture of their countries of origin, but rather deploying a double-sided critical strategy in which, instead of pursuing Frantz Fanon's invitation to abandon the European game, they have been utilizing identical postmodern strategies and ways of thinking to produce alternative theater forms. They bring about a double subversion that strives to elude "wild difference," working across borders of different epistemologies and artistic practices belonging to self and other. The urge to rewrite our theater histories from decolonial perspectives highlights not only the uncomfortable reality of previous narratives but also the political connotations of thinking across borders.

Notes

1 Anna Lowenhaupt Tsing, *Friction: An Ethnography of Global Connection* (Princeton, NJ: Princeton University Press, 2005), 4.
2 The annual conference *Performing Tangier* is organized by the International Centre for Performance Studies (ICPS) in Tangier, Morocco. It performs the city—from the actors onstage to those on the street, everyone together creating "the hereandthenow"; empowering the margins, challenging political divides and stretching our limits; searching, resisting and listening anew, halfway around the world and half a century after the sensation began; and most importantly, it negotiates the future and asks, what kind of world do we want to live in and how will we create it? The past *Performing Tangier* conferences were all fueled by diverse intellectual contributions from colleagues in many parts of the world and in many areas of research.
3 "The postcolony," according to Achille Mbembe, "identifies specifically a given historical trajectory—that of societies recently emerging from the experience of colonialism and the violence which the colonial relationship, *par excellence*, involves. To be sure, the postcolony is chaotically pluralistic, yet it has nonetheless an internal coherence." Achille Mbembe, "Provisional Notes on the Postcolony," *Africa: Journal of the International African Institute* 62, no. 1 (1992): 3.
4 Erika Fischer-Lichte, "Introduction: Entangled Performance Histories: New Approaches to Theater Historiography," 2.
5 Abdelkébir Khatibi (1938–2009) was a Moroccan sociologist, philosopher, critic, playwright, novelist and poet. Khatibi defines "double critique" in the following terms: "So, I call for a double critique: which is centered on us as it is centered on the West and which should take place between us and them. Its aim is to deconstruct both the concept of unity and entirety that we are burdened with. Double critique aims at a demolition of divinity and ideology which are based on origin and absolute unity… I believe that this is the only effective way which can support our strategy. The countries which are subjugated by the West, what-

ever the subjugation is, could know the foundation of Western domination and ask a very critical question away from the delusive assumptions of origin and unity." Abdelkébir Khatibi, *An-Naqdu al-Muzdawij* (Rabat: Oukad, 1990), 12, my translation. My own deployment of Khatibi's double critique aims at foregrounding what Khatibi has termed "the affirmation of a difference." The first implication of such critique is an attempt to decolonize Western logocentrism as manifested in the history of dramatic art. As to the second implication, it is affirmation itself as proposed by Khatibi. In other words, the Arabs have their own performance cultures, yet they are different from the Western traditions of theater making. See ibid., 143.

6 Mustapha Hamil, "Interrogating Identity: Abdelkébir Khatibi and the Postcolonial Prerogative," *Alif: Journal of Comparative Poetics*, no. 22 (2002): 75.

7 The Global South, being an epistemological entity rather than a physical reality, is an invitation to plunge into the poetics and politics of resistance against domineering, exclusionist and, at times, Eurocentric paradigms, theatrical and otherwise, whose very existence hinges on dismissing and discarding as irrelevant any alternative trials to graft newer elements onto a body said to be in full swing. As the site of diverse historical, literary, cultural and artistic convergences, the Global South has been and continues to be the quintessential decolonial space for created hybridities and cultural pluralism.

8 Walter D. Mignolo, *Local Histories/Global Designs: Coloniality, Subaltern Knowledges, and Border Thinking* (Princeton, NJ and Oxford: Princeton University Press, 2012), 71.

9 Ibid., xvi.

10 Ibid., ix.

11 Georg Wilhelm Friedrich Hegel, *The Philosophy of History* (New York, NY: Dover, 1956), 99.

12 Aníbal Quijano, "Coloniality and Modernity/Rationality," *Cultural Studies* 21, no. 2–3 (2007): 170.

13 Dipesh Chakrabarty, *Provincializing Europe: Postcolonial Thought and Historical Difference* (Princeton, NJ: Princeton University Press, 2000), 254.

14 Mignolo, *Local Histories/Global Designs*, xvi.

15 Chakrabarty, *Provincializing Europe*, 27.

16 Walter D. Mignolo admits that "modernity is a European narrative that hides its darker side, 'coloniality.' Coloniality, in other words, is constitutive of modernity—there is no modernity without coloniality." Walter D. Mignolo, "Coloniality: The Darker Side of Modernity," in *Modernologies: Contemporary Artists Researching Modernity and Modernism*, ed. Sabine Breitwieser (Barcelona: MACBA, 2009), 39.

17 On 22 August 1799, Napoleon wrote an important note to his successor, General Kléber, explaining the imperative of theater activity: "I have already asked several times for a troupe of comedians. I will make a special point of sending you one. This item is of great importance for the army and as the means of beginning to change the customs of the country." Quoted in P. C. Sadgrove, *The Egyptian Theatre in the Nineteenth Century, 1799–1882* (Reading: Ithaca Press, 2007), 28.

18 Mohamed Youssef Najm, *Al Masraḥiya fi al-Adhab al-'Arabi al-Ḥadīth*, 2nd ed. (Beirut: Dar Athaqāfa, 1967), 17, my translation.

19 Ali Al-Rai, *Al-Masraḥ fi Al-Watan Al-'Arabi*, 2nd ed. (Kuwait: Alam al Maarifa, 1999), 29, my translation.

20 Ibid., 496.

21 Homi K. Bhabha, *The Location of Culture* (London: Routledge, 1994), 7.

22 Lenin El-Ramly describes the first Arabic reception of Western theater: "Discussing the French Expedition to Egypt of which he was a witness, Egyptian Chronicler Abdel-Rahman al-Jabarti wrote that the French had constructed at al-Azbakiyya quarter special buildings where men and women would gather to engage in unrestricted entertainment and acts of licentiousness. It was theater that he was describing. As we get to know later, Egyptian natives would go out of their way to steal a look at what took place inside." Lenin El-Ramly, "Comedy in the East, or the Art of Cunning: A Testimony," trans. Hazem Azmy, in *The Performance of the Comic in Arabic Theatre: Cultural Heritage, Western Models, Postcolonial Hybridity*, ed. Mieke Kolk and Freddy Decreus (Amsterdam: Amsterdam University Press, 2005), 166.

23 Mignolo, "Coloniality," 42.

24 See Jacob M. Landau, *Studies in the Arab Theater and Cinema* (Philadelphia, PA: University of Pennsylvania, 1958); John Gassner and Edward Quinn, eds., *The Reader's Encyclopedia of World Drama* (New York, NY: Crowell, 1969); Peter J. Chelkowski, *Ta'ziyeh: Ritual and Drama in Iran* (New York, NY: NYU Press, 1979); M. M. Badawi, *Early Arabic Drama* (New York, NY: Cambridge, 1988).

25 Oscar G. Brockett and Franklin J. Hildy, *History of the Theatre*, 9th ed. (Boston, MA: Allyn and Bacon, 2003), 69.

26 Mohammed Al-Khozai, *The Development of Early Arabic Drama (1847–1900)* (London and New York, NY: Longman, 1984), 4.

27 See Mohammed Aziza, *Al-Islam wal-Masrah* (Riyadh: Oyoun al-Maqālāt, 1987), 21, 45, 211. Much of such historionic interventions are based on a flawed argument produced by some Muslim orthodox scholars, the so-called guardians of Islamic faith. Indeed, the Moroccan Ahmed Ben Saddik (1901–1961) was the first to publish a whole book against theater: *Iqāmatu ad-Dalīli 'alā Ḥurmati at-Tamtīli*, published first in Cairo in the 1940s, then edited and republished by the Cairo library in 2004. Ben Saddik, who studied at Al-Qarawiyyin and Al-Azhar universities, provided 48 facts against theatrical activity. In his third argument, he even displayed a strong animosity against other enlightened *Fuqaha* (the literate and learned elites in the Islamic tradition) who encouraged theater as a moral institution. Among these is Mustafa al-Maraghi (1885–1945), who was appointed rector of Al-Azhar University in 1928 and began a series of reforms, and the enlightened Cheikh Mustapha Abderrazaq (1885–1947), who led Al-Azhar between the years 1945 and 1947. Abderrazaq studied in Al-Azhar with the renowned Islamic modernist Mohammed Abdu (1849–1905) and taught at the University of Lyon in France. Ben Saddik, however, goes beyond the limits of scholarly debate to call these moderate Azhari leaders who support theatrical activity "the most ignorant people of their religion." Ben Saddik, *Iqāmatu ad-Dalīli 'alā Ḥurmati at-Tamtīli* (Cairo: Cairo Library, 2004), 7. Ironically, Ben Saddik's many fatwas were ineffective even inside their home city, Tangier, which was one of the theater centers in North Africa at the beginning of the twentieth century. See Ahmed Ben Saddik, *At-Tankīlu Awi Taqtīlu liman Abāḥa Tamtīl* (Beirut: Dar al-Kutub al-Ilmiyah, 2002).

28 Frantz Fanon, *The Wretched of the Earth*, trans. Constance Farington (New York, NY: Grove Press, 1963), 312–16. See also Homi K. Bhabha, "Foreword: Remembering Fanon: Self, Psyche and the Colonial Condition," in *Black Skin, White Masks*, ed. Frantz Fanon (London: Pluto Press, 1986), vii–xxvi.

29 Mignolo, *Local Histories/Global Designs*, xxi.

30 Chakrabarty, *Provincializing Europe*, 255.

31 Dipesh Chakrabarty, "Postcoloniality and the Artifice of History: Who Speaks for 'Indian' Pasts?," *Representations* 37, Special Issue: Imperial Fantasies and Postcolonial Histories (Winter 1992): 2.

32 Rustom Bharucha, "Foreign Asia/Foreign Shakespeare: Dissenting Notes on New Asian Interculturality, Postcoloniality, and Recolonization," *Theatre Journal* 56, no. 1 (2004): 21.
33 "Border thinking," Mignolo emphasizes, "requires dwelling in the border." Mignolo, *Local Histories/Global Designs*, xv.
34 Ibid., 67.
35 Ibid., x.
36 Ibid., 74.
37 "Let us name 'wild difference,' the fake separation which casts the Other into the absolute outside. Wild difference definitely leads to frenzied identities: cultural, historical, ethnic, racial, national [...]. It has condemned the West and made it a captive of hostility." Khatibi, *Double critique*, 30, my translation.
38 Abdelkebir Khatibi, "Double Criticism: The Decolonization of Arab Sociology," in *Contemporary North Africa: Issues of Development and Integration*, ed. Halim Barakat (Washington, DC: Center for Contemporary Arab Studies, Georgetown University, 1985), 14.
39 Ibid., 13.
40 Mignolo, *Local Histories/Global Designs*, 67.
41 Ibid.
42 Martin Heidegger, "What Is Metaphysics?," in *Basic Writings*, trans. David Farrell Krell (San Francisco, CA: HarperCollins, 1993), 100.
43 On 12 January 2015, I curated a conference at the 7th edition of the Arab Theatre Festival in Rabat, Morocco, under the auspices of the Arab Theatre Council. The conference was on "Interweaving Performance Cultures: The North–South Dialogue"; and among the distinguished participants were Erika Fischer-Lichte, Stephen Barber, Maroua Mahdi and Khalid Jalal. Abu Al-Kacem El-Gour from Sudan was supposed to present a synthesis of the debate at the end of the panel. Instead, his presentation under the title "The Structure of European Hegemony" voiced out many of the attitudes and opinions articulated by those Pan-Arabists, Pan-Islamists, Pan-Africanists, etc. These so-called gatekeepers of tradition are actively promoting xenophobia, demonization of the West (as if this "west" is one single entity), conspiracy libels, etc. El-Gour seems to celebrate the divide between East and West as if there is no Global North in the South: "The modern state of human rights from Thomas Hobbes, John Locke and Jean-Jacques Rousseau to the emergence of the League of Nations, the Universal Declaration of Human Rights, the Geneva Conventions and Treaties, and the development of the International Bill of Rights within all national constitutions affirms the inequality of this so-called dialogue," he argued (unpublished manuscript, 1, my translation). El-Gour concluded by fusing and confusing the intercultural paradigm and the interweaving prospects: "The hegemonic European system is a highly complex and interconnected system of signs, particles and dynamics. Accordingly, it can be said that some elements of the European hegemonic patterns are reflected in 'intercultural theater' and the fallacy of 'interweaving performance cultures.' While the theoretical and epistemic foundations of Western European theory are based on Western philosophy, the paradigm of 'interweaving performance cultures' reflects also the crisis of the European theater establishment, which has been centered since the beginning of the twentieth century on attempts at injecting its wasteland. The experiences of Peter Brook and others can be seen as cultural invasions, as Western history says, justifying the invasion of Sudan (for money and men); and the word 'men' here means 'slaves'" (3). Briefly, El-Gour's report was all in all a deliberate misrepresentation of what Erika Fischer-Lichte, Stephen Barber and Khalid Amine were saying on the panel.

44 Youssef Aydabi, "A-Ḥadhitu Khurāfa!" *Arab Theatre Institute*, 16 February 2020, https://tinyurl.com/4b8utbhv.
45 Fanon, *Wretched of the Earth*, 316.
46 *Jemaa el-Fna* is one of the famous sites of popular culture in Morocco. It is a huge and open square in the city of Marrakesh wherein storytelling and other performance behaviors rooted in Moroccan popular culture are practiced as licensed and free oral performances. In brief, the square marks a site of popular orality and ritualistic formulae as well as an archive of Moroccan performance cultures. The square is classified by UNESCO as a site of Intangible Cultural Heritage of Humanity.
47 *Al-Ḥalqa* contitutes a managed environment that stands in stark contrast to the European proscenium tradition. Its audience is called upon "to drift" spontaneously into an area surrounding the performance from all sides. The space required by the *hlayqi* (the maker of spectacle) is not specified, and neither is the timing of the performance. No fourth wall with hypnotic fields is erected between stage and auditorium. The entire marketplace and medina gates can be transformed into a stage; the entire circle may serve as performance space, as open as its repertoire of narrative performances, acrobatic games, songs and dances. In retrieving this performance tradition, theater in Morocco has become more and more improvisational and self-reflexive, even as this retrieval is negotiated within the paradoxical parameters of appropriating and disappropriating the Western models of theater making that were introduced to the country at the turn of the twentieth century.
48 See Erika Fischer-Liche, "Introduction: Interweaving Performance Culture—Rethinking 'Intercultural Theatre': Toward an Experience and Theory of Performance beyond Postcolonialism," in *The Politics of Interweaving Performance Cultures: Beyond Postcolonialism* (New York, NY and London: Routledge, 2014), 11–15.
49 Claudia Breger, *An Aesthetics of Narrative Performance: Transnational Theater, Literature, and Film in Contemporary Germany* (Columbus, OH: The Ohio State University Press, 2012), 5.

Bibliography

Al-Khozai, Mohammed. *The Development of Early Arabic Drama (1847–1900)*. London and New York, NY: Longman, 1984.
Al-Rai, Ali. *Al-Masraḥ fī Al-Watan Al-'Arabi* [*Theater in the Arab World*]. 2nd ed. Kuwait: Alam al Maarifa, 1999.
Amine, Khalid, and Marvin Carlson. *The Theatres of Morocco, Algeria and Tunisia: Performance Traditions of the Maghreb*. Basingstoke: Palgrave Macmillan, 2012.
Aziza, Mohammed. *Al-Islam wal-Masrah*. Riyadh: Oyoun al-Maqālāt, 1987.
Aydabi, Youssef, "A-Ḥadhitu Khurāfa!" ["What Idle Talk!"]. *Arab Theatre Institute*, 16 February 2020. https://tinyurl.com/4b8utbhv.
Badawi, M. M. *Early Arabic Drama*. New York, NY: Cambridge, 1988.
Ben Saddik, Ahmed. *At-Tankīlu Awi Taqtīlu liman Abāḥa Tamtīl* [*Torturing or Killing Those Who Permitted Acting*]. Beirut: Dar al-Kutub al-Ilmiyah, 2002.
———. *Iqāmatu ad-Dalīli 'alā Ḥurmati at-Tamtīli* [*Substantiating Evidence against Acting*]. 3rd ed. Cairo: Cairo Library, 2004.
Bhabha, Homi K. "Foreword: Remembering Fanon: Self, Psyche and the Colonial Condition." In *Black Skin, White Masks*, by Frantz Fanon, vii–xxvi. London: Pluto Press, 1986.

———. *The Location of Culture*. London: Routledge, 1994.
Bharucha, Rustom. "Foreign Asia/Foreign Shakespeare: Dissenting Notes on New Asian Interculturality, Postcoloniality, and Recolonization." *Theatre Journal* 56, no. 1 (2004): 1–28.
Breger, Claudia. *An Aesthetics of Narrative Performance: Transnational Theater, Literature, and Film in Contemporary Germany*. Columbus, OH: The Ohio State University Press, 2012.
Brockett, Oscar G., and Franklin J. Hildy. *History of the Theatre*. 9th ed. Boston, MA: Allyn and Bacon, 2003.
Chakrabarty, Dipesh. "Postcoloniality and the Artifice of History: Who Speaks for 'Indian' Pasts?" *Representations* 37, Special Issue: Imperial Fantasies and Postcolonial Histories (Winter 1992): 1–26.
———. *Provincializing Europe: Postcolonial Thought and Historical Difference*. Princeton, NJ: Princeton University Press, 2000.
Chelkowski, Peter J. *Ta'ziyeh: Ritual and Drama in Iran*. New York, NY: NYU Press, 1979.
Cochrane, Claire, and Jo Robinson, eds. *The Methuen Drama Handbook of Theatre History and Historiography*. London: Methuen, 2020.
El-Ramly, Lenin. "Comedy in the East, or the Art of Cunning: A Testimony." Translated by Hazem Azmy. In *The Performance of the Comic in Arabic Theatre: Cultural Heritage, Western Models, Postcolonial Hybridity*, edited by Mieke Kolk and Freddy Decreus, 166–80. Amsterdam: Amsterdam University Press, 2005.
Fanon, Frantz. *The Wretched of the Earth*. Translated by Constance Farington. New York, NY: Grove Press, 1963.
Fischer-Liche, Erika. "Introduction: Interweaving Performance Culture—Rethinking 'Intercultural Theatre': Toward an Experience and Theory of Performance beyond Postcolonialism." In *The Politics of Interweaving Performance Cultures: Beyond Postcolonialism*, edited by Erika Fischer-Lichte, Torsten Jost and Saskya Iris Jain, 1–21. New York, NY and London: Routledge, 2014.
———, Torsten Jost and Saskya Iris Jain, eds. *The Politics of Interweaving Performance Cultures: Beyond Postcolonialism*. London and New York, NY: Routledge, 2014.
Gassner, John, and Edward Quinn, eds. *The Reader's Encyclopedia of World Drama*. New York, NY: Crowell, 1969.
Hamil, Mustapha. "Interrogating Identity: Abdelkebir Khatibi and the Postcolonial Prerogative." *Alif: Journal of Comparative Poetics*, no. 22 (2002): 72–86.
Hegel, Georg Wilhelm Friedrich. *The Philosophy of History*. New York, NY: Dover, 1956.
Heidegger, Martin. "What Is Metaphysics?" In *Basic Writings*, translated by David Farrell Krell, 89–110. San Francisco, CA: HarperCollins, 1993.
Khatibi, Abdelkebir. "Double Criticism: The Decolonization of Arab Sociology." In *Contemporary North Africa: Issues of Development and Integration*, edited by Halim Barakat, 9–19. Washington, DC: Center for Contemporary Arab Studies, Georgetown University, 1985.
———. *An-Naqdu al-Muzdawij [Double Critique]*. Rabat: Oukad, 1990.
Landau, Jacob M. *Studies in the Arab Theater and Cinema*. Philadelphia, PA: University of Pennsylvania, 1958.
Mbembe, Achille. "Provisional Notes on the Postcolony." *Africa: Journal of the International African Institute* 62, no. 1 (1992): 3–37.

Mckenzie, Jon, Heike Roms and C. J. W. -L. Wee, eds. *Contesting Performance: Global Sites of Research*. Basingstoke: Palgrave Macmillan, 2010.

Mignolo, Walter D. "Coloniality: The Darker Side of Modernity." In *Modernologies: Contemporary Artists Researching Modernity and Modernism*, edited by Sabine Breitwieser, 39–49. Barcelona: MACBA, 2009.

———. *Local Histories/Global Designs: Coloniality, Subaltern Knowledges, and Border Thinking*. Princeton, NJ and Oxford: Princeton University Press, 2012.

Sadgrove, P. C. *The Egyptian Theatre in the Nineteenth Century, 1799–1882*. Reading: Ithaca Press, 2007.

Tsing, Anna Lowenhaupt. *Friction: An Ethnography of Global Connection*. Princeton, NJ: Princeton University Press, 2005.

Quijano, Aníbal. "Coloniality and Modernity/Rationality." *Cultural Studies* 21, no. 2–3 (2007): 168–78.

Youssef Najm, Mohamed. *Al Masraḥiya fī al-Adhab al-'Arabi al-Ḥadīth* [*The Play in Modern Arabic Literature*]. 2nd ed. Beirut: Dar Athaqāfa, 1967.

PART II
Hidden Histories—Forgetting and Remembering

3

WILLIAM KENTRIDGE'S *THE HEAD & THE LOAD*

Theatrical Collage and the Color of Memory

Catherine M. Cole

> When the whites feel [that] they have become too mechanized, they turn to [the] men of color and ask [them] for a little human sustenance.
> —*Frantz Fanon, Black Skins, White Masks; or William Kentridge*[1]

What makes a particular history hidden? Hidden from whom? How is it hidden? And what does it mean to uncover such histories, especially when their concealment is entangled with racism, colonialism and violence?[2] An estimated four million people of color were involved in WWI, including more than two million Africans and a million Indians who served in the British army.[3] Africans, often serving as porters, literally carried the war—its weaponry, provisions and necessary implements. Many of them died. Some violently, others by accident. Many more were felled by dysentery, exhaustion, typhus, yellow fever, pneumonia, heart failure, cerebral malaria and a host of other maladies. African loss of life was significant, estimated at 255,000 soldiers and laborers and over 740,000 civilians.[4] While the role of Africans in the Great War has been documented and studied by Africanist social historians for some time, the story has been largely absent from European public consciousness.[5] "The color of first World War memory remains largely white," says historian Santanu Das.[6] Sometimes this is due to underlying omissions that were deliberate and systematic, as is evident in the 2019 report of the Commonwealth War Graves Commission which found that hundreds of thousands of African casualties were either commemorated unequally (as compared to Europeans), improperly (i.e., not by name), or not at all.[7] Public memory is also shaped by narrative preferences: heroic tales about individuals are easier to grasp than messy stories of a collective ordeal, and whites

DOI: 10.4324/9781003353461-6

generally have had greater access to such singular narratives.⁸ As a result, David Olusoga contends,

> More words have been written over the past century about the few dozen middle-class officers who wrote their war memoirs and penned their war poetry than about the 4 million non-white, non-European soldiers who fought for Britain, France, and their allies, let alone the millions of civilians who laboured and suffered hardships and loss when the war swept through their communities.⁹

As a corrective to this historic erasure and to mark the Great War's centennial in the years 2014–2018, several artists created new works by engaging archival sources that documented the role of Africans, Indians and other non-Europeans in the war. Two artists in particular, John Akomfrah and William Kentridge, used the medium of collage. "Can we think about history as collage, rather than as narrative?," asked South African Kentridge as he created his landmark performance *The Head & the Load* (*H&L*).¹⁰ While audiences often desire that epic stories be conveyed through a singular protagonist and linear narrative (think Anne Frank), Kentridge wanted to work against this tendency, to explore instead whether it was possible to connect and have a sense of affect without a clear narrative, to grasp a massive and missing history through fragments presented in a three-dimensional, enacted collage.¹¹

Kentridge's *H&L* and Akomfrah's video installation *Mimesis: African Soldier* were part of the UK-based arts program "14–18 NOW," a five-year-long reflection on the WWI centenary. The program aimed to put the world—especially the non-European world—back into the history of the first World War.¹² *H&L* did so in particularly intercultural ways, both in terms of its eclectic cultural referents as well as its cosmopolitan performers and production team, which included artists from South Africa, America, Belgium and Germany. *H&L* was meant as neither a history lesson nor a lecture. Nor was it, in Kentridge's view, an opera, theater piece, or oratorio—though it had elements of all three. It was, rather, "something in between"—a time-based, multimedia collage with vocal and instrumental music, dance, projections, and spoken words.¹³ Critics hailed this historical pageant as a "fever dream," a "carnage cabaret."¹⁴

Tracy C. Davis and Peter W. Marx in their introduction to *The Routledge Companion to Theatre and Performance Historiography* single out *H&L* as exemplary. What interests Davis and Marx about this production is both its polyphonic historiography and critical media methods, the way *H&L* is a "discourse *of*, and not merely *through*, media."¹⁵ Polyphonic historiography is evident in Kentridge's surprising and revelatory juxtapositions in this theatrical collage: a performer on a ladder representing Kaiser Wilhelm II placed in proximity to an African musician playing the kora (a 21-stringed instrument often used by West African bards to tell epic history). Both are seen against a theatrical backdrop that includes projections of lists of figures and facts about the Great War.[16] These unreconciled fragments help us to perceive WWI history differently: we can see that Africa intersected with Germany; we can hear one country screeching its history while another plucks its epic tales on a lute; and we can feel affectively how war is lived both in the symbolic realm—through figureheads like the Kaiser and his imperial coat of arms—and in mundane objects like pairs of mittens and packets of ink powder.

H&L's polyphonic historiography and self-reflexive mediated spectatorship can offer new insights about the past, especially about eclipsed histories. But what might be the limitations of this approach, especially in relation to both past and present anti-Black racism? Collage was an apt form for this production for several reasons. Invented in 1912, coincident with the inception of the Great War itself, collage formed an important critique of modernism. As Christine Poggi contends, collage undermined notions of unity, "subverted (rather than affirmed) the role of the frame of the pictorial ground and brought the languages of high and low culture into a new relationship of exchange."[17] Kentridge's adoption of collage for this production similarly disrupted previous historiographic unities, deprivileged narrative as a primary means of accessing the past, and brought the cultures of Africa and Europe into a new relationship and exchange. A guiding question for Kentridge in creating this production was whether we can think about history as collage rather than narrative. I want to pose a different set of questions: *Why* use collage to represent a formerly hidden, culturally entangled, and racialized history, and to what end? What does this method accomplish? What might be its boundaries? And what implications might collage as a method have for the writing about hidden and entangled performance histories?

Whiteness/Trajectory Without Narrative

WWI's first and last shots were fired on African soil, in Togo and Zambia respectively. While the Great War is generally perceived as a European affair, John Akomfrah reminds us that Europe in 1914 was far larger than it is today.[18] At the war's outbreak in 1914, Europe controlled over 90 percent of Africa, its dominance having been established at the Berlin Conference of 1884, during which Belgium, Britain, France, Germany, Italy and Spain divided Africa like a "magnificent cake."[19] Three decades later, colonizing powers called upon their African subjects to serve in the Great War. From the beginning, their involvement was both compelled and repressed. Imperial powers desperately needed the conscription of their colonial subjects to win the war. However, equipping non-Europeans with guns and providing conditions for heroism in battle could sow the seeds of anti-colonial unrest. Asking Africans to kill Europeans ran counter to white supremacy, the foundation of colonial rule.

And then there was the question of history: What would be remembered? Black South African Sol Plaatje described in 1916 the reasons African conscripts were prohibited from bearing arms: "Nor must they carry arms, lest their behavior should merit recognition; their heroic deeds and acts of valour must, on account of their colour, not be recorded."[20] In other words, there was a deliberate decision to limit Africans' potential to be history's protagonists by casting them not as combatants but instead as porters, a supporting role. History is not interested in the baggage carriers.

While African participation in the Great War was constrained, nevertheless many Africans served both as soldiers and laborers, and archives documenting their experiences *do* exist. For instance, African soldiers held as prisoners of war in German camps left behind 2,000 audio recordings.[21] Archives in Senegal, Ghana and Kenya possess enough cinematic evidence to contribute to John Akomfrah's 75-minute, 3-channel video installation *Mimesis* depicting African, Asian and Black American soldiers and porters "being signed up, feeding supply lines, and converging on fronts, from Flanders mud to jungle, desert, and veld."[22] A much wider set of archival sources informed David Olusoga's *The World's War*, a history of WWI's multiracial dimensions. Why were these archives not heretofore more widely known or consulted? John Akomfrah approaches the question of concealed history provocatively. When people talk to him about hidden history, he reflects on the many WWI-era documents of Black life he has accessed. He imagines speaking directly to these sources:

> Since you exist as pieces of film with figures of color in it, how come you've been hidden? Why are you hidden? And the reasons are fairly obvious [...]. They are not hidden because they are literally locked up. There was something else standing where they would have been, which basically said to them, "OK, I got this. I got this." In other words, there is a whole bunch of archival material from the war; most of it has, frankly, white people, because they were the majority. And the way whiteness functions in these spaces of authority is to inadvertently exclude others by simply standing in the place of everything. It just says, "I've got this. I can *do* this for us."[23]

In Akomfrah's view, what often makes Black history hidden is that it is upstaged by whiteness. Whiteness claims centrality, takes center stage, crowds out everything else. Whiteness bathes in the spotlight of history so intense and narrow that it obscures everything around it.

Artworks like Akomfrah's multimedia collage installation *Mimesis* and Kentridge's *H&L* face a challenge. If uncovering for the public a hidden history of Black participation in the Great War is done through the medium of collage using fragments from archives that are generally dominated by documentation of white people, there is a danger that whiteness will once again overwhelm, conveying, in effect, "I've *got* this." How did Kentridge's *H&L* fare in this regard? Did whiteness once again claim the spotlight?

Premiering in 2018 in London, *H&L* was an intensely collaborative work staged by an army of musicians, singers, actors, designers and technicians from South Africa, Europe and America. Among its intercultural cast of over 45 performers, the majority were Black South Africans. Meanwhile, behind the scenes, the show's production staff was overwhelmingly white. Together, this multiracial artistic collective mediated the gulf between the production's monumental and incidental realms, which at times felt as unreconciled as the gulf between Africans and Europeans during the Great War. Lacking a single narrative or protagonist, *H&L* produced cacophony: multiple languages, mutually unintelligible. A jumble that did not cohere—and that was the point. The goal was not simply to represent the contending claims, hubris, manifestos and ambitions that both incited and fueled the war, but to "show the limits of our hearing and to allow other voices to start to emerge," said Kentridge.[24] It is precisely the question of these "other voices" that most interests me. Whose voices, in the end, did this production allow audiences to hear?

H&L mined the power of paradox, putting incongruent elements in juxtaposition, often to absurd effect. Its premise was that because the past itself is fragmented and because history (the writing of the past) is "a construction of fragments that make a provisional understanding of the past," collage is a form that can expose these ruptures and reveal disparate perspectives.[25] More importantly, a performed collage has the capacity to highlight the viewer's agency in creating—indeed choosing—meaning. "Here we have a choice," says Kentridge, either "to hide the joints between the different fragments, or to show the white scars of the joints of the reconstructed vase and to show the completed vessel made up of so many shards. Our task was to make a piece of theatre that has a trajectory rather than a narrative."[26] Densely wrought from historic remnants and samplings from African and European musical and aesthetic movements of the early twentieth century, *H&L* staged jarring contrasts. On one hand was the show's massive scale: at its premiere at the Tate Modern's Turbine Hall, the stage measured 55 meters wide (which is over half the size of an American football field).[27] *H&L* instilled a visceral sense of foreboding as we witnessed the inexorable machinery of empire and war barreling ahead. The mammoth stage, layered scenography, and frenetic staging catered to no one perspective. No matter where you sat in the audience, you had to keep turning your head. One simply could not take it all in. This may have been one of the performance's most forceful means of persuasion: the past is too big for us to perceive.

H&L was grand, yes, and even grandiose, but at the same time, the work's scope was constantly undercut. As much as *H&L* emphasized enormity with its yawning stage, throng of performers, gigantic projections, and abundance of heady historical, literary, musical, philosophical and visual citations, the production also valorized the quotidian and banal: shoes, mosquitos, a list of musical instruments and sporting equipment sent to the troops by a British welfare committee, a recitation of someone giving directions on how to march. A mélange of musical shards and tidbits of very specific aspects of material culture (pairs of socks, a portable organ, pen holders) were put in dynamic tension. The monumental was shot through with the incidental. A big picture full of minute and seemingly random details. The story of Africans in the Great War was important, yes, but how do we decide which details of history deserve our focus?

Despite lacking a storyline, there was an overall directionality to the work, most notably in the form of processions, usually from left to right across the stage, the same direction in which one reads European languages. An iconic feature of Kentridge's oeuvre, processions have featured in his previous works such as: *Arc/Procession: Develop, Catch Up, Even Surpass* (1990), a charcoal and pastel arc-shaped drawing on 11 pieces of paper; *More Sweetly Play the Dance* (2015), an eight-channel video installation of people processing from left to right across the expanse; and the site-specific work *Triumphs and Laments: A Project for Rome* (2016), a 500-meter-long frieze created on the banks of the River Tiber. Each of these iterations of processions was larger, more performative, dimensional and embodied than the previous one.[28] In that sense, *H&L*'s processions were a culmination of this technique, here instantiated by live actors walking slowly in single file across a cavernous stage. Dressed in khakis and dusky-hued muslins, they wore boots and hand-crafted caps and carried silhouette cutouts mounted on sticks, holding them aloft like signboards at a protest march. High-powered footlights shining on the actors from the edge of the stage cast enormous shadows on the back wall, creating looming silhouettes both of the actors and their disparate loads: cannons, megaphones, ships, airplanes, typewriters, jumbles of indeterminate things, and busts of past and future African and European leaders. Superimposed on these projected shadows were other projected images—photographic, cinematic, and stop-motion animations. Video clips, montages, drawings and charcoal sketches leapt into animated sequence: monochromatic color schemes of words, texts and maps dotted with flourishes of red; snatches of historic black-and-white filmstrips replayed in loops. One short film showed a dancer's legs as she clicked her black heels together like Dorothy in *The Wizard of Oz* trying to go back home. Another clip depicted a lone soldier as he saluted the camera, his face obscured by cut-out geometric shapes. Archival footage of a phalanx of African soldiers wearing fezzes and marching toward the camera repeated, caught in a loop—a circuit of loyalty? Recurrent trauma? entrenched muscle memory? You decide.

While collage as a form suggests openness, *H&L*'s scale and density worked against this. Its trajectory felt inexorable, its intertexts cerebral. Orchestrating this many people and objects required a squadron of staff and carefully choreographed cues. The production left little to chance. As one reviewer commented, "The production team keeps all that talent and the profusion of spinning wheels coordinated with the aplomb of a Barnumringmaster."[29] *H&L*'s many allusions (to Dada, the European avant-garde, Frantz Fanon, Tristan Tzara, Wilfred Owen, isiZulu proverbs, African activist John Chilembwe) were unmarked and unexplained. As reviewer Justin Davidson commented in *New York* magazine, *H&L* "is a 90-minute collage that, if it doesn't rattle you into existential despair, may at least send you to consult a Wikipedia entry to see what the whole thing's about."[30] Kentridge was adamant that he wanted to "avoid an essay, to not give a lecture. By that I mean to not start with a series of facts and knowledge that the makers of the piece have, which they give to an audience who they assume knows less than them."[31]

H&L did seem to have a lesson, but it refused to tell you what it was, which some found frustrating: "I don't mind having the world deconstructed before my eyes in a nonlinear artistic experience," wrote critic Davidson, "but when it feels like I'm supposed to be digesting a historical argument at the same time, my brain goes on the fritz."[32] Yet for literary scholar Homi Bhabha, *H&L*'s dense citationality was a hermeneutic playground for exercising his interpretive agility.[33] Negative reviews of *H&L* were the exception, for critics generally lavished praise. Writing in the *Daily Telegraph*, David Hudson enthused, "Like everyone else there I was utterly engrossed and fabulously transported."[34] The *New Yorker* likened *H&L* to a "fusillade of arrows hitting not one but many bull's-eyes."[35] The *Opera Wire* critic wrote, "The magnitude of the proportions and their corresponding complexity never overwhelm our emotional connectivity or interest."[36]

H&L's deeply layered pastiche put fragments side-by-side without explanation. These very gaps stimulate one's mental inclination to make sense of things, to find connection among discrete elements, to reconcile, to discover meaning in the absurd. However, the collage form constantly frustrated this cognitive impulse. Recurrent images of scissors, tearing and cutting reminded us that the history of the Great War—including its maps and the borders drawn within Africa—were all constructions. And constructions are always vulnerable to destruction. Images that seemed to be whole—like a beautiful ink drawing of a bird (projected on the wall while soprano Ann Masina sings Erik Satie's sentimental waltz *Je te veux*)—visually exploded into bits, torn up into fragments, and filmed via stop-motion animation sequence to display the remnants of the drawing scattering like autumn leaves in a wind. Other projections depicted lines arbitrarily drawn on maps during a part of the show that evoked the Berlin Conference of 1884, at which Africa was divided up among European powers. Colonialism drew boundaries across African ethnolinguistic groups in ways that made no sense. In *H&L*, the African continent was divided on a map while three actors spoke nonsense. They declaimed portions of Kurt Schwitters's Dada sound poem *Ursonate* saying sounds without sense: "rakete rinnzekete," "fümmsböwötääzääUu pöggiff" and "rrummpff tillff toooo?"[37] Just as colonial borders were both real and fictional, arbitrary and deliberate, penetrating and fragile, language too could quickly degenerate into a collection of indecipherable consonants and vowels, a jumble of plosives and fricatives. The first page of the published libretto for H&L simply begins: "eeeeeeeeeeeee," with the letters getting gradually larger as they move from left to right across the page. This is what trajectory without narrative feels like. But where does the trajectory take us?

Setting Things Right/Trying Not to Be Right

John Battersby writing in South Africa's *Daily Maverick* rhapsodically gushed, "Using his unique brand of interactive collage, Kentridge has in one flourish restored the humanity of the descendants of Africans lost in the war and accommodated the need of the colonial descendants to restore their own dignity by acknowledging the humanity of others."[38] This sweeping claim was preposterous. How could one theatrical performance serve as a reparation for over a million African war dead? Kentridge is known as an artist of the irresolute, who favors process and the peripatetic over arrivals and political positions. As Ashraf Jamal argues, "He challenges each and every attempt to fix his art as something monumental, or worse, as a window onto a country's history. Rather, Kentridge puts categorical imperatives under erasure. This process is both aesthetic and ethical."[39] While Kentridge would likely disavow Battersby's claim of reparation through this performance, something about the production led to such an interpretation. What was it?

H&L began with a segment on "Manifestos," which concluded with an invitation to embrace the provisional, the incorrect: "Let's try for once not to be right."[40] Was this the production's aim? While it tried not to be right, to not claim superior knowledge, at the same time, the project had a moral claim, one attempting to acknowledge what had historically been denied: the participation of Africans in the Great War. Can one really do both at the same time—not be right and help make something right? Located in a no-man's-land between forms, genres and nations, between Europe and Africa, between then—the "then" of history—and now, H&L summoned during its 90-minute duration a discordant onslaught. While trying not to be right, it nevertheless invited and frustrated our impulse to make sense. It unleashed a babel of untranslated languages: German, Swahili, French, English, isiZulu, Shangaan, Hungarian, Morse code, Italian, Setswana and Kurt Schwitters's nonsense Dadaist language, Ursonate. To this were added other aesthetic grammars and modes: fragmentation, procession, shadows, projections, manifestos, letters and proverbs.

Intercultural entanglement was evident not just in the subject matter of this production but also in its form, especially its sonic landscape. The musical score by composers Philip Miller and Thuthuka Sibisi fused snippets from a Viennese waltz by Austrian Fritz Kreisler with melodies from French composers Erik Satie and Maurice Ravel. African musical influences included West African kora music, which often accompanies the telling of oral epics about history, conquerors and wars—a particularly apt musical form for a tale about a massive world war. One also heard, saw and felt the percussive rhythms of South African Pedi stomping dances, performed by Black dancers wearing white skirts that resembled Scottish kilts.[41] The stage itself became a percussive instrument as the troupe of soldiers stomped and marched with such vehemence that spectators felt vibrations through their seats. Even the projectors began to shudder. Just as the stage became an instrument, actual musical instruments were played unconventionally: a sort of pitchless breathing rasp into brass instruments evoked a human cry, and drumsticks struck on a double bass produced an unnerving tap. One also heard war chants; a bugle call played on violin strings. The English anthem *God Save the King* was chopped up, performed as though its broadcast signal was faltering, while the phrase "God Save…" reverberated as if in a cathedral. The effect some found "spine-chilling."[42]

Interrupted trajectory was evident in the physical staging as well. At one point, the show's musical ensemble was propelled on a mobile cart across the stage as they repeatedly launched the upbeat melody of a classic and deceptively cheery South African *kwela* ditty, one often featured in documentaries about South African popular music under apartheid. But the path of this melody kept being halted by kazoo-like whistles, a sound inspired by historic audio recordings of detonated artillery. These comic sounds were intermixed with projections of charcoal-drawn animations of explosions. *H&L* was not just intercultural but also interspecies in its aural referents, with piercing vocal screeches reminiscent of a bird of prey shrieked by Joanna Dudley and a war poem by Wilfred Owen, translated into French, delivered as though it were the barking of a dog.

Key to deciphering the sense in the nonsense, the quiet at the center of the show's sonic and visual storm, was the importance of *not* knowing the answers, of trying, for once, *not* to be right.[43] The production satirized the hubris of manifestos and proclamations that assert unequivocable meaning. The nationalist obsessions behind the war were manifest as a screeching imperial German eagle of war, played by Joanna Dudley, careening across the stage on a wagon, as well as through a preposterous disposition on the magnificence of French vowels performed by Luc De Wit:

> *Parlez le français. Parlez le français de la France*
> *Le français français des Françiases de la France.*
> *Les magnifiques voyelles.*
> *Le grande AAAAAAAA.*
> *Le noble eeeeeeeee, uuuuuuuuuuu, le è!*
> *MOLIÈRE!*

These fleeting caricatures expressed little in terms of narrative or content, but one thing was clear: they believed they were right.

Collage as an aesthetic form is modest and, therefore, well suited to a production that is trying not to be right. Collage draws from other sources rather than claiming sui generis originality, thereby conveying a nonhierarchical ethos. It displays multiple perspectives without necessarily asserting one point of view. It relies more on assembly than mastery of artistic craft, which feels collaborative and inclusive. So, all in all, collage seemed to be an effective aesthetic vessel for this subject matter. In answer to Kentridge's question about whether we can think about history as collage rather than as narrative, I would answer: yes, of course. History writing has always been, to some extent, a collage: disparate sources are assembled into a whole that is always fabricated. History's perspective is always partial, even if presumed not to be. Scholars may downplay the selectivity and partiality of their sources. But artists working with archival sources through the medium of collage may choose instead to foreground the partial and incomplete, as Kentridge does here. Or to use the archive to tell not what was but what might have been. Or to envision different futures through what Asbjørn Skarsvåg Grønstad, writing about John Akomfrah, calls the "elsewhere of the image."[44] *H&L* was self-consciously and overtly constructed as collage, revealing rather than disguising the cuts and its arbitrary perspectives.[45] In this way, it was very different from the defacto collage of formal WWI histories, which have for so long occluded the African presence and participation in the war and so often glossed over these gaps and erasures rather than laying them bare.

While *H&L* was a revelation of what had been missing from the Great War's historiography, the production at the same time erased its own historiographic tracks. As critic Justin Davidson commented, "Performers from a variety of African nations declaim what we're told are bits of Frantz Fanon in siSwati and Tristan Tzara in isiZulu, though I'll have to take Kentridge's word for that."[46] Its assemblage of borrowed images, redeployed texts and purloined melodic riffs was reproduced with little, if any, attribution. Near the start of the show, narrator Mncedisi Shabangu declaims, "When the whites feel they have become too mechanized, they turn to men of color and ask for a little human sustenance." In various interviews about the production, Kentridge attributes this quote to Frantz Fanon, the Black Martinican anti-colonial theorist. Does it matter that Fanon's words are lifted and spoken in *H&L* without attribution, or that there is no citation included in the published libretto? Fanon's words become, by default, Kentridge's, if one cites this line from the libretto, as I have done in this chapter's epigraph. Of course, no playwright is expected to offer footnotes. But how should we think about the inequality of value placed on the many intertexts of *H&L*? Ghanaian proverbs and Tristan Tzara do not exist on an even playing field, after all.

Here the limits of collage begin to reveal themselves. While collage as an aesthetic form routinely appropriates sources without permission and attribution, in the history of relations between Europeans and Africans, the habit of appropriation without permission, attribution or even understanding has been a problem. For instance, the European inception of the collage form, which typically dates to 1912, is often told as a story about Picasso's inspiration from the forms of Grebo and Fang West African masks in which he had an aesthetic interest, although Grebo and Fang *peoples* themselves held little interest.[47] Colonized aesthetics often evacuate an "exotic" form while jettisoning the source's content, cultural context and indigenous meaning, as well as indigenous people themselves.

Let us consider the title *The Head & the Load*, which is attributed by Kentridge to a Ghanaian proverb that apparently says, 'The head and the load are the troubles of the neck'—the head being, perhaps, the ideologies and ambitions of Europeans that incited and drove the war; the load may indicate the war's machinery and violent weight—its ships, guns, gas and trenches. And the neck, in this reading, could be those several million Africans who served in the Great War, who bore its heavy weight and profound physical consequences. Structurally, "the head and the load are the troubles of the neck" sounds like it could be a Ghanaian proverb. But is it? Experts who I consulted could not recall such a Ghanaian proverb.[48] Nor is this saying listed in various Ghanaian proverb compendiums. The closest West African link to a proverb like this I could find comes from a collection of Hausa proverbs from 1905: "*Da kai da kaia duka malakka'n wuya.* The head and the load are both the possession of the neck."[49] George Merrick, the editor of that volume, was a captain with the British Royal Garrison Artillery stationed in Nigeria with the Bolewa people, which leads me to think the proverb is more likely Nigerian than Ghanaian (though Hausa spans both countries).

But does the proverb even mean what the title *The Head & the Load* seems to suggest? The title implies that the neck must carry the burden of the head and the load. Yet the Hausa proverb reverses this hierarchy, saying rather the head and the load are not the *troubles* but the *possessions* of the neck. This rendering of the proverb is consistent with one offered by Mohammed Bashir Salau, who has researched the history of slavery in Kano, Nigeria. He quotes from an interview conducted by Yusufu Yunusa in 1975: "If my slave buys a slave, the Hausas have a saying: The head and the load are all under the jurisdiction of the neck. Then it implies that my slave's slave is my slave?" To which his interlocutor, Malam Isyaku, an ex-slave who was 90 years old at the time of the interview, replied, "Yes"!ature [50] Here a proverb is used to discuss who owns who, which indicates the importance and seriousness of this linguistic form, being used here to discuss possession and enslavement. Power in these two versions of the Hausa proverb goes in the opposite direction of what is suggested by Kentridge's *H&L*. Does that matter? The production exhorts,

"Let's try for once not to be right." But in the appropriation of African content, Europeans have historically not worked very hard to get things right. Is now not the time to do better?

Proverbs are essential to West African rhetoric and communication. They are notoriously multivalent, condensing wisdom, insight, advice and criticism into brief aphorisms. Proverbs can simultaneously flatter and criticize, both bite and embrace, for they leverage language's power of indirection.[51] Their use requires skill and precision. Misuse of a proverb in a chief's palace in Ghana can lead to a fine, according to Chief Linguist Kwame Frimpong Manso Adakabre.[52] While proverbs are multivalent, they do hold meaning. And they challenge the recipient to unpack their dense repositories of communication. Hence my desire to learn more about the supposed Ghanaian proverb referenced in *The Head & the Load*'s title. If this performance was intended to "show the limits of our hearing and to allow other voices to start to emerge," let us hear those previously repressed African voices and take time to understand their words.[53]

Production History as Palimpsest

Kentridge as an artist favors the journey more than the destination, the trajectory more than the end point, the question more than the argument. "Let us avoid not the bite of a word, the vertigo of a question mark," begins *H&L*.[54] In line with this, let us consider the path by which this production came to be. I have provided thus far a critical analysis of the production and its reception. Let us now consider the performance's path of creation, going behind its intermedial layers of images, bodies and shadows to examine its creative process as palimpsest, one that contains its own hidden histories in the smudged erasures and faded lines. Can we hear, for once, more African voices?

As with all things Kentridge, the creative tributaries that flow into *H&L* are multiple. Many of its core ideas were salvaged from the cutting-room floor during his preparation for another production: Alban Berg's opera *Wozzeck* for the New York Metropolitan Opera in 2019, which first premiered at the 2017 Salzburg Festival. Kentridge decided to set Berg's opera just before the start of WWI. To develop his opera's concept, he conducted a workshop in his studio in Johannesburg. South African composers, dancers, actors, musicians—most of them Black—served as creative porters for this project, enabling Kentridge's ambitious conceptualization of *Wozzeck*. Through improvisation, the artists surfaced shards of ideas, some of which ended up in *Wozzeck*, a production that would not involve these African performers at all. Their work was generative and conceptual but limited to the studio, not the stage. However, some of the concepts they prototyped ended up having a whole other life: they eventually became *H&L*. Material that had very specific African inflections and roots generally did not make it into *Wozzeck*, for the role of Africans in the

Great War was not its focus. Some of these Africa-specific concepts came from archival provocations, such as a recording of a Portuguese WWI soldier saying of African recruits: "They are not men because they have no names. They are not soldiers because they have no numbers. They are not to be called but counted."[55] Other ideas came from material culture: while Africans went to war often hoping that their willingness to die for their colonial masters would finally lead to an acquisition of rights, they generally received no invitation to a victory parade, no medals, and certainly survivors did not acquire greater political agency back in Africa at the war's end. What some received instead was a bicycle and an overcoat. One of the South African performers working in the studio realized, "Oh my God, now I understand. My grandfather had a bicycle and a coat, and no one in the family was ever allowed to touch them. They were his most precious possessions. He would never wear the coat, and no one could ride the bicycle. They stood there."[56] Seemingly no one in his family had previously understood the connection between these objects, their grandfather's behavior and WWI.

Several of the improvisations from the *Wozzeck* workshop were so illuminating and affectively potent that they clearly deserved a life onstage, even if their African specificity was not well suited to the Berg opera. For instance, dancers Gregory Maqoma and Thulani Chauke created a haunting processional duet of a soldier falling from exhaustion and injury who is propelled forward. His trajectory is compelled in part by habit, even as his body falters. He moves across the stage in a sort of collapsing crawl, occasionally resurrected to attention by his more alert companion through gestures that alternate between compassionate embrace and violent slaps. The core movement vocabulary of this vignette Kentridge later labeled as a "spasm of history," and it became the essence for the creative project that eventually became *H&L*.[57] "In the sequence of the wounded man, we have the feeling of the body following and not following an order—a wounded man falling and catching himself," said Kentridge. "The moment we saw the wounded man dance, we knew we had the emotional heart of the piece. For me, that moment was a talisman."[58]

The contradictory impulses in the duet—its push and pull—encapsulated with great potency the African response to the Great War itself. The dynamics of this "spasm of history," as Kentridge labeled it, go in multiple directions. On the one hand was someone like the historic figure of John Chilembwe from Nyasaland (present-day Malawi), who wondered in a letter he sent in 1915 to the *Nyasaland Times* whether anything good would come to the natives by the end of the war. Entitled "The Voice of African Natives in the Present War," his letter is quoted extensively in *H&L* as Chilembwe asks whether Africans' loyalty and service would be recognized. If Africans stood on the firing line and "played a patriot's part, with a spirit of true gallantry," if they shed blood as a matter of honor and loyalty, "shall we be recognised as anyone in the best interests of civilisation and Christianity, after the great struggle is ended?"[59] The question was rhetorical. While equality was paramount in wartime, Chilembwe knew that in peacetime everything was "for Europeans only." The voice of the African natives in the Great War, as represented by Chilembwe, was not just suppressed. His letter was never published in his lifetime, Chilembwe was executed, those who followed him were hanged, and the Baptist Church he led was blown up. Whereas some Africans like Chilembwe questioned the call to serve in WWI and did not wish to die for a cause that was not theirs, others saw the Great War as their cause, their pathway to full citizenship. They agitated for the *right* to participate: "We demand the right to serve in the army as all French citizens do. We offer a harvest of devotion."[60] These conflicted and oscillating reactions—to opt out or in, to step forward or back, to lean in or withdraw—cut to the core of the African response to the Great War. Since African participants in the *Wozzeck* workshop were serving as proxies, stand-ins for the European and American actors who would eventually perform in this opera abroad, one wonders if they too had similarly conflicted responses to the call to create for a production in which they would have no billing.

While African-specific creative ideas generated for the creation of *Wozzeck* ended up on the cutting-room floor, these ideas nevertheless had "legs" and became the generative seed for *H&L*. As Kentridge says,

> There's something remarkable about the improvisations that were done by the team of largely black, African performers that I work with. […] So, when the invitation came from the Armory, [I had] the thought of using some of the improvisations and material that never found its way into the opera but was very rich in itself. So […] we had the sense of the look and partly the cast of characters I wanted to be in the piece.[61]

When Maqoma and Chauke's duet finally did make it into *H&L*, critics readily identified it as the affective core of the production: "A soldier attempting to hold a wounded comrade in military posture in Act 3, Running & Falling, plays out the link between tenderness and violence, writ large in their twenty-foot high shadows. Finally, unable to stand, he collapses in death," wrote Ann McCoy.[62] "Probably the most affecting new piece of choreography I have seen in a very long time," wrote Patricia Zohn.[63]

H&L's multidisciplinary, multiracial team of artists worked in highly collaborative ways. In public interviews and his own documentation of the project, Kentridge makes clear that the creative process was shared. He speaks often in the first person plural: "We needed to be led not only by books and texts"; "We would improvise with many different rhythms of percussion"; "We did not want dialogue: one character speaking to another"; "Our starting point was the width of the stage."[64] However, in most feature articles and reviews written about both the London and New York productions of *H&L*, Kentridge himself is the primary focus. The *Wall Street Journal* and *American Theatre Magazine* ran lengthy profiles on Kentridge to coincide with the production.[65] Critics called the production electrifying, mind-bending and extraordinary, typically identifying Kentridge as the sole auteur and creator. Some saw *H&L* as "by far his most ambitious work," predicting it "will be hailed as a tour de force."[66] As with the historiography of the Great War, the color of memory about this production, as evidenced in its production archive, trends white and favors the singular individual. In the publicity spotlight is Kentridge as solo genius, the hero. His African collaborators receive marginal mention, they are part of the army but not the generals of this production's "tour de force." How does this happen? How do whiteness and individual heroism so effectively dominant memory yet again?

The creative process dictated that inclusivity and collaboration had limits. The vetting of ideas generated in the studio involved conversations among the artistic team, and this sometimes led to intensive debates. In particular, the decision to conclude *H&L* with a montage of images of twentieth-century leaders of independent Africa was hotly contested among cocreators. However, while the creative process was collaborative, there were limits, as Kentridge explained: "The actors are engaged, and feel like it is theirs, but at a certain point I say, 'If each of you gets to take out something you don't like we'll be left with nothing. So, I decide.'"[67] Two articles on *H&L* begin to touch upon the delicate issue of intellectual property and racial ethics. Jo Livingston, writing in the *New Republic*, said,

> Kentridge's continual reference to abstract traditions in European art, like Dadaism, and the remoteness of his practice from contemporary struggles in South Africa, make his work a little less urgent. Meanwhile, opera, which features so heavily in this performance, has a very specific cultural valence in South Africa: Many of the best opera singers there come from townships or poor rural villages, even though it is a form that still caters to the most elite audiences. Watching *The Head and the Load* [*sic*], there is a sense that his collaborators bathe him in a kind of unearned, reflected glory.[68]

Murray Whyte noted in the *Guardian* that "exhuming stories is tricky work, particularly now, as history unravels less as fact than perspective, with those typically shoved to the margins finding space closer to the centre."[69] In a rare case of any journalist speaking directly to any of the cocreators of *H&L*, Whyte asked Thuthuka Sibisi, the show's Black cocomposer and music director, to comment on whether the story of the role of Africans in the Great War should not be told by artists of African rather than European descent. Sibisi responded, "On the one hand, yes, I think it's important that black stories be told by black artists. [...] But I think certain stories can only find room through certain kinds of artists. This story, at this scale, happens because of William, and who he is—it becomes a global story, and that's really important."[70] Sibisi believes that the magnitude of Kentridge's international stature and artistry overrides the imperative of Black artists to tell this particular Black story.

While a collage can show many perspectives, these are finite in number. And they are also particular. What perspective did Kentridge bring to the project? For him, *H&L* was about his personal commitment to rectify his own ignorance. When he was a child growing up in South Africa, history lessons in school were generally silent on the role of Africans in the Great War: "We learned nothing, absolutely nothing, about the participation of the porters in the war. This piece, 'The Head and the Load,' was a way to answer an ignorance in myself. We did learn that, in 1917, the S.S. Mendi had sunk, with great loss of life, with many Africans aboard. But there was no discussion about what they were doing there, in the English Channel."[71] Kentridge says the project began in "a frustration at my own ignorance about the material"—an ignorance, he notes, that other participants on the project also shared.[72] So ultimately the work became a meditation about different kinds of ignorance. For several Black South African artists involved in the show, such as lead actor and director of song and dance Nhlanhla Mahlangu, the project was about addressing both ignorance and systems of concealment: "This history was hidden from Africans because of the framing of the education system."[73] Black South Africans who have the rare privilege of access to advanced higher education might learn about prominent resistance figures like John Chilembwe. Or they may have heard about the SS Mendi, a ship that carried the Fifth Battalion of the South African Native Labour Corps that sank in 1917 in the English Channel on its way to France, killing 616 South Africans. However, "for the everyday men and women," according to Mahlangu, "this is not common knowledge."[74]

Yet for some of the show's Black performers, *H&L* was not primarily about correcting ignorance. Nor was it an experiment in the potential of collage, or the importance of trajectory over narrative. Nor was it even primarily about history. It was rather a sacred ritual in the now honoring the dead—the thousands of Africans who died, often unacknowledged, unmourned and without proper burial. To unearth their story for any reason is to call these ancestors forth yet again. For what purpose are they being summoned today? Mahlangu, who played the role of the chief carrier, said that he came to see these unsettled ancestors, those Africans who died during WWI, as inhabiting temporarily the bodies and voices of the living performers in *H&L*. The performance was a gift of the living to the dead "so that they rise and speak."[75] Approaching each performance as a kind of spirit possession took a heavy psychological toll on some of the performers, both on and off stage. During a reception after the New York production that I attended, I witnessed two of the lead performers conferring about the personal mental, emotional and spiritual cost of showing up each night to carry this load.

Actor Nhlanhla Mahlangu told me later in an interview that he had two favorite moments in *H&L*. These stories are a previously hidden history of this production—something that, as he says, "the audience never gets to see."[76] He played the chief carrier who leads people to war. There were moments in the show when actors must cross backstage behind the curtain as they moved from one side of the stage to another in the endless procession:

> They walked slowly, as you're going to change your costume and pick up a different prop. During those moments when I meet a stage manager or fellow performer crossing, I usually give them a salute. And that salute, the stage manager says, "Everytime you give me that salute, I feel so special. I know you do a lot of salutes on stage. That one is different. It's private. It's mine."[77]

Mahlangu also saluted backstage every member of the choir. "The audience is not seeing this. It's how we carry the story from one place to another. The contemplating happens." His second favorite moment was the last song of *H&L*, when the names of the deceased are recited to the accompaniment of a haunting chorus:

> People [spectators] don't know the words. But it's more than just the words of the song. What we are doing there, which is what I try to inspire the choir and all other performers to say "This story is a true story. We are actors. And we're going to get paid for performing this story. But this story is about the real lives of dead people. They died. And they never got to tell their side of the story. So just for that moment, can we lend them our bodies and our voices so that they speak for themselves, for once?" And that is why it is so emotional for me. And because it's not us singing. But we have to submit ourselves, so that they rise and speak.[78]

While the libretto begins with the exhortation "Let's try for once not to be right," Mahlangu's call to his fellow Black performers was different: let's lend the ancestors our bodies and our voices so that they speak for themselves, for once.

Returning to the Hausa proverb—the head and the load are the possession of the neck—we can see that for the performers, the ancestors may be the "neck," inasmuch as they literally take possession of the head and the load—that is, the performers and this production's story. Mahlangu found the spiritual aspect of *H&L* to be at once deeply meaningful and totally exhausting:

> Yes. It is. Because the conversation I've been having a lot this week with my colleague [is]: "What is an ancestor?" And my new understanding is not that it's someone who is dead and buried. It's not the spirit hovering somewhere—a simplistic explanation of an ancestor with a European gaze. Every time when words are translated, they lose meaning a little bit. Yet ancestors are our DNA itself. For that, I carry my mother and father, who carried her mother and her father, who carry their parents—these are my great-grandparents continuing today. We are constantly questioning ourselves. Obviously, we see our ancestors as those who passed. Yet whether you know it or not, they are here.[79]

Choreographer and lead dancer Gregory Maqoma concurs: "Every night it feels like you are paying homage."[80] Maqoma speaks of *H&L* not as collage or history, but rather as a ritual, something that is performed by the cast, especially when the names of the deceased are recited at the end. This ritual is done "so that their souls don't just roam." Maqoma continues,

> It was for me to embody their spirit and to be able to walk that path, and to give, and to dance that path, to recognize their part and to evoke the sense of spirit, and to bring them home. And that was for me important. And the same with when these names are being called [in *H&L*]. It's about bringing them home because most of them died ... of diseases, of hunger, and they were never returned. So, it's about taking them back home, returning them to their home, and to give them a little bit of dignity.[81]

These narratives, too, are a hidden history of *H&L*. While some collaborators are trying to address their own ignorance, others are trying to carry home their dead ancestors so that their souls "don't just roam." Yet this later story, the African cocreators' perspective on *H&L*, has been upstaged in the archive, once again by whiteness.

Conclusion

Now let us embrace the vertigo of the question mark: Can collage withstand the moral and ethical imperative that this production frames—that is, to address the historic wrong of the erasure of Africans from the historiography of the Great War? Can a contemporary theatrical production about the largely unknown and actively obscured African involvement in the Great War represent this history without reinscribing its inequities? Can it depict the refusal to listen, or the reduction of humans to numbers, the conflation of people with objects, or the sacrifice of Africans to a cause not their own without repeating these very patterns? And why were audiences for this show so very *white*? If whiteness functions in places of authority by inadvertently excluding others by simply standing in the place of everything—if it says, essentially, "OK. I got this. I got this," does collage even have the capacity to break such entrenched pathologies?

Racialized histories can be hidden for many reasons. To unearth such histories requires care and thought. Kentridge's approach sought to work against narrative, to refuse coherence among disparate elements. *The Head & the Load* elevated the fragment, juxtaposed unreconciled archival shards. All these are valuable techniques to disrupt longstanding historiographic trends toward the heroic and the singular with regard to the Great War. Kentridge's polyphonic historiography and intermedial methods broke a historiographic frame, allowing spectators to become aware of previously untold stories about the Great War, and of our own role in making choices about where we look and what we see. However, collage has limits. While as Scarlet Higgins argues, collage is fundamentally disruptive and anti-narrative, it may be less fundamentally disruptive than we assume. "Politically, collage is a means with no inherent ends, and while it may contain revolutionary potential, it can also be domesticated toward conservative ends," Higgins writes.[82] Joshua Clover takes the critique of collage further by focusing on what he calls "ambiguity and theft" at its core, contending that collage as political practice can lead us "nowhere but to theft itself."[83] And it is here, on the question of theft, that the history of racism and hidden histories entangled in colonialism and violence introduces a potent toxicity that collage cannot easily diffuse through simple cut-and-paste techniques. Appropriation without permission, attribution or even understanding haunts any historiography enmeshed with anti-Black racism, especially when so little about that racism has changed between past and present.

Collage both reveals and conceals. In taking from multiple sources and placing elements together, collage typically appropriates and disguises the process of taking. Likewise, collage seems to offer many perspectives at once, yet its points of view are nevertheless particular and finite. Using the medium of performed collage, *H&L* wove together imperial monumentality, archival fragments, colonial legacies, and African images, actors and voices into a landmark intercultural production, one that surely persuaded many people for the first time that Africans participated in the Great War, died for a cause not their own, and deserve to be honored, respected and remembered for their contributions. However, despite the intention to substitute trajectory for narrative and to put African voices at the center, this production's reception tended to replace the former hegemony of Wilfred Owen's poetry in the literary memory of the Great War with the singularity of William Kentridge as the genius behind this twenty-first-century theatrical rendering. In other words, the color of memory remained notably white. Collage as a method for unearthing hidden histories holds promise, but it is by no means a panacea.

As Santanu Das argues, "While it is essential to challenge the colour of war memory, it is also important to keep a watch on the way it is being done."[84] The ways of whiteness are wily and insidious.[85] Perhaps the key lies not in any one aesthetic method or historiographic technique, per se, but rather in our answer to the question of whether the head and the load are the troubles of the neck or its possessions. We may also need to step back and consider whether this story of Africans in the Great War is even in the past, whether we can safely call it "history." As chief carrier Nhlanhla Mahlangu said, "Obviously, we see our ancestors as those who passed. Yet whether you know it or not, they are here."[86] We must submit ourselves so that they rise and speak, Mahlangu urges. He was referring to the performers in *H&L*—that they needed to submit themselves through their performances so that the ancestors could rise and speak. What would it mean for performance historians, too, to submit ourselves so that the unheard voices of history can both speak and be heard? It might entail asking different questions: What is missing? What is left out? What is standing in the way? What methods can work against the force of whiteness? This might involve talking to different people, putting previously marginalized voices and perspectives into the record, creating for the archive documents that will more fully reflect a diversity of viewpoints. The creative method that produced *H&L* was overtly collaborative, drawing upon the wisdom, creativity and insight of a large, racially diverse team. Yet ironically, contemporary reviews and feature articles rarely quoted anyone besides the lead white "author," Kentridge. To counter this bias in the defacto archive created around this production, I asked where were African voices, and what did they have to say? My method for this chapter led me to talk to people—including several Black performers and collaborators on this production as well as with key African scholars who study orality such as Kwame Anthony Appiah, Kwasi Ampene and Kwesi Yankah. The perspective on *H&L* I have presented here is still partial, particular and incomplete—as all histories are. But it is a perspective that deliberately aimed to center and document Black voices. The insidious and persistent force of whiteness, which seems always to claim center stage, will only be counteracted and disrupted when we deliberately ask what color of memory our scholarship is leaving behind. Let us aim for once that this memory not be primarily white.

Notes

1 Unattributed quote, both spoken and projected in William Kentridge's production *The Head & the Load*. See William Kentridge, *The Head & the Load* (London: Prestel Verlag, 2020), 19, libretto. The source of the quote is likely Frantz Fanon's *Black Skin, White Masks*, trans. Charles Lam Markmann (New York, NY: Pluto Press, 1986), 98.

2 Special thanks to this volume's coeditors, Leo Cabranes-Grant, and colleagues in the University of Washington African Studies reading group for their critical feedback on the chapter.
3 Santanu Das, "The First World War and the Colour of Memory," *Guardian*, 22 July 2014, https://www.theguardian.com/commentisfree/2014/jul/22/first-world-war-whitewashed-eurocentric.
4 Joe Harris Lunn, "War Losses (Africa)," *1914–1918 Online: International Encyclopedia of the First World War*, last updated 22 June 2015, https://encyclopedia.1914-1918-online.net/article/war_losses_africa.
5 For an introduction to the African participation in World War I, see David Olusoga, *The World's War: Forgotten Soldiers of Empire* (London: Head of Zeus, 2014). See also the research of historians such as Norman Clothier, Joe Lunn and Timothy Parsons.
6 Santanu Das, quoted in Tim Kirby, dir., "Martial Races," episode 1 of *The World's War: Forgotten Soldiers of Empire*, BBC Worldwide, 2014, https://video.alexanderstreet.com/watch/martial-races.
7 See the 2019 "Report of the Special Committee to Review Historical Inequalities in Commemoration," *Commonwealth War Graves Commission*, accessed 21 March 2021, https://www.cwgc.org/non-commemoration-report/. Special thanks to Taylor Soja for drawing my attention to this report.
8 As historian Santanu Das contends, "Today, one of the main stumbling blocks to a truly global and non-Eurocentric archive of the war is that many of these 1 million Indians, or 140,000 Chinese, or 166,000 West Africans, did not leave behind diaries and memoirs." Das, "The First World War."
9 Olusoga, *The World's War*, 40.
10 Kentridge, quoted in the program for the Park Avenue Armory's production of *The Head & the Load*, 4.
11 Kentridge, "In Conversation: William Kentridge & Paul Gilroy [Full]," Centre for the Less Good Idea, 9 March 2018, Vimeo video, 52:08, https://vimeo.com/259299630.
12 "14–18 NOW" also sponsored other artistic works including Isango Ensemble's performance piece *SS Mendi: Dancing the Death Drill*, about a ship full of South African volunteers that sank in the English Channel in 1917, and British-Bangladeshi choreographer Akram Khan's solo work *XENOS*, about Indian colonial soldiers, estimated to be 1.4 million in number, who were, like African soldiers, quite systematically erased from the historical record and from public memory. For more on these works, see Sabine Sörgel, "Poppies, Ropes, and Shadow Play: Transcultural Memories of the First World War during Brexit," *New Theatre Quarterly* 37, no. 2 (2021): 174–89; see also Angela Koo, ed., *14–18 Now: Contemporary Arts Commissions for the First World War Centenary* (London: Profile Editions, 2019).
13 Kentridge, quoted in Donald Hutera, "Exhibition Review: The Head & the Load at Tate Modern," *Times*, 12 July 2018, https://www.thetimes.co.uk/article/exhibition-review-the-head-the-load-at-tate-modern-ln8hqrjnb.
14 See Cynthia Zarin, "'The Head and the Load,' William Kentridge's Homage to Africa in the Great War," *New Yorker*, 16 December 2018, and also Murray Whyte, "The Carnage Cabaret: Tate's High-Octane Tribute to Africa's Forgotten War Dead," *Guardian*, 10 July 2018, https://www.theguardian.com/artanddesign/2018/jul/10/carnage-cabaret-tates-high-octane-tribute-to-africas-forgotten-war-dead-head-load-william-kentridge.
15 Ibid., 2, 24, italics in the original.
16 Tracy C. Davis and Peter W. Marx, "Introduction: On Critical Media History," in *The Routledge Companion to Theatre and Performance Historiography*, ed. Tracy C. Davis and Peter W. Marx (New York, NY: Routledge, 2020), 1–3

17 Christine Poggi, *In Defiance of Painting: Cubism, Futurism, and the Invention of Collage* (New Haven, CT: Yale University Press, 1992), xi.
18 Anette Hoffmann, "Echoes of the Great War: The Recordings of African Prisoners in the First World War," *Open Arts Journal*, no. 3 (2014): 9, https://openartsjournal.files.wordpress.com/2014/09/hoffmann_v3_p7-23.pdf.
19 Attributed to Belgian King Leopold II, quoted in Adam Hochschild, *King Leopold's Ghost: A Story of Greed, Terror, and Heroism in Colonial Africa* (New York, NY: Houghton Mifflin Company, 1998), 58.
20 Sol T. Plaatje, *Native Life in South Africa: Before and Since the European War and the Boer Rebellion* (New York, NY: Negro Universities Press, 1969), 266–67. In *The Head & the Load*, this quote is unattributed and rewritten: "Lest their actions merit recognition, their deeds must not be recorded." Kentridge, *The Head & the Load*, 118.
21 See Hoffmann, "Echoes of the Great War."
22 Maya Jaggi, "Decolonizing Commemoration: New War Art," *New York Review of Books*, 14 November 2018, https://www.nybooks.com/daily/2018/11/14/decolonizing-commemoration-new-war-art/?printpage=true.
23 John Akomfrah, "Artist, John Akomfrah, in Conversation with Skinder Hundal and Jenny Waldman," posted by New Art Exchange, 17 October 2019, YouTube video, 18:30. https://youtu.be/P6XThuKYCgQ.
24 Centre for the Less Good Idea, "Kentridge & Gilroy," 11:30.
25 Kentridge, *The Head & the Load*, 283.
26 Ibid.
27 Vincent Dowd, "Africa's WWI Effort Recognised in New Tate Modern Exhibit," *BBC News*, 15 July 2018, https://www.bbc.com/news/entertainment-arts-44792194.
28 For more on Kentridge's signature use of processions, see Homi K. Bhabha, "Processional Ethics: William Kentridge's *More Sweetly Play the Dance*," *Artforum International* 55, no. 2 (October 2016): 230–37, 292; and Michael Rothberg, "Progress, Progression, Procession: William Kentridge and the Narratology of Transitional Justice," *Narrative* 20, no. 1 (2012): 1–24.
29 Justin Davidson, "Opera Review: The Unseen Great War, in William Kentridge's *The Head and the Load*," *New York Magazine*, 7 December 2018, https://www.vulture.com/2018/12/unseen-ww-i-in-william-kentridges-the-head-and-the-load.html.
30 Ibid.
31 Kentridge, *The Head & the Load*, 283.
32 Davidson, "The Unseen Great War."
33 Homi K. Bhabha, "Theater of War: *Din und Drang* in *The Head & the Load*," in *The Head & the Load*, by William Kentridge (London: Prestel Verlag, 2020), 301–16.
34 Mark Hudson, "Vast, Ambitious and Transporting Tribute to Fallen African Soldiers," *Daily Telegraph*, 13 July 2018.
35 Zarin, "'The Head and the Load.'"
36 Xenia Hanusiak, "Park Avenue Armory 2018 Review: The Head and The Load," *Opera Wire*, 13 December 2018, https://operawire.com/park-avenue-armory-2018-review-the-head-and-the-load/.
37 *This Week in New York*, "William Kentridge: Let us Try for Once," 16 April 2019, http://twi-ny.com/blog/2019/04/16/william-kentridge-let-us-try-for-once/.
38 John Battersby, "Op-Ed: The Head and the Load, William Kentridge's Epic Production on Imperial Indifference in WWI, Premieres in London," *Daily Maverick*, 13 July 2018, https://www.dailymaverick.co.za/article/2018-07-13-the-head-and-the-load-william-kentridges-epic-production-on-imperial-indifference-in-wwi-premieres-in-london/.

39 Ashraf Jamal, "The Necessary Accidental," *The Thinker: A Pan-African Quarterly for Thought Leaders* 87, no. 2 (2021): 8.
40 Kentridge, *The Head & the Load*, 27.
41 According to scholar Deborah James, "Pedi men, when they dance this style of dancing are commemorating both their own involvement in both World Wars, in which they were soldiers fighting on the Allied side, but also commemorating their history as members of the Pedi Empire, which in fact basically ruled over the entire Transvaal during the late nineteenth century." "South Africa: Why Do the Pedi Tribe Wear Scottish Kilts?," posted by AP Archive, 21 July 2015, YouTube video, 1:15, https://www.youtube.com/watch?v=MKOtmzMcuL0.
42 Zo Anderson, "The Head & the Load, Tate Modern, London, Review: William Kentridge's Piece about Africans in WWI Is Electrifying," *Independent*, 12 July 2018, https://www.independent.co.uk/arts-entertainment/theatre-dance/reviews/the-head-and-the-load-review-tate-modern-william-kentridge-dance-first-world-war-a8443756.html.
43 See Centre for the Less Good Idea, "Kentridge & Gilroy," 50:00.
44 See Asbjørn Skarsvåg Grønstad, "Archival Ghosts, or the Elsewhere of the Image: John Akomfrah," in *Rethinking Art and Visual Culture: The Poetics of Opacity*, ed. Asbjørn Skarsvåg Grønstad (London: Palgrave Macmillan, 2020), 77–101.
45 Productions of H&L included a development workshop at MassMOCA in North Adams, Massachusetts, 3–4 May 2018, and the premiere at the Tate Modern Turbine Hall in London, 11–15 July 2018. Thereafter, it appeared at the Ruhrtriennale, Duisburg, Germany, 9–12 August 2018; the Park Avenue Armory in New York City, 4–15 December 2018; and at the Holland Festival in Amsterdam, 29–31 May 2019. A production was scheduled at the Johannesburg Theatre in South Africa, 1–9 May 2020; however, the COVID-19 pandemic has postponed this performance indefinitely. The author attended the MassMOCA workshop on 4 May 2018 and the New York Park Avenue Armory production on 14 December 2018. Analysis in this chapter is based on those two viewings, as well as a video of the London Tate production.
46 Davidson, "The Unseen Great War."
47 See Poggi, *In Defiance of Painting*.
48 Kwame Anthony Appiah, coeditor of *Bu Me Be*, a collection of Akan proverbs, in personal communications with the author on 10 August 2021. Author also corresponded electronically with Kwasi Ampene, author of *Asante Court Music and Verbal Arts in Ghana*, on 10 August 2021 and with Kwesi Yankah, author of *The Proverb in the Context of Akan Rhetoric*, on 31 August 2021.
49 George Merrick, *Hausa Proverbs* (London: Kegan Paul, Trench, Trübner & Co., 1905), 54.
50 Mohammed Bashir Salau, "Slavery in Kano Emirate of Sokoto Caliphate as Recounted: Testimonies of Isyaku and Idrisu," in *African Voices on Slavery and the Slave Trade*, vol. 1, *The Sources*, ed. Alice Bellagamba, Sandra E. Greene and Martin A. Klein (Cambridge: Cambridge University Press, 2013), 98.
51 Kwesi Yankah, *Speaking for the Chief: Okyeame and the Politics of Akan Royal Oratory* (Bloomington, IN: Indiana University Press, 1995), 51–52. See also Yankah, *The Proverb*.
52 Kwame Frimpong Manso Adakabre, "Akan Proverbs and Their Meaning," yenkassa, 8 June 2017, YouTube video, 33:21, https://www.youtube.com/watch?v=wTf-nNTr1aA.
53 Centre for the Less Good Idea, "Kentridge & Gilroy," 11:00.
54 Kentridge, *The Head & the Load*, 4.

55 Eileen Blumenthal, "Carry That Weight: William Kentridge's Epic 'The Head and the Load' Honored the Million-plus Black Africans Dead in World War I," *American Theatre* (February 2019): 34.
56 Kentridge, quoting an unnamed collaborator from the development workshop, in "An Evening with William Kentridge and Homi Bhabha," Museum of Fine Arts, Boston, 13 December 2019, YouTube video, 53:00. https://www.youtube.com/watch?v=c2wuK3eHOWA.
57 Centre for the Less Good Idea, "Kentridge & Gilroy," 45:00.
58 Kentridge, quoted in Zarin, "'The Head and the Load.'"
59 Quoted in William Kentridge, *Six Drawing Lessons* (Cambridge, MA: Harvard University Press, 2014), 35.
60 Uncredited source, quoted in Kentridge, *The Head & the Load*, 140, likely adapted from statement of Blaise Diagne and Gratien Candace in 1916: "The war against Germany and her allies has kindled in the colonies the most beautiful harvest of devotion to France that history has ever known. Muslim Algeria, Morocco, black Africa, Madagascar, and Indochina have, along with Tunisia, provided the assistance of their indigenous populations, either in the army or in munitions factories. The country—metropole and colonies—has thus affirmed its complete unity above any question of origin or race." Quoted in Richard S. Fogarty, *Race and War in France: Colonial Subjects in the French Army, 1914–1918* (Baltimore, MD: Johns Hopkins University Press, 2008), 1.
61 The "armory" refers to the Park Avenue Amory in Manhattan which commissioned *H&L*. Kentridge, quoted in Julie Belcove, "William Kentridge Tackles History of Apartheid and Colonialism in His Latest Production," *Wall Street Journal*, 4 December 2018, https://www.wsj.com/articles/william-kentridge-tackles-the-history-of-apartheid-and-colonialism-in-his-latest-production-1543940205.
62 Ann McCoy, "Pulled from the Shadows: William Kentridge's African Dance of Death," *PAJ: A Journal of Performance and Art* 41, no. 2 (May 2019): 24.
63 Patricia Zohn, "The Head and the Load: William Kentridge Pulls Focus on Africa and WWI," *Culturezohn* (blog), 7 December 2018, https://www.culturezohn.com/culturedpearls/2018/12/7/the-head-and-the-load-william-kentridge-pulls-focus-on-africa-and-ww-i.
64 Kentridge, *The Head & the Load*, 285, 289; Centre for the Less Good Idea, "Kentridge & Gilroy"; Museum of Fine Arts, Boston, "An Evening."
65 See Belcove, "William Kentridge Tackles History"; Blumenthal, "Carry That Weight."
66 Battersby, "Op-Ed."
67 Zarin, "'The Head and the Load.'"
68 Jo Livingstone, "*The Head and the Load* Is a Kaleidoscopic Tour of Africa's Colonial History," *New Republic*, 7 December 2018, https://newrepublic.com/article/152544/head-load-kaleidoscopic-tour-africas-colonial-history.
69 Whyte, "Carnage Cabaret."
70 Thuthuka Sibisi, quoted in ibid.
71 Zarin, "'The Head and the Load.'"
72 Kentridge, *The Head & the Load*, 292.
73 Nhlanhla Mahlangu, in telephone interview with the author, 23 November 2019.
74 Ibid.
75 Ibid.
76 Ibid.
77 Ibid.
78 Ibid.
79 Ibid.
80 Gregory Maqoma, in discussion with the author, New York City, 14 December 2018.

81 Ibid.
82 Scarlett Higgins, *Collage and Literature: The Persistence of Vision* (New York, NY: Routledge, 2019), 26.
83 Joshua Clover, "Ambiguity and Theft," in *Cutting Across Media: Appropriation Art, Interventionist Collage, and Copyright Law*, ed. Kembrew McLeod and Rudolf Kuenzli (Durham, NC: Duke University Press, 2011), 89.
84 Das, "The First World War."
85 As are the ways of patriarchy and the elitist global art market—both surely additional factors in the reception of this performance.
86 Mahlangu, telephone interview.

Bibliography

Adakabre, Kwame Frimpong Manso. "Akan Proverbs and Their Meaning." Posted by yenkassa. 8 June 2017. YouTube video, 33:21. https://www.youtube.com/watch?v=wTf-nNTr1aA.
Akomfrah, John. "Artist, John Akomfrah, in Conversation with Skinder Hundal and Jenny Waldman." Posted by New Art Exchange. 17 October 2019. YouTube video, 1:06:15. https://youtu.be/P6XThuKYCgQ.
Ampene, Kwasi. *Asante Court Music and Verbal Arts in Ghana: The Porcupine and the Gold Stool*. London: Routledge, 2020.
Anderson, Zo. "The Head & the Load, Tate Modern, London, Review: William Kentridge's Piece about Africans in WWI Is Electrifying." *Independent*, 12 July 2018. https://www.independent.co.uk/arts-entertainment/theatre-dance/reviews/the-head-and-the-load-review-tate-modern-william-kentridge-dance-first-world-war-a8443756.html.
Appiah, Peggy, Kwame Anthony Appiah and Ivor Agyeman-Duah. *Bu Me Be: Proverbs of the Akans*. Oxfordshire: Ayebia Clarke Limited, 2007.
Battersby, John. "Op-Ed: The Head and the Load, William Kentridge's Epic Production on Imperial Indifference in WWI, Premieres in London." *Daily Maverick*, 13 July 2018. https://www.dailymaverick.co.za/article/2018-07-13-the-head-and-the-load-william-kentridges-epic-production-on-imperial-indifference-in-wwi-premieres-in-london/.
Belcove, Julie. "William Kentridge Tackles History of Apartheid and Colonialism in His Latest Production." *Wall Street Journal*, 4 December 2018. https://www.wsj.com/articles/william-kentridge-tackles-the-history-of-apartheid-and-colonialism-in-his-latest-production-1543940205.
Bhabha, Homi K. "Processional Ethics: William Kentridge's *More Sweetly Play the Dance*." *Artforum International* 55, no. 2 (October 2016): 230–37, 292.
———. "Theater of War: *Din und Drang* in *The Head & the Load*." In *The Head & the Load*, by William Kentridge, 301–16. London: Prestel Verlag, 2020.
Blumenthal, Eileen. "Carry That Weight: William Kentridge's Epic 'The Head and the Load' Honored the Million-plus Black Africans Dead in World War I." *American Theatre* (February 2019): 34–37.
Centre for the Less Good Idea. "In Conversation: William Kentridge & Paul Gilroy [Full]." 9 March 2018. Vimeo video, 52:08. https://vimeo.com/259299630.
Clover, Joshua. "Ambiguity and Theft." In *Cutting Across Media: Appropriation Art, Interventionist Collage, and Copyright Law*, edited by Kembrew McLeod and Rudolf Kuenzli, 84–93. Durham, NC: Duke University Press, 2011.

Commonwealth War Graves Commission. "Report of the Special Committee to Review Historical Inequalities in Commemoration." Accessed 21 March 2021. https://www.cwgc.org/non-commemoration-report/.

Das, Santanu. "The First World War and the Colour of Memory." *Guardian*, 22 July 2014. https://www.theguardian.com/commentisfree/2014/jul/22/first-world-war-whitewashed-eurocentric.

Davidson, Justin. "Opera Review: The Unseen Great War, in William Kentridge's *The Head and the Load*." *New York Magazine*, 7 December 2018. https://www.vulture.com/2018/12/unseen-ww-i-in-william-kentridges-the-head-and-the-load.html.

Davis, Tracy C., and Peter W. Marx. "Introduction: On Critical Media History." In *The Routledge Companion to Theatre and Performance Historiography*, edited by Tracy C. Davis and Peter W. Marx, 1–39. New York, NY: Routledge, 2020.

Dowd, Vincent. "Africa's WWI Effort Recognised in New Tate Modern Exhibit." *BBC News*, 15 July 2018. https://www.bbc.com/news/entertainment-arts-44792194.

Fanon, Frantz. *Black Skin, White Masks*. Translated by Charles Lam Markmann. New York, NY: Pluto Press, 1986.

Fogarty, Richard S. *Race and War in France: Colonial Subjects in the French Army, 1914–1918*. Baltimore, MD: Johns Hopkins University Press, 2008.

Grønstad, Asbjørn Skarsvåg. "Archival Ghosts, or the Elsewhere of the Image: John Akomfrah." In *Rethinking Art and Visual Culture: The Poetics of Opacity*, edited by Asbjørn Skarsvåg Grønstad, 77–101. London: Palgrave Macmillan, 2020.

Hanusiak, Xenia. "Park Avenue Armory 2018 Review: The Head and The Load." *Opera Wire*, 13 December 2018. https://operawire.com/park-avenue-armory-2018-review-the-head-and-the-load/.

Higgins, Scarlett. *Collage and Literature: The Persistence of Vision*. New York, NY: Routledge, 2019.

Hochschild, Adam. *King Leopold's Ghost: A Story of Greed, Terror, and Heroism in Colonial Africa*. New York, NY: Houghton Mifflin Company, 1998.

Hoffmann, Anette. "Echoes of the Great War: The Recordings of African Prisoners in the First World War." *Open Arts Journal*, no. 3 (2014): 7–23. https://openartsjournal.files.wordpress.com/2014/09/hoffmann_v3_p7-23.pdf.

Hudson, Mark. "Vast, Ambitious and Transporting Tribute to Fallen African Soldiers." *Daily Telegraph*, 13 July 2018.

Hutera, Donald. "Exhibition Review: The Head & the Load at Tate Modern." *Times*, 12 July 2018. https://www.thetimes.co.uk/article/exhibition-review-the-head-the-load-at-tate-modern-ln8hqrjnb.

Jaggi, Maya. "Decolonizing Commemoration: New War Art." *New York Review of Books*, 14 November 2018. https://www.nybooks.com/daily/2018/11/14/decolonizing-commemoration-new-war-art/?printpage=true.

Jamal, Ashraf. "The Necessary Accidental." *The Thinker: A Pan-African Quarterly for Thought Leaders* 87, no. 2 (2021): 4–12.

James, Deborah. "South Africa: Why Do the Pedi Tribe Wear Scottish Kilts?" Posted by AP Archive. 21 July 2015. YouTube video, 2:13. https://www.youtube.com/watch?v=MKOtmzMcuL0.

Kentridge, William. *Six Drawing Lessons*. Cambridge, MA: Harvard University Press, 2014.

———. *The Head & the Load*. London: Prestel Verlag, 2020.

Kirby, Tim, dir. "Martial Races." Episode 1 of *The World's War: Forgotten Soldiers of Empire*. BBC Worldwide, 2014. https://video.alexanderstreet.com/watch/martial-races.

Koo, Angela, ed. *14–18 Now: Contemporary Arts Commissions for the First World War Centenary*. London: Profile Editions, 2019.

Livingstone, Jo. "*The Head and the Load* Is a Kaleidoscopic Tour of Africa's Colonial History." *New Republic*, 7 December 2018. https://newrepublic.com/article/152544/head-load-kaleidoscopic-tour-africas-colonial-history.

Lunn, Joe Harris. "War Losses (Africa)." *1914–1918 Online: International Encyclopedia of the First World War*. Last updated 22 June 2015. https://encyclopedia.1914-1918-online.net/article/war_losses_africa.

McCoy, Ann. "Pulled from the Shadows: William Kentridge's African Dance of Death." *PAJ: A Journal of Performance and Art* 41, no. 2 (May 2019): 19–26.

Merrick, George. *Hausa Proverbs*. London: Kegan Paul, Trench, Trübner & Co., 1905.

Museum of Fine Arts, Boston. "An Evening with William Kentridge and Homi Bhabha." 13 December 2019. YouTube video, 1:13:36. https://www.youtube.com/watch?v=c2wuK3eHOWA.

Olusoga, David. *The World's War: Forgotten Soldiers of Empire*. London: Head of Zeus, 2014.

Plaatje, Sol T. *Native Life in South Africa: Before and Since the European War and the Boer Rebellion*. New York, NY: Negro Universities Press, 1969.

Poggi, Christine. *In Defiance of Painting: Cubism, Futurism, and the Invention of Collage*. New Haven, CT: Yale University Press, 1992.

Rothberg, Michael. "Progress, Progression, Procession: William Kentridge and the Narratology of Transitional Justice." *Narrative* 20, no. 1 (2012): 1–24.

Salau, Mohammed Bashir. "Slavery in Kano Emirate of Sokoto Caliphate as Recounted: Testimonies of Isyaku and Idrisu." In *African Voices on Slavery and the Slave Trade*, vol. 1, *The Sources*, edited by Alice Bellagamba, Sandra E. Greene and Martin A. Klein, 88–114. Cambridge: Cambridge University Press, 2013.

Sörgel, Sabine. "Poppies, Ropes, and Shadow Play: Transcultural Memories of the First World War during Brexit." *New Theatre Quarterly* 37, no. 2 (2021): 174–89.

This Week in New York. "William Kentridge: Let us Try for Once." 16 April 2019. http://twi-ny.com/blog/2019/04/16/william-kentridge-let-us-try-for-once/.

Whyte, Murray. "The Carnage Cabaret: Tate's High-Octane Tribute to Africa's Forgotten War Dead." *Guardian*, 10 July 2018. https://www.theguardian.com/artanddesign/2018/jul/10/carnage-cabaret-tates-high-octane-tribute-to-africas-forgotten-war-dead-head-load-william-kentridge.

Yankah, Kwesi. *Speaking for the Chief: Okyeame and the Politics of Akan Royal Oratory*. Bloomington, IN: Indiana University Press, 1995.

———. *The Proverb in the Context of Akan Rhetoric*. 2nd rev. ed. New York, NY: Diasporic Africa Press, 2012.

Zarin, Cynthia. "'The Head and the Load,' William Kentridge's Homage to Africa in the Great War." *New Yorker*, 16 December 2018.

Zohn, Patricia. "The Head and the Load: William Kentridge Pulls Focus on Africa and WWI." *Culturezohn* (blog), 7 December 2018. https://www.culturezohn.com/culturedpearls/2018/12/7/the-head-and-the-load-william-kentridge-pulls-focus-on-africa-and-ww-i.

4

HIJIKATA TATSUMI AT THE OSAKA WORLD EXPOSITION'S PEPSI PAVILION, 1970

Multiple Historiographies of a Lost Performance

Stephen Barber

Writing the Lost Histories of Hijikata Tatsumi's Dance

The histories of performance cultures are constelled with lost or forgotten events, in which a performance—often perceived as exceptional in its time—slips through its tangible traces and commemoration, via an archival eroding, or else a parallel process of documentational malfunction, or else because the performance itself contained an inbuilt resistance to its representation, or for other reasons. Whenever a "lost" performance is evoked in this chapter, "loss" indicates one or other of the multiple and diverse ways in which performances are subtracted from immediate visibility, tangibility and memory, and must then be relocated in order for that loss to be amended or canceled; whenever a performance is "almost" lost, surviving only by a fragile margin of evidence, as with Hijikata's performance at the Osaka Exposition, it is precisely that margin and the precarious, narrow interval of the "almost" which is vital in reactivating the performance, since its extreme dearth of traces imparts a special intensity and concentration to that interval between the definitively lost and the wholly representational, which operates notably as a receptive location for interweaving strategies. Performances require an active conservation—in memory, language or moving-image media—in order to possess a secure, future-oriented grounding in their time and space. Interweaving approaches call for a writing of performance histories which both investigates and intersects—across cultural, historical and aesthetic terrains—different practices of conserving performances, thus gathering and substantiating the multiply dispersed, often fragile traces of an apparently "lost" performance, while also investigating the reasons why performances become exposed to a process of forgetting in the first place.

DOI: 10.4324/9781003353461-7

The knowledge of a performance that has "expired" can never be comprehensive and often requires new approaches to its writing and that of its historical moment in order to illuminate its intentions and dimensions. Existing knowledge of a performance may be fissured to the point of becoming contradictory or of relying primarily on one medium, such as that of contemporary eyewitness accounts. The writing of a performance history may insightfully comprise an investigation and an interweaving of the different, even contradictory, historiographic regimes which originally surrounded or accompanied a performance, and consequently an intersecting of those residues, incorporating overlooked and excluded archival materials, vocal accounts of participants and witnesses, the visiting of the performance venue (if it still exists), and the social and political contexts of the performance—especially when those contexts indicate acute crises—in order to compact such residues into a historical projection which may serve to reactivate that performance. Writing on lost performances is simultaneously a spectral process which confronts an event's vanishing, and also a corporeal process that attempts to anatomize and reassemble the dispersed fragments of a performance's multiple, diverse histories. Writing on performance is always a contemporary act that pivots on the imperatives of current understandings of performance cultures, even when it is engaged in resuscitating a lost performance of several decades ago, thereby enabling that performance to survive into the future. Writing on performance histories necessarily exacts a transmutation of the original intentions and understandings of lost, neglected or abandoned events; that process of writing oscillates between a performance's historical moment and the contemporary act of writing, necessarily entailing an in-depth transmutation of that act of writing itself; that transformative oscillation between a performance's historical moment and the contemporary act of "writing that moment" may only result in an ensured survival for a performance if it is able to weave together that performance's traces with the intricacy and openness which they demand.

In March 1970, the choreographer and dance theorist Hijikata Tatsumi (1928–1986)—renowned for his development, at the end of the 1950s in Japan, of an experimental performance form named *Butoh* or *Ankoku Butoh* (dance of utter darkness)—gave a performance of his work in one of the many pavilions that comprised the Osaka World Exposition. At that time, Hijikata was one of Japan's most prominent contemporary artists and was invited to participate for that reason. The Osaka Exposition drew the then largest number of visitors to any event in human history, with an attendance, over its six-month span, of 64,218,770 (it would be surpassed only 40 years later by the 2010 Shanghai World Exposition), with each pavilion receiving millions of visitors.[1] Even so—and in defiance of that immense proliferation of attentive visitors—Hijikata's performance is an almost entirely forgotten one, which generated virtually no known surviving evidence or traces. In view both of Hijikata's artistic prominence at that time and of the unusually vast public audience that surrounded his appearance at the Osaka Exposition, his performance's forgetting constitutes a seemingly anomalous event and an exemplary opportunity for the writing of lost histories of performance.

In investigating Hijikata's performance, it is immediately clear that two antithetical historiographic regimes conjoin within that performance, whose conceptual disparity provides an exceptionally valuable opportunity for a strategic methodology of interweaving, written from the contemporary moment with its own historiographic perspective incorporating intersections of archival, topographical and vocal traces. Those two regimes are Hijikata's own experimental choreographic and historiographic work, and the historiography of the Osaka Exposition itself, conceived by its alliance of governmental and corporate organizers as forming an "experimental metropolis,"[2] its space intensively guarded and under surveillance through new technologies, in an era of fierce dissident unrest in Japan's cities. The exposition's pavilions and their contents were designed to direct global attention toward Japan's ascendant technologies and industries while also involving the active international participation of performers, artists and musicians from many fields.[3] In that sense, Hijikata's performance is a combination of corporeal history and urban history, with his body in its unique act of dance (he performed only once), contained within a complex space of multiple urban experimentations that included visitors' transits through it.

Although Japan's prominent artists and performers were invited to take part in the exposition—in order to accentuate its contemporaneity and its aura of innovation and thereby to provide artistic prestige for the corporations that commissioned performances and artworks—that alliance of the artistic and the corporate misfired in the response to Hijikata's performance, in ways that serve enduringly to illuminate current encounters between art and corporate cultures. Hijikata's performance at the Pepsi Pavilion, undertaken as a "preview" event shortly before the exposition's opening, was evaluated as deficient by its Pepsi Corporation commissioners, who annulled envisaged future performances in their pavilion, both by Hijikata and other artists, and amended their plans for the pavilion's events program, which had been developed in direct competition with those of pavilions throughout the exposition. In that sense, Hijikata's performance forms an urban malfunction as well as an aberrant spectacle, and that perceived unsuitability of the performance—mismatched with its commissioners' aesthetic expectations as well as with the technologically innovative city that encompassed it—contributed directly to its public profile's annulling. No photographic or filmic images appear to have survived of the performance, even in the Osaka Exposition's dedicated archive. Additionally, the performance slipped through the wider knowledge and awareness of Hijikata's work as a choreographer, despite the performance's special significance (it was, for example, his final solo performance).

The writing and potential revivification of such a performance requires a delicate tracing and juxtaposition of the multiple histories that comprise it. Most histories are supplemented by imageries, but in this instance, no images subsist, and it appears likely that none existed in the first place through the performance's controlled status as a private "preview" event. The performance was subject to an act of forgetting, more through institutional and corporate neglect—together with an ambivalent perception of the performance as corporately commissioned "art" and therefore only worth conserving to further corporate imperatives, if at all—than as the result of a coordinated intention: not only Hijikata's performance but all of the Osaka Exposition pavilions' contents (and those of all previous exposition events) formed predominantly unpreserved entities, consigned to ruination in their material dimensions and to a voiding in their memorial dimensions. Hijikata's performance at the Pepsi Pavilion belonged to the wider regime of World Expositions' culture of rapid redundancy and was never intended to possess a long-term survival, even if it had been perceived positively by its commissioners. However, to reconstitute that performance, against the grain, it was possible to locate at least one witness of the event—the choreographer Murobushi Kō—with a clear memory of it, as well as to conduct archival research into it, such as architectural investigations of the Pepsi Pavilion's distinctive domed performance space. Such a process of locating historical knowledge of a lost performance may operate not in a linear way but as an accumulation of fragments that can also generate a revealing aperture into the dynamics of contemporary performance cultures.

In evaluating the residual historical fragments of Hijikata's lost performance, their disparity is apparent. Rather than filmic or photographic documents, or choreographic scores and notes, what remains—alongside vocal accounts of the performance—are the remnants of practices that could be perceived as peripheral to the historiography of performance, such as the architectural and urban spatial design of the performance venue, as well as the wider cultural history of the exposition event that determined its corporations' commissioning approach. The urban history of unrest—with the city of Osaka (directly to the south of the immense "experimental metropolis" of the exposition's site) as a prominent location of student protests at the time of the exposition—forms a key element in the dynamics by which the performance can be approached, in its corporeal and sensorial dimensions as well as its architectural and urban aspects.

In its distinctive combination of residual traces, Hijikata's performance at the Osaka Exposition also provides insights into how any seemingly unknown performance has been rendered "lost," as an entity beyond linear performance histories, which characteristically depend upon the certainty that any performance, along with its time and space, can be entirely represented, in any of the visual media that may be deployed to encompass and contain it. Any and every performance is subject to its own disintegration, immediately upon its elapsing as a live event. In distinction from the representational context of 1970, the record and memory of a contemporary work of theater, performance art or dance will almost invariably become transferred to its documentation in digital photographic or moving-image media, either through its recording by its own organizers and participants, or else, more informally, by audience members using smartphones or digital cameras. Performance thereby acquires a documentational or archival record, in the form of a seemingly definitive and authorized representation—antithetical, in many ways, to Hijikata's own historiographic practices—which may well supersede the individual memories of its witnesses. For its future survival, a contemporary performance must lose the live physicality of its occupation of time and space, becoming transformed into sequences of images, often in an abbreviated or reduced form. That close interconnection, between a performance and its registration or preservation as a sequence of images, has existed for as long as the media of photography and film have respectively existed since the 1840s and the 1890s. Moving-image media, in particular, were invented largely in order to record—and then to project—performance, as in the moving-image sequences of dance and performative actions which the moving-image innovator Eadweard Muybridge (1830–1904) projected publicly in Europe's cities in the early 1890s. Performances may also be undertaken solely in order to be filmed and photographed. As a result, a performance whose history indicates that it was contrarily not filmed or photographed, or whose visual documentation has vanished or become lost, possesses an exceptional status; it may, for example, have been undertaken in notably volatile circumstances, or have been so daunting to its audience that they hesitated to film or photograph it.

Alongside performances which have eluded being filmed or photographed, or whose images are "lost," many performance works were never intended in the first place to hold a visual dimension, such as works of sound art or of radio performance. The loss of a performance does not solely depend on the eventual erasure or degradation of its images; sonic performances are equally subject to loss or to erasure from history. An example is the final work of the performer and theorist Antonin Artaud (1896–1948), with his vocal project commissioned by the French national radio station in 1947, *Pour en finir avec le jugement de dieu* (To Have Done with the Judgement of God), which consisted of readings of texts, together with cries and percussion, undertaken with three collaborators. Artaud specifically viewed that vocal, nonvisual medium as one entailing the opportunity for its own intentional loss, through its resistance to what he perceived as banalizing media of representation. He intended the performance to exist only for its duration of transmission, as a kind of intense sensory conflagration. During his preparations for the recording, he noted, "There is nothing I abominate and execrate so much as this idea of representation [...] attached to all that is produced and shown."[4] He attempted to configure his performance as one which would both transmit his preoccupations to an envisaged audience of around one million auditors but would simultaneously retain a "lost" status in its avowed resistance to representation.

As with Hijikata's performance at the Pepsi Pavilion, the commissioners of Artaud's work rejected it; they declined to broadcast it, and its status as a multiply lost work was exacerbated by its near disappearance: unheard for several decades and surviving only on one fragile reel-to-reel audiotape. Eventually, that tape was archived. In one of Jacques Derrida's last interviews, in 2004, he imagined Artaud's vocal recording existing in a unique archival space of its own, comprising a solitary "one-artifact" archive: "The voice of Artaud […] when you've heard it, you can no longer silence it. And so you have to read him with *his* voice, the phantom of his voice that you have to keep inside your ear. For me, the archivization of the voice is something that is profoundly moving. Contrary to photography, the archivized voice is 'alive.'"[5] Artaud had died immediately after his performance's censoring. However, that single, vocal archival artifact could still be multiplied through interviews with two of Artaud's collaborators on his radio performance, who were still living in the 1990s, and also through wider historical accounts of the censorship of performances in France during the era when Artaud's vocal performance remained both intentionally lost, in his resistance to representation, and almost lost, in its banning by the radio station from transmission.

The example of Artaud's radio performance and its self-willed loss indicates the multiple historical dynamics at stake in a performance's apparent disappearance. As with Hijikata's performance at the Pepsi Pavilion, Artaud's work possessed provocative dimensions that ensured it would be viewed negatively by its commissioners. Any performance can appear to have become almost definitively neglected but retain the capacity always to re-emerge unexpectedly, either through a new relevance of such provocative dimensions or via an archival rediscovery of its traces. The "loss" of a performance, with its subsequent and apparently definitive erasure from performance histories, requires a particular approach to its writing, involving a flexible, non-exclusionary interweaving of the diverse historiographic regimes which accompanied that performance and the traces they produced; its vital history may appear detrital or to emerge at the last moment, as with a witness's last-breath evocation of it. Bringing together traces from diverse and even contradictory historiographic regimes generates an amalgam of historical sources for the launching of a performance history into the future.[6] Such sources may appear unusual ones and to demand unprecedented conjunctions in order to carry through a performance's restitution from loss. Whenever a performance appears near definitively lost, reduced to its last-ditch traces of recuperability, such unforeseen interconnections of histories become resilient constellations, generating the survival of a performance which would otherwise appear in danger of being forgotten altogether. In the instance of a performance such as that undertaken by Hijikata, in the context of a World Exposition event—with that event's characteristic regime of rendering its performances and artifacts obsolescent—such historiographical constellations form especially imperative ones.

To research and reconstitute Hijikata's lost (or almost lost) performance at the Pepsi Pavilion generates a historiographic regime of its own, in the act of its writing, that in some ways operates, at first sight, against Hijikata's own intentions, in his desire actively to forget that performance since it risked contaminating his work with corporate affiliations that are otherwise absent from that body of work, and as part of his wider wariness or repudiation of representation, which is allied to that of Artaud. That research is necessarily a historiography of fragments; fragments form optimal receptacles for writings embodying interweaving processes since fragments are never enclosed, and any fixed hierarchical strata they once possessed have transmutated, in the contemporary moment, into a multidimensional transparency. A historiography of performance's fragments may also demand a corporeal and topographical excavation into a performance's spatial locations, especially when a performance has attained a lost status, as with Hijikata's exposition performance, and needs both to be substantiated and revivified, as well as opened out to the interweaving of its own moment's diverse and contrary historiographic regimes.

The Osaka World Exposition as a Performance Location

Historiographies of performance are often mappings of locations, of urban space, and of the venues which a performer selected as the ideal locus for the time and space of a performance. In many instances, as for example with the performance art works of the Viennese Actionists, the ideal performance space is one that is subterranean, away from the public or police gaze, such as a tenement building's cellar able to hold 20 or 30 spectators. Contrarily, whenever a performance is commissioned, the performer may not participate at all in determining the performance's location, as with Hijikata's performance at the Osaka Exposition's Pepsi Pavilion in March 1970. Although the Pepsi Corporation had commissioned a New York-based group of experimental artists and architects—the E.A.T. (Experiments in Art and Technology) collective—to design the interior of the performance space, and had accorded them complete freedom both in that and in the development of a program of performances and music events to occupy the pavilion's interior, that location remained entirely under the jurisdiction of the Pepsi Corporation, which could alter and annul the space and its performance culture according to their own priorities. In such a situation, a performance's evidence and memory can be especially vulnerable to loss or vanishing since the performer cannot carry away the event's documentation (in the way that the Viennese Actionists took away the photographs and films of their subterranean, cellar-located performances and subsequently archived them). Hijikata took nothing from his performance, and appears never to have spoken about it to any of his collaborators in the remaining 16 years of his life. In charting the multiple historiographies of lost performances, it becomes evident that it is often the performer who has also cast the performance into oblivion. By contrast, many of Hijikata's other performances subsist through the films made of them, often recorded by associates to whom he directly conveyed his own obliviousness or ambivalence towards his work's representation, as a distinctive historiographic regime which, in part, emphasizes the live moment of performance far above its residues. By contrast, many performers and artists—such as Muybridge, with his strategy of obsessive self-documentation, notably in scrapbook media—meticulously archive and selectively "edit" the entirety of their histories, paradoxically emphasizing the special dimensions of malfunctioned performances or events by attempting intentionally to erode their traces and thereby render them "lost." And despite Hijikata's own concerted attempts to dissipate or annul the historiographic dimensions of his own work, its amassed traces (scrapbooks, notes, posters, films, photographs, sound recordings) now contrarily occupy a large posthumous archival space at Keio University's Art Center in Tokyo and are gathered under a name: The Hijikata Memorial Archive.

The Osaka Exposition was always intended as an immense, spectacular event, prepared intensively for many years in advance, as with all previous World Expositions. The exposition's "experimental metropolis" possessed a vast, intricate infrastructure, extending from the transport network carrying visitors to and through it, to the corporeal infrastructure of its many thousands of guards and hostesses. The event was intended as a forum for the display of future-oriented technological innovation as well as of cutting-edge contemporary arts. At the same time, it was conceived as a finite spectacle, to be dissolved as rapidly as possible after its elapsing. The exposition's archive, established in the site's former administrative building in 1971, manifests that tension between the intensive preparations and operation of the exposition, and its immediate obsolescence, including that of the documentation of the event's performances. That historical archive is one, at least in part, of its own dissolution and neglect since it demonstrates how a globally high-profile event could be actively forgotten.

Within a few months of the exposition's closure in the autumn of 1970, almost the entire site had been emptied and razed to the ground (the participating corporations were contractually obliged to ensure that their pavilions were rapidly destroyed). No specific plans had been formulated by the exposition's organizers for the future of that huge site; it had been constructed over the course of three years through the anti-ecological deforestation and leveling of a region of pine tree groves. Since that deforestation proved irreparable, the site then remained empty as a wasteland for over a decade, before a semi-wild public park and adjacent shopping center were installed on the site.

Alongside its archive, the exposition's commemoration extended only to the eventual opening in the park of a display exhibition installed in the one pavilion remaining from the event.

The history of the post-exposition site, with its abrupt transition from the finite "live" event to the indefinite neglect of its vulnerable traces, mirrors that of many performances in which the performer is not the proprietor or instigator of the event's memory. At the same time, fragile or lost traces of a performance or event may resurge unexpectedly, generating new, excavatory historiographies of what has appeared forgotten. In November 2018, the decision was taken to allocate a new World Exposition to the city of Osaka to take place in 2025. Although that future event will occupy a different space to the 1970 exposition, through the creating of an artificial island alongside the city, its pavilions' plans closely resemble those of the earlier exposition, in a direct referencing; as a result, new historical engagement with the 1970 exposition, including its performance culture, resurged in Japan at the end of 2018. Among the preoccupations of that new engagement is the exploratory interconnection between the original, near lost performances of 1970 (such as that of Hijikata at the Pepsi Pavilion) and the future performances for 2025, focused—in their tentative initial plans—on robotics, post-human simulations and spectrally inhabited digital screens. An apparently annulled, voided history may unexpectedly transmutate into a vital future-history.

At the 1970 exposition, performances were undertaken either in the uniformly domed interiors of corporate-sponsored pavilions, or within a large outdoor "Festival Plaza" designed by the architect Isozaki Arata, who knew many of Japan's contemporary artists and proposed performances such as that of Hijikata's as being suitably innovative for inclusion in the exposition. Commissioned performers were expected to adapt their work to its external and internal locations. The Gutai group of artists were commissioned to present a sequence of nocturnal outdoor performances in the Festival Plaza; they undertook nine "Night Event" spectacles (each starting at 9 p.m.) performed by overall-wearing figures, with titles such as *Plaza of Mobile Arts and Light*, *Mad Robot* and *Constellation Event*. The group also staged a "Gutai Fine Arts Spectacle," mainly conceived by Shiraga Kazuo, in 11 parts, filmed in color across three days toward the end of the exposition's span, from August 31 to September 2. Many of the pavilions, such as the Pepsi Pavilion, were intended to hold experimental lighting systems and unprecedented multichannel sound environments. The Pepsi Pavilion's large interior space was entirely coated by its E.A.T. group designers in reflecting aluminum foil, which had the effect of inversing the appearance of its occupants, so that all figures in that space were perceived as being upside down. As a result, Hijikata performed in a spatial environment which had already been determined, with an emphasis on technological and especially sonic innovation, and toward which his performance was expected to respond (though Hijikata appears to have been entirely indifferent to that demand). In that sense, the Osaka Exposition forms a precursor to contemporary, global performance festivals for which the thematic agenda and spatial design have already been inflexibly set, along with audiences' preconceptions, even before the performances begin.

Although the Osaka Exposition was held under the patronage of the Japanese government and imperial family, its primary financial regime was determined by the prominent Japanese technology corporations—JP Fuji Group, Toshiba Inc., Midori Group and others—which commissioned the construction and operation of individual pavilions. Almost all of the pavilions took the form of windowless domed constructions, inspired by the geodesic dome designed by Buckminster Fuller for the previous World Exposition in Montreal in 1967, but also by the experimental domes designed by the young Italian architect Dante Bini, which could be rapidly assembled by air inflation (and, crucially, disassembled after the event). Bini attended the exposition in order to supervise the construction of several of his domes that formed elements of the JP Fuji Group Pavilion as well as to license his technology to Japanese corporations. In an interview I conducted with him in 2016, he evoked the profound impression which that "experimental metropolis" had on him, and how he was convinced that he was witnessing the origins of a new urban history; he recalled standing alongside his domes while helicopters hovered overhead to drop vast quantities of orange paint onto them.[7]

The Pepsi Pavilion was located within an annex, Expo Land, at the southeastern periphery of the main exposition site. Pavilions within the main site could only be operated by Japanese corporations, but since the exposition was intended as an international event, global corporations were also invited to commission pavilions, solely on the annex site, and the Pepsi Corporation took up that opportunity. Expo Land was designed as a direct successor to the Midway Plaisance annex site, which had formed part of the 1893 World's Columbian Exposition held in Chicago and had encompassed pavilions intended to display innovations in moving-image media (Muybridge designed and constructed his Zoopraxographical Hall projection auditorium on the Midway Plaisance). The centerpiece of Expo Land was a Ferris wheel, offering its riders a panorama of the entire exposition site, as had been the case too with the Midway Plaisance. In order to induce visitors of the Osaka Exposition to exit the main site and enter Expo Land, its pavilions' organizers had to present their buildings and the spectacles held in their interiors as extraordinarily innovative and enticing. Alongside their hiring of the E.A.T. group to design the pavilion's striking interior and sonic environment, the Pepsi Corporation's executives were ready to invite Japan's prominent artists, such as Hijikata and Terayama Shūji, to perform there. The allocation to Hijikata of the "preview" performance occasion indicates the depth of expectation that he would present a performance that could give the Pepsi Pavilion its required aura of exceptional artistic innovation as it prepared to open to the public.

Most performers, artists and writers who contributed to the exposition did so for financial reasons, or else to reach a vastly greater audience for their work; Hijikata's performances in the 1960s were invariably undertaken for relatively small audiences, and he required funding to maintain his studio, the Asbestos Studio, in Tokyo's Meguro district.

Deep tensions had emerged during the preparations for the exposition between its corporate- and art-focused imperatives, between the artists who agreed to participate and those who refused to do so and also, more widely, between the exposition as a global corporate spectacle and Japan's dissident cultures of resistance, which included terrorist factions. During the preparations for the opening of the Pepsi Pavilion, the president of the Pepsi Corporation's operations in Japan, Alan Pottasch (renowned for having promoted the slogan "the Pepsi Generation") was interviewed about his intentions in envisaging an intimate alliance between corporate culture and contemporary art—embodied in the design and performance program of the Pepsi Pavilion—for a promotional film, *Great Big Mirror Dome*, and commented,

> Being alive and being with it and being here today and a part of things going on means paying attention to the artists, the engineers, that are trying to say something, trying to do something, trying to communicate with people all around them, today, and we feel that our contribution to what is going on, as a corporation, is to see that those people have a platform from which they can express themselves and their ideas, to a great mass of the people.[8]

Pottasch's comments, viewed in the context of the conjoined US and Japanese dimensions of the Pepsi Corporation alongside the US postwar occupation of Japan (1945–1952), still recent in 1970, highlight the relevance of "entangled" or "crossed" histories which Erika Fischer-Lichte analyzes in the introduction to this volume, and which oscillate between historical and performance cultures in interweaving maneuvers, as they did across the space of the Expo grounds; authors such as John Dower and Furuhata Yuriko[9] have explored the complexity of such entanglements in the wider US-Japan postwar context, across urban history, performance and moving-image cultures.

Opposition to the Expo's agenda, as it was articulated by Pottasch, took many forms, from street-demonstration performances by the prominent Japanese performance-art group Zero Jigen—intended to denounce the exposition and the artists complicit with it—to combative interventions within the space of the exposition itself. The siting in time of the exposition emerged at the very end of a decade of great political and social turmoil in Japan, exemplified in the form of immense battles between student activists and the riot police, in the central avenues of Tokyo, Osaka and other cities, as well as in contested rural locations, such as the site of the future Narita International Airport; visitors from outside Japan, such as the writer Jean Genet and the filmmaker Chris Marker, actively took part in those protests. The primary focus of the protests, across the 1960s, had been on a postwar security treaty perceived as subjugating Japan to the United States military priorities, such as the ongoing war in Vietnam, and the use of air bases in Japan to supply that war. But by 1970, many of the protestors had become exhausted and disillusioned, while others believed that more radical action was now necessary, in the form of terrorist cells.

Despite the immense presence of security guards and surveillance systems within the exposition grounds, a member of one terrorist group, the Japanese Red Army Faction, successfully infiltrated one of the exposition's principal buildings, a large tower in the form of a surreal masked figure with eyes, the Tower of the Sun. The exposition's official report, published in 1972, gave a retrospective account of that infiltration:

> Around 5:05 pm on 26 April, 1970, a young man intruded into the Tower of the Sun. He climbed to the Golden Mask of the Tower and entered the right "eye." He wore a red helmet bearing the inscription "Red Army." The invasion was first discovered by a guard of the Central District Unit stationed at the "Theme" Pavilion. The intruder stayed in one or the other of the "eyes" for 159 hours and 30 minutes, sometimes shouting "Down with Expo" until he finally allowed himself to be arrested on the 3rd of May.[10]

In many ways, the Osaka Exposition site—as the location of Hijikata's lost performance at the Pepsi Pavilion—transmits directly the profound tensions of Japan at a time of corporate consolidation and social fracture, despite the intended isolating of that "experimental metropolis" away from the riot-torn streets of Japan's cities such as Tokyo and Osaka. Since the architecture of World Exposition sites, from the 1893 Chicago Exposition to more recent instances such as the 2010 Shanghai Exposition, is invariably intended to become obsolete and to vanish at each event's elapsing, the performances undertaken within exposition sites become correspondingly magnified, provided that at least some trace or resonance of those performances subsists into the future. An instance of such performances is the sequence of "performance lectures" given by Muybridge at his Zoopraxographical Hall pavilion, standing directly alongside his moving-image sequences' projection. Muybridge's pavilion was a financial failure, and he was ejected from it, mid-exposition, leaving little evidence of his appearances there. Even so, bare or fragmentary traces, located within or beyond archives, are all that is needed to survive in order for those 1893 performances to be reconstructed, as with Hijikata's

1970 performance at the Pepsi Pavilion. Both Hijikata's performance and Muybridge's performance lectures were undertaken at extreme variance from the agendas of the encompassing events in which they were situated. That friction in itself generates the historiographic momentum to separate out the eroding and vanishing of those performances' wider contexts from the seminal inspiration ignited by such performances themselves.

The location of the Pepsi Pavilion in the Osaka Exposition's Expo Land site is now occupied by a multistory shopping mall (Expo City), positioned between the channel of an inner-city highway, which itself occupies part of the route of the monorail constructed to allow visitors to circuit the exposition site, and the neglected concrete building that houses the exposition's archives. As with all of the exposition pavilions, the Pepsi Pavilion was razed immediately after the event's closure. Even so, in inhabiting the shopping mall's environment of sonic cacophony and digital screens, resonances of the Pepsi Pavilion, and fragments of Hijikata's performance, appear embedded there.

Hijikata's Two Presences at the Osaka Exposition

The involvement of Hijikata in the Osaka Exposition has an intricate and contradictory history, with many elements of his performance that were undocumented in the first instance or whose traces have been lost from sight; after a half-century, key participants are no longer able to evoke the event, with the result that the writing of that performance's history forms an accumulation of interconnected strata drawn from archival, memorial and architectural sources, with many strata in a fragmentary form or missing altogether. A crucial element of that complexity is that Hijikata was present at the exposition in two distinct, antithetical ways: with his unique live performance at the Pepsi Pavilion on the exposition's peripheral annex site, and also through his body's filming for an immersive moving-image projection experiment, shown repeatedly every 20 minutes on an immense 360-degree concave screen encompassing the domed interior of one of the Japanese corporate pavilions on the exposition's main site, the Midori Pavilion.

The primary intentions of the Midori Group were to gain prestige for their corporation through an alliance with experimental art and media, and to test and promote their new film-projection technology, Astrorama, which proved to be too expensive to adapt for existing cinemas and became defunct as soon as the exposition ended. The Midori Group's commissioning of Hijikata to participate in that project emerged, as with the Pepsi Pavilion's commission, solely from their desire to hire well-known or notorious contemporary artists in order to heighten their pavilion's public profile. The Astrorama projection experiment, compacting choreography and moving-image media, attracted an immense audience at the exposition; ticket sale records indicate that around 8,000,000 visitors experienced Hijikata's performance, across the event's six-month span, in its filmic rendering. Very few spectators would have identified Hijikata, whose reputation extended, in 1970, only within Japan's experimental art and dance, and not to a wider public. Audiences queued for many hours to enter the pavilion. Those visitors were entirely surrounded by the projection, via five separate film projectors, of Hijikata's figure dancing across the screen's expanse. A promotional film shot for the Midori Group inside the auditorium shows the crammed, standing spectators in a state of disorientation, their bodies and heads revolving erratically in order to follow Hijikata's filmed performance; when spectators were interviewed on leaving the pavilion after the projection's 15-minute span, they expressed vertigo and shock.

Although Hijikata's body possessed a pervasive presence at the Midori Pavilion in its filmic projection, he was corporeally absent from that space and appears not to have visited the pavilion during the exposition's span. His performance had been filmed in color almost a year before the exposition's opening, in June 1969, on the slopes of an active volcano, Mount Io, on Japan's northern island of Hokkaido. Hijikata's oscillating absence and presence at the exposition parallels that of his figure in the surviving celluloid reels of the Astrorama film, whose sole copy was consigned to a storage warehouse immediately after the exposition's closure and was abandoned there; it was rediscovered only 40 years later, in a condition of acute deterioration. Hijikata's figure had either become desiccated to the point of near erasure, or else remained still visible but discolored entirely to red. In the "memorial" archive in Tokyo, in which it is now conserved, that film's decayed nitrate celluloid reels transmit a tangible smell of the performance's loss.

By contrast with that ruined olfactory trace of Hijikata's filmed performance at the exposition's Midori Pavilion, the fragile trace of his presence at the Pepsi Pavilion was voiced by the prominent choreographer Murobushi Kō. I knew nothing whatsoever of that performance of 11 March 1970 until Murobushi vocally conjured it during an interview I conducted with him in London in 2004. Although Murobushi was a determinedly autonomous choreographer with a fractious, tangential rapport with Butoh, he had worked as an assistant to Hijikata for a year, from 1969 to 1970, living at Hijikata's Asbestos Studio, and had traveled with him from Tokyo to Kyoto, where Hijikata was engaged in choreographing sequences for horror and pornographic films (such as *Hot Springs Spa Maid Pimps* [1969], in which Murobushi appeared), and to the Osaka Exposition in March 1970. Murobushi assisted with arranging Hijikata's performance space within the foil-coated interior of the Pepsi Pavilion, and then stood to one side, attentive to any malfunction which would have required his intervention during the 30-minute performance.

Murobushi especially remembered the sonic environment of Hijikata's performance, with recordings of funeral chants, thunderstorms, and the cawing of crows. Alongside Hijikata's body, alone in the performance space, he recalled the hanging of many metal panels and of wedding robes, suspended from the pavilion's ceiling, all of them revolving, and multiply reflected, in inversion, by the pavilion's mirrored interior. All he remembered of Hijikata's performance itself was a relentless sequence of collisions of Hijikata's body against the metal panels. Murobushi remembered the performance's "preview" audience as including numerous figures from the Pepsi Corporation as well as executives of the Expo Land site, and their evident displeasure at Hijikata's performance. Hijikata, on leaving the Pepsi Pavilion, had complained to Murobushi about having to meet the corporate executives, though he had been professionally cordial to them at the event, just as—in Murobushi's memory—he had always been dutifully professional in his work on pornographic and horror films, always appearing promptly each morning in his working overalls provided by the Kyoto film studios.[11]

That vocal trace of Hijikata's Pepsi Pavilion performance formed a unique but precarious, last-gasp one; Murobushi died unexpectedly in 2015 at Mexico City's airport, and investigations into his own extensive performance archive (conserved informally by Watanabe Kimiko as an archive-café, Café Shy, in Tokyo's Waseda district) reveal no further trace of his experience of witnessing Hijikata's performance at the exposition. The architectural space of the Pepsi Pavilion itself remains vividly recalled by many witnesses, especially those who visited it as children, such as the performance theorist Uchino Tadashi. The pavilion's architectural form was unexceptional, in that it conformed to the domed design, which was pervasive across the exposition's grounds. But on approaching that white dome, visitors would see the entire pavilion abruptly disappear from sight through the regular activation of clouds of water vapor designed by the young artist Nakaya Fujiko, who was associated with the E.A.T. group and continued to deploy that art of architectural vanishing almost a half-century later, in 2017, at the Tate Modern art museum in London, during a dance performance by Hijikata's collaborator, Tanaka Min. On entering the Pepsi Pavilion, visitors were handed a portable sonic device by uniformed hostesses and could interact with the sonic installations designed by the composer David Tudor as they transited the pavilion's interior. They witnessed their own figures cast upside down and grotesquely distorted by the dome's mirror casing.

In contrast to most pavilions at the Osaka Exposition, the Pepsi Pavilion was entirely empty, other than through its occupation by visitors' bodies. It was one of the very few corporate pavilions which did not contain moving-image projection experiments. As a result of Pottasch's negative response to Hijikata's "preview" performance, the program of evening performances and concerts envisioned by its E.A.T. curators was annulled, and the group's members returned to New York. At the pavilion's opening, three days after Hijikata's performance, the president of the global Pepsi Corporation, Donald Kendall (a close ally of the US president of that era, Richard Nixon), gave a speech in which he declared, "We believe that the Pepsi Cola pavilion will set a precedent in new corporate participation in the arts."[12] Despite Kendall's optimism, the Pepsi Pavilion rapidly faced dual problems of its relative dearth of visitors (in the context of the millions who were streaming through the main site's pavilions) and of a lack of content. Two months after the pavilion's opening to the public, Sebastian T. Hiraga, the deputy commissioner of Expo Land, wrote to Hayashi Mitsui, the operations director for the exposition as a whole, on 9 May 1970, lamenting what he saw as poor, impeded visitor access to the Pepsi Pavilion and to the Expo Land annex in general, "because of [the] total failure of your design of visitors' flow." Shiraga requested approval from Hayashi for nightly dance events within the Pepsi Pavilion's interior and on its exterior terraces, thereby replacing the annulled program of experimental choreography and sound art. The Pepsi Pavilion's new theme, replacing its previous emphasis on "World Without Boundaries," would be "Theme: Outdoor rock dancing."[13] Nocturnal go-go dancing was also planned. In contrast to the absence of photographs or film footage of Hijikata's Pepsi Pavilion performance, photographic slides exist of teenagers dancing wildly on the pavilion's terrace.

Future Historiographies of Lost Performances

The Osaka Exposition's Documentation Center forms a unique repository of performance's lost cultures, alongside its detrital traces of the entire exposition. The dilapidated former administrative building of the exposition appears entirely deserted on first entry, with immense but empty reception rooms and corridors. In many ways, that environment forms an anti-archive, devoted to the pinpointing of voids, losses and intentional destructions, extending from that of the pine forests that occupied the area prior to the exposition era, to the near comprehensive erasure of the exposition's pavilions and their contents. The archive exists in occluded fragments, as though in resistance to its infiltration. Although both the archive's current director and its now retired archivist from the 1970s spent many days attempting assiduously to locate materials on the Pepsi Pavilion and the Midori Pavilion, and of Hijikata's presence at the exposition, they unearthed only a scattering of relevant documents and images.

Finally, the archivists allowed me to enter the upper story's storage areas myself, and I ascended the elevator to a vast ghostly room of piled-up artifacts, obsolete film projectors, cracked artworks, collapsed architectural models and faded photographic slides. From a window at one end of the room, I could look over to the adjacent Expo City shopping mall that occupied the Pepsi

Pavilion's site, and further north to the semi-derelict but surviving Tower of the Sun, with its gilt eyes through which an unarmed terrorist, having ascended the tower's interior stairway, had expelled his vocal denunciation of the exposition to its thousands of enthralled visitors, to the point of exhaustion, before finally surrendering to the site's guards.

Hijikata's lost performance of 11 March 1970 at the Pepsi Pavilion possesses almost no tangible traces, though it may simultaneously be located within the amassed strata of the exposition's archival detritus. Hijikata himself had no active strategy by which to ensure the future survival of his work. His Pepsi Pavilion performance can be excavated through the interwoven materials of vocal memory, architectural investigation and archival exploration but resiliently remains a distinctively lost performance. Its past as an event is fast-eroding (as with the loss of Murobushi's voice as one of its last witnesses), but it may conceivably be reactivated in unforeseen ways, as a spectral entity, through the future-historical event of the forthcoming 2025 Osaka Exposition and its enhanced technologies of vision.

The act of writing performance histories often operates with scarce residual materials that deflect a linear narration and demand instead the adroit weaving-together, from disparate sources, of memories and raw materials, in a process that possesses a close parallel with that in which performances themselves are imagined and devised. Hijikata's performance at the Pepsi Pavilion notably generates insights into the process by which a performance occurring within a situation of prominent visibility—that of a World Exposition, with many millions of attentive visitors—can be consigned to a state of forgetting, through an intricate combination of social, political and cultural imperatives. That process of forgetting illuminates and accentuates the special turmoil held by a moment of intensive transformation in Japan's history, and such moments of historical unrest—as the frameworks for performance—can also be placed in revealing intersections, both with one another and with the contemporary moment. After the Osaka Exposition had ended and its traces were being razed or consigned to neglect, Japan moved from its 1960s era of artistic experimentation and activist ferment into a prolonged era dominated by corporate and institutional cultures of surveillance and stasis. For many performers—including Hijikata, who maintained a reclusive existence at his Asbestos Studio from the early 1970s until his death in 1986—that social and artistic stasis ended their vital work.

A historically "lost" performance about which little can definitively be known, as with Hijikata's performance at the Pepsi Pavilion, simultaneously opens up exceptional ground for contemporary research investigation and for the exploratory writing of performance cultures' histories, revealing pivotal moments in performances' historiographic frameworks and isolating the surviving memories and traces of performances which may intentionally have become occluded. Lost performances, from seminal historical moments such as Japan in 1970, form prescient ones for contemporary digital representations of performance, whose easily erased technologies may be far more precarious ones in the future preservation of performances' traces than the media that caught performances' histories in prior decades. A dynamic interdependence exists, across time, between historically lost performances such as that of Hijikata at the Pepsi Pavilion and those of the contemporary moment.

Notes

1. Nihon Bankoku Hakurankai Kyōkai, *Japan World Exposition, Osaka, 1970: Official Report* (Suita City, Osaka Prefecture: Commemorative Association for the Japan World Exposition 1970, 1972), Green volume, 11.
2. The presentation of the Expo as an "experimental metropolis," as well as a "model metropolis," is highlighted in ibid., Red volume, 11.
3. Ibid.
4. Antonin Artaud, "Notes for *Pour en finir avec le jugement de dieu*," in *Oeuvres complètes*, vol. 13 (Paris: Gallimard, 1988), 258, my translation.
5. Jacques Derrida, "Les voix d'Artaud (la force, la forme, la forge)," interview by Évelyne Grossman, *Magazine littéraire*, no. 434 (September 2004): 36, my translation.
6. The performance theorist Khalid Amine has noted that the English-language and German-language word "amalgam" is very probably derived from an Arabic word, "al-malgham," with alchemical as well as medicinal historical resonances.
7. Dante Bini, in discussion with the author, Arezzo, 26 June 2016.
8. Alan Pottasch, interview for the film *Great Big Mirror Dome*, dir. Eric Saarinen, 1970.
9. See John Dower, *Embracing Defeat: Japan in the Aftermath of World War II* (London: Penguin, 2000); and Yuriko Furuhata, *Cinema of Actuality: Japanese Avant-Garde Filmmaking in the Season of Image Politics* (Durham, NC and London: Duke University Press, 2013).
10. Nihon Bankoku Hakurankai Kyōkai, *Official Report*, Green volume, 20.
11. Murobushi Kō, in discussion with the author, London, 15 February 2004.
12. Donald Kendall, typed transcript of speech at the opening of the Pepsi Pavilion, 14 March 1970, Pepsi-kan files, Documentation Center of the Osaka World Exposition.
13. Sebastian T. Hiraga, typed letter to Hayashi Mitsui, 9 May 1970, Pepsi-kan files, Documentation Center of the Osaka World Exposition.

Bibliography

Artaud, Antonin. "Dossier: *Pour en finir avec le jugement de dieu*" ["Dossier Materials: To Have Done with the Judgement of God"]. In *Oeuvres complètes* [*Complete Works*], 229–84. Paris: Gallimard, 1988.

Derrida, Jacques. "Les voix d'Artaud (la force, la forme, la forge)" ["The Voices of Artaud (The Force, the Form, the Forge)"]. Interview by Évelyne Grossman. *Magazine Littéraire*, no. 434 (September 2004): 34–36.

Dower, John. *Embracing Defeat: Japan in the Aftermath of World War II*. London: Penguin, 2000.

Furuhata, Yuriko. *Cinema of Actuality: Japanese Avant-Garde Filmmaking in the Season of Image Politics*. Durham, NC and London: Duke University Press, 2013.

Hiraga, Sebastian T. Typed letter to Hayashi Mitsui, 9 May 1970. Pepsi-kan files, Documentation Center of the Osaka World Exposition.

Kendall, Donald. Typed transcript of speech at the opening of the Pepsi Pavilion, 14 March 1970. Pepsi-kan files, Documentation Center of the Osaka World Exposition.

Nihon Bankoku Hakurankai Kyōkai. *Japan World Exposition, Osaka, 1970: Official Report*. 3 volumes color-coded in Red, Blue and Green. Suita City, Osaka Prefecture: Commemorative Association for the Japan World Exposition 1970, 1972.

Pottasch, Alan. Interview for the film *Great Big Mirror Dome*. Directed by Eric Saarinen, 1970.

PART III
Entanglements between Drama, Theater and Colonial Historiographies

5
DISENTANGLING COLONIAL ARCHIVES

The Combustible Affair of Ensuring/Insuring Theater Safety in Colonial Singapore

meLê yamomo

Reading Along the Archival Order

In 2010, I came for the first time to the Singapore National Archive as a starting doctoral student of theater history researching for my dissertation. I was writing about traveling music and theater troupes in nineteenth-century Southeast Asia. At the time, the colonial documents collection of the archive was still in the process of digitization. Being my first foray into the territory, I was faced with an epistemological challenge unapparent to my naivete at the time. I had the assumption that the British colonial government would have organized documents pertaining to the performing arts in such a section labeled specifically so. However, clearly demarcated theater, dance or music sections—as we would label them now in contemporary taxonomies of artistic practices—do not exist in British colonial Singapore's bureaucracy. After two weeks of persistent scrolling through microforms—of colonial municipal reports, government gazettes and the limited arts-related documents—searching for traces and reverberations of theater and performances in the British Crown colony in vain, I was ready to leave in resignation. On the last day of my research trip, I strayed toward unfamiliar sections of the archive—to the police and the fire departments. My inadvertent trip down these aisles of then unfamiliar file drawers would open a rift in my older understandings of history and the archive.

Annual reports of the fire department are replete with accounts of theater building fire safety investigations—the theater being the most combustible structure of nineteenth-century cities. Numerous noise grievances and complaints of disorderly conduct at the Chinese and *wayang*[1] theaters were filed under the office of the police chief. My wandering offtrack made me question

DOI: 10.4324/9781003353461-9

how I understand theater history. On my trip back to Munich, where I was doing my PhD, the rift unraveled: colonial history is a historiographic enterprise. Archive, especially the colonial archive, is not an objective repository of historical sources. Rather, it is a site of contradicting attempts of the empire to order and create knowledges of the constructed *Other*. This chapter is a historiographical reflection of archival materials on theater regulations implemented in British Colonial Singapore between 1890 and 1920. The archival documents at the National Archives of Singapore and historical newspapers demonstrate the interweaving of colonial governance, fire safety management, and the local theater culture.

Being the global medium—a cultural technology—of the nineteenth century, theater disseminated a global imagining of modernity. Modern aesthetics, as it is mediatized through theatrical representation, circulated the interconnecting world conjoined by the early global technologies of the steam engine and the telegraph. By the end of the nineteenth century, modern theater buildings became requisite facilities in the urban capitals across the world—ones that would be able to host the demands of the concomitant global migration of theater, opera, circus and music troupes. Theater, however, cannot just be thought of as a purveyor of aesthetic ideas of modernity. As these buildings were physically and materially enmeshed into the daily lives of modern cities across the globe, they were instrumental in the training and policing of the urban citizens and colonial subjects in the social practices of modernity.

The colonial modernization agenda in Singapore was entangled with the self-affirmation of British superiority. This civilizing mission justified the colonial government's need to administer the local cultural practices, building and space management protocols, and social control. The theater—the management of the building, space and its public—was subsumed under the police and the institutionalization of fire prevention laws. What was previously feared of—namely, uncontrollable fire and outbreak of sicknesses—was conquered by modernist reason and science, which were then used as means to control the subjugated Asian working classes. The employment of the social technologies of fire mitigation and insurance policies, however, instigated further power and racial hierarchies in the city. As a colonial society, the number of local inhabitants was disproportionate to the European residents of British Malaya.[2] As British Empire historian Lynn Hollen Lees points out, Europeans in British Malaya "not only composed a minute proportion of town populations, but their absolute numbers were so small that even in the 1920s only in a few places could Europeans constitute a critical mass for the creation and maintenance of social institutions."[3] Thus, considering this, a clear distinction is marked by who benefited from these policies as a public service and who was being policed, levied and penalized in its implementation.

I came to this topic through accidental diversions in the archive. Epistemological detour here also serves as a hermeneutic methodology. I write this chapter straddling a journey in understanding the theater history of British colonial Singapore alongside and within the archival framework that circumscribes it. This is as much a historiographical analysis of theater's subjugation to the municipal fire control department as it is a reflection on the archival materials of the vestiges of the theatrical social lives of the Chinese and Malay citizens of colonial Singapore. To understand theater history through the colonial British Singapore archive, one needs to think within the logic of the mind of the colonialists. Colonial historian and archive scholar Ann Laura Stoler's turn of phrase to read the colonial archives *along the archival grain* reframes colonial history within a bigger imperial historiographical project.

Stoler considers the colonial archives as subjects themselves and not just as sources, refocusing the scholarly analysis from archives-as-things to archiving-as-process.[4] Her methodology endeavors to unpack colonialism in "the principles and practices of governance lodged in particular archival forms." "Archival form," for Stoler, refers to "prose style, repetitive refrain, the arts of persuasion, affective strains that shape 'rational' response, categories of confidentiality and classification, and not least, genres of documentation."[5]

This chapter examines the British colonial project of policing and fire prevention through the "archival forms" of theater ordinances. The extant documents rarely include information about artists, performances or discussions of aesthetic qualities. The lack of documentation about the local theater houses and companies' artistic content signifies the colonial regime's disinterest in local cultural and artistic expressions that needed documentation. Rather, the archival form circumscribes the bureaucratic logic of these colonial administrative departments. The local cultural practices were negligible in the bigger enterprise of subsuming them within the social technologies of the colonial engineering of civilizing missions in the guise of imperial modernity. However, this social ordering, as we will see in this chapter, was less absolute and was formed dynamically—often erratically—in response to local cultures and circumstances. While imperial historiography paints an ostensible narrative of well-orchestrated statecraft, the archive is replete with anxieties in the form of nuisance, riots, immoralities and disruptions to colonial administration and businesses figured polemically to the Victorian values and morality of the time. And this is the reason why when local theater and performance cultures appear in the colonial archive, they are mostly in the police, fire and sanitation departments—the colonial state's regulatory apparatuses.

I read these documents alongside newspaper reports of the time which made public colonialism's underlying epistemic anxieties.[6] In the mid-nineteenth century, newspapers formed the inter-imperial "mediascape" of the urban capitals in colonial Southeast Asia. Singapore readers read in their local newspapers about the latest news, entertainment, technological advancements, political unrests, and tragedies of neighboring cities—Batavia, Penang, Manila, Hong Kong, Saigon, Shanghai, Tokyo—as well as of the European metropoles. In following through the news, opinions and even advertisements in these newspapers, one could surmise that the urban modernization projects in these colonial capitals were not just the importation from Europe of the latest fashion, technologies and social engineering policies. Newspaper opinion articles across the region reveal that the colonialist project is not infallible and consistent. As in the case of the Singapore municipal ordinances on theater, which I shall analyze here, the conflicting imperial policies, local and colonial business interests, and the varying theater cultures interweave into a paradoxical entanglement of the enterprising local Singaporean theater owners and capricious imperialist aspirations.

To set the historical context, it is important to note how colonial Singapore was interconnected with the global economic and cultural network. In the nineteenth century, Singapore served as a major transportation hub between Europe, Africa and Asia. Since the opening of the Suez Canal, steamship travel between London and Singapore via Ceylon took only 30 days. Onboard these ships also came theater, opera and music troupes, which toured along the steamship route in the Mediterranean Sea as well as the Indian and Pacific Oceans. Some took residencies for month-long theater seasons in the colonial capitals of the Dutch Indies, Spanish Philippines, and the French territories in Southeast Asia, and further to the east in Shanghai, Japan and Australia.[7] In the last two decades of the nineteenth century and at the beginning of the twentieth century, Singapore may not have attracted long-term residencies of European performing companies. Still, its role as a transit point between the Indian Ocean and the Asia Pacific saw steady traffic of itinerant performers passing through the city and doing short theater runs. This sets the background for this chapter's narrative.

Incendiary Issues

The newspaper and its network of distribution within the imperial metropolis and the colonial territories brought together the world in its collective social fears—of fire tragedies and infection outbreaks. Since the mid-nineteenth century, newspapers were also replete with sensational news of human tragedies. Searching through the digitized newspaper archive, one could easily see how sensationalized accounts of fire disasters were a recurring theme of yellow journalism in the United States and the United Kingdom since the mid-nineteenth century. These news reports were typically reprinted in newspapers in the colonial territories. Theater fires that transpired in crowded urban centers and resulted in big casualties were reported in gory details and circulated on print worldwide. The 1882 Ringtheater fire in Vienna—the most disastrous fire in the Western world—was intensively reported in newspapers in colonial Southeast Asia. Singaporean newspapers reported on the news for several months and were referred to again together with the news of the theater fire in Milwaukee in 1883. In 1893, during the discussion of the fire insurance of the Singapore town hall, which served as the venue for visiting "European" theater troupes in the Straits Settlements, the Vienna Ringtheater recirculated in the local news. In the years to come, news of the disastrous burnings of the theaters circulated in print in the Straits Settlements: a makeshift theater in Bombay (1886), the Theatre Royal in Exeter and the Opéra-Comique in Paris (1887), the Central Theatre in Philadelphia (1892), a theater in Ningpo that killed 200 (1893), another in Foo Chow that killed 400 (1896), a fire that burnt down a theater in Shanghai (1901), the big fire that razed the entire theater street in Yokohama (1899), a temporary bamboo theater in Canton that claimed the lives of 400 (1901), the Iroquois Theatre in Chicago (1904), a theater at Sam Kong in Sun Wui District that killed 500 (1907), and Meininger Theater and the Drury Lane Theatre (1908). Many of the reports contained very graphic descriptions of the corpses and the traumatic experiences of the survivors. The accounts often included the causes of the fire (sudden combustion of the flying battens, foot lights, or the flammable materials of the makeshift theaters), but also the overcrowding and lack of exits that caused the many deaths.

The fear invoked by these tragedies arguably led to a global interest toward more deliberate policies and practices in theater building and operations, such as the efforts of Edwin Thomas Sachs in England in Western Europe and further by William Paul Gerhard in the United States.[8] Fire and its prevention as it is submitted into scientific inquiry and method constituted new epistemes of modernity and subsumed it within the modernist project of controlling "nature." The theater as a public structure was crucial for this, in that, as theater historian Tracy Davis points out, "[u]nlike state edifices or privately owned factories, warehouses, and residences (which also feature in the fire prevention literature) theatres demonstrate the risk to entire populations at the vital heart of metropolises."[9] She further argues,

> In theatres, it was not cotton bales or nitrate stockpiles that ignited but scenery, ballet-girls, and soft furnishings; it was not just wealth that went up in smoke but people enjoying culture. Metonymously, it was not a merchant-trading network that perished but The Public itself, not just in that vicinity but by implication everywhere entertainments were enjoyed.[10]

In 1887, Singapore enacted the Municipal Ordinance 1887, a set of bylaws to control and supervise theaters, wayangs, concerts and other public exhibitions and entertainments. A revised version of the law was issued in 1895, which intended "to give the necessary control to the Chief Police Officer in each Settlement [...] especially those carried on by Chinese and Malays."[11]

The new ordinance requires any person opening a theater or carrying out theater performances to obtain a license from and pay the prescribed fees to the chief police officer in the settlement where the theater is located.[12] The legislation also stipulates that

> The Chief Police Officer may withdraw any license if in his opinion the theatre licensed is a public nuisance or is an annoyance to the persons living near or having their place of work or business near or if any riot, unlawful gaming or misbehavior has taken place therein or if any performance therein is of an indecent immoral or improper nature or if the theatre has been kept open beyond the hours stated in the license. The Chief Police Officer shall if required furnish the license with the grounds of such withdrawal in writing. Notice of such withdrawal shall be served on the license if he can be found and shall also be affixed to the theatre.[13]

The penalty for breaches of the ordinance are fines of up to 500 dollars and terms of imprisonment up to six months.[14]

A further revision was implemented in 1897, which stipulated a detailed ordinance on how theater buildings were to be built and managed. Section 2 of the bill qualifies what it covers in its definition of theater, which includes "any theater, room, booth […] or other place open to public, or any class of the public, in which there is carried on any stage play, circus, conjuring, dancing, wayang, mayang, mundu, joget, ronggeng, or other operatic or theatrical performance of any sort whatever."[15] I cite this section of the bill to look into the building regulations, but I also annotate here what this policy consequentially reveals. I opened this chapter with my reflection on how one might think "through the mind" of the colonial administration to find where the indigenous theaters might be recorded. While doing my archival research 12 years ago, documentations about the repertoires, descriptions and analyses of the local performances were difficult to find in the surviving colonial archival documents and historical newspapers. Nineteenth-century newspaper archives, however, were replete with documentations of visiting Italian, French and British theaters, concerts and operas. In the administrative files, only in this so-called "theater law" do I find a list that reveals the diversity of the theatrical forms and performance traditions available to the theater-going public in Singapore. They appear precisely in the records because they were the local cultural practices requiring control.

The 1897 theater law explicates the architectural ordering of how theaters should be organized and controlled so that they adhere to the social ordering imagined by the colonial administration. The bylaw stipulates "that every building used as a theater shall be self-contained or, if the theater forms part only of the building, the part used as a theater shall be completely separated by party walls from the rest of the building, shall have separate doors and shall in no way communicate with any other building or part of the building."[16]

The bylaw also indicates the rules for the width of gangways and the maximum distance between the gangways and the seats. Something worth noting here is how the requirement for fixed theater seating is organized specifically for audience seats to permanently face the stage, thus architecturally engineering theater spectatorship that is less intertwined with other forms of socialization, but rather reinforces the theater production as a commodity that requires focused consumption.

The bill also reinforces fire mitigation policies in how it indicates that exits are to be provided for every balcony, tier or floor which accommodates no more than 500 persons. Additional exits are required for every 250 persons above 500. The bylaw also dictates the materials that are to be used in the construction of theaters. Only through compliance with these bylaws can a license be issued to theater owners or operators.[17]

The legislation of such laws can be construed as a consequence of earlier reports by the Municipal Engineer, Thomas Cargill, submitted on 25 February 1883 and published in the *Straits Times* on 10 March. The report surveys the status of town thoroughfares, bridges, drains, waterworks, pumping stations and public infrastructures. It also included an extensive commentary on the situation of the Chinese theaters of the city. From this report, we also draw some idea of what theaters existed and were operated by the Chinese community at the time. The report included six theaters in five different locations: in North Bridge Road, New Bridge Road, Smith Street, North Street and two on Merchant Road.

The report summarizes the fire safety compliance of the theater buildings. With the exception of the theater on the North Bridge Road, all the buildings were "wedged between adjoining houses, so that there is no possibility of providing additional entrances at the sides or back of the building."[18] Five of the theaters included a secondary or side entrance provided for the female audiences—what would be a common practice at the time. In the event of fire or any sudden panic, Cargill opines that "the women would have little difficulty in finding a ready and rapid means of exit by the staircase and door set apart for them, without being liable to get mixed up and confused with the rest of the audience."[19] The theater on the corner of North Street was indicated to have no distinctly separate entrance for the women. The building itself "has no pretensions to be strictly regarded as a theatre" and was described as "merely a large upper room converted and adapted for the purpose."[20] Censuring its lack of public safety provisions, the report pointed out that exits "are scarcely adequate and are moreover difficult of approach, the staircase being small and badly lighted and badly constructed"[21] Cargill mentions "a peculiar feature in the design of these theaters is that part of the front side or the ground floor is usually occupied by shops, which are either ranged on each side of the street entrance, or, as in one case in North Bridge

Road, are set back, leaving a small quadrangle or court between them and the main entrance."[22]

Of the six theaters, Cargill took special attention to the architectural details of the largest theater—the one located on North Bridge Road, describing it as "well built, large commodious building and capable, when full, of containing, as I was informed, 1,500 or 1,600 people."[23] This particular theater is seen to have more public safety features, with its "five entrances from the shops, leading from the building into the small courtyard."[24] Cargill further indicates that "[t]hese entrances might be termed the doors, and the main entrance, which is about 10 feet in width and communicating directly with the street, the gate of the building."[25]

Based on the observations of how these theaters were constructed and relate to their immediate surrounding, Cargill presents some criticisms:

> The practice of construction shops and eating-places along the front wall of theatres is not one to be recommended. Even in the theatre in North Bridge Road, where the shops are provided with doors which could be opened so as to allow additional means of exit, and in which case the shops themselves would constitute regular thoroughfares for egress, there still remains the uncertainty whether the doors would be opened at the right time. Those who are familiar with fires are well aware how difficult it is to open, upon an emergency, windows and doors that as a rule are disused. There is either something piled up against them, or if they are locked the key is not to be found, and nine times out of ten the only resource is to break them open. Obviously the situation becomes aggravated when the shops have no proper entrance towards the street, and virtually block up and take the space which should be allotted to doors in the front wall of the theatre, thereby establishing direct communication between the interior of the building and the street outside.[26]

Cargill further recommends that

> Taking into consideration the facilities which a Chinese Theatre, from its general design and construction, as well as from the character of the audience, presents for a speedy clearance in the event of any panic, I am not prepared to say—with the exception of the one theatre at the corner of North Street, already alluded to—that the present means of exit are absolutely inadequate and insufficient to allow of the people making a rapid escape should a fire occur within the building. At the same time, I would suggest that, when practicable, a separate entrance should be attached to the stage, and that in the plans of all future theatres the dimensions and positions of such a number of doors as may be

reasonably demanded should be distinctly marked on the plans, and the owner required to adhere to them.²⁷

If we are to situate these policies within the bigger colonial civilizing ambition, we may find such legislations resonating within the bigger social engineering project of the British Empire. As medical historian Brenda S. A. Yeoh explains in her book, *Contesting Space in Colonial Singapore: Power Relations and the Urban Built Environment*:

> [I]n order to combat overcrowding and its attendant "house diseases," it was necessary to control the spatial arrangement and built form of housing in the city. In one sense, the control of spatial form as a technique of power was simply a reworking of the strategy of surveillance. The municipal "inspecting gaze" had shifted from overseeing the daily practices of the Asian population carried out in specific spaces (such as the house, street, market, or a public place) to controlling the dimensions, arrangements, and legibility of particular spaces (such as the house, the building block, and ultimately, the city as a whole) in order to influence the practices of those who inhabited or used such spaces.²⁸

She also argues that the study of colonial sanitation focuses "on the capacity of colonial power, through its complex of the institutional and legislative machinery, to order, regulate, and sanitize the subordinated society."²⁹ This is clearly seen in how the British expatriates were compelled to a civic duty of socially controlling the colonial subjects through public opinions and letters to editors on their observations of the fire hazards and unsanitary conditions of the local "Chinese theatre" and "wayangs."Complicating the imperial aspiration for modernity and safety is not just a society's ability to mitigate fire but in how its public behaves socially under stress.³⁰ In the middle of the 1890s, the danger of panic entered the public discourse on issues of theater and safety. German-American sanitation engineer William Paul Gerhard's books on theater safety have been referred to in opinion articles in the *Straits Times*. A reprint of "When Panic Threaten" [sic] from *Cassell's Saturday Journal* appeared in the *Straits Times* on 24 February 1897.

> "Except a fire," said a theatrical manager, "there's nothing we managers dread in our theaters so much as a panic, which, by-the-bye, has more than once arisen in when there has been no fire at all—one, for instance, occurred about three years ago in a provincial theater, through the bursting of a water pipe and some miserant [sic] shouting 'fire.'"³¹

British residents of the city visiting the local theaters felt inclined to report, in print media, their disapproval of the nonadherence of these venues to the already circulated concepts of building fire safety and public control—while injecting racially prejudiced comments to validate the superiority of the colonialists' agenda. An anonymous contributor who called himself the Spectator wrote to the editors of the *Straits Times* on 17 June 1903 about his recent visit to the Wayang Kassim. He condemned, in his letter, how dangerously crowded and unsafe the theater was and pointed out that the peril for loss of life in this theater was most likely to happen not through fire itself but through fire panic—particularly with the "fact that Orientals are, as a rule, easily panic stricken."[32]

The announcement of the revision of the theater bylaw in the *Government Gazette* in July 1895 reveals the motivation behind the revision of the Theatre Enactment Law: "The statements of objects and reasons alleges that the Police have long felt the want of some power of control over theatres, wayangs, and similar performances, especially those carried on by Chinese and Malays."[33]

In Stoler's critique of the colonial archive, we are made to consider how the records "register confused assessments, parenthetic doubts about what might count as evidence, the records of eyewitnesses with dubious credentials, dismissed rumors laced with pertinent truths, contradictory testimonies called upon and quickly discarded."[34] The grand civilizing metanarrative of the fire prevention laws reveals personal conflicts by the municipal commissioners, who legislated the laws and who were stakeholders of the burgeoning fire insurance industry in the city.

Ensuring/Insuring Theater Safety

One month after Municipal Engineer Thomas Cargill's report was published in the newspapers, a lecture by Cornelius Walford published in the *Overland Mail* was reprinted in the *Straits Times*. Walford had made a reputation as a British insurance scholar in Europe and the United States at the time with the publication of his influential article "Fires and Fire Insurance Considered under Their Historical, Financial, Statistical, and National Aspects," published in the *Journal of the Statistical Society of London* in 1877. The lengthy article provides a comprehensive overview of early modern European fire policies and eventually focuses on eighteenth and nineteenth British fire mitigation laws and fire insurance regulations.[35]

The growing intercontinental flow of theatrical and musical entertainments in Southeast Asia in the nineteenth century saw the increase of the usage of the Singapore town hall—which, at the time, had a multipurpose hall used as a theater.[36] In an opinion article that appeared in the *Singapore Free Press and Mercantile Advertiser* on 2 April 1892, the town hall was described as "a nondescript sort of Building, serving partly as Offices for the Municipality, and partly as a Music Hall."[37] The writer also comments on how "it has been used for theatrical performances of varied kind, some three times a week chiefly by strolling companies not over particular as to how the place is left after a performance, or whether the building catches fire from badly guarded lights or carelessly arranged scenery."[38] This newspaper commentary was published amidst the heated debate on the insurance policy of the town hall, which was publicly circulated in the local newspapers between 1890 and 1892.

The disputation was triggered by the competition between the recently established Straits Fire Insurance Company and the England-based insurers who had previously covered property indemnities in the colonial territories. The Straits Fire Insurance Company was established by British capitalists living in Singapore in 1889, some of whom were members of the municipal commission. In 1892, the Municipal Council received a quote from London insurers for a lower premium compared to the local Straits Company, which was at this time the insurer of the town hall.[39] I include here details and financial figures of the conversation regarding the insurance rates, which have implications in making distinctions between town halls, music halls, and theaters—cultural categories of urban modernity that the British were trying to import into the colony.

The quote indicates a net premium of $141.75 ($157.50 minus the 10% commission) offered for a building appraised at $90,000 by the London company, including all contents, which puts the building at a rate of 3/6d% (that is 3 shillings and sixpence).[40] An anonymous letter to the editor on 15 April 1892 in the *Straits Times* explains how "foolish" such acceptance by the insurance office was. This has to do with the town hall being used as a music hall and theater. The distinction in name and usage of the hall spells a difference in the insurance premium. Music halls in England were rated at 10/6d% to 24/6d%, but such buildings were not allowed to hold theatrical performances or representations that require sceneries. Theater buildings were typically rated at 31/6d% and further in the upwards of 150/6d%. Further remarking on the municipal commissioner's skewed perception, the writer comments on how the "Town Hall in Singapore may think itself slighted being called a music hall, but if it aspires to the grander name of 'Theatre' then is still more lucky in being covered for 3/6d%, the rates on Home theatres commencing at 31/6d and going up as high as 150/6d."[41]

This debate, however, as would become apparent, is not purely rooted in the municipal commissioners' interest in safety. In a small colonial town such as Singapore, the local capitalists who were members of the municipal governing board were also the founders of local private corporations providing commercial, public services. This often created conflicts in corporate and public interests, which the same people administered. The municipal board member Theodore Sohst was also the chair of the board of the Straits Fire Insurance Company. In the dispute over the town hall insurers, where the board was leaning toward employing the cheaper premiums offered by the London-based company, Sohst questioned the provision in the policy that allowed theatrical performances in the town hall during the 30 March and 2 April 1892 board meetings.[42] Considering that the town hall had hosted performances by traveling troupes performing on occasions three times a week and had already had fires more than once, Sohst had strong grounds for arguing that the absence of such clause rendered the policy null and void and that in considering the new policy, the theatrical use of the town hall had to be made clear to the foreign insurers. On 13 April, the decision to continue the use of the two halls in the town hall as theater was left to the president (Mr. Alexander Gentle)—which in any case was agreed upon by the board to be allowed the use of footlights.[43]

The Town Hall theater insurance controversy reveals the colonial government's inconsistencies in its assumed superiority. Amidst the insurance debate, the British residents of Singapore were quick to pass the ridicule toward the Chinese, as was the case in what is supposed to be a humorous social commentary on the "By the Way" section in the *Straits Times* in July 1901:

> Singapore is frequently misunderstood, and so are the ways of its people to the great chagrin of the latter. Still it is only a person who has been in a Chinese theatre, and remembers its appointments, that will appreciate the solicitude of the head of office at home of an insurance company whose local agents had issued a policy on one of the Celestial playhouses. The head office wrote to enquire whether the drop curtain was fire-proof, and also was smoking allowed in any part of the building other than the bar.[44]

The irregularity in the implementation of the theater regulations is also seen in how it took almost a decade before the municipality-owned theater adhered to its own regulations of separating the theater from the municipal offices. With the revised Theatre Ordinance that included fire safety guidelines put in place in 1897, the fire-related risk of the town hall, which shared the colonial government office and entertainment hall, became patently a civic concern. With such a bylaw in place, a building dedicated to theater, separate from the town hall, was proposed in 1899. After the death of Queen Victoria in 1901, the municipal commissioners decided to build a memorial hall honoring the deceased monarch, which coincided with the interest of building a new theater. After deliberation, the municipal commissioners decided that "a theatre might not be universally regarded as an appropriate memorial to our late Queen."[45] The Victoria Memorial Hall was finished in 1905 and served as a concert hall. With the need for a bigger and fire-protected theater, the town hall (which seated 370) was renovated and was completed in 1909. The renovated hall, which seated 850 was renamed the Victoria Theatre. The two performance halls were eventually joined by a clock tower to form a two-winged structure.

After the completion of its renovation, the Victoria Theatre was not just exemplary for its architecture and facilities. The 1912 Municipal Report publishes that new lighting equipment has been procured and that the "stage is furnished with a set of stock scenery specially made for it in London."[46] The theater was also the very model of theater safety and sanitation. The same 1912 report also indicated that "a fire-proof curtain and automatic sprinkler have been provided."[47] The city council also paid for its insurance, and the annual municipal reports publicize that fire safety staff were present in all performances, functions and rehearsals at the venue, free of charge. The distinction of the "premiere" municipal theater, which houses visiting European theater and music companies receiving fire safety public service stands, signifies a stark difference in how, in the same municipal report, the city fire department indicates earnings of $2,870.35 (1917) and $1,954.49 (1916) for servicing the "native theatres" and cinematographs.[48] The report also states that "[l]icensing arrangements for these theaters were not satisfactory."[49]

The annual municipal reports also publish the engagements at the Victoria Theater and the Victoria Memorial Hall—wherein theatrical performances and concerts in the venue were staged by traveling and local amateur European performing companies. Within the colonial records, information about the Chinese, Malay and Indian theatrical activities are undocumented, save for reports on violations of the theater ordinances and summary of license fees collected. An exception appeared in the 1915 and 1917 municipal reports, wherein a summary of the number of performances in the indigenous theaters was included. The report also showed comparative numbers from 1914. These figures, however, were primarily included to show the accounting of the fees collected for the services of the fire protection department. The report also included a commentary on licensing due to a complicated ticketing system in the Chinese theaters. I include here a section of the 1917 report:

Fire Protection

Firemen were on duty during all performances and rehearsals at the Victoria Theatre and at all functions in the Memorial Hall: no charge is made for this service.

1,560 short, 2,039 long, and 32 matinee turns of duty were undertaken in the Native Theatres and Cinematograph Halls: charges for this service amount to $2,011.80: compared with 1,335: 2,180:50 [*sic*] and $1,988 for 1914.

Periodical and surprise inspections were made of all Theatres and Cinematograph Halls: a lot of overcrowding still occurs in the Chinese Theatres, principally owing to the system of selling ticket for entrance and another for a seat. New By-Laws were in preparation with a view to dealing with this and other questions, but the Theatre Ordinance and the system of licensing require alteration first.[50]

These reports also make legible how the ordinances took different controls over the indigenous theaters, and how theater owners created more administrative problems in the long run. Already in 1912, the Fire Protection report indicated that the superintendent considered "precaution taken against fire in theatres and cinematograph halls insufficient, but it is difficult to remedy matters so long as a dual control over such buildings exercised."[51] The conflicting jurisdictions refer to the theater regulations being under the power of the municipal commissioners, whereas the licensing authority is the chief police officer.[52] The report recommends that "[i]t would be more satisfactory if the Commissioners were the licensing authority and the functions of the police were restricted to the maintenance of order within the buildings."[53] Five years later, the 1917 report still indicated that the problem had not been solved, stating that "[t]he arrangements for licensing the Theatres are still not satisfactory, there is dual control and no control; the President of the Municipal Commissioners should be the Licensing Officer under a new Theatre's Ordinance."[54]

Conclusion: Disentangling Colonial Archives

This chapter was less an exposition of what indigenous theaters transpired parallel to the more visibly documented touring shows by European troupes and companies. Rather, I examined how the policing of the theaters—the most flammable buildings in nineteenth-century urban centers—unravels the British administration's entanglement with the local performance cultures and publics. This risk management policy was implemented while betting on the insurance plans of the very cultural modernization they were setting up in colonial Singapore.

In this historical entanglement, one of the threads reveal the sites of local theater in the nineteenth and early twentieth centuries. My research within the British colonial archive did not reveal much about the aesthetics and accounts of artistic practices—the common themes of theater historiography. However, the theater fire and sanitation policies and reports became supplementary sources to the locations, building details, and operations of the local theaters of the time. Here I found archival pieces of the colonial theater history puzzle sitting in unexpected places. In thinking of postcolonial historiography as a collective work, I hope that these puzzle fragments could connect with pieces other theater historians might uncover in other unlikely corners of the archive.

Finding the history of local and indigenous theaters in British Singapore was not easy to find in the colonial archive. An accident borne of desperation led me to what, for me, were unlikely records sections of the police, fire and sanitation departments, which inadvertently compelled me to think deeper into the colonial archival logic. In this "failed attempt" to map out indigenous Singaporean theater history, I draw from postcolonial theorist Homi Bhabha's notion of "double vision" generated by the colonial encounter[55] to reread the interweavings of colonial Singapore's entangled past. Another historical thread in this entangled history reveals how the local performance cultures are circumscribed within the social policing system of the colonial government. The task of colonial theater historiography is a task of disentangling the colonial intentions of the social ordering of the colonized *Other* as they are embedded in the archive; and of finding, from within the colonial archives, the extant presence of local performance histories.

Notes

1 *Wayang* is a traditional form of puppet theater play originating from Indonesian and popular in the Malay-speaking archipelago. The term wayang refers to the entire dramatic performance, although there are different types of puppets with their specific terms such as the *wayang kulit*, or the shadow puppets made from leather, and the *wayang golek*, which are three-dimensional puppets. The archival documents and newspaper documents that I consulted only indicated the general term wayang.
2 "British Malaya" loosely refers to a group of states on the Malay Peninsula and the island of Singapore that was under British control since the late eighteenth to the mid-twentieth century. These states include the Federated and the Unfederated Malay States, which were British protectorates governed by local rulers, and the Straits Settlements, which were initially governed by the East India Company and were later ruled directly under the British Crown from 1867.
3 Lynn Hollen Lees, "Discipline and Delegation: Colonial Governance in Malayan Towns, 1880–1930," *Urban History* 38, no. 1 (2011): 51.
4 See Ann Laura Stoler, *Along the Archival Grain: Epistemic Anxieties and Colonial Common Sense* (Princeton, NJ and Oxford: Princeton University Press, 2009), 20.
5 Ibid.
6 Ibid.
7 For further accounts on itinerant performing companies in Southeast Asia in the nineteenth century, see Michael McClellan, "Performing Empire: Opera in Colonial Hanoi," *Journal of Musicological Research* 22, no. 1–2 (January 2003): 135–66; meLê yamomo, "Global Currents, Musical Streams: European Opera in Colonial Southeast Asia," *Nineteenth-Century Theatre and Film* 44, no. 1 (2017): 54–74; and *Theatre and Music in Manila and the Asia Pacific, 1869–1946: Sounding Modernities* (Cham: Palgrave Macmillan, 2018).
8 See Tracy C. Davis, "Brokering Best Practices: International Advocacy for Fire Prevention," *Popular Entertainment Studies* 6, no. 2 (2015): 38–55.
9 Ibid., 41.
10 Ibid., 43.
11 *Straits Times*, 15 July 1895, 3.
12 Ibid.
13 Ibid.
14 Ibid.
15 Ordinance to Make Provisions for the Better Regulation of Theatres and Theatrical Performances, Singapore Municipal Bylaw on Theatres, 1895.
16 Ibid.
17 "Amendments of Sections 85111 (i) (v) (vi) and 153(1) of Municipal Ordinance No. XV of 1896 Bylaws for Regulating the Construction of Theaters and for the Control and Supervision Thereof," Special Meeting of 3 June 1897, Minutes of Singapore Municipal Commissioners' Meetings, 2945–48.

18 "Municipal Engineer's Office," *Straits Times*, 10 March 1883, 3.
19 Ibid.
20 Ibid.
21 Ibid.
22 Ibid.
23 Ibid.
24 Ibid.
25 Ibid.
26 Ibid.
27 Ibid.
28 Brenda S. A. Yeoh, *Contesting Space in Colonial Singapore: Power Relations and the Urban Built Environment* (Singapore: NUS Press, 2003), 146.
29 Ibid., 81.
30 See William Paul Gerhard, *Theatre Fires and Panics: Their Causes and Prevention* (New York, NY: John Wiley & Sons, 1896).
31 "When Panic Threaten" [*sic*], *Straits Times*, 24 February 1897, 3.
32 "Crowded Theatres: Wayang Kassim," *Straits Times*, 17 June 1903, 5.
33 This quote was taken from the reprint of the *Government Gazette* in the *Straits Times*, 15 July 1895, 3.
34 Stoler, *Along the Archival Grain*, 23.
35 See Cornelius Walford, "Fires and Fire Insurance Considered under Their Historical, Financial, Statistical, and National Aspects," *Journal of the Statistical Society of London* 40, no. 3 (1877): 347–432.
36 yamomo, "Global Currents," 59.
37 "Philanthropical Fire Insurance," *Singapore Free Press and Mercantile Advertiser*, 4 April 1892, 3.
38 Ibid.
39 The Royal Insurance Company offered $90,000 at a quarter per cent net. See *Straits Times*, 15 April 1892, 13.
40 I am grateful to the help of Christopher Balme, Tracy Davis and Jane Frecknall-Hughes for explaining the nineteenth-century British currency. For more information regarding the old English money system before the 1971 decimalization of the pound, see "Old English Money," *Project Britain*, accessed 12 April 2022, https://projectbritain.com/moneyold.htm.
Between 1867 and 1903, with Singapore becoming a British Crown colony, the Straits Settlements Legislative Council created the Legal Tender Act of 1867, which made the Mexican, Hong Kong, Spanish, Peruvian and Bolivian silver dollars the recognized legal tender currencies in the territory; this is why the currency symbol is $. For more information, see Stephanie Ho, "History of Singapore Currency," 9 March 2016, https://eresources.nlb.gov.sg/infopedia/articles/SIP_2016-03-09_114438.html. See also Sheng-Yi Lee, *The Monetary and Banking Development of Singapore and Malaysia* (Singapore: NUS Press, 1990).
41 Ibid.
42 "Municipal Commission," *Singapore Free Press and Mercantile Advertiser*, 14 April 1892, 3.
43 "Minutes of Proceedings of the Municipal Commissioners," *Straits Times Weekly Issue*, 4 May 1892, 261.
44 "By the Way," *Straits Times*, 20 July 1901, 3.
45 *Straits Times*, 28 November 1901, 2.
46 Singapore Municipal Report, 1912, 18.
47 Ibid.
48 Singapore Municipal Report, 1917, 10.

49 Ibid.
50 Singapore Municipal Report, 1915, 4.
51 Singapore Municipal Report, 1912, 14.
52 Ibid.
53 Ibid.
54 Singapore Municipal Report, 1917, 5.
55 See Homi K. Bhabha, *The Location of Culture* (London: Routledge, 1994).

Bibliography

Bhabha, Homi K. *The Location of Culture*. London: Routledge, 1994.
Davis, Tracy C. "Brokering Best Practices: International Advocacy for Fire Prevention.'" *Popular Entertainment Studies* 6, no. 2 (2015): 38–55.
Gerhard, William Paul. *Theatre Fires and Panics: Their Causes and Prevention*. New York, NY: John Wiley & Sons, 1896.
Ho, Stephanie. "History of Singapore Currency." *Singapore Infopedia*, 9 March 2016. https://eresources.nlb.gov.sg/infopedia/articles/SIP_2016-03-09_114438.html.
Lee, Sheng-Yi. *The Monetary and Banking Development of Singapore and Malaysia*. Singapore: NUS Press, 1990.
Lees, Lynn Hollen. "Discipline and Delegation: Colonial Governance in Malayan Towns, 1880-1930." *Urban History* 38, no. 1 (2011): 48–64.
McClellan, Michael. "Performing Empire: Opera in Colonial Hanoi." *Journal of Musicological Research* 22, no. 1–2 (January 2003): 135–66.
Project Britain. "Old English Money." Accessed 12 April 2022. https://projectbritain.com/moneyold.htm.
Singapore Free Press and Mercantile Advertiser. "Municipal Commission." 14 April 1892, 3.
———. "Philanthropical Fire Insurance." 4 April 1892, 3.
Stoler, Ann Laura. *Along the Archival Grain: Epistemic Anxieties and Colonial Common Sense*. Princeton, NJ and Oxford: Princeton University Press, 2009.
Straits Times. "By the Way." 20 July 1901, 3.
——— "Crowded Theatres: Wayang Kassim." 17 June 1903, 5.
———. "Municipal Engineer's Office." 10 March 1883, 3.
———. "When Panic Threaten" [sic]. 24 February 1897, 3.
Straits Times Weekly Issue. "Minutes of Proceedings of the Municipal Commissioners." 4 May 1892, 261.
Tener, Robert H. "Breaking the Code of Anonymity: The Case of the Spectator, 1861–1897." *The Yearbook of English Studies*, vol. 16, Literary Periodicals Special Number (1986): 63–73.
Walford, Cornelius. "Fires and Fire Insurance Considered under Their Historical, Financial, Statistical, and National Aspects." *Journal of the Statistical Society of London* 40, no. 3 (1877): 347–432.
yamomo, meLê. "Global Currents, Musical Streams: European Opera in Colonial Southeast Asia." *Nineteenth-Century Theatre and Film* 44, no. 1 (2017): 54–74.
———. *Theatre and Music in Manila and the Asia Pacific, 1869–1946: Sounding Modernities*. Cham: Palgrave Macmillan, 2018.
Yeoh, Brenda S. A. *Contesting Space in Colonial Singapore: Power Relations and the Urban Built Environment*. Singapore: NUS Press, 2003.

Historical Newspapers

The Daily Advertiser
Mid-day Herald
The Singapore Free Press and Mercantile Advertiser
The Straits Times

Archives

National Archives of Singapore
The National Archives (United Kingdom)

6

THE THORNY ENTANGLEMENTS OF THEATER AND COLONIAL HISTORIOGRAPHY IN THE NETHERLANDS

Anti-colonial Critique and Imperial Nostalgia in J. Slauerhoff's Play *Jan Pieterszoon Coen* (1931)

Sruti Bala

Of Rogue Heroes

In the wake of the massive world-wide protests under the banner of Black Lives Matter, a group of demonstrators gathered in the main square of the city of Hoorn in the Netherlands in late June 2020, calling for the removal of the massive bronze statue of the seventeenth-century colonial figure of Jan Pieterszoon Coen, prominently placed in Coen's city of birth.[1] The demonstration, not the first of its kind, followed a series of petitions and appeals to the municipal government, which gained significant media attention. In a gesture that can only be termed a publicity stunt, the Dutch parliamentarian and leader of the right-wing party *Forum voor Demokratie*, Thierry Baudet visited the square in Hoorn in mid-June 2020, demonstratively placing a bouquet of flowers at the base of the statue, tweeting that such an act marked his "adoration for a national hero" and "pride towards a site of national historical importance."[2]

The very same Jan Pieterszoon Coen (1587–1629), erstwhile Governor-General of the Dutch East India Company in the seventeenth century, is also the protagonist of a play by the Dutch writer J. (Jan Jacob) Slauerhoff, published in 1931, which is the subject of investigation of the present chapter.[3] Through a reading of the play and its curious production history, the chapter seeks to investigate some of the thorny entanglements between theater and colonial historiography in the Netherlands. The chapter addresses the concerns of this volume through the specific question of staging the colonial past. Dealing with colonialism and its aftermaths is not only a matter of material reparations or setting historical records straight but also a complex process of collective cultural introspection, intimately tied to the present. The arts play a significant role in this process, influencing the narratives, images, vocabularies and attitudes with which a society comprehends its colonial pasts and grapples with its post-colonial conditions. At the same time, the arts in general, and theater more specifically, have also served as ideological stages for the mobilization and legitimization of territorial conquest and civilizational missions.

The present chapter underlines the need to think theater historiography in terms of multiple pasts, and reflects on how every staging of the play compels an interweaving of these plural pasts, to speak with the call of this volume. The chapter examines the politics of this interweaving, or rather entanglement, from two angles: first, it considers how every attempted staging of Slauerhoff's play brought the Dutch colonial past to bear upon the immediate political circumstances, thus raising questions of legitimizing current agendas with a selective understanding of the past, as well as questions of comparability and shared histories. Second, the chapter pays attention to the gendered and sexualized dimensions of performance historiography. It examines how the play articulates the relation between colonizers and colonized in gendered terms, thereby emphasizing the importance of feminist perspectives on performance historiography. The choice of this play has to do with the fact that it was one of 100 play texts selected as part of an initiative to revive the Dutch and Flemish language theater canon.[4] The inclusion of any play in a canonical list is based on the assumption of its long-term "stageworthiness," that it deserves to be part of the Dutch repertoire in the present and in the future. I leave aside, for the moment, the question of the underlying assumptions of canonization and the role of canons in educational and cultural policy, no doubt a subject of intense discussion but one that exceeds the scope of the current chapter. I rather set out to ask what it might mean to stage a play such as Slauerhoff's *Coen* at a time when public debates in the Netherlands and other European urban sites emphasize the need for the decolonization of art history and for the dismantling of colonial hero worship in public spaces? How might the play and its production history be interpreted today in a way that constructively contributes to a historicized understanding of the colonial project, beyond the simple polarities of heroism and despotism? How does the play reveal prevalent self-conceptions of Europe that are entangled with its colonial pasts?

Jan Jacob Slauerhoff's only play, *Jan Pieterszoon Coen*, written in 1931, is a fast-paced tale of imperial fantasies and the anxieties that accompany them. With its central narrative woven around the historical figure of Jan Pieterszoon Coen, the play dislodges Coen from his mythical status as national hero and moves in episodic strides through various phases and facets of his decline. In doing so, it touches on the easily wounded nerve that ties national pride to greed, masculinity, and racial and religious supremacy. The play's canonical status is contested on several counts. Early appraisals of the play all seem to broadly agree that it is not of the literary caliber of the rest of the writer's oeuvre.[5] Slauerhoff (1898–1936) was a Dutch poet and novelist who travelled around the world as a naval doctor. His works are regarded as belonging to the late romantic tradition, yet refreshing in terms of his anti-authoritarian and cosmopolitan worldview, characterized by adventure, a search for the unknown, and a longing for faraway places.[6] Though he was a celebrated writer during his lifetime, the publication of his only play did not particularly excite reviewers at the time. One reviewer chides it as being characterized by a narrative rather than dramatic approach, as being unsuitable for staging because of its frequent change of scenes and, thus, as being dramaturgically flawed.[7] Another reviewer cites the use of antiquated language as making the play inaccessible to theatergoers of the twentieth century.[8] Others worry that the play contains historical imprecisions and misrepresents certain events.[9]

Yet, despite the formal criticisms, there remains an abiding fascination in several early reviews and readings of the play with the way in which Slauerhoff approaches the historical figure of Jan Pieterszoon Coen, chipping away at the image of the daring[10] and uncompromising statesman, and unravelling a psychically wrecked and megalomaniac tyrant behind the figure. Notwithstanding its open criticism of Coen, Slauerhoff's play was received according to the tenor of the rising nationalist wave in the Europe of the tumultuous interbellum years, as evidence of Coen's status as a big man of the Dutch Golden Age. This is no doubt the case in H. P. Geerke's 1929 hagiography of Coen, read by Slauerhoff, in which Coen is positively compared to Mussolini, "both humans, powerful figures, who sought to advance their fellow beings."[11] Indeed, one might argue with Benedict Anderson that the formation of a Dutch nationalism required the manufacture of a glorious past to which it could anchor itself, as well as a mythical hero, no matter how despotic, who represented the quest for territorial expansion and the imperial conquest of other, larger European powers such as the Spaniards.[12] This would explain why the first statue of Coen was thus erected 250 years after his death, in 1867, in what was then called Batavia, today's Jakarta; or what motivated Coen's hometown of Hoorn in the Netherlands to install a statue in his honor with much pomp and ceremony as late as 1893. The popularity of colonial figures such as Admiral de Ruyter, Witte de With, Maurice of Nassau, or Peter Stuyvesant grew in Dutch national literature and public culture in the late nineteenth century and remained till the Second World War. Literary scholars refer to the emergence of a genre of apologetic literature in the interbellum period, observing a correlation between works referring to the Dutch colonies and a growing patriotic nationalism at the cusp of the war in Europe and the expanding decolonization movements across Asia and Africa.[13] Against this body of writing, Slauerhoff's choice of this hero-cum-tyrant of Dutch colonial history as the protagonist of the play might thus be seen as a means of reckoning with the nationalist fervor of his times through the diverted route of a figure from colonial history.

On the Play's Production History

The play's controversial production history further elevated its place in the canon. *Coen* was never publicly staged till 1986, after earlier productions in 1937, 1943, 1948 and 1961 had been cancelled at the last minute or refused permission.[14] The details around these cancellations offer intriguing insights into how the play evidently suggested an entanglement of the colonial past with the public affairs of the current time.

One of the first known attempts at performing the play was by a group of students of Indology from the University of Leiden in 1937. The students approached the writer Edgar du Perron, who held the rights to Slauerhoff's literary estate, for permission to stage the play, sending him a copy of the adapted version of their script. In two letters dated 1937 to his friend, the writer Menno ter Braak, Du Perron notes that he refused to give permission to a performance which distorted the substance of the play and had nothing to do with the spirit of the writer:

> I just received this jaw-dropping blabber [...] with an adaptation by the gentlemen. Not only has the entire sadistic scene been scrapped, but in fact every single indelicate or unseemly word in the entire play has been removed. For example, where it should be "wedded and bedded spouse" [...] the word "bed" is gone! [...] Cortenhoeff is not allowed to have "the Spanish pox" [...]. When Sara imitates the voice of God "with a heavy distilled gin-laced voice," the gin is taken out.[15]

While it has not been possible to trace the script adapted by the students, it is evident from Du Perron's comments that the performance was motivated by a puritan attempt at rehabilitating Coen's image as a hero of the East Indies, which Du Perron found appalling and tasteless. That it was undertaken by a group of Indology students is not insignificant in this connection and can be read as an indication of the apologetic inclination of the Orientalists of the time toward the colonial territories.

Another production was announced in 1943 at the Gemeentelijk Theaterbedrijf (Municipal Theater Company) in Amsterdam, an agency set up to coordinate theater and performance activities during the war under German occupation. This performance too did not take place, because "the authority considered the portrayal of the pioneer of the Indies to be too rough and not ideal enough."[16] In the case of the annual book gala event in 1948, the performance was cancelled by the Mayor of Amsterdam, d'Ailley, a week before the event, leading to much uproar, since the program brochures had already been printed. Although no reasons were officially given, the cancellation was no doubt connected to the way the play might have been received in the light of the Dutch military interventions in the East Indies in the 1940s and the war crimes and mass violence that began in 1945. A play that placed Dutch colonial history in a negative light was deemed as inappropriate at a time that the Dutch sought to retain their grip on the Dutch East Indies.[17]

The 1961 production by the student theater group Kothurne was meant to coincide with Slauerhoff's twenty-fifth death anniversary and the anniversary of the Amsterdam Female Student Association. The performance was eventually restricted to a strictly closed, invited audience, following an order from the Amsterdam Mayor, Van Hall, who appealed to national interest in claiming that a performance of the play would touch on a sensitive nerve and undermine national unity. The play's anti-colonial sentiment was deemed as detrimental to public opinion at a time when the Netherlands was embroiled in the so-called New Guinea dispute.[18]

Dutch audiences first watched the play only in 1969, indeed not on stage but as an adaptation for television by Jan Blokker, with documentary inserts and several omissions in the script, such as the scene featuring two deserters of the Dutch colonial army. A similarly edited radio-play version was aired in 1981.[19] The first full public performance of the play took place in 1986 by the Dutch Repertory Company in an adaptation by Hans Bakx in the basement or Soeterijn Theater of what was then known as the Colonial Institute, today renamed the KIT Royal Tropical Institute in Amsterdam.[20]

For a play so evidently concerned with a figure from the seventeenth century, it is remarkable that its staging in the twentieth century evoked such intense nationalist sentiments and a fair deal of attention from local authorities. As Coen biographer Jur van Goor has argued, the reasons for the controversies around the play have less to do with its contents and more to do with the public debates around the end of Dutch colonialism in the East Indies and the aftermath of the Second World War.[21] However, it is the play that allows for these entanglements to come alive, as it were, for its staging inevitably begs the question of its connection to the present, whether it be a matter of historical continuity or of the mode of writing history, remembering and judging past events.

Between Violence and Desire

Slauerhoff's play focuses on the last months of Coen's life. Since Coen's wife, Eva Ment, is pregnant at the beginning of the play, and delivers a girl child at the end, it can be deduced that less than nine months elapse in the fictional time of the play. The play takes the license to conflate facts relating to the first and second historical invasions of Batavia (1628 and 1629) in one incident, thereby dramatically sharpening the downfall of Coen. The play is structured in 11 acts (in Dutch: *tafereel*, a term originating from the Old French, carrying the connotations of scene, description, enactment and surface of projection), each subdivided into short, chronological scenes. Its episodic structure references the form of Shakespearean tragedies. The play is located in different sites of the colonial establishment in Batavia, with the crucial scenes taking place in the board room of the Dutch East India Company. Almost precisely halfway through the play (act 5) is a scene in a churchyard, which rather explicitly references the canonical graveyard scene in *Hamlet*, including a reflexive monologue.

The play opens with Coen's secretary and personnel gossiping about his poor health and fiery temperament. Within the first four scenes of the first act, the central elements of the plot are rapidly introduced. We are informed that the mighty Governor-General of the Dutch East Indies suffers from nightmares and numerous ailments. He announces plans to destroy the surplus harvest of spices to prevent it from being sold to the British. The arrival of a delegation of "native" rulers from Bantam is anticipated. The territory has been occupied by the Mataram army. Coen dictates a letter to the heads of the East India Company in Europe, by whom he feels abandoned, frantically appealing for more personnel and resources. He partly attributes the financial and territorial losses of the Company in the Indies to the lack of discipline and morale amongst his personnel. In particular, he is increasingly worried about the lasciviousness and immodesty of those in his custody, notably Sara, the daughter of East India Company Officer Jacques Specx and a Japanese woman. Coen seeks to "resolve" the situation by arranging the marriage of a number of his officers to young white women brought to the colony from the Netherlands. Sara, however, is to marry the bald, sweaty-palmed and bad-breath pastor Hurnius, who is "to erase any heathen traces in her."[22] The conflicts escalate at different levels in the course of the play: we learn that the Dutch troops in Fort Parel and Fort Orange are successively attacked by the reigning monarch of Mataram, with whom Coen was expecting to strike a spice trade deal. Several officers desert the Company; others are held hostage. Coen's position as Governor-General is increasingly under question. Meanwhile, Sara, who manages to postpone her marriage to the pastor by seeking permission to be of assistance to Coen's wife, Eva Ment, until she delivers her baby, is discovered in her room in the amorous company of the young officer Cortenhoeff,[23] an act deemed as criminal, "a villainous dalliance."[24] Coen is enraged and orders their immediate death. Cortenhoeff is executed, but Sara escapes death in the last minute, thanks to the arrival of her father, Jacques Specx, who also brings with him the news that he is to succeed Coen as Governor-General of the Indies. The play ends with the news of Coen's death in bitterness, resentment, loneliness and defeat. Coen is rarely alone on stage; he is surrounded by personnel and company officers of various ranks, almost all of whom fear, loathe, envy or plot against him, even as they bow in obeisance to his orders.

Françoys Blaeu, Coen's secretary, appears throughout the play as commentator and observer—"I am but an interested spectator"[25]—trusted by Coen enough to question him and speak truth to him, yet himself mistrustful of Coen and envying his powerful position, willing to defend Coen to the end, if only in order to retain the right to appoint his successor.

The "Specx Affair"

While the play revolves around the figure of Coen, it curiously places the figure of Sara Specx and the so-called Specx Affair center stage. The historical figure of Saartje or Sara Specx was the daughter of an unknown Japanese woman and Jacques Specx (1585–1652), head of the East India Company establishment in Hirado, Japan and, later, Governor-General in Batavia (1629–1632). Since Company policy at the time sought to prevent what was then termed the "bastardization" of the Dutch population in Asia, children born out of extramarital liaisons between Dutch Company officers and indigenous women were sent to Batavia to be raised under the supervision of the Company.[26] When Saartje's father, Jacques Specx, was repatriated from his appointment in Japan, she was left under the guardianship of Jan Pieterszoon Coen and his wife, Eva Ment. The "scandal" around Saartje took place in 1629, when she was probably barely 13 years old, and was found in the company of Pieter Kortenhoef, a 16-year-old reserve officer in the Company's service, himself raised as a mixed-race subject in the Company establishment in Batavia.[27] Coen, appointed as their guardian, was furious about this affair and announced that Kortenhoef would be sentenced to death, a punishment that was executed the very next day. Sara was initially sentenced to death by drowning, but since she was under 14, her punishment was reduced to a public whipping. Although Sara escaped death, her father, Jacques Specx, later appointed as the successor of Coen in Batavia, fought the case at a high level, with the financial support of Kortenhoef's uncle in the Netherlands, revealing that the case was a matter of concern and debate in metropolitan Europe as well.[28]

Slauerhoff's play dramatizes several elements of this historical event, largely in line with archivally documented facts. Sara's affair with Cortenhoeff and the scandal it caused become the catalyst of climax and catastrophe in Slauerhoff's play. Coen's response was no doubt considered harsh and disproportionate even at the time, not only because of their young age, or because they were both under his guardianship, but also because Kortenhoef had, in fact, officially asked for her hand in marriage, which should have technically acquitted him of the accusation of *crimen maiestatis* (high treason). Slauerhoff, however, introduces another twist in the plot, namely that Sara is figured as the object of desire of not only the minor character of Cortenhoeff, and the lustful pastor Hurnius, but also of Coen's chief secretary, Blaeu, and indeed Coen himself: "We all are in love with her, possess her in our nightly lustful thoughts. Each in his own way. [...] And you, who had the most power and did not use it in battle, eventually used your power to take revenge, to kill the one who knew to possess her."[29] This figuration of Sara Specx in relation to Coen and other characters in the play is suggestive of some of the core concerns of the play, which happen to resonate with recurrent themes of colonial discourse, such as the tension between colonial violence and desire, nostalgia, the fear of "miscegenation" and the imagination of the relation between colonizer and colonized in gendered and sexualized terms. For if colonialism, as Anne McClintock has pertinently observed, is "as deeply concerned with violence and power as it is with questions of fantasy, desire and difference,"[30] then Slauerhoff's play offers an opportunity to explore this uncomfortable ambivalence in a manner that remains relevant to the present day.

Fantasy of Conquest and Fear of Engulfment

The setting of the play is in and around the East India Company's council chambers and quarters in Batavia, the name given to the Dutch East India Company's colonial headquarters in what is today Jakarta, which Coen wants to rename as New Hoorn, after his hometown in Holland. Batavia, however, always remains in the backdrop, sometimes as the fantasy of a conquered territory, at other times as the site of threat and hostility. In the play text, Batavia does not feature center stage but rather appears in the italics of stage directions and scenographic indications: "Outside a canal, over which a bamboo bridge, flanked by palm trees on the side. Malays slink past, back and forth, catching cockroaches and sprinkling water."[31] The colonial territory is figured in the play both as mysterious, beautiful and desirable, holding promises of immense treasures, and simultaneously as threatening, potentially contaminating, inflammable. The colony is imagined at some distance from the scene of action of the play, outside of it, yet engulfing it. "Why are you afraid?" Coen's wife, Eva Ment, asks Sara, "the natives will not come here. The Governor is the terror of the entire archipelago"[32]—as if it were not the East India Company that were invading the Indies but rather the Indies that were menacing to the Company. This tension between the imagined safe, intimate, domestic "inside" of the colonial headquarters and the rough, unpredictable and threatening "outside" of the colonies is scenographically indicated in the play. What we mainly see on stage is the life on the "inside," yet rather than affirming this imagined uniform society, Slauerhoff sets it up as a façade in order to chip away at its supposed stability and homogeneity.

The play does not primarily address the resistance and insurgence of the colonized, but it does reveal the internal tensions within the Company establishment in Batavia as well as the asymmetries on racial, economic and social grounds within and amongst the colonizers. The colonizers are not depicted as one homogenous community. Not all is well with the powerful

Governor-General as the play begins. Coen is surrounded by officers who despise him and desert the Company, servants who gossip behind his back, and subjects under his guardianship disobeying his will. The European directors of the Company are deaf to his pleas, as they are primarily concerned about the profits Batavia brings, and less so about the welfare of the colonies. "I don't count on anything anymore. I know what we can expect: delays overseas, betrayal all around us, barely any troops and a perennial scarcity of cannonballs. In this nothing will ever change."[33] Slauerhoff's depiction of Coen, however, does not mention anything about the massacre of Banda in 1621, in which tens of thousands were killed in the battle over the monopoly of the spice trade, nor of his involvement in the Indian Ocean slave trade.[34] Yet the play is not an apologetic appraisal of the human side and personal qualities of this tyrannical ruler. Rather, we become audience to the pathetic and crumbling foundations of power and its ambivalent attraction to that which it seeks to conquer or vanquish.

One instance of this internal tension in the Company is the conflict between Coen and Specx, which is not only a battle over imperial power but also over domestic control and prescriptions of how Europeans ought to behave in the colonies in the domestic sphere. Coen is the guardian of Specx's mixed-race daughter, Sara, and his inability to discipline her and her desires, or place her in the grip of missionary Christianity and white supremacy, becomes emblematic of his political failure to keep the European model intact, as it were. Whereas Coen's dread of racial and religious contamination stands for the loss of colonial power, Specx, on the other hand, can be associated with the proud fantasies of masculine territorial conquest and the rewards that come to men when crossing racial boundaries in the form of concubinage or domestic sexual servitude. In both cases, paranoia and megalomania go together.[35] The obsession with maintaining and patrolling the racial, religious and spatial boundaries between colonizer and colonized as well as the nostalgia for the European homeland are paradoxically accompanied by an intense fascination for and attachment of the colonizer to the colonies, its people and its products, an aspect that Homi Bhabha has famously theorized as the ambivalence of colonialism.[36] Sara is figured as the focal point of this fascination, as nearly every male character in the play turns out to be infatuated with her. "She has the soul of her land, she is coaxing, charming, pliant, but also sly as a fox."[37] She is desired and simultaneously also mistrusted and loathed.

"Tell me," Sara questions Eva Ment in a moment of intimate conversation, "don't you also long to be from here?"[38] That rhetorical question is, of course, addressed equally to herself, who imagines herself as belonging more to the local population than to the Dutch colonial environment in which she is brought up. Sara's fantasies of becoming a geisha in Japan seem to have more to do with Slauerhoff's orientalist projections of her longing for submission and being desired by the European as other, than with a quest for cultural belonging by a mixed-race subject under colonialism. This is worth noting because of its theater historiographical implications, namely when we imagine what a staging of the play might look like in our own times. I would like to argue that it is the historiographical task of any contemporary adaptation of the play to self-reflexively comment on these layers of fantasy that are projected onto the colonial past, which extend to the present day. In what way historiographical? Because every staging assumes a relationship of the subject of the play to the contemporary moment of its staging. Staging a historical play about an event and a figure from seventeenth-century Dutch colonial history suggests that there is a resemblance or continuity between that historical-fictional time, the time of writing the play and the present time, or that there is something to be learnt from those pasts that is of relevance to the present. The task of performance becomes historiographical to the extent that it is not only a work of interpreting sources but also, in doing so, a work of critically investigating the position of the observer in relation to these historical pasts.

The racialized, gendered and sexualized connotations of these male power fantasies are evident in the play, and they are typical tropes of colonial discourse. Feminist scholars of colonial historiography have pointed out that the assertion of the rulers' supremacy in the colonies is often done in terms of virility, patriotic masculinity and racial purity.[39] Slauerhoff, too, repeatedly employs these tropes: natives tend to be figured as naked, sensual, either sleepy or mercurial in temper, either lazy or bogged down by the conditions of manual labor—in any case, bodies perceived and imagined through the vantage point of colonial power: "below the bridge, one sees a pirogue passing by with half-naked natives"[40]; or "An *alang-alang* field. Troops from Mataram squat along the roadside, chewing betel leaves, smoking corn leaf cigars, or sleeping."[41] In his references to the landscapes and the natural environment of the colonies, Slauerhoff seems to unwittingly adopt the colonial depiction of nature as simultaneously inert and extravagant, made available for human extraction and consumption.[42] As scholars have pointed out, this figuration of nature rose in popularity in the seventeenth century through the genre of still life paintings that characterize the art historical period known as the Dutch Golden Age. However, regardless of whether or not the playwright affirmatively uses these as nostalgic imaginations of the colonial period, it is important for any interpretation or staging of the play to unravel the ambivalences between colonial violence and colonial desire.[43] This might be done by paying more dramaturgical attention to the ways in which the "inside" and "outside" of colonial power are represented and how unstable the boundaries between them are.

In his critique of Benedict Anderson's *Imagined Communities*, Partha Chatterjee questions Anderson's assumption that all anti-colonial nationalist movements imagined their nation along the lines of models offered to them by Europe.[44] He argues instead that in their social institutions and practices, these movements often distinguished between an "outside" sphere of statecraft, economy and technology, where the European model was adopted as required, and an "inside" domain of cultural uniqueness and identity, which governed language, family and gender relations and which sought to carve out a sovereignty and autonomy, untouched by colonial power. In reading Slauerhoff's play in the light of Chatterjee's argument, it is interesting to ask how colonial discourse conversely also developed its own distinctions between "inside" and "outside." The play invites such a historiographic shift of perspective, wherein one might investigate not only how the colonies are shaped by Europe but also how Europe's self-conception is shaped by its colonies.

Colony as Woman and Woman as Colony

In her study on the figure of Pocahontas in American colonial historiography, Helen Carr argues that the relationship between colonizer and colonized is often modeled in terms of the power relationship between men and women, specifically that the analogy "provided a fund of images and topoi by which the difference European/non-European could be politically accommodated."[45] For instance, the colonized land is often rendered as the passive, feminized recipient of male custodianship.[46] "You need not go into the interior territories in search of conquest,[47] Coen tells his officers, with the allusive linking of territorial conquest to the acquisition of women. "Decent ladies are in absence of their natural guardians,"[48] he continues, figuratively linking women with nature and, by implication, with unconquered territory, both requiring, indeed waiting for, masculine colonial protection and custodianship. Interestingly, the Dutch word *voogd* stands for both governor and guardian; it refers to the male role as both the guardian of land as well as of children. It is noteworthy, in this context, that in colonial discourse, both colonial subjects and women are often represented as children.[49]

The play offers an explicit commentary on the place of women in the colonial project. "If only there were enough women, the bulk of East Indian trade would be yours [...]. We must plant a colony, women must be sent expressly for this purpose,"[50] remarks Blaeu with reference to Coen's plea to the directors of the Dutch East India Company to send white Dutch women to the Indies. It is historically documented that it was common practice to send poor or orphaned white women and girls to the colonies in the early part of the seventeenth century, on the one hand as a measure to increase the population of the white settlers and create a social life and environment that emulated the European bourgeois model, but, on the other hand, it was also a measure to supposedly prevent sexual encounters between white men and indigenous women.[51] The policy was thus shaped by a fear of "miscegenation" or racial intermingling, which was widely regarded as a threat to the civilizational mission of colonialism. In one of several monologues of self-doubt and self-deprecation, Coen laments the crumbling of his power and ambitions:

> The house of Nassau has fallen. Orange is faltering. If it collapses, we are done for and everything will once again be as it was before we arrived; with only some additional ruins, graves and bastards. A somewhat lighter tinted Javanese, an occasional blue-eyed one, that is all that will remain as a reminder of us. Our shame![52]

Coen is depicted here as not merely concerned about the material profits of the East India Company but equally obsessed about the civilizational mission of establishing a powerful, white ruling class in the colonies. The fact that Slauerhoff picked up on this might also be connected to the resurgence of Nazi eugenics in the period when he wrote the play, and this might have been a way to critique the racism and petty moralism of his times. In reading these lines against the current backdrop of a resurgent, aggressively masculine, racialized nationalist politics in different parts of the world, not only in the Global North but also in formerly colonized countries such as India and Brazil, as well as in other imperial contexts such as Russia, Slauerhoff's figuration of *Coen* needs to be interpreted with a reflexive and historicized positioning of the present in relation to the colonial pasts.

The position of the white woman in the colony is a curious one in this regard. The white woman in the colony—in this case, Eva Ment—is both subordinate to as well as an active upholder of colonial norms.[53] Ment fiercely defends her husband and his civilizational mission, though she also admits to his being "irascible and somewhat rough."[54] In speaking about herself, she has no doubts that a woman's role is in being obedient and subservient to her husband: "She must be where her husband is, bear and raise his children, obey, and if it must be, suffer."[55] What suffering implies for the wife of the Governor-General of the Dutch East Indies is, of course, a relative question. Eva, however, despite distancing herself from the "natives," also compares her fate to that of all women elsewhere in the world. It is the fate of women everywhere to suffer, she concludes, hoping thus to bring the conversation with Sara to an end. "And that is not just here, it is also the case in Holland, and in Japan even worse. Don't you know that the woman is the slave of man there?"[56] Here again, the relation between man and woman is drawn in terms of a political economy that is tied at once to the colonial enterprise as well as to the Calvinist ethic of suffering. The white woman in the colony recognizes that the control of women's bodies and sexualities is part of the maintenance of colonial power.[57] She imagines herself as both necessary to the preservation of the system, as a beneficiary of it, and, at the same time, as universally allied with those enslaved in colonialism. This universalist white feminist position would need to be carefully taken apart and complicated in any staging of the play.[58]

As a mixed-race subject under colonialism, Sara occupies a slightly different position, straddling between the colonial environment of Batavia and her imagined affinity to Japan. She refuses the Calvinist ethic of suffering, insisting she would rather be indulgent and ornamental rather than subject herself to feminine tasks of labor such as serving, washing and cleaning. "I have not yet learned to make and serve tea, but I know thirty-three dances, and I can play the *samisen* too."[59] In choosing Cortenhoeff over the pastor Hurnius, she defies Coen and, with him, the politics of respectability that was part and parcel of the civilizational mission of colonialism. A staging of the figure of Sara would thus need to take into account the numerous orientalist and nostalgic projections that Slauerhoff endows her with and unpack these in a historically responsible way.[60] The task of interweaving performance histories can thus be interpreted as a feminist task, questioning established, canonized understandings of colonial histories and paying attention to the gendered dimensions of their asymmetries and hierarchies.

Questions of Interpretive Methodology

The above reflections about Slauerhoff's play are informed by the curious circumstance that it is a play that has been censored and cancelled more often than it has been performed. The production history reveals important insights into how performance is a form of historiographic practice. Performance as the lived life of a play text is not only a means of challenging culturally canonized understandings of the historical subject of the play but an active intervention in the present, an interweaving of the present with multiple pasts. In the best case, it can complicate and offer nuanced understandings of the past as well as shape the relationship between the past and present into a multidirectional one. In the worst case, it is an exercise in manipulating and manufacturing history to suit some limited agendas of the present. The absence of a large number of performances is, however, not a major hindrance to the study of the play, as this chapter adopts a speculative approach to performance historiography. It is concerned with ways of bringing historical facts and events to life in the present, thus also anticipating possible future ways of representing pasts. Considering the implications of the inclusion of Slauerhoff's play in a list of 100 most important plays in the Dutch/Flemish language, the chapter seeks to imagine what would be required for possible future stagings of the play, to do justice, as it were, to the representation of colonial pasts.

The chapter investigates how Slauerhoff's play invites, indeed insists, on an interpretation, which would connect its historical subject to the contexts of the times in which it is staged. Because the play is entangled with its interpreters and the contexts of interpretation, and the historical events it portrays seep into the contemporary and past interpretations of these events, the play is suggestive of multiple performance frames, connecting different times and histories. It does not therefore suffice to speak of these multiple frames in terms of comparison, as in: What was it like then, and how is it like now? What are the commonalities and differences between the spatio-temporalities of the Dutch East India Company era and our own time, or between Dutch and other colonial sites? Such an approach suggests a point of view that postulates that the interpreter can be separated from the comparable times and spaces, and summons a "we" that begs the question of its own history. Such comparative moves are never straightforward or innocent. They demand a certain self-positioning of the reader, artist or the audience toward the play and its subject as well as toward the play's production history. They imply choices about the scale of comparison and the inherent logic of comparison. They call for setting up or recalibrating the frames of reference.[61] The play compels such a self-positioning.

The question is thus not only how to but why stage a play such as Slauerhoff's *Coen* in a contemporary setting. What promises or challenges does this interweaving of different histories offer? The play is intriguing in the way it unravels the ambivalences and gradations of colonialism. It is valuable for the way it places the historiography of Dutch colonialism in the East Indies in relation to Slauerhoff's own time, which we now know as the interbellum period between the wars of the twentieth century in Europe. Its production history reveals how the play resonated with and created frictions with the hegemonic views of the post-war and postcolonial Netherlands. A twenty-first-century staging of the play would ideally need to retain and explore those ambivalences and contradictions, not just in the way they pertain to the historical event of colonialism but also in their traces in the present time and space, and no doubt dependent on whether the interpretation is undertaken in Leiden or Jakarta or Curaçao. For instance, what is to be done with certain parts of the script that would no doubt be considered as racist or offensive if used on the contemporary stage? Ought these parts to be skipped or eliminated in order not to offend anyone in the audience? How might such an erasure be different from the 1937 version of the play, where Indology students in Leiden deleted certain parts of the script, which they felt would depict the protagonist in too negative a light? How might the exoticized depictions of women and natives in the play be translated to a contemporary context? What kind of a casting practice might complicate the script? How might a performance sensitize us to certain absences such as that of enslaved persons in the play? Such questions must not be quickly brushed aside with liberal arguments that seek to mobilize freedom of expression or easy condemnations of the past as conservative and backward. Sometimes, as in the instance of the absence of the Banda massacres in Slauerhoff's play, it is the task of a possible future staging to explicitly comment on or redress this absence, for ambivalence in this case would only reinforce the erasure. However, in other instances, such as the manner of Slauerhoff's depiction of the domestic lives of colonial administrators, a possible staging would need to retain and explore the ambivalence with which they are portrayed in the play. For it is this ambivalence that allows for a connection of the colonial past with the present time to realize this present as entangled with these histories. Any possible future adaptation of the play would necessarily need to confront theater makers and audiences with these uncomfortable questions.

Notes

1 I acknowledge with gratitude the valuable research inputs and feedback I received from Rob van der Zalm and Veronika Zangl. An earlier, Dutch version of this text was published in Sruti Bala, "'Een Kolonie Moeten Wij Planten': Over Het Toneelstuk 'Jan Pietersz. Coen' (1931) van J. Slauerhoff," in *In Reprise: Tweeëntwintig Nederlandse En Vlaamse Toneelstukken Om Opnieuw Te Bekijken*, ed. Rob van der Zalm et al. (Amsterdam: Amsterdam University Press, 2020), 63–75.
2 Thomas Borst, "Jan Pieterszoon Coen Wekt Wrevel in Hoorn; Gemeente Weigert Betoging Rondom Beeld," *De Volkskrant*, 16 June 2020, https://www.volkskrant.nl/nieuws-achtergrond/jan-pieterszoon-coen-wekt-wrevel-in-hoorn-gemeente-weigert-betogingrondom-beeld~beb95cb7. My translation.
3 J. J. Slauerhoff, *Jan Pietersz. Coen* (1931; repr., Amsterdam: De nieuwe toneelbibliotheek, vol. 150, 2012).
4 The ongoing initiative *In Reprise* (In Revival) has assembled a longlist of 100 and a shortlist of 25 plays in the Dutch/Flemish language from different historical periods. The process involved a broad range of experts in Dutch and Flemish theater, an extensive survey of public opinion as well as an empirical analysis of historical statistics about the popularity of plays in terms of ticket sales and production figures. The initiative has resulted in an extensive website with historical documentation on each play and its production history, a book-length publication with essays on select plays, and a partnership with theater companies to stimulate and support the staging of these plays and an inclusion in their repertories. See http://www.inreprise.org.
5 For a selection of reviews of the play, see the website of the project, "De Lijst van 100," *In Reprise*, accessed 7 January 2022, http://www.inreprise.org/lijst_100?s=t&id=dwslau001janp001.
6 See a biography of the writer in *Koninklijke Bibliotheek*, "J. J. Slauerhoff (1898–1936)," Royal Dutch National Library Online Resources, accessed 7 January 2022, https://www.kb.nl/themas/nederlandse-literatuur-en-taal/schrijversalfabet/jj-slauerhoff-1898-1936.
7 Ben van Eysselsteijn, "Jan Pietersz. Coen in Drama Uitgebeeld: Een Nieuw Nederlandsen Tooneelstuk," *Bataviaasch Nieuwsblad*, sec. Kunst en Letteren, 8 January 1932, Delpher.
8 Ibid.
9 "Toneelspel 'Jan Pieterszn. Coen' Verboden Door Burgemeester van Amsterdam," *Leeuwarder Courant: Hoofdblad van Friesland*, 20 February 1948, Delpher.
10 The Dutch word *koen* means daring, doughty, fearless.
11 H. P. Geerke, *Jan Pieterszoon Coen: De Baanbreker in Ons Indië* (Utrecht: De Haan, 1929), my translation; Jur van Goor, "Sara Specx En de Reputatie van Jan Pieterszoon Coen," in *Het Koloniale Beschavingsoffensief: Wegen Naar Het Nieuwe Indië, 1890–1950*, ed. Marieke Bloembergen and Remco Raben (Leiden: KITLV, 2009), 145.

12 "He may have been a rogue, but he was our very own rogue," a Dutch politician is said to have remarked about Coen. The quote was visualized in a 2012 exhibition on Coen in the West Friesian Museum in Hoorn; see Westfries Museum, Vind Magazine, and Polder Vondsten, eds., *Coen! Geroemd En Verguisd* (Hoorn: Westfries Museum, 2012), accessed 4 March 2022, https://wfm.nl/coen. It is noteworthy that Benedict Anderson argues that anti-colonial movements such as in French Indochina adopted a model of nationalism taken from the Dutch colonial model of *beamtenstaaten*, a point I will return to later in this chapter. Benedict Anderson, *Imagined Communities: Reflections on the Origin and Spread of Nationalism*, 2nd ed. (London: Verso Books, 2006), 99.

13 W. H. van Helsdingen, *Daar Werd Iets Groots Verricht …. Nederlandsch-Indie in de XXte Eeuw* (Amsterdam: Elsevier, 1941). This is a widely cited instance of such apologetic literature, published 10 years after Slauerhoff's play. See J. M. Pluvier, "Recent Dutch Contributions to Modern Indonesian History," *Journal of Southeast Asian History* 8, no. 2 (1967): 202.

14 Westfries Museum, Vind Magazine, and Polder Vondsten, *Coen! Geroemd En Verguisd*, 81; J. H. W. Veenstra, "Slauerhoff, Coen En de Oorlogsmisdaden," *Maatstaf* 17, no. 6 (1970): 337–50.

15 Edgar du Perron to Menno ter Braak, Tjitjoeroeg, 8 February and 14 April 1937, in *Briefwisseling tussen Menno ter Braak en E. du Perron 1930–1940*, rev. ed., Literary Museum in the Hague in Cooperation with Foundation Menno ter Braak (DBNL, 2009), my translation.

16 M. Wolters, "Het Nederlandsche Repertoire," *De Waag*, 27 October 1944, 596. At the time of publication of this article, the periodical *De Waag* was still under the editorship of the National Socialists, and Wolters happened to be the acting Head of Theatre and Dance in the Department of Public Education and Arts. In the article, he defends both Slauerhoff as well as Coen as "unique, unrivalled figures" and expresses regret about the banning of the play. This instantiates how, even within National Socialist circles, the historical legacy and value of J. P. Coen remained malleable and contested.

17 Apart from the above instances, Aalders presents evidence for a failed attempt at performing the play in the 1950s by a student theater company in Utrecht. See Hein Aalders, "Een 'ploertig Stuk' En de Openbare Orde, De Wereldpremière van Slauerhoffs 'Jan Pietersz. Coen,'" *De Parelduiker* 22, no. 1 (2017): 48. See also Wim Hazeu, *Slauerhoff: Biografie*, 4th ed., Open Domein 28 (Amsterdam: De Arbeiderspers, 2018).

18 "Na Lang Beraad Toch Opvoering," *De Tijd De Maasbode*, 5 October 1961; Aalders, "Een 'ploertig Stuk.'"

19 Tom Rooduin, "De Beul van Banda," *Radio Doc*, 19 March 2017, https://www.nporadio1.nl/radio-doc/onderwerpen/399724-de-beul-van-banda.

20 Hazeu, *Slauerhoff*, n556, n564.

21 Jur van Goor, *Jan Pieterszoon Coen, 1587–1629: Koopman-koning in Azië* (Amsterdam: Boom, 2015).

22 Slauerhoff, *Coen*, 16, my translation.

23 Cortenhoeff is the name of the character in the play, which is based on the historical figure of Pieter Kortenhoef. The spellings used throughout the text indicate this distinction.

24 Ibid., 104.

25 Ibid., 47.

26 Ann L. Stoler, "Making Empire Respectable: The Politics of Race and Sexual Morality in 20th-Century Colonial Cultures," *American Ethnologist* 16, no. 4 (1989): 637.

27 Jur van Goor cites sources that mention the presence of enslaved women and other servants in the room, apart from Cortenhoeff. The presence-absence of enslaved persons in the play is another aspect that deserves attention; see Van Goor, "Sara Specx," 151.
28 Adrienne Zuiderweg, "Sara En Pieter, Een Bataviase Liefdesaffaire," *Indische Letteren* 22 (2007): 2–15; Michiel van Groesen, "Specx, Sara (1616/1617–ca. 1636)," *Digitaal Vrouwenlexicon van Nederland*, 13 January 2014, http://resources.huygens.knaw.nl/bwn1780-1830/DVN/lemmata/data/Specx.
29 Slauerhoff, *Coen*, 99–100.
30 Anne McClintock, *Imperial Leather: Race, Gender, and Sexuality in the Colonial Contest* (New York, NY: Routledge, 1995), 15.
31 Slauerhoff, *Coen*, 7.
32 Ibid., 22.
33 Ibid., 38–39.
34 Only one line in act 1, scene 4 mentions the existence of thousands of dead in broad terms: "While you traversed the Indian Ocean, they were beaten, thousands were killed, many rioters were reduced to ashes, leaving the Sultan indebted to you." Ibid., 15.
35 Peter Hulme has argued that this coming together of paranoia and megalomania is a recurrent trope in male imperial discourse; see "Polytropic Men: Tropes of Sexuality and Mobility in Early Colonial Discourse," in *Europe and Its Others: Proceedings of the Essex Conference on the Sociology of Literature*, vol. 2, ed. Francis Barker et al. (Colchester: University of Essex Press, 1985), 26–27.
36 Homi Bhabha, "Of Mimicry and Man: The Ambivalence of Colonial Discourse," *October* 28 (1984): 125–33.
37 Slauerhoff, *Coen*, 101.
38 Ibid., 23.
39 Stoler, "Making Empire Respectable"; McClintock, *Imperial Leather*.
40 Slauerhoff, *Coen*, 10.
41 Ibid., 50.
42 In this regard, a contemporary staging of the play would ideally engage with the critique of colonial modernity's conceptions of nature. In a series of brilliant essays departing from the story of the nutmeg in Dutch colonial history, Amitav Ghosh pleads for a vitalist politics, one that pays attention to the entanglements of human history with non-human forces. *The Nutmeg's Curse: Parables for a Planet in Crisis* (London: John Murray Publishers, 2021), 40. In an essay in this volume titled "The Fruits of the Nutmeg Have Died," Ghosh references the work of art historian Julie Berger Hochstrasser, which relates the rise of the genre of still life paintings to the colonial enterprise: "The Conquest of Spice and the Dutch Colonial Imaginary: Seen and Unseen in the Visual Culture of Trade," in *Colonial Botany: Science, Commerce, and Politics in the Early Modern World*, ed. Londa Schiebinger and Claudia Swan (Philadelphia, PA: University of Pennsylvania Press, 2007), 169–86.
43 Sarah de Mul, "Nostalgia for Empire: 'Tempo Doeloe' in Contemporary Dutch Literature," *Memory Studies* 3, no. 4 (2010): 413–28.
44 Partha Chatterjee, "Whose Imagined Community?," *Millennium: Journal of International Studies* 20, no. 3 (1991): 521–25.
45 Helen Carr, "Woman/Indian: 'The American' and His Others," in *Europe and Its Others: Proceedings of the Essex Conference on the Sociology of Literature*, vol. 2, ed. Francis Barker et al. (Colchester: University of Essex Press, 1985), 46.
46 Hulme, "Polytropic Men," quoted in McClintock, *Imperial Leather*, 26.
47 Slauerhoff, *Coen*, 16.
48 Ibid.

49 See, for example, a study on respectability politics in the Dutch Caribbean context by Rose Mary Allen, "Biba Un Bida Drechi: Living a Respectable Life," in *Di Ki Manera? A Social History of Afro-Curaçaoans, 1863–1917* (Amsterdam: SWP Publishers, 2007), 215–34.
50 Slauerhoff, *Coen*, 98.
51 Stoler, "Making Empire Respectable."
52 Slauerhoff, *Coen*, 74.
53 For an extensive analysis of this subject, see McClintock, *Imperial Leather*.
54 Slauerhoff, *Coen*, 22.
55 Ibid., 23.
56 Ibid.
57 McClintock, *Imperial Leather*.
58 This could be done with the help of studies such as Gloria Wekker, *White Innocence: Paradoxes of Colonialism and Race* (Durham, NC: Duke University Press, 2016) and Philomena Essed and Isabel Hoving, eds., *Dutch Racism* (Leiden: Brill/Rodopi, 2014). These studies speak to the ways in which race, class, gender, sexuality and colonial history intersect in the Netherlands.
59 Slauerhoff, *Coen*, 19.
60 This might serve as an opportunity for theater makers to engage with recent scholarship, offering insightful guides in the process of historicizing a play, such as Reggie Baay, *De njai: het concubinaat in Nederlands-Indië* (Amsterdam: Athenaeum-Polak & Van Gennep, 2008); Pamela Pattynama, *Bitterzoet Indië: Herinnering En Nostalgie in Literatuur, Foto's En Films* (Amsterdam: Prometheus/Bert Bakker, 2014); and Ann Stoler, *Carnal Knowledge and Imperial Power: Race and the Intimate in Colonial Rule* (Berkeley, CA: University of California Press, 2002).
61 In this emphasis on self-reflexivity and positioning, I believe the *histoire croisée* approach is a valuable contribution to performance historiography; see Michael Werner and Bénédicte Zimmermann, "Beyond Comparison: *Histoire Croisée* and the Challenge of Reflexivity," *History and Theory* 45, no. 1 (2006): 30–50.

Bibliography

Aalders, Hein. "Een 'ploertig Stuk' En de Openbare Orde, De Wereldpremière van Slauerhoffs 'Jan Pietersz. Coen'" ["A 'Shabby' Piece and the Public Order, the World Première of Slauerhoff's 'Jan Pietersz. Coen'"]. *De Parelduiker* 22, no. 1 (2017): 44–59.

Allen, Rose Mary. "Biba Un Bida Drechi: Living a Respectable Life." In *Di Ki Manera? A Social History of Afro-Curaçaoans, 1863–1917*, 215–34. Amsterdam: SWP Publishers, 2007.

Anderson, Benedict. *Imagined Communities: Reflections on the Origin and Spread of Nationalism*. 2nd ed. London: Verso Books, 2006.

Baay, Reggie. *De njai: het concubinaat in Nederlands-Indië [The Njai: Concubinage in the Netherlands East Indies]*. Amsterdam: Athenaeum-Polak & Van Gennep, 2008.

Bala, Sruti. "'Een Kolonie Moeten Wij Planten': Over Het Toneelstuk 'Jan Pietersz. Coen' (1931) van J. Slauerhoff" ["A Colony We Must Plant": On J. Slauerhoff's Play "Jan Pietersz. Coen" (1931)]. In *In Reprise: Tweeëntwintig Nederlandse En Vlaamse Toneelstukken Om Opnieuw Te Bekijken [In Revival: A New Appraisal of Twenty-Two Dutch and Flemish Plays]*, edited by Rob vander Zalm, Anja Krans, Bart Ramakers and Veronika Zangl, 63–75. Amsterdam: Amsterdam University Press, 2020.

Bhabha, Homi. "Of Mimicry and Man: The Ambivalence of Colonial Discourse." *October* 28 (1984): 125–33.

Borst, Thomas. "Jan Pieterszoon Coen Wekt Wrevel in Hoorn; Gemeente Weigert Betoging Rondom Beeld" ["Jan Pieterszoon Coen Festers Resentment in Hoorn; Municipality Refuses Demonstration around Statue"]. *De Volkskrant*, 16 June 2020. https://www.volkskrant.nl/nieuws-achtergrond/jan-pieterszoon-coen-wekt-wrevel-in-hoorn-gemeente-weigert-betogingrondom-beeld~beb95cb7.

Braak, Menno ter, and Edgar du Perron. *Briefwisseling tussen Menno ter Braak en E. du Perron 1930–1940* [*Correspondence between Menno ter Braak and Edgar du Perron 1930–1940*]. Rev. ed. Literary Museum in the Hague in Cooperation with Foundation Menno ter Braak. DBNL, 2009.

Carr, Helen. "Woman/Indian: 'The American' and His Others." In *Europe and Its Others: Proceedings of the Essex Conference on the Sociology of Literature*, vol. 2, edited by Francis Barker, Peter Hulme, Margaret Iversen and Diana Loxley, 46–60. Colchester: University of Essex, 1985.

Chatterjee, Partha. "Whose Imagined Community?" *Millennium: Journal of International Studies* 20, no. 3 (1991): 521–25.

De Mul, Sarah. "Nostalgia for Empire: 'Tempo Doeloe' in Contemporary Dutch Literature." *Memory Studies* 3, no. 4 (2010): 413–28.

De Tijd De Maasbode. "Na Lang Beraad Toch Opvoering" ["Play Staged after Prolonged Deliberations"]. 5 October 1961.

Essed, Philomena, and Isabel Hoving, eds. *Dutch Racism*. Leiden: Brill/Rodopi, 2014.

Eysselsteijn, Ben van. "Jan Pietersz. Coen in Drama Uitgebeeld: Een Nieuw Nederlandsen Tooneelstuk" ["Dramatic Portrayal of Jan Pietersz. Coen: A New Dutch Play"]. *Bataviaasch Nieuwsblad*, sec. Kunst en Letteren [*Batavian Newspaper*, Art and Literature Section], 8 January 1932. Delpher.

Geerke, H. P. *Jan Pieterszoon Coen: De Baanbreker in Ons Indië [Jan Pieterszoon Coen: Pioneer of Our Indies]*. Utrecht: De Haan, 1929.

Ghosh, Amitav. *The Nutmeg's Curse: Parables for a Planet in Crisis*. London: John Murray Publishers, 2021.

Goor, Jur van. "Sara Specx En de Reputatie van Jan Pieterszoon Coen" ["Sara Specx and the Reputation of Jan Pieterszoon Coen"]. In *Het Koloniale Beschavingsoffensief: Wegen Naar Het Nieuwe Indië, 1890–1950* [*The Colonial Civilizational Offensive: Paths to the New Indies, 1890–1950*], edited by Marieke Bloembergen and Remco Raben, 143–68. Leiden: KITLV, 2009.

Goor, Jur van. *Jan Pieterszoon Coen, 1587–1629: Koopman-koning in Azië [Jan Pieterszoon Coen, 1587–1629: Merchant King in Asia]*. Amsterdam: Boom, 2015.

Groesen, Michiel van. "Specx, Sara (1616/1617–ca. 1636)." *Digitaal Vrouwenlexicon van Nederland* [Digital Women's Lexicon of the Netherlands], 13 January 2014. http://resources.huygens.knaw.nl/bwn1780-1830/DVN/lemmata/data/Specx.

Hazeu, Wim. *Slauerhoff: Biografie [Slauerhoff: A Biography]*. 4th ed. Open Domein 28. Amsterdam: De Arbeiderspers, 2018.

Helsdingen, W. H. van. *Daar Werd Iets Groots Verricht .... Nederlandsch-Indie in de XXte Eeuw* [*Great Deeds Were Done There .... The Netherlands Indies in the 20th Century*]. Amsterdam: Elsevier, 1941.

Hochstrasser, Julie Berger. "The Conquest of Spice and the Dutch Colonial Imaginary: Seen and Unseen in the Visual Culture of Trade." In *Colonial Botany: Science, Commerce, and Politics in the Early Modern World*, edited by Londa Schiebinger and Claudia Swan, 169–86. Philadelphia, PA: University of Pennsylvania Press, 2007.

Hulme, Peter. "Polytropic Men: Tropes of Sexuality and Mobility in Early Colonial Discourse." In *Europe and Its Others: Proceedings of the Essex Conference on the Sociology of Literature*, vol. 2, edited by Francis Barker, Peter Hulme, Margaret Iversen and Diana Loxley, 17–32. Colchester: University of Essex Press, 1985.

In Reprise. "De Lijst van 100" ["The List of 100"]. Accessed 7 January 2022. http://www.inreprise.org/lijst_100?s=t&id=dwslau001janp001.

Koninklijke Bibliotheek. "J. J. Slauerhoff (1898–1936)." Royal Dutch National Library Online Resources. Accessed 7 January 2022. https://www.kb.nl/themas/nederlandse-literatuur-en-taal/schrijversalfabet/jj-slauerhoff-1898-1936.

Leeuwarder Courant: Hoofdblad van Friesland. "Toneelspel 'Jan Pieterszn. Coen' Verboden Door Burgemeester van Amsterdam" ["Staging of Play 'Jan Pieterszn. Coen' Banned by Mayor of Amsterdam"]. 20 February 1948. Delpher.

McClintock, Anne. *Imperial Leather: Race, Gender, and Sexuality in the Colonial Contest*. New York, NY: Routledge, 1995.

Pattynama, Pamela. *Bitterzoet Indië: Herinnering En Nostalgie in Literatuur, Foto's En Films* [*Bittersweet Indies: Memories and Nostalgia in Literature, Photography and Films*]. Amsterdam: Prometheus/Bert Bakker, 2014.

Pluvier, J. M. "Recent Dutch Contributions to Modern Indonesian History." *Journal of Southeast Asian History* 8, no. 2 (1967): 201–25.

Rooduin, Tom. "De Beul van Banda" ["The Killer of Banda"]. *Radio Doc*, 19 March 2017. https://www.nporadio1.nl/radio-doc/onderwerpen/399724-de-beul-van-banda.

Slauerhoff, J. J. *Jan Pietersz. Coen*. 1931. Reprint, Amsterdam: De nieuwe toneelbibliotheek, vol. 150, 2012.

Stoler, Ann L. "Making Empire Respectable: The Politics of Race and Sexual Morality in 20th-Century Colonial Cultures." *American Ethnologist* 16, no. 4 (1989): 634–60.

Stoler, Ann L. *Carnal Knowledge and Imperial Power: Race and the Intimate in Colonial Rule*. Berkeley, CA: University of California Press, 2002.

Veenstra, J. H. W. "Slauerhoff, Coen En de Oorlogsmisdaden" ["Slauerhoff, Coen and the War Crimes"]. *Maatstaf* 17, no. 6 (1970): 337–50.

Wekker, Gloria. *White Innocence: Paradoxes of Colonialism and Race*. Durham, NC: Duke University Press, 2016.

Werner, Michael, and Bénédicte Zimmermann. "Beyond Comparison: *Histoire Croisée* and the Challenge of Reflexivity." *History and Theory* 45, no. 1 (2006): 30–50.

Westfries Museum, Vind Magazine, and Polder Vondsten, eds. *Coen! Geroemd En Verguisd* [*Coen! Praised and Reviled*]. Hoorn: Westfries Museum, 2012. Accessed 4 March 2022. https://wfm.nl/coen.

Wolters, M. "Het Nederlandsche Repertoire" ["The Dutch Repertory"]. *De Waag*, 27 October 1944, 596.

Zuiderweg, Adrienne. "Sara En Pieter, Een Bataviase Liefdesaffaire" ["Sara and Pieter, a Batavian Love Affair"]. *Indische Letteren* 22 (2007): 2–15.

PART IV
Emergence and Transformation of Genres

7

REVERSIBILITY AS HISTORIOGRAPHICAL METHOD

Japanese Theater and Its Doubles

Carol Fisher Sorgenfrei

"The past is a foreign country: They do things differently there."[1] So begins L. P. Huntley's 1953 novel *The Go-Between*. But just how foreign is the past? Can we ever know it, or will it remain forever alien? Historians continually attempt to answer that question, often guided only by the equivalent of faded snapshots or blurry, inaccurate maps.

A related question might be, can the past invade the present, reside in the present, even transform the present? This question is especially relevant for Japanese theater, often historicized as a virtually unbroken, changeless tradition. This idea, however, is a misconception. As Erika Fisher-Lichte notes in the Introduction to this volume, Japan has always been welcoming of innovation, whether imported or native. At the same time, ancient, even obscure, genres continue to be performed along with newer ones. For example, the multiday Kasuga Wakamiya festival in Nara, celebrated each mid-December since 1136, is essentially a living museum of rarely performed, pre-*nō* genres. Originally religious rituals, these performances were offered as prayers to end a fierce plague and insure a good harvest. While retaining its sacred aspects, the festival (which today includes such audience-pleasing events as processions of costumed samurai, horseback archery, *sumo* wrestling, etc.) also serves as a valuable resource for theater researchers.

Although numerous early Japanese performance genres endure as vital forms, they are not and never have been frozen in time. For example, *nō* is now performed at a far more leisurely pace than in the fourteenth century (perhaps as much as two or three times slower), and supposedly unchanging *kabuki* has always been, and continues to be, in a state of perpetual transformation.[2]

In addition, new genres periodically appear, both rebelling against and being influenced by older, still active genres. The ancient genres seen in the Kasuga Wakamiya festival were crucial in the creation of fourteenth-century

DOI: 10.4324/9781003353461-12

nō and *kyōgen*, which continued to flourish while influencing the development of seventeenth-century kabuki and *bunraku*, which in turn thrived while influencing the development of nineteenth- and twentieth-century *shimpa* (a transitional genre), the *Takarazuka* Revue (an all-female genre) and *shingeki* (modern drama that intentionally rejects but cannot escape the influence of traditional forms). All these genres are alive today and typify the traditions against which the young, experimental artists of the postwar generation defined themselves, simultaneously rejecting and mining older genres for style and content. Those originally experimental works are now part of the multilayered "traditions" against which even newer, post-1990s genres (for example, quiet theater and robot theater) define themselves. It is thus clear that Japan's performance history exhibits entanglement between ancient, traditional, modern and contemporary genres within a single culture. As we will see, these already internally entangled genres have always encountered and welcomed foreign actors, technologies and practices, adding an additional layer of entanglement to interweaving with an outside "Other."

In contrast, for much of Euro-American theater history, while ancient genres may exist as dramatic texts, the modes of performance (such as acting and staging) are matters of conjecture and scholarly reconstruction, requiring digging out lost bits of evidence, whether in libraries or in physical archeological sites. For example, the size of the audience, the style of stage decor, and the modes of speech, movement and music in historical genres such as ancient Greek or Elizabethan Theater remain debatable.[3]

Even with persistent change, the continuity of Japanese performance might suggest that historians have greater resources than those dealing with Western theater. Although true to a certain extent, many questions remain unanswered.[4] For this chapter, I will consider the crucial but relatively neglected (at least by theater scholars) Japanese aesthetic theory of reversibility, followed by a discussion of reversibility as historiographical method. Reversibility helps explain why so many key innovators and artists in every era were members of "outsider" groups, including (at various times) foreigners, females, Christians, the blind or disabled, apparently supernatural beings, the lower classes, and even inanimate objects. Due to space limitations, I will confine the discussion to nō, but the theory of reversibility is valid for all periods, as I hope to demonstrate in a future, longer work. This chapter concludes with a brief discussion of the relationship between reversibility and entanglement, and queries if reversibility might be useful in analyzing contemporary, non-Japanese performance.

Reversibility and Otherness

The term "reversibility" as used here is derived primarily from the ideas of contemporary philosopher and aesthetician Sakabe Megumi (1936–2009).[5] Reversibility is a condition in which apparently incongruous opposites simultaneously co-exist and reflect (or mirror) each other. In this chapter, I will focus on the relationship between the self (personal and national) and what I call its double (or other).

Reversibility's key dyads include *omote/ura* and *soto/uchi*.[6] "Omote" means visible, open, or public, and can also denote face or mask. "Ura" means inside, secret, hidden, back, or private. The related dyad *tatemae* (outward, formal appearance; the social consensus and conventions by which humans enact a public life) and *honne* (true inner feelings, unexpressed or concealed emotions) has been felicitously translated as "onstage/backstage."[7] In public, people mask their feelings by displaying omote and behave according to onstage tatemae. In contrast, they hide their deepest ura, exhibiting backstage honne only to intimate relations. However, there is always an element of secret ura in the most outward facing omote, and of hidden honne in the most public tatemae. Omote/ura and tatemae/honne are primarily personal and deal with the individual or psychological sense of self, but because omote also means mask, the concepts are especially useful in performance theory.[8]

In contrast, soto/uchi refers to broader social relationships. "Soto"(outside) implies "not in the house," while "uchi"(inside) can also mean house––both a dwelling and also one's family, clan and even nation. There is thus a continuum of relationships from the most intimate of groups to which one belongs (the immediate family) to the most extended of groups (such as school, employment, city, nation, race or even "human being").

Sakabe emphasizes that "omote" and "ura" are reversible and reciprocal; the outside exists only because the inside exists, and the outside can be substituted for the inside. Sakabe notes that

> in traditional Japanese thought, there is neither the category of Cartesian substance nor any kind of rigid or fixed dualism between soul and body, exterior and interior, seen and unseen. It seems to me that nothing is more alien to Japanese thought than Cartesian dualism. [...] In short, in Japanese traditional thought there is nothing but surfaces [...] that are, at least in principle, strictly reversible, the one into the other.[9]

Sakabe continues,

> on the nō stage (including the "Kagami no Ma" [room of the mirror]), which is surrounded several times symbolically and physically by the structure of the mirror, there is nothing but the play of various surfaces or various reflections (including, of course the song *"utai"* [performed by the main actor] and the chorus *"ji-utai"* [the chorus performs the main actor's lines when he dances, often using first-person voice]). [...] There is nothing but a play of identity and difference, without any strictly fixed

identity. Even the "persons" (first, second and third personal pronouns) are not strictly fixed....

On the nō stage, even the world of the dead *"yukai"* and our world, the terrestrial world, the unseen and the seen, finally put themselves in a relationship of reversibility and reciprocity. [...]

Nothing exists but surfaces, grids of surfaces. Nothing but *"omote."* Nothing but reflections. Nothing but shades. Therefore, there are no substantial beings, no being that has been fixed in its sameness. Nothing exists but a world of diverse and infinite metamorphosis.[10]

Reversibility therefore posits the simultaneous existence of the material and the nonmaterial. In indigenous Japanese ways of thinking, ideas such as cause and effect, absolute morality, or inevitable progress are absent. Rather, indigenous thought (including Shintō) emphasizes harmony and purity; evil is due to demonic forces that require exorcism. These early Japanese ideologies remain potent despite Buddhism's (imported in the sixth century) emphasis on personal karma (cause and effect) and its goals of ending eternal rebirth and attaining enlightenment (progress toward perfection). Sakabe's theory of reversibility helps elucidate the links between Buddhism and pre-Buddhist Japanese thought.

Because this chapter emphasizes the social status/class of "others," it may be useful to note key similarities and differences between my use of reversibility and materialist historiography. Materialism, derived from Marxism, emphasizes the impact on human history of material social conditions such as economics and class. Materialist historiography posits that the concrete, day-to-day factors of everyday life (not grand, philosophic ideas) fuel historical change. Thus Marx discarded Hegel's Christian Idealism while borrowing his dialectic methodology. The current chapter likewise demonstrates that ideological convictions spring from the requirements of daily life. Marx contradicted himself regarding the question of whether history progresses toward an inevitable goal (the classic Eurocentric and Buddhist views); contemporary proponents of historical materialism likewise differ.[11] Most significantly, materialism's emphasis on facts rather than ideas or beliefs ties it to the scientific method, which aims to prove or disprove a thesis.[12] Thus "either/or" is crucial to both the scientific method and materialist historiography. In contrast, reversibility emphasizes "both/and," the simultaneous co-existence and mutuality of apparent opposites. This is the most significant difference between materialist historiography and reversibility.

Using reversibility, this chapter will focus on people or entities (including certain nominally inanimate objects) often seen as "outsiders," including those whose social status would traditionally be considered so low as to verge on being "nonhuman." By the reversible, transformative processes described

Reversibility and Foreigners

At first glance, the concept of the incorporation of the double or other into the self seems to contradict commonly held conceptions of Japan. Despite genetic evidence,[13] there remains a stubborn belief, both inside and outside Japan, that the Japanese people and culture are unique and homogeneous. This concept is central to the ideology of Japanese exceptionalism, called *nihonjinron* (the study of Japaneseness), fostered by right-wing nationalists. Beginning in the seventeenth century, and especially since the Meiji era (1868–1912), cultural nationalists have emphasized the Emperor's direct descent from supreme Shintō deity Amaterasu Omikuni. However, after Japan's defeat in World War II, then Emperor Hirohito was forced to publicly renounce his divinity. Although the Japanese classic *Nihongi* (Chronicles of Japan, seventh century) states that the imperial family is at least partially of Korean origin, advocates of nihonjinron deny it. They were thus dismayed when then Emperor Akihito embraced his Korean heritage on his sixty-eighth birthday in 2001.[14]

Historically, Japanese self-concepts in relation to other cultures have wavered between superiority and inferiority. China was a significant influence, more so in certain periods. By the late fourteenth century, when nō was being developed, Chinese culture was again making inroads. The nō play *Haku Rakuten* responded by implying Japanese superiority. In the play, the great Chinese poet Bai Juyi (aka Po Chü-I, 772–847), known in Japan as Haku Rakuten, attempts to enter Japan via boat. Two Japanese fishermen, one of whom is the Japanese god of poetry, sail out to meet him. Through dance and song, they demonstrate the superiority of Japanese over Chinese poetry. The divine wind (*kamikaze*) generated by their dancing sleeves blows the would-be invader back to China.

The notion that foreign "others" were crucial to the development of Japanese culture is thus a fraught one. However, since ancient times, the Japanese have welcomed and feared *marebito* (rare strangers), supernatural visitors who came from across the waters bringing gifts and happiness. They were often associated with sorcery and the keeping of witch animals; even today, folk rituals feature performers dressed and masked as marebito, who offer blessings at village festivals and harvests (see Figure 7.1).

Spanish Japanologist Alfonso Falero notes, "According to [Japanese ethnologist Origuchi Shinobu (1887–1963)], the people incarnating the marebito belonged to three classes: people with the appearance of *kami* [gods or entities partaking of sacredness], performers, and beggars."[15] Situating Origuchi's concept of "marebito" in relation to discussions of otherness, American anthropologist Emiko Ohnuki-Tierney (b. 1934) writes, "the marebito, or

FIGURE 7.1 A dancing drummer wearing a Namahage costume, performing Namahage-Daiko in Akita Station (2010).

Source: Wikimedia Commons.

stranger-outsider deities who come from outside a settlement or outside of Japan, constitute the semiotic *other* for the Japanese, which is symbolically equivalent to their transcendental self, that is, the *self* perceived at a higher level of abstraction than a reflective self."[16]

While marebito were imagined as looking Japanese or East Asian, making entry into the uchi relatively easy, all foreigners partake of a similar ambiguity. Japanese cultural anthropologist Yoshida Teigo (b. 1923) remarks that

> Japanese attitudes toward foreigners who came to Japan from the West during the sixteenth and following centuries also contained much that was ambiguous. The foreigners were often attributed by Japanese as having mystical powers. On the one hand, they were seen as mystically dangerous; yet, on the other hand, they were often considered to have some supernatural ability, e.g., the power to find miraculous stones which could bestow longevity and even eternal life.[17]

The power of marebito is also evident in legends about miraculous masks that are caught in fishermen's nets, or that drift ashore, or that fall from heaven.[18]

The traditional origin of theater, recounted in the myth of Amaterasu (goddess of the sun, supreme deity of Shintō, and the supposed ancestor of the imperial family), equates performers with "sacred others." Angry at her mischievous brother, Amaterasu hid herself in a cave and blocked the entrance with stone, depriving the universe of the life-giving sun. In the darkness, another goddess, Uzume, leaped onto an overturned rain barrel, disarranged her clothing to reveal her genitals, and began a lewd dance. The assembled deities roared with laughter, causing the curious sun goddess to peek out. Whereupon, they seized her, displayed ritual objects, and forced her to look at herself in a mirror. Thus entranced by her own reversed image, she was lured out, saving the world from eternal darkness and sterility. This myth demonstrates that performance, divinity, female sexuality, inside/outside, and reversed mirror images form the heart of Japanese conceptions of a national self.

Nō founder Zeami Motokiyo (ca. 1363–1443) discusses this myth to suggest that his art, while created by members of the lowest class, partakes of holiness.

Reversibility and Masks

Sacred objects can be dangerous. In 1594, nō actor Kongō Ujimasa, to impress the emperor, cut off the face of a Fudō statue to use as a mask.[19] After the performance, the mask remained glued to his face, so that removing it drew blood, which is said to stain the back of the mask to this day.[20]

Such stories suggest an immutable connection between divinity and performance, demonstrating both the mask's power and the unity of actor and character (and omote and ura). From the Buddhist perspective, they also suggest that defacing a sacred object results in punishment. Such ideas are absent in indigenous Japanese thought. For example, Shintō focuses on the creation of harmony and purity rather than on obedience to moral rules.

This legend also implies that carved wooden masks, though nominally inanimate, are sentient. Any observer of nō will attest that the mask seems to come alive in performance. At one moment, it may appear to be smiling; at another, it appears to be crying. This transformative ability is due partly to the skill of the mask-maker and partly to the skill of the actor (see Figure 7.2).[21]

Nō masks can also be doubles, simultaneously two things in one. Japanese nō scholar Yokomichi Mario (1916–2012) notes that the *hannya* demon mask embodies the duality of nō's view of females. When the upper half of the mask is covered, the jaw, with its open mouth and pointed teeth, reveals demonic rage; when the bottom is covered, the forehead seems to be a furrowed brow, suggesting a deeply anguished, heartbroken woman.[22] The origin of nō masks

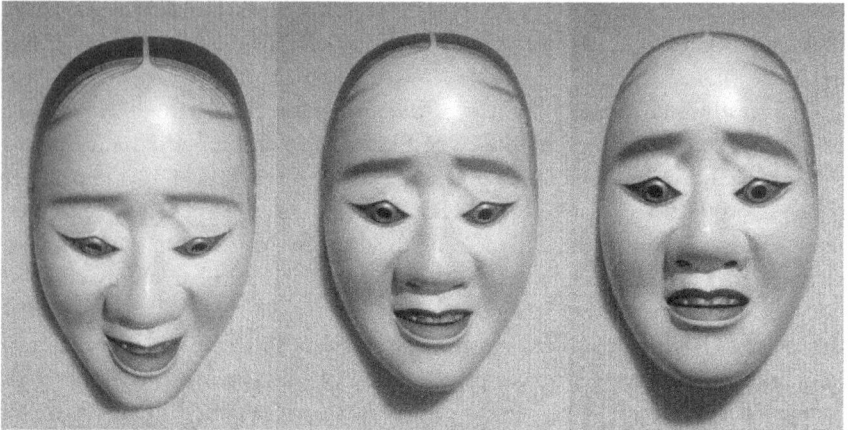

FIGURE 7.2 This image of a *nō* mask shows how the expression changes with the tilting of the head.

Source: Wikimedia Commons.

is inconclusive, but one theory suggests derivation from large masks used in some pre-nō genres. Zeami may have been thinking of these when he wrote in his treatise *Sarugaku dangi* that, to create a pleasing visual image, "the top of the forehead of a long mask should be cut off."[23]

Regardless of origins,[24] the crucial question is how nō masks were used in performance and how the audience responded.[25] To consider these issues, we turn to the creation of nō.

Reversibility and Class

Part 1: Performing Social Roles

Korean monks brought Buddhism to Japan in 538 or 552. Thereafter, the Buddhist term "*hinin*" (literally, nonhuman) was used to signify vagrants, actors, dancers, beggars and others who lived in "non-spaces"—for instance, at crossroads or under bridges. Because these denizens of the soto world lacked a fixed or settled abode (a home or inside area, uchi), they were considered "nonhuman." The traditional outcasts (*burakumin* aka *eta*) are also hinin but with even lower status. The position of women varied, from high in an earlier gynocentric (not matrilineal) society to lower in periods that excluded women from power. Priests and the imperial family were not included in any class.

The twelfth and thirteenth centuries were filled with clan warfare, the alternating rule by (and usurpation of) the imperial family, the growing power of warrior monks, the transformation of the samurai class, the Genpei War (1180–1185, a civil war between rival clans), earthquakes, famines, rebellions, epidemics and two attempted Mongol invasions (1274 and 1281). Memories of these traumas, especially the Genpei War, are the defining beacons of medieval Japan. The Genpei War was immortalized in the crucial epic *Heike Monogatari* (Tales of the Heike, thirteenth century), the origin of many nō and kabuki plays. It displays an empathic focus on noble losers rather than victorious warriors, and includes powerful tales of female bravery and sacrifice. The stories were originally oral recitations performed by blind biwa players (the biwa is a stringed instrument). The Genpei War ended with the defeat of the Taira by the Genji (aka Minamoto) clan, marking the first time that the samurai became the undoubted rulers of Japan (the emperors remained in name but were powerless). Finally, after sixty years of rival imperial courts, the Ashikaga shōgunate (the *shōgun* was the supreme military ruler) took control, opening the Muromachi era (1336 or 1338–1573, also called the Ashikaga era), a time of peace and artistic brilliance.

These new rulers, formerly despised but necessary soldiers, now displaced or joined the ranks of the hereditary aristocrats who had fostered (since 795) a distinctive Japanese culture incorporating both native (often female-centered) and imported (primarily Chinese, often male-centered) elements. Thus, by the time Zeami Motokiyo was born, the normative or controlling Japanese "self" would have been perceived as a healthy male samurai, with the newly defeated aristocrats only slightly diminished in status. Foreigners, supernatural beings (including the dead), apparently supernatural objects (including masks), women, the blind or disabled, and the lower classes (including performers) were outside this self, and thus considered "others." Yet, it is these others who reflected and "doubled" the self, and whose incorporation into the self permitted the creation of new ideas and new forms of artistic expression, here exemplified by nō. Singaporean Japanologist Lim Beng Choo (b. 1962) emphasizes the often-overlooked significance of outsiders shifting to the inside:

> The process by which the *sarugaku* noh, a genre that once belonged to the "social outcasts," emerged to be one that was embraced by all members of the society has often been taken for granted. [Lim provides a lengthy endnote of examples] A close examination of this change, however, shows that it is no accident that noh theatre developed the way it did. Both the audience and the performers participated, consciously or unconsciously, in redefining the noh theatre. The performers performed what they deemed most appropriate, incorporating both their own creativity and the anticipated preferences of the audience. The audience, on the other hand, came to see the show with certain expectations that were closely related to the élite members' artistic taste. In an abstract sense, "negotiations" as to what the best show might be took place constantly between the two parties.[26]

Zeami's father, Kan'ami Kiyotsugu (1333–1384), headed a popular troupe of *sarugaku* actors. Sarugaku (monkey music) was a masked genre consisting of skits and circus-like acts. Derived primarily from mainland Asian imports, sarugaku was sometimes performed in conjunction with Buddhist prayers for the dead. An even more popular masked genre, *dengaku* (field music), was derived from native fertility and planting rituals, and thus was associated with female sexuality and the dance of Uzume.

At least since the eleventh century, the imperial family and other nobility had enjoyed viewing peasants performing ritual dengaku. In one famous instance, the nobility literally looked down on the dancing farmers from a discrete height in their palatial pavilion, both as entertainment and possibly as a way to reinforce class distinctions and the dominance of urban over rural culture.[27]

Dengaku eventually became interwoven with colorful, urban processions (*furyū*) meant to placate the angry spirits, demons and deities assumed responsible for Kyoto's numerous disasters (fires, earthquakes, drought, etc.). Israeli Japanologist Jacob Raz (b. 1944) suggests that dengaku's interweaving with furyū encouraged a positive relationship between rural (peasant) and urban (including nobility) society, aiding in strengthening the emperor's (and diminishing the regents') power during the late eleventh century.[28]

Although it became ever more raucous and out of control, furyū dengaku was patronized by audiences from all classes. An account from 1096 "notes that the performance was seen 'by all classes, high and low,' and [...] that it 'drove everyone crazy.'"[29] Raz goes on to describe

> a wave of licentiousness and curiosity towards new forms of art. [...] In 1127, at the Gion festival, daimyō [heads of samurai clans], miko [Shintō priestesses], [Buddhist] priests, children, dengaku players and others marched in the streets in gorgeous costumes. With the growing intercourse between upper and lower classes, the latter used various occasions to wear extravagant attire in showy parades, in imitation of the nobles' costumes and customs. This craze, using religious parades and expressing the imitation instinct, developed sometimes from mass dances to mass violence and disorder.[30]

Diaries closer to Zeami's time relate shocking, often dangerous dengaku performances, filled with exotic, terrifying masks and costumes, out-of-control audiences who danced (sometimes naked) as though possessed for days, drunkenness, lewd behavior, and even a riot following the collapse of a seating structure.[31]

It is therefore hardly surprising that in 1375, courtiers of the seventeen-year-old Yoshimitsu (1358–1408), the third Ashikaga shōgun, encouraged him to patronize sarugaku rather than dengaku. Entranced (perhaps sexually) by the eleven-year-old Zeami, Yoshimitsu invited Kan'ami's troupe to reside at his palace, thereby transforming commoner (actually classless) actors into de facto members of the court. They would live with and perform for the aristocrats, not for the common people they previously entertained. However, the tastes of these aristocrats, formerly used to the refined delicacy of the emperor, conflicted with those of the high-spirited, brash, rather vulgar shōgun.

Although the courtiers viewed class mingling with disdain, they were realists who needed samurai support. They saw the young Zeami, the shōgun's new favorite, as a key to refining Yoshimitsu's style. Under the tutelage of poet/courtier Nijō Yoshimoto (1320–1388), Zeami gradually focused his art more on *yūgen* (refined, idealized elegance) and less on *monomane* (the imitation of things). While retaining performance elements suggestive of Shintō,[32] nō's content became more clearly Buddhist. Eventually, Zeami and other actors tied to the court were given the status of Buddhist priests, allowing the upper classes to more comfortably associate with them.

As nō was developing, Yoshimitsu reestablished trade with China, encouraged improvements in agriculture, and shifted the system of inheritance away from widows and toward sons. While these changes created prosperity, they also created anxieties, including the need to placate the unruly spirits of displaced women and defeated clan members. As the following example shows, these conflicts and this need are crucial aspects of many nō texts.

In *Atsumori* (inspired by *The Tale of the Heike*), the tormented but victorious warrior-turned-monk Kumagai prays for the soul of the defeated Atsumori, asking his forgiveness. Many years have passed. Now, he meets a simple, lower-class reaper, actually the ghost of Atsumori in disguise. Atsumori, a delicate, flute-playing, fifteen-year-old noble has delayed retreating from battle to retrieve his beloved flute, thus unintentionally meeting his death at the hands of Kumagai, a mature warrior lacking Atsumori's cultivation. Now, the two suffering men (one living, one dead) relive their most passionate moment of mutual warfare, victory and defeat, and together find Buddhist peace. Their souls will be joined eternally on the same lotus. They are simultaneously mirror images and opposites, reflections of the brash new samurai regime forced to work with the defeated aristocracy.

The flute's music alerts Kumagai to the reaper's true identity, tying the play to marebito; as Falero notes, "[…] a striking point in [Origuchi's] text […] is that, as spiritual entities, marebito [*sic*] are heard and not seen."[33] Zeami himself wrote that in nō, the auditory takes precedence over the visual:

> As a general rule, it is on the basis of the meaning that all stage action should come into being. That which manifests the meaning is words. For that reason, vocal music constitutes the causal agent, and acting, its effect. Therefore, the natural order is for bodily movement to arise out of the vocal music. It is backward to perform the vocal music on the basis of the bodily expression.[34]

In performance, music and words precede and inspire acting and dance; the immaterial precedes and evokes the material.[35] Before seeing him, Kumagai mistakenly assumed the flute player would be an aristocrat. He says, "one does not look for such music from men of your condition."[36] Just as invisible marebito chant sacred words, Atsumori's disguised ghost offers Kumagai a chance at salvation. Atsumori is simultaneously a peasant reaper and a delicate noble; Kumagai is simultaneously a wandering monk and a hardened warrior. Without Kumagai's intervention, Atsumori could not reach salvation, just as Kumagai is doomed without Atsumori's forgiveness.

The next part of my analysis is complicated by the linguistic identity (and consequent ambiguity) of "omote" as both "face" and "mask." Atsumori's personal reversibility is most clearly demonstrated by being unmasked in the first part of the play, thus revealing ura (his true nature) but hiding (masking) his class identity, which would normally be visible in the features of his physical face (omote). In the second part, Atsumori wears a wooden mask (omote), having chosen to reveal his identity upon hearing Kumagai's prayers. Thus his normally outward-facing omote (his corporeal face) is literally covered, represented by (or identical with) the wooden mask (omote) that hides it. The wooden mask (omote) of the second part reveals his true identity, while the corporeal face (omote) of the first part hides his identity but reveals (in conjunction with the flute) his hidden ura.

The unmasked reaper's ura and the masked aristocrat's ura are mirror images, identical and reversible. Similarly, the older, tormented Kumagai (who, as the *waki* or secondary character remains unmasked throughout the play, his ura always visible due to his anguished need for forgiveness) mirrors and reverses the delicate, defeated Atsumori.

Although the nō Atsumori is unusual in that the *shite* (main character) and *waki* (secondary character) share a prior connection, the play typifies how transformation is used to reveal and reverse class structure. For example, plays about the poetess Ono no Komachi (ca. 825–900) often depict her as a decrepit beggar woman who is revealed to have been a beautiful aristocrat. Others depict the innate elegance and nobility of anguished, lower- or middle-class women deprived of child or lover. Such Buddhist-inflected nō plays suggest the reversibility not only of class but of age and youth, beauty and ugliness, victory and defeat, spirituality and materiality, life and death.

Part 2: Acting

As an actor training other actors, Zeami often writes of doubleness. For example, he insists that

> when an actor plans to express the emotion of anger, he must not fail to retain a tender heart. [...] On the other hand, in a performance requiring

[yūgen], an actor must not forget to remain strong. [...] When he moves himself about in a powerful way, he must stamp his foot in a gentle way. And when he stamps his feet strongly, he must hold the upper part of his body quiet.[37]

Unlike the display of omote and ura in daily life, when ura can only be revealed to one's closest intimates, onstage acting demands the ability to shift ura as needed. Such doubleness/otherness and reciprocity are crucial to both masked or unmasked roles. Revealing too much ura creates vulgarity.

In nō, the actor remains himself while simultaneously permitting the other to enter him; it is as though the mask (omote) is an open window (or more aptly, a semi-translucent sliding *shōji* screen) between the outside world (soto) and the inner sanctum (uchi), which is the abode of ura. Sakabe writes,

> In the Kagami-no-Ma [Room of the Mirror], the actor puts on the mask; he sees in the mirror his own face or his own mask; at the same time, he is seen by his mask in the mirror and, finally, he sees himself transmogrified in some deity or demon. Afterward [...] the actor enters the stage as a self transmogrified into an other or as an other transmogrified into the self. [...] What is important to notice now is the fact that the structure of "*omote*" is evidently the structure of the mask, as we have seen, but at the same time, it is also the structure of the face. The reason is that the face also is what is seen by the other, what sees itself, and what sees itself as the other.[38]

For Zeami, the key point is the actor's relationship to the audience, "the other." For Zeami, the viewer's perception is more important than the actor's experience. He emphasizes "*riken no ken*," or a detached view. The actor must imaginatively see himself as though from a distance, even from the rear:

> As concerns the dance, it is said that "the eyes look ahead and the mind looks behind." This expression means that the actor looks in front of him with his physical eyes, but his inner concentration must be directed to the appearance of his movements from behind. [...] In order to see himself from a detached point of view [riken no ken], the actor must put himself in the audience's place. [...] If the actor cannot somehow come to a sense of how he looks from behind, he will not be able to become conscious of any possible vulgarities in his performance. [...] To repeat again, an actor must come to have an ability to see himself as the spectators do, grasp the logic of the fact that the eyes cannot see themselves, and find the skill to grasp the whole—left and right, ahead and behind.[39]

The emphasis on the audience as "other" is crucial to understanding Zeami's place at court. Despite elevation to priestly status, as actors, Zeami and his troupe would always be classless. Therefore, in various ways, Zeami insists that his art is for all types of audiences. This point is made clear by Japanese literary scholar Nishio Minoru (1889–1979), who interprets riken no ken as implying "caring for the common folk," presumably because the actor is concerned not only about his own acting but, more importantly, about how his art is perceived by the audience.[40]

In the *Fūshikaden*, Zeami maintained that the actor must modify his acting depending on the mood and makeup of the audience; in *Nōsakusho*, he insisted that the goal was equalitarian: to delight the audience, whether city dwellers or village peasants.[41] Certainly, as he became more attached to the court, his aesthetics exhibited greater elements of aristocratic taste, but this basic concept—that nō was for the audience, regardless of class—remained.

Yusa Michiko (b. 1951), an expert on Japanese religion and philosophy, writes, "*Riken no ken* is the mental eye by which the actor knows what the audience sees of him and identifies his viewpoint with that of the audience."[42] Zeami wrote, "He who understands noh sees it with his mind; he who does not, sees it with his eyes."[43] He maintained that the actor's mind "renders his appearance beautiful."[44] In considering the connection of riken no ken to class (or specifically, to classlessness), Yusa explains that

> Zeami compares the actor capable of the ultimate art [...] to the authentic Zen person—what Zen Master Rinzai [d. 866] called "the true person of no fixed rank," a free person unattached to any stationary "abode." Just as an enlightened Zen-person dwells on no fixed point but manifests his or her dynamic subjectivity, so the noh actor of this caliber manifests himself as the authentic "doer," the *shite*, or the main actor in noh terminology.[45]

The Zen master possesses ultimate spiritual power, making him stronger than any secular ruler. It is thus intriguing to remember that Yoshimitsu, addicted to worldly pleasure, spent large sums to transform a dilapidated villa into a luxurious retirement palace, mandating that it be dedicated as a Zen temple upon his death. This temple is Kyoto's Kinkakuji (the Golden Pavilion), simultaneously a symbol of sybaritic extravagance and spiritual purity. This dual consciousness suggests that Yoshimitsu desired to be (or considered himself) both insider and outsider, secular ruler and holy mendicant. Of course, Yoshimitsu might also simply be covering his bets regarding the afterlife.

One of Zeami's most famous dictums demonstrates his sensitivity to the possibility of shifting between classes. In discussing the nine stages of the actor's art, Zeami maintains that crudeness should only be performed by an actor who has attained the highest level of *hana* (the flower), *yūgen* and skill. As Yusa summarizes,

> This theme of "going beyond perfection," or the idea of [...] "returning to the starting point after perfecting the ultimate stage," explains, for instance, the art of *ran'i*, a "free rank" or "free state," wherein the actor intentionally blends the imperfect into the highly polished art, thereby effecting a new, unexpected sense of delight. Zeami describes the actor who can freely move up and down the nine stages of the art of noh as a man of "wide awareness"; similarly, the spectators who can appreciate varieties of "flowers" and not merely the cherry blossoms are the superior spectators who have "expansive vision."[46]

In this chapter, we have seen how the theory of reversibility as historiographical method opens a door to new ways of viewing how the past exists in the present, how the local infuses the global, and how the popular interweaves with the elite. These processes occur in all periods and genres.[47] Using the examples of Zeami, masks, and nō, we have seen how Japan's "others" are inextricably tied to the notion of the Japanese self, and how the inner and outer worlds merge while simultaneously remaining unique. In an earlier article,[48] I argued that Asian artists often injected Euro-American aesthetics into their own cultures to move toward modernization/Westernization. In the following, however, I would like to reverse the perspective: In the spirit of riken no ken, I will ask whether the concept of "reversibility" can be usefully applied outside Japan, not only as an approach in theater historiography but also as a tool for performance analysis.

Reversibility and International Performance

Although most classical Western philosophies and the three Abrahamic religions emphasize cause and effect and inevitable progress toward a higher goal, ideologies derived from "other" cultures offer opposing ideas. Thus, despite the discomfort felt by some people schooled in traditional Western thought, concepts such as cultural, temporal or gender ambiguity are gaining ground.

It appears, then, that the current moment (unlike the Western past) permits (or demands?), almost unconsciously, the acceptance of concepts such as "non-duality" or "reversibility." If this is so, can reversibility be usefully applied to analyses of contemporary, non-Japanese performance?

To consider this question, I will use the example of Berlin's Deutsches Theater's production of *Drei Schwestern* (Three Sisters), based on Chekhov, adapted and directed by Karin Henkel, which opened on 12 November 2018 (seen 26 May 2019). The cast is reduced to five performers. The three sisters are all portrayed by masked males, who also (unmasked) portray the major male characters of the play. These four male actors are joined at the end by an unmasked actress who portrays Irina after she decides to marry the doomed Tusenbach.

Each actor, masked or unmasked, embodies a single sensibility while inhabiting dual genders. They are both omote and ura, and also quite eerie doppelgängers. Olga (masked), the oldest and a spinster, loves and supports her sisters, thus her dual role as Masha's (unmasked) male lover. Despite this energizing love, Masha (masked) is inextricably bound to her boring husband, portrayed by the same actor unmasked. Similarly, their brother Andrei (unmasked) and his wife Natasha (masked), as different as they are, and although the marriage was clearly a mistake, have become two sides of the same being, played by a single male actor. In contrast, Irina (masked), the other side of her would-be fiancé Tusenbach (unmasked), is at first ambivalent about love, but once she decides to marry, she opens herself to emotion and is transformed. She is then portrayed by a different performer, an unmasked actress (the indomitable Angela Winkler, b. 1944). Thus, body and soul are united at the conclusion. In each case, the director/adaptor seems to imply that males are incapable of deep emotion, that the frozen, unhappy women in this world are nothing but males in disguise until, like Irina, they are freed by love.

Chekhov's story is interpreted from the perspective of Irina, who is clearly traumatized by the death of Tusenbach. It opens with Irina's inner monologue, a flashback years later. During the memory, the house tilts radically to one side, everything slips or falls over, and the bloody body of Tusenbach slides into the room. It is terrifying. Rather than the Chekhovian focus on getting away to Moscow, the focus here seems to be the powerful need to find one's true self, unmasked and whole. The memory of Tusenbach—the potential for love, the trauma of death—brings Irina's multiple selves or genders together. As in Chekhov, the security of the house (specifically the playroom) is inviolate; characters only leave the safety of uchi and venture into the terrifying world of soto during moments of crisis, transformation or trauma (the fire, Irina's acceptance of Tusenbach's love, Tusenbach's death, and the departure of the military).

At several other traumatic moments, the room tilts, causing objects to fall and actors to slide to the side (see Figure 7.3). It is unlikely that Henkel intentionally referenced kabuki, but nonetheless, this choice seems to do so. The origin of the term "kabuki" is the verb "*kabuku*," which means off-kilter, tilted radically to the side. It referred originally to young people who behaved in an outrageous manner, and was soon applied to the shocking, anti-establishment performances of cross-dressing, class-crossing actors. While not using masks, kabuki toys radically with gender and identity. Kabuki is also an all-male genre in which star actors sometimes portray multiple characters and genders in a single play. However, the point of doubling in kabuki is to display the actor's skill rather than to suggest psychological subtext. It demonstrates

FIGURE 7.3 Angela Winkler, Benjamin Lillie in Karin Henkel's *Drei Schwestern* (*Three Sisters*), Deutsches Theater Berlin, 2018.

Source: Photo by Arno Declair.

versatility, offering surprise and pleasure to the audience, by using impossibly quick changes and doubles (who sometimes appear onstage together with the main actor, so that his two characters can perform simultaneously). Of course, it also references the actor's doubleness as discussed above. In this version of *Drei Schwestern*, in contrast, the rationale for doubling is primarily psychological.

All genres of Japanese theater, regardless of historical period, seem to have emerged in response to social or cultural trauma.[49] For example, kabuki developed during a period of isolation from the rest of the world, but memories of traumatic events from both the distant and recent past are embedded in kabuki's present. Similarly, traumatic memory is key to Henkel's version of Chekhov. Might the traumatic memories in this *Drei Schwestern* reflect or reference German memory (and anti-memory) of the country's traumatic twentieth century? Might the masking and unmasking suggest the reversibility and nonduality of past and present, approved public self and hidden, guilty self? Possible historical reflections within this production might include an ambivalent love/hate for the military (the garrison is stationed in the town, and both Masha's and Irina's lovers are soldiers) and desire for a lost, distant but glorious past (longing for Moscow, vanished childhood, and a time before the father's death). In addition, the trauma of fire as depicted by copious and long-lasting smoke is suggestive, perhaps, of a German victim/perpetrator dual mentality: the memory of wartime firebombing (Germany as victim) and the smoke rising from gas chambers (Germany as perpetrator).

Returning to the quotation that opens this chapter, "The past is a foreign country: They do things differently there," we can conclude that reversibility is a historiographical methodology that is closely aligned with entanglement—in this case, between Germany's past and present, and between theatrical memory and theatrical innovation. The production is both an example of the past invading the present (within the world of the play and, potentially, in the minds of the audiences) and a radical rethinking and interweaving of a Russian (soto) classic with the German (uchi) self. Like the Japanese model discussed in the main portion of this chapter, it illustrates how performative interweaving can be understood through the historiographical methodologies of reversibility and entanglement.

The past and the present, male and female, mask and face, victim and perpetrator, nō, kabuki and postmodernism, Chekhov and Henkel—all exist simultaneously as doubles, interwoven in the world of reversibility. Although it seems that some types of contemporary Western theater can comfortably accept reversibility and nonduality, classic or pre-modern Western theater productions (and texts) may not be amenable to analysis using these Japanese concepts, due to the stranglehold of "both/and" thinking.

Notes

1 L. P. Hartley, *The Go-Between* (1953; repr., New York, NY: New York Review of Books, 2002), 17.
2 For example, the late James C. Brandon demonstrated that wartime kabuki included new works featuring nationalistic propaganda, contemporary costumes and even biological women performing female roles. See, for example, James R. Brandon, *Kabuki's Forgotten War: 1931–1945* (Honolulu, HI: University of Hawai'i Press, 2009). In nō, kyōgen, kabuki and bunraku, performers both past and present create and discard supposedly "traditional" gestures, staging, costuming and so on. Samuel L. Leiter documents kabuki's continuous self-reinvention (past and present) in his books, articles and ongoing blog. See, for example, Samuel L. Leiter, *Rising from the Flames: The Rebirth of Theater in Occupied Japan, 1945–1952* (Lanham, MD: Lexington, 2009) and the weblog *Kabuki Woogie* at http://kabukiwoogie.blogspot.com.
3 Occasionally, of course, archeology and other new discoveries radically transform our relationship to and understanding of the past. The ongoing excavations of London's Elizabethan playhouses is one example. Another is how our perception of nō was totally overturned in 1908 by historian/geographer Yoshida Tōgo (1864–1918), who discovered Zeami's *Fūshi Kaden* (also known as *Kadenshō*) in a private library in Japan. Previously, only nō actors and a few samurai had access to this work.
4 For example, why do so many Japanese genres develop in response to cultural trauma?
5 East Asian names are traditionally written with the family name first. I will use this traditional pattern unless the person normally uses the Western name order. For details on Sakabe's career and significance, see James W. Heisig, Thomas P.

Kasulis and John C. Maraldo, *Japanese Philosophy: A Sourcebook* (Honolulu, HI: University of Hawai'i Press, 2011), 979.
6 Omote/ura has been popularized by Japanese psychoanalyst Doi Takeo, and soto/uchi is commonly discussed by sociologists/anthropologists. In this chapter, I will focus primarily on the use of these terms in aesthetic analysis, focusing on the ideas of philosopher Sakabe Megumi.
7 Nancy R. Rosenberger, "Introduction," in *Japanese Sense of Self*, ed. Nancy R. Rosenberger (Cambridge: Cambridge University Press, 1992), 14.
8 The mask in nō is sometimes referred to as *"nōmen"* or *"nohmen,"* but "omote" is also used.
9 Megumi Sakabe, "Mask and Shadow in Japanese Culture: Implicit Ontology in Japanese Thought," in *Modern Japanese Aesthetics: A Reader*, ed. Michele Marra (Honolulu, HI: University of Hawai'i Press, 1999), 247.
10 Ibid. The emphasis on surface and reversibility is not unique to nō. In a 2000 catalogue for a group exhibition at Los Angeles' Museum of Contemporary Art, visual artist Murakami Takeshi (b. 1962) first proposed his "superflat" theory as a defining characteristic of Japanese art and culture. He noted that traditional and contemporary Japanese art and popular culture (including *ukiyo-e, manga* and *anime*) emphasize two-dimensional, flat surfaces, in contrast to the Western emphasis on the illusion of three-dimensionality; in addition, he proposed that contemporary Japanese culture "flattens" distinctions between high and low art, between upper and lower classes. Murakami implied that this contemporary flattening is new, but the history of Japanese art and culture reveals otherwise. High and low art, aesthetic and utilitarian or commercial creations, traditionally co-existed, mingled, reflected each other and were in many cases literally inseparable. Well-known theatrical examples include woodblock images of kabuki actors, fabric designs, makeup, tattoos and set design. In certain eras, class distinctions also dissolved, flattened, and were reversible. The distinction between the scientific method's either/or and reversibility's both/and does not imply the rejection of factual evidence or science.
11 For an excellent discussion, see Michael Löwy, "Marx's Dialectic of Progress: Closed or Open?" *Socialism and Democracy* 14, no. 1 (2000): 35–44, esp. 39.
12 Marx consistently maintained that his method was scientific, in contrast to Idealism or religion. For an intriguing analysis, see John Bellamy Foster, Brett Clark and Richard York, *Critique of Intelligent Design: Materialism versus Creationism from Antiquity to the Present* (New York, NY: Monthly Review, 2008) and John Bellamy Foster, Brett Clark and Richard York, "The Critique of Intelligent Design: Epicurus, Marx, Darwin and Freud and the Materialist Defense of Science," *Theory and Society* 36, no. 6 (2007): 515–46. By referencing these articles, I am in no way suggesting any connection of reversibility to beliefs such as "intelligent design."
13 According to recent genetic evidence, the Japanese people are not native to Japan but originated in Northeast Asia, probably the Baikal region of Siberia. See Matsumoto Hideo, "The Origin of the Japanese Race Based on Genetic Markers of Immunoglobulin G," *Proceedings of the Japan Academy, Series B Physical and Biological Sciences* 85, no. 2 (2009): 69–82. Previously, the most accepted theory was the "dual structure model," based primarily on archeological evidence, suggesting that settlers from Southeast Asia and then later from Northeast Asia overran the earlier Ainu and Ryūkūan inhabitants. See Hanihara Kazuro, "Dual Structure Model for the Population History of the Japanese," *Japan Review*, no. 2 (1991): 1–33.
14 See Jonathan Watts, "The Emperor's New Roots," *Guardian*, 28 December 2001, https://www.theguardian.com/world/2001/dec/28/japan.worlddispatch.

15 Alfonso Falero, "Origuchi Shinobu's *Marebitoron* in Global Perspective: A Preliminary Study," in *Frontiers of Japanese Philosophy: Japanese Philosophy Abroad*, ed. James W. Heisig and Rein Raud (Nagoya: Nanzan Institute for Religion and Culture, 2010), 280.
16 Emiko Ohnuki-Tierney, *Rice as Self: Japanese Identities through Time* (Princeton, NJ: Princeton University Press, 1994), 54.
17 Yoshida Teigo, "The Stranger as God: The Place of the Outsider in Japanese Folk Religion," *Ethnology* 20, no. 2 (1981): 88.
18 See Manabu Ogura, "Drifted Deities in the Noto Peninsula," in *Studies in Japanese Folklore*, ed. Richard M. Dorson (Bloomington, IN: Indiana University Press, 1963), 133–44.
19 Fudō Myō-ō is the Japanese name of a fierce-looking Buddhist guardian deity, called Acala in Sanskrit.
20 Solrun Hoaas Pulvers, "The Noh Mask and the Mask Making Tradition" (master's thesis, Australian National University, 1978), 38–39, available online at b1224871x_Pulvers_Solrun_Hoaas.pdf.
21 In contrast, pre-nō Japanese masks, such as those seen at the Kasuga Wakamiya festival or those used in village festivals, do not share this quality. Non-nō masks are often extremely exaggerated, grotesque and often brightly painted, characteristics that to a lesser extent apply only to certain demonic or supernatural nō masks but not to the crucially human-like ones considered here. In addition, nō masks are slightly smaller than the typical adult's face, another factor that sets them apart from earlier Japanese and non-Japanese masks, which are often quite large, sometimes even covering the entire head.
22 See Frank Hoff and Willi Flindt, "The Life Structure of *Noh*: An English Version of Yokomichi Mario's Analysis of the Structure of Noh," *Concerned Theatre Japan* 2, no. 3–4 (Spring 1973): 210–56.
23 Nose Asaji, *Zeami jurokubushū hyōshaku*, 2 vols. (Tokyo: Iwanami shoten, 1971), 535, quoted in Hoaas Pulvers, "The Noh Mask," 34.
24 One likely source for the realism of many nō masks, especially old men, is the portraiture sculpture of the Kamakura era (1185–1333). Zeami's son, Motomasa (d. 1432), donated such a personalized, realistic mask to a temple in 1430 (Hoaas Pulvers, "The Noh Mask," 40–41). The first nō mask-makers were probably Buddhist monks skilled in creating Buddhist imagery. Similarly, there is a Shintō portrait sculpture of a young woman at Yoshino Mikumari Shrine in Nara that suggests such images might have influenced the mysterious faces of young women's nō masks. Significantly, unlike Buddhist sculpture, images of Shintō deities were often hidden from public view. As Hoaas Pulvers astutely notes, "The knowledge of the figures' presence would be enough to inspire awe" (ibid., 45).
25 For an incisive discussion of class and audience in early nō, see Lim Beng Choo, "They Came to Party: An Examination of the Social Status of the Medieval Noh Theatre," *Japan Forum* 16, no. 1 (2004): 111–33.
26 Ibid., 112.
27 See Jacob Raz, "Popular Entertainment and Politics: The Great Dengaku of 1096," *Monumenta Nipponica* 40, no. 3 (1985): 283–98.
28 Ibid.
29 Jacob Raz, *Audience and Actors: A Study of Their Interactions in the Japanese Traditional Theatre* (Leiden: Brill, 1983), 58.
30 Ibid., 59.
31 Cf. Patrick G. O'Neill, *Early Nō Drama: Its Background, Character and Development, 1300–1450* (London: Lund Humphries, 1958), 75–77.
32 The architecture of the stage, appearance of multiple pine trees, foot stamping ("demon-quelling") dances, and the almost shamanistic relationship between actor and character/mask (see my discussion of mirrors) evoke Shintō shrines and practices.

33 Falero, "Origuchi Shinobu's *Marebitoron*," 278.
34 Zeami, quoted in Shelley Fenno Quinn, *Developing Zeami: The Noh Actor's Attunement in Practice* (Honolulu, HI: University of Hawai'i Press, 2005), 116.
35 This is another instance of how analysis of nō using a strictly materialist historiography would be mistaken. In nō, as in other aspects of indigenous Japanese thought, the immaterial precedes the material. In life, however, the material often dominates, further demonstrating the power of "both/and."
36 "Atsumori by Seami," *Sacred Texts*, accessed 10 July 2019, https://www.sacred-texts.com/shi/npj/npj08.htm.
37 Zeami, "Teachings on Style and the Flower (*Fūshikaden*)," in *On the Art of the Nō Drama: The Major Treatises of Zeami*, trans. J. Thomas Rimer and Yamazaki Masakazu (Princeton, NJ: Princeton University Press, 1984), 58.
38 Sakabe, "Mask and Shadow in Japanese Culture," 245.
39 Zeami, quoted in ibid., 246.
40 Nishio Minoru, quoted in Yusa Michiko, "Riken no Ken: Zeami's Theory of Acting and Theatrical Appreciation," *Monumenta Nipponica* 42, no. 3 (1987): 332.
41 Yusa, "Riken no Ken," 333.
42 Ibid., 335.
43 Ibid.
44 Ibid.
45 Ibid., 341.
46 Ibid.
47 See Jane M. Law, *Puppets of Nostalgia: The Life, Death, and Rebirth of the Japanese Awaji Ningyō Tradition* (Princeton, NJ: Princeton University Press, 1997), 201–2. Consider, for example, contemporary robot performance, such as those by Hirata Oriza. Robots may appear to be totally modern, but their history in Japan goes back to imported and native *karakuri* (mechanical or trick objects, including dolls and puppets). Puppets (*ningyō*, human form, also translated as doll) have a long tradition in Japanese ritual and theatrical performance, where they are vessels for receiving the divine presence, which originates in the outside (uchi) world. Until the late nineteenth century, puppets retained this sense of holiness and even life-likeness; dilapidated puppets, like deceased humans, were buried in cemeteries. While most puppets, including Japan's highly complex *bunraku* puppets, are manipulated by humans (either visible or hidden), their ancestors, cousins and descendants include various mechanical devices or automata. The earliest Asian automaton was the third century BCE Chinese South Pointing Chariot (a kind of compass). The Chinese also adopted Babylonian water clocks. Such devices were later imported into Japan via Korea. See "Karakuri Origins," *karakuri*, 14 January 2008, http://www.karakuri.info/origins/index.html. European traders and missionaries were active in Japan from 1543 until 1639, when Japan was finally closed to all foreign contact (a situation that lasted until 1853, when Japan was forced to open for trade). During that intense century of contact, St. Francis Xavier missionized Japan. In 1551, he brought with him the first mechanical clock (called karakuri); while that clock is lost, another brought to the shōgun Tokugawa Ieyasu (1543–1615) fifty years later still exists and currently resides in Ieyasu's mausoleum. According to a 1796 Japanese source, all karakuri are derived from clockwork mechanisms. European clocks were the driving force in the development of stage karakuri, which included not only mechanized puppets and realistic *bunraku* dolls with various moving parts (eyes, fingers, eyebrows, etc.) but mechanical stage machinery that ultimately influenced kabuki's famous revolve, flying mechanisms, and various other seeming magical stage tricks. From the seventeenth to the nineteenth century, household karakuri dolls, such as the tea-serving doll, were popular among the middle classes. For further discussion, see Timon Screech, *The Lens Within the Heart: The Western Scientific Gaze and Popular Imagery in Later Edo*

(Honolulu, HI: University of Hawai'i Press, 2002); and Jennifer Robertson, *Robo Sapiens Japanicus: Robots, Gender, Family and the Japanese Nation* (Oakland, CA: University of California Press, 2018).
48 See Carol Fisher Sorgenfrei, "Countering 'Theoretical Imperialism': Some Possibilities from Japan," *Theatre Research International* 32, no. 3 (2007): 312–24.
49 Nō and kyōgen appeared in the fourteenth century during a period of cultural brilliance following long, devastating clan warfare and natural disasters; kabuki and bunraku developed in the seventeenth century during a period of total isolation from the rest of the world following civil war and attempted incursions by cultural, national and religious others; shimpa, shingeki and Takarazuka were created in the late nineteenth and early twentieth centuries, following the end of forced national isolation, and the imposition of rapid modernization/Westernization and of Japanese colonization/militarization; butō and *angura* arose after 1945, following total defeat in World War II, atomic bombings, military occupation, and violent political protests; and in the late twentieth to early twenty-first centuries, following social and natural traumas including financial upheaval, terrorist attacks within Japan, earthquakes, tsunamis and nuclear meltdown, various contemporary genres (including quiet theater and robot theater) emerged.

Bibliography

Brandon, James R. *Kabuki's Forgotten War: 1931–1945*. Honolulu, HI: University of Hawai'i Press, 2009.

Falero, Alfonso. "Origuchi Shinobu's *Marebitoron* in Global Perspective: A Preliminary Study." In *Frontiers of Japanese Philosophy: Japanese Philosophy Abroad*, edited by James W. Heisig and Rein Raud, 274–304. Nagoya: Nanzan Institute for Religion and Culture, 2010.

Fenno Quinn, Shelley. *Developing Zeami: The Noh Actor's Attunement in Practice*. Honolulu, HI: University of Hawai'i Press, 2005.

Foster, John Bellamy, Brett Clark and Richard York. *Critique of Intelligent Design: Materialism versus Creationism from Antiquity to the Present*. New York, NY: Monthly Review, 2008.

———. "The Critique of Intelligent Design: Epicurus, Marx, Darwin and Freud and the Materialist Defense of Science." *Theory and Society* 36, no. 6 (2007): 515–46.

Hanihara Kazuro. "Dual Structure Model for the Population History of the Japanese." *Japan Review*, no. 2 (1991): 1–33.

Hartley, L. P. *The Go-Between*. 1953. Reprint, New York, NY: New York Review of Books, 2002.

Heisig, James W., Thomas P. Kasulis and John C. Maraldo. *Japanese Philosophy: A Sourcebook*. Honolulu, HI: University of Hawai'i Press, 2011.

Hoaas Pulvers, Solrun. "The Noh Mask and the Mask Making Tradition." Master's thesis, Australian National University, 1978. Available online at b1224871x_Pulvers_Solrun_Hoaas.pdf.

Hoff, Frank, and Willi Flindt. "The Life Structure of *Noh*: An English Version of Yokomichi Mario's Analysis of the Structure of Noh." *Concerned Theatre Japan* 2, no. 3–4 (Spring 1973): 210–56.

Karakuri. "Karakuri Origins." 14 January 2008. http://www.karakuri.info/origins/index.html.

Law, Jane M. *Puppets of Nostalgia: The Life, Death, and Rebirth of the Japanese "Awaji Ningyo" Tradition*. Princeton, NJ: Princeton University Press, 1997.

Leiter, Samuel L. *Rising from the Flames: The Rebirth of Theater in Occupied Japan, 1945–1952*. Lanham, MD: Lexington, 2009.
Lim Beng Choo. "They Came to Party: An Examination of the Social Status of the Medieval Noh Theatre." *Japan Forum* 16, no. 1 (2004): 111–33.
Löwy, Michael. "Marx's Dialectic of Progress: Closed or Open?" *Socialism and Democracy* 14, no. 1 (2000): 35–44.
Manabu Ogura. "Drifted Deities in the Noto Peninsula." In *Studies in Japanese Folklore*, edited by Richard M. Dorson, 133–44. Bloomington, IN: Indiana University Press, 1963.
Matsumoto Hideo. "The Origin of the Japanese Race Based on Genetic Markers of Immunoglobulin G." *Proceedings of the Japan Academy, Series B Physical and Biological Sciences* 85 no. 2 (2009): 69–82.
Mignolo, Walter D. "Epistemic Disobedience, Independent Thought and De-Colonial Freedom." *Theory, Culture & Society* 26, no. 7–8 (2009): 1–23.
Nose Asaji. *Zeami jurokubushū hyōshaku [Zeami's Sixteen Treatises]*. 2 vols. Tokyo: Iwanami shoten, 1971.
Ohnuki-Tierney, Emiko. *Rice as Self: Japanese Identities Through Time*. Princeton, NJ: Princeton University Press, 1994.
O'Neill, Patrick G. *Early Nō Drama: Its Background, Character and Development, 1300–1450*. London: Lund Humphires, 1958.
Raz, Jacob. *Audience and Actors: A Study of Their Interactions in the Japanese Traditional Theatre*. Leiden: Brill, 1983.
———. "Popular Entertainment and Politics: The Great Dengaku of 1096." *Monumenta Nipponica* 40, no. 3 (1985): 283–98.
Robertson, Jennifer. *Robo Sapiens Japanicus: Robots, Gender, Family and the Japanese Nation*. Oakland, CA: University of California Press, 2018.
Rosenberger, Nancy R. "Introduction." In *Japanese Sense of Self*, edited by Nancy R. Rosenberger, 1–20. Cambridge: Cambridge University Press, 1992.
Sacred Texts. "Atsumori by Seami." Accessed 10 July 2019. https://www.sacred-texts.com/shi/npj/npj08.htm.
Sakabe Megumi. "Mask and Shadow in Japanese Culture: Implicit Ontology in Japanese Thought." In *Modern Japanese Aesthetics: A Reader*, edited by Michele Marra, 242–51. Honolulu, HI: University of Hawai'i Press, 1999.
Screech, Timon. *The Lens within the Heart: The Western Scientific Gaze and Popular Imagery in Later Edo*. Honolulu, HI: University of Hawai'i Press, 2002.
Sorgenfrei, Carol Fisher. "Countering 'Theoretical Imperialism': Some Possibilities from Japan." *Theatre Research International* 32, no. 3 (2007): 312–24.
Watts, Jonathan. "The Emperor's New Roots." *Guardian*, 28 December 2001. https://www.theguardian.com/world/2001/dec/28/japan.worlddispatch.
Yoshida Teigo. "The Stranger as God: The Place of the Outsider in Japanese Folk Religion." *Ethnology* 20, no. 2 (1981): 87–99.
Yusa Michiko. "Riken no Ken: Zeami's Theory of Acting and Theatrical Appreciation." *Monumenta Nipponica* 42, no. 3 (1987): 331–45.
Zeami. "Teachings on Style and the Flower (Fūshikaden)." In *On the Art of the Nō Drama: The Major Treatises of Zeami*. Translated by J. Thomas Rimer and Yamazaki Masakazu, 3–63. Princeton, NJ: Princeton University Press, 1984.

8

PLUMBING THE PAST TO PROJECT INTO THE FUTURE

The Entangled Trajectories of Flamenco's Twenty-First-Century Avant-Garde

Catherine Diamond

The Scream

"It's an evening that screams avant-garde!" wrote the *Guardian* critic Judith Mackrell of Israel Galván's 2017 *Fla.Co.Men*,[1] her use of "scream" implying that the flamenco dancer-choreographer exploited outrageous self-mocking juxtapositions associated with the early twentieth-century art movement as attention-getting gimmicks. The term "avant-garde" itself traverses a difficult borderline between buffoonish self-indulgence and radical innovation, and combining it with flamenco only complicates both, as guitarist John C. Moore observes: "Given that flamenco, like any living art form, changes over time and is subject to trends, it is difficult to objectively distinguish cheap commercial tricks from honest artistic innovations."[2]

What does "avant-garde" mean in the twenty-first-century context when most performances that arise in, or travel to, the capitals of globalized culture strive to be novel or cutting-edge? The label "avant-garde" might be particularly apt for flamenco's current explosive experimentation, as it breaks out of its traditional folkloric stereotypes to interact with other forms of contemporary music and dance, thus becoming an international medium of artistic expression. Some dancer-choreographers are also finding inspiration in iconoclasts of the past, such as flamenco's first contact with the European avant-garde of early twentieth-century Paris or the post-Franco emergence of gender parity in Spain. Although flamenco, like other highly developed classical and folk arts, adheres to its historical legacies and legendary performers of previous eras, thereby acknowledging their contributions, it is also constantly innovating, often by incorporating elements from outside the "tradition" of the time. The present generation of internationally known flamenco dancers have all adopted aspects of modernity or externality into their locally learned styles—from the "rock star" persona of Joaquín Cortés and the Celtic "Firedance" of María Pagés to the cross-dressing of Manuel Liñan and the intellectual abstractions of Belén Maya—and some deconstruction of the traditional norm is now expected of them. Israel Galván (b. 1973) and Rocío Molina (b. 1984), however, are recognized both in and out of Spain as *vanguardistas*.[3] They push flamenco to extremes in all directions, dissecting and parodying flamenco's popular image—its costuming, music, emotional appeal, flamboyant beauty, ethnic identity, gendered eroticism—and opt for an abstraction and theatricality that is both new and, yet, has precedence in the flamenco legacy. Galván adapts the twentieth century's fascination with the machine to alter the presentation of the male body. Molina takes inspiration from former rebels and charts new territory for the previously hidden female body. They invoke their predecessors' revolt to denude the flamenco body, stripping it of its eroticism—exploited by international popular media—to explore a vaster range of expressions (and ideas) suited to their own individual creative drives and relevant to their contemporary world.

The art currently known as "flamenco" has a recorded history of about 250 years, but its roots go back much earlier, as it absorbed both the casual and formal fusions of Spanish folk, Arabic, Sephardic, Byzantine, African, Cuban, Latin American, and then later, classical *escuela bolera*, American jazz and pop, cakewalk, modern dance and, most recently, hip-hop. Developing into a complexly interwoven art whose multiple influences impact each artist differently, flamenco also remains deeply rooted in a single ethnic community, the Spanish Roma (Gitanos), living primarily in Andalusia. Thus flamenco retains both its core characteristics and a plasticity that absorbs, and adjusts to, the foreign and new, expanding its boundaries to incorporate them, as well as imbuing them with those characteristics. Over the past 250 years, flamenco has altered but remained discernibly "flamenco," but the two vanguardistas are challenging that discernibility by inventing their own movement vocabularies, rupturing the traditional bond between dance and music, dispensing with former notions of beauty, and experimenting with nondramatic theater. To some, they are creating exciting new paths for flamenco as a global medium, and for others, they transgress its essential qualities and destroy its sources of powerful visceral appeal.

Traditionally in the pueblos, the *cante* (singing) reigned supreme, but when flamenco was increasingly performed for outsiders in town venues, dance became ascendant. Although the touring troupes composed group choreographies and narrative works to fill out an evening's entertainment, flamenco dance was, and is, primarily a solo art, created and performed by the dancer to express an emotion in the context of a specific time and place. Accompanied by musicians, the *cantaor* (singer), *tocaor* (guitarist) and *palmero* (hand-clapper), the dance is built around the *compás*, the rhythmic structure of accented beats within a cycle that determines the *palo*, the genre within the flamenco canon. Flamenco is an art of the individual's personal negotiation with tradition, demonstrating knowledge of a legacy from a teacher or family mentor, and at the same time adding to it with personal innovations. At informal or private gatherings, such negotiations are spontaneously improvised to match the occasion. Increased professionalism meant less improvisation and more set choreography. However, as every dance is uniquely composed and performed, each artist creates his or her own authenticity—a quality based not only in style but in their artistic integrity, acknowledged by informed audiences judging their counterbalance of legacy and novelty.

While flamenco has become an international art form, and dancers and musicians all over the world have adapted it to their own cultural milieus, they preserve the heart of its authenticity in Andalusia, *la cuna* (the cradle) and its Gitano cultural identity as the touchstone of that authenticity, because this is where flamenco is not merely an art but a way of life. Many of the current flamenco stars are not Gitanos, but while all other people may study and perform it, flamenco remains the unique cultural expression of Gitanos. Only they employ it as individuals to express and define themselves both within and outside their communities.

Flamenco's Historical Dimensions

As flamenco developed into a theatricalized art at the end of the nineteenth century, two parallel and distinct strains evolved: that which is performed for each other within the close-knit and marginalized Gitano community, and that which is performed in commercial venues for outsiders. The former was an expression of emotion—of joy, grief, sorrow, humor and rage—to be shared only with intimates, while the latter was often a theatrical simulacrum of emotion expressed behind a mask of disdain that protected the inner self while appearing to expose it. This situation had foundational roots in the earlier history of eclectic receptivity, resistance and resilience, as Gitanos suffered oppression ever since their arrival in Spain at the end of the fifteenth century.

Twentieth-century flamenco reveals a complex dynamic between three forces:(1) a conservative strain that, while open to individual innovation within the Gitano community, was resistant to technological and outside influences, and which was idealized by the poet-playwright Federico García Lorca; (2) the commercialization of the art in the form of operettas as well as the *tablao* (nightclub) performances, which was later approved by the dictator Francisco Franco for tourism and export; and (3) the influence of foreign music and dance encountered by the flamenco artists touring around the world and presented on concert stages.

In the mid-twentieth century, flamenco was engaged in arguments over preserving local purity that grew increasingly contentious in response to commercialization, cultural cliché and corrupt representation, especially that of the eroticized Gitano and Gitana. The combination of Spain's political isolation and Franco's reactionary cultural policy (1939–1975) resulted in his appropriation of flamenco as a national dance, the *nacional flamenquismo*, and its commodification as a major source of income for the country.[4] Post-Civil War Spain did not experience art movements such as modern dance, or social revolutions such as feminism taking place in some parts of Europe, thus flamenco dance remained tied to the coded gestures of the local people and valorized expressions of exaggerated sexual difference. However, elements of modern dance's freedom and abstraction filtered into the work of Spanish choreographers who toured Paris and New York, where they also collaborated with exiled Spanish painters and composers.[5] During the period of 1937–1945, not only were the largest number of flamenco and Spanish dance shows touring the Americas; they were also being featured in popular Spanish, Hollywood and German films, which firmly established the stereotype of the passionate gypsy for foreign consumption.[6]

After Franco's death in 1975, socialist Felipe González's rise to power (1982) and Spain's entry into the European Union (1986) spurred *La Movida Madrileña*—the Spanish counterpart to the 1960s counterculture movements in Europe and the United States. It signaled a new trajectory for Spanish society and its arts. Flamenco practitioners were divided, some held back while others opened up to the influences of jazz and rock, and female dancers began to perform independent of male management. A younger generation freed from the reactionary time warp of Franco's dictatorship revived the spirit of the Republican era (1931–1939) with the restitution of Lorca (1986) and the homecoming of Picasso's painting *Guernica* (1981). Spain's reference point for much eccentric experimentation was the pre-Civil War avant-garde painting, literature, theater and dance adapted to 1980s sensibilities as captured in the early films of Pedro Almodóvar.

In twenty-first-century Spain, flamenco exists in many concurrent formats—the tablaos, where young performers get exposure, a steady income, and hone their technique; the Seville and Jerez festivals showcasing new work by established artists; the flamenco ballets produced by famous soloists as guest choreographers at the Ballet Nacional de España in Madrid; the neighborhood *peñas* in the Andalusian towns, which feature local performers and stress cante more than dance; Flamenco Empírico in Barcelona, which provides a platform for the most radical flamenco performance art; and the private *juergas*, such as wedding parties, where Gitano families and friends congregate to celebrate with spontaneous music and dance.

Flamenco as Protest

Henri de Saint-Simon's adoption of the military term "avant-garde" to describe the rebellious art movements in the late nineteenth century had distinct political and philosophical implications—artists were to spearhead social change: "In the act of disrupting the cultural construction of that [earlier] order, avant-garde art drew its public [...] into new relationships with experiential performance."[7] What it protests and why it provokes is not always straightforward, but in this manner, the avant-garde overlaps with flamenco, which grew out of the Gitano community's response to ethnic persecution and to celebrate its resilience and solidarity. Flamenco, within the Gitano community, has usually been a form of protest; whether in sorrow or joy, it is an aesthetic response to injustice. Comprised of singing, rhythmic clapping, body slapping, foot stamping and *jaleo* (calls of encouragement), flamenco is a form of body music with which poor people could entertain and express themselves anytime, anywhere, even without guitar or shoes. It was not always the crying lament of *canto jondo*, the deep song, but also ribald, burlesquing, and joyous empowerment, affirming an individual's vitality and communal ties. There was always space allowed for individual creativity within the context of community, but contemporary flamenco adopts the avant-garde's directive to present "a self as person, persona, and icon engaged in an on-going reflexive critical examination, inviting the audience to participate in the creation of meaning [...]."[8] What was formerly understood is now being wrenched open for simultaneous and multiple interpretations of flamenco itself. Flamenco was protest and endurance in the face of discrimination and poverty; its subversive satiric character—unlike the early avant-garde movement—was not modern, for the Gitano community was deeply conservative. But the current vanguardistas are "avant-garde" because they combine the element of protest with a postmodern self-reflexivity. They use other forms of contemporary dance and progressive ideas to reject the prior aesthetic, sometimes by retrieving and adapting an even earlier one.

Twenty-first-century experimental flamenco has uncovered the subliminal protest that made flamenco a powerful passionate medium, and applied it directly to a wide range of social ills—migration, racism, economic exploitation and gender inequality—exemplified by the flash-mob action of the group Flo6x8. Israel Galván and Rocío Molina protest the limiting definitions of flamenco, pushing it further in stylistic distortions. The subject matter of their choreographies far exceeds the former parameters, as they aim not only at social problems but also to disrupt preconceptions of flamenco as well as expanding its repertoire. Developing highly idiosyncratic movements within a theatrical framework, Galván has opened old wounds in Gitano history, and Molina has burst the restraints placed on female performers.

Rediscovering Roots

After Franco's death, Spain began recouping its pre-Civil War trajectory and asserting its relevance in the world of contemporary performance. Vanguardistas like Israel Galván and Rocío Molina not only project into the future but hark back to innovators of past eras, using former radical departures to pose anarchic challenges to its signification codified during the fascist era. One source is the revitalization of the *tanztheater* brought about by Pina Bausch. Initially, it would be hard to imagine a genre more antithetical to traditional flamenco that had become the quintessential "anti-modern" dance and music, presenting assertive confidence, earthy beauty, and untrammeled emotions expressed in dramas of love rivalry and jealousy, such as those presented in the films by Carlos Saura. But as Galván and Molina move away from pure dance into the world of ideas, their longer works take on aspects of Bausch's theatrical style. Their fully developed tanztheater productions—Galván's *Lo Real/Le Réel/The Real* (2012) and Molina's *Bosque Ardora* (2014)—break new ground in Spanish nondramatic performance.

The early twentieth-century tanztheater refers to a genre in which trained dancers combined dance, speaking, singing and chanting, conventional theater and the use of props, set and costumes: "Usually there is no narrative plot; instead, specific situations, fears, and human conflicts are presented. Audiences are stimulated to follow a train of thought or to reflect on what the tanztheater piece expresses."[9] However, because flamenco originated in a close-knit ethnic community and preserves its original intent to communicate intimately within that community, much of the movement is gestural rather than symbolic. As dancer Illeana Gomez says, in traditional flamenco performance, motifs are musical rather than visual because the dance is based in the music.[10] But Galván and Molina incorporate many visual and symbolic motifs into their theatricalizations, both changing the nature of the presentation and appealing to younger Spanish and foreign audiences not as familiar with how the music, song and dance interrelate, a key pleasure offered to the connoisseur aficionados.

In addition, Bausch's aesthetics provided Molina and Galván with a new perspective on the body in performance:

> For her [Bausch], the individual's experience is the critical component and is expressed in bodily terms, thus creating a new type of body language. By doing this, *the role of the body is redefined from one in which it disappears into the function of creation and is objectified, as is typical in ballet and most dance, to one in which it becomes the subject of the performance.* Each dancer's body tells its own story based on what it has experienced."[11]

Both Molina and Galván explore and stress the unique qualities of their bodies—neither of which conforms to the current standard of the dancer's "body beautiful." Their bodies are literally instruments upon which they play.

In commercialized flamenco, the body is culturally objectified, and that is the carapace which Galván and Molina burst apart as they redefine their own bodies' role and present themselves as independent artists, not flamenco representatives. Galván takes a uniquely cerebral and abstract approach to portraying figures and features from the flamenco past, filtering them through Dada aesthetics and his own ironic attitude that gives his work a keen sense of the absurd. Molina deconstructs, with both mockery and radical exposure, the clichés of female beauty the dancer was expected to exemplify. More visceral and imagistic than Galván, she expresses her own inner contradictions between self and body while satirizing external stereotypes. Tapping into the literature, music, photography and philosophy of other cultures, as well as improvising in Roma ghettos, prisons and parks, the two dancer-choreographers dispense with all restraint, pushing their ideas and bodies ruthlessly, as if trying to turn themselves and their worlds inside out.

Galván Resurrects Rebels of Times Past

In 1973, Israel Galván was born into a family of flamenco dancers, and in 1994, he joined the company of Mario Maya, who was not only one of the foremost flamenco dancers of the time but one who in the 1960s studied modern dance in the New York studios of Alwin Nikolais and Alvin Ailey. Moved by the Civil Rights struggles of American black people, Maya depicted the oppression of the Gitano in his dramatized *martinete*—danced without guitar accompaniment to the beat of the anvil—in *Ay! Jondo* (1977).[12] Maya's work, along with that of other innovators of the period, expanded flamenco with new narrative themes and movement patterns but did not go beyond the stylistic boundaries of flamenco.

Galván furthered Maya's venture into the theatricalization of social critique with his first dramatic work, *Mira!/Los Zapatos Rojos* (1998), which combined Hans Christian Andersen's "Red Shoes," about the Devil tempting the dancer, with the unhappy true story of Félix Fernández García "El Loco" (1893–1941), a brilliant but destitute young Gitano dancer. Discovered by Léonide Massine and Sergei Diaghilev while the Ballets Russes was touring Spain, Félix, who believed he had been incorporated into the company, taught Massine the *farruca* (male dance in 4/4 rhythm). When Massine danced the piece in *El Sombrero de Tres Picos* (1919) in London, and Félix saw that his name was not even on the bill, he fell into a fit and wildly danced his farruca in the church St Martin-in-the-Fields. Diagnosed with dementia, he was incarcerated in a British asylum, where he remained until his death in 1941.[13]

The moving story was introduced to Galván by artist and flamenco scholar Pedro G. Romero, who serves as Galván's dramaturge, artistic director, and interpreter. Embodying El Loco, Galván represented the exploited genius of the whole impoverished community. Inspired by, and learning from, El Loco's frustrated desire, Galván decided that, from then on, only he would determine what he danced: "And so it was [that] with Félix's beautiful madness began my other career, which if I had not put on the red shoes and run with them, perhaps I would not have continued dancing, for through them I found the madness of being free."[14] When Galván dances "temptation," his bright red shoes move independently to improvised piano music. They take control of him as he descends into madness. Dancing with unrelenting intensity, Galván gets inside of El Loco's psyche of despair and presents the world from that vantage through the use of projections and puppets. Galván dances the final farruca, restoring it to its rightful owner.[15]

The most important figure for Galván has been Vicente Escudero (1888–1980), the "cubist" flamenco dancer who achieved acclaim among avant-garde artists in the 1920s and 1930s. Laughed off the Spanish stage early in his career because he could not command the compás, he went to Paris, where, associating with Picasso and other cubist painters, Escudero created a cubist body and cultivated a style of revolt by adopting "modernity" as his theme. He interpreted the sounds he heard around him, his first piece being *El Tren* (1906), mimicking the sounds of a train departing and arriving. Moreover, Escudero insisted on the improvisational quality of his solos and deplored planned and rehearsed performance.

Escudero had a problem with music and the compás, which is one of the core characteristics of flamenco performance. Despite the ascendency of dance, music still dictates the tenor, or *sentido*, of the palo performed, and as Gomez comments, "many contemporary choreographers feel that 'good' dance can stand alone, without musical stimuli…flamenco dance always references the music, especially the compás, or rhythmical structure. It does not ever exist for itself."[16] Even when dancing without guitar accompaniment, the body moves to the internalized rhythm and becomes a musical instrument with stamps, slaps and snaps.

Romero credits Escudero with being the first to divorce dance from music:

> Vicente Escudero conceived the idea of dance without music, but on the other hand, it's something intrinsic to flamenco because the music is the body of the *bailaor* [flamenco dancer] itself. And he [Escudero] conceived it thirty years before Merce Cunningham performed the great revolution of dance without music.[17]

Escudero created dances in which he embodied the struggles between the human and the machine, the restriction of technique and the freedom of improvisation, as well as flamenco's capacity for juxtaposing gravity and mockery, a quality that Galván readily exploits. Galván imposes his internalized compás on nontraditional music and music-less performance in four choreographies inspired by Escudero, pushing a wedge between dance and its traditional musicality.[18] Galván quotes Escudero's angular cubist positions with arms overhead, his palms held flat, wrists slightly bent, his poker face, his rigid verticality, to then deconstruct it via its antithesis in flexible fluid contortions. He adopts, yet makes fun of, his own and Escudero's machismo by constantly readjusting its frames. Galván, like Escudero, is intrigued by Dada, incorporating its philosophy and poetry and, in particular, its absurdity.

In 1924, Escudero presented a Dada performance to a small audience in the Théâtre de la courbe. According to an anonymous source, the scene was set in a bar, the stage decorated with paintings of Spanish cliché picturesque, and the music was dissonant jazz. Escudero later ecstatically wrote that he had never danced with such vivacity and inspiration, delighted that his feet found the rhythm for his "geometric farruca" without his "searching" for it.[19] Galván adapts the event for *La Curva* (2010) and positions himself between a traditional cantaora and palmero, on one side, and a contemporary pianist who plucks the strings of her instrument on the other. Galván states, "This show takes flamenco out of its natural habitat. We are free to experiment in a timeless space without start or finish, without concessions. In this show, we are that room and the spectator observes us through the keyhole."[20] This freedom is directed at ripping apart the symbiosis between music and movement, and converting everything in the environment to become a sounding board for pure rhythm. Galván says, "*La Curva* is born out of my familiarity with silence, from my need to remove the structure from flamenco recitals, where song, music and dance are intimately linked. I wanted to see each element on its own and show the silence."[21]

Flamenco critic Estela Zatania, however, "found it produced an abstract feeling of coldness that is uncharacteristic of flamenco. Depressing in spite of some comic details that Galván always likes to insert. It's as if the dancer wanted to overcome a dislike of the traditional flamenco with which he was inculcated from a very young age [...]."[22] Galván is frequently taken to task for "disliking flamenco," as he so consciously dismantles its familiar character. He insists that he is a flamenco dancer but does not want to dance it like anyone else.

The Reality of Samudaripen

Though inured to such criticisms, Galván was shocked by the outraged reaction to his *Lo Real/Le Réel/The Real* (2012) in Madrid's Teatro Real, calling it the worst day of his life because spectators shouted for the performers to get off the stage.[23] The work also marks Galván's foray into flamenco tanztheater.

He achieved a new level of synthesis, complexity and emotional intensity due both to the subject matter and his collaboration with 15 performers, including two famous female soloists. *Lo Real* is an ambitious multilayered production that addresses the contradiction within the Nazi attitude toward the Roma people: on one hand, they were despised non-Aryans doomed for extermination in the *Samudaripen* (mass killing), and on the other, they were the orientalized, primitive Other, a race of atavistic passion and raw vitality that was deeply attractive to many within the National Socialist hierarchy. Galván builds upon Tony Gatlif's short film, *Canta Gitano* (1982), portraying the Roma people being rounded up to be put on the trains destined for the camps. It shows Galván's mentor, Mario Maya, surrounded by barbed wire dancing defiantly before being taken away and shot.

During the 1940s, Franco sent two film directors to Germany to make five films based on the Spanish Gitano community, especially its female dancers, for German audiences.[24] In addition, German film director Leni Riefenstahl (1902–2003) persevered for two decades to complete *Tiefland* (1954, *The Lowlands*), in which she starred as Marta, the gypsy dancer. When Marta dances in a tavern, among the gypsy extras that were brought in from nearby internment camps, she captivates first the villain, Don Sebastian, who is depriving the lowland farmers of water and abducts her, and then the hero, Pedro, the upland blond shepherd who rescues her to live with him in the high mountains.[25]

Galván contrasts the image of the German director filming and portraying the erotic Gitana with the actual Roma women in the camps. Belén Maya, whom he knew from his time in her father's company and whose experimental work predates his own, reprises the tortured young female counterpart to her father's representation of the Gitano oppressed in Spain, with similar pain and stoic dignity. Dressed in a short skirt and her head in a kerchief, she pounds flamenco rhythms in wooden clogs. Trapped between taut elastic strands, she dances as if tangled in electrified wire. Galván says that with Belén, he wanted to show "the scourge of genocide and at the same time, survival through dance, desire to dance even in the worst conditions."[26]

To contrast with Maya's victimization, he chose Isabel Bayón because of her beauty and charisma with the public to play Riefenstahl, both behind and in front of her camera. Galván's motivating image for his own role was the lyric "from the corpses flowers grow" from Antony and the Johnsons' song "Hitler in My Heart" (2000), even though the final image of the performance is not of flowers but the complete walling off and silencing of the people inside the camps, as the Roma genocide is rarely referred to even by the Roma themselves.

Including a variety of musicians, dancers and actors, such as several residents from Tres Mil Viviendas, a Gitano ghetto in Seville, *Lo Real* operates on many levels visually, aurally and symbolically as it combines contemporary saxophone and piano music with traditional guitar palos, cante and palmas. Steel girders serve as prison bars and railroad crossbars, and the sound of them crashing and screeching across the floor resonates with the closing of train car and gas chamber doors. Galván writhes with cubist angular moves and robotically abrupt torso isolations, along with his characteristic drumming, tapping and eliciting sound from every surface, but within the context of the camp, the grotesque contortions take on more potent and poignant meaning. Hanna Weibye remarks that "Israel Galván is angry about the way gypsy culture is glamorised, sexualised, commercialised, orientalised (and not just by Nazis); angry not only because it has done violence to the people and the culture, but because it problematises all attempts to speak through that culture."[27] By removing the popular folkloric elements, Galván uncovers the protest in flamenco, but then he intellectualizes it. In *Lo Real*, he makes a frantic and intense attack on a piano as if it symbolized all bourgeois culture, and then, with detached curiosity, taps and drums his fingers all over Bayón's body. In his own dancing, instead of his customary aloofness, he expresses exhaustive emotional commitment and gives his most visceral performance.

Galván and his director, Txiki Berraondo, do not so much delve into the paradox of fascination and extermination but layer it with multiple forms of representation, juxtaposing and mixing references, overlapping visual symbols and musical motifs—many of which cannot be discerned without the program notes—but nonetheless create a potent demonstration of torment, endurance, and an insistence on this voice being heard. As Galván dances on top of the metal girders lying like train tracks, he seems to comment sardonically on Escudero's innocently optimistic *El Tren*, or as critic Roger Salas noted, the concentration camps resulted from the same technological advances Escudero celebrated in 1906.[28]

Rocío Molina, Exploding Restraints of Beauty

All female flamenco dancers today are indebted to the Barcelonan Gitana, Carmen Amaya (1913–1963), who not only brought a forceful uncompromising Gitano style to the stage, but she frequently danced in trousers and included more *tacaneo*, the fast foot work, formerly the province of the male dancer. Critics of the day found her passion and technique too powerful to be seductively beautiful and called her a "force of nature," indicating that her dance transcended and transgressed the gender divide. Unlike Galván, Rocío Molina did not have a Vincente Escudero providing her with an alternative path, but she later adopted a figure whose career resembled that of Félix El Loco, confirming her decision to follow only her own compulsion. Molina's "spiritual godmother" is Antonia Santiago Amador "La Chana" (b. 1946), who in the 1960s and 1970s garnered international renown. Antonio Ruiz Soler "Antonio el Bailarín" (1921–1996) said that, in her heyday, "La Chana was *performing flamenco of the future. She used rhythmic combinations that were far from traditional at a speed that was unprecedented.*"²⁹ Current flamenco artists not only acknowledge that the self-taught La Chana uniquely transformed rhythm into art, but they also express profound admiration for her spirit after the 2016 film *La Chana* revealed she had been brutalized by her husband of 18 years, who destroyed her career at its height and then robbed her of all possessions. As the patriarchal Gitano community imposed a code of silence upon her, La Chana later spoke of the freedom she found inside the dance, because her life offstage was a nightmare. Making a stage comeback after the success of the film, she is now only able to dance seated in a chair, but still dazzling spectators with the rapidity of her rhythmic feet, she has become an icon of "strength, speed, and soul." Emilio Belmonte's film *Impulso* (2018) about Molina's artistry casts the younger woman dancing in homage to La Chana, establishing a lineage of female dance as protest against patriarchal control and silence.

Born in 1984, Rocío Molina is neither Gitana nor from a flamenco family, though her mother was a ballet dancer. She belongs to the first generation in twentieth-century Spain to mature without the constraints of dictatorship and assumes the freedom to express herself as a birthright. Molina's career takes a similar trajectory to Galván's after she trained at the Real Conservatorio de Danza de Madrid. She joined the company of María Pagés, who is well known for expanding the subject matter for flamenco group choreographies. As a soloist, she appeared in a *Mujeres* (2008, *Women*), which also featured Mario Maya's daughter, Belén Maya, an innovator who paved the way for women to break the mold of feminine dance.³⁰ In Carlos Saura's film, *Flamenco* (1995), Maya danced a minimalist *bulerias* displaying a linear and geometric style, marking her as the first female cubist dancer. She was also among the first to recognize the even greater daring of Molina, commenting, "Ugliness doesn't exist in flamenco. Well, except for Israel. Can you imagine a woman doing what he does? Rocío will do it. She'll do it because it is in her. She is unique."³¹ As Galván separated his dance from music, Molina separates her dance from conventional images of beauty. Countering both allure and modesty, she explores her body as an instrument the way Galván taps his environments as sounding boards.

She first acknowledged her aesthetic debt to her predecessors in *Oro Viejo* (2008, *Old Gold*), presenting a range of classical and folk styles, but also exhibited her nascent individual vocabulary as a modernist in quirky mechanical ticks and jerks. In one dance, *Malagueña*, her male partners wore shoes while she, in a *bata de cola* (train), danced barefoot so that it resembled a modern dance performed to flamenco music with balletic lifts and assisted turns. *Oro Viejo* was a balanced integration of preserving flamenco characteristics while expanding them with modern dance. Molina was still working within the realm of the conventionally beautiful, even while she satirized some of its clichés.

The change came the following year with *Cuando las Piedras Vuelen* (2009, *When Stones Fly*), in which she literally "undresses" flamenco, stripping to a minimal costume of gym-wear and divorcing sound from movement as she danced barefoot while the singers tapped her shoes on stones. The mise-en-scène projected images of owls flapping in cages as a metaphor of flamenco attempting to free itself. As she relates, "'Oro Viejo' was still a rather traditional piece…but from that moment on, I began to concentrate on my own path […] I was prepared to take a risk by turning to a contemporary style."[32] The shift occurred when she met the director Carlos Marquerie in 2009: "He came from a theatre background and helped me to find an entirely new approach. He opened my eyes, so to speak."[33] Marquerie functions as a designer and dramaturge for Molina, as Romero does for Galván, providing sources beyond flamenco, from all world cultures. Molina says, "He made me understand how important the stage was. I also realised I didn't have to rely only on dance as a starting point, that I could use other references. […] What we developed is a kind of carnal, poetic dramaturgy."[34]

She further demonstrates this new dramaturgy in *Caída del Cielo* (2016, *Fallen from Heaven*), in which she assumes one gendered guise after another, toying with each but allowing none to represent her. Luke Jennings of the *Guardian* wrote, "Flamenco has always proposed a fierce and proud femininity, but as embodied by Molina in *Fallen from Heaven* (Caída del Cielo), it becomes a feminist scream, an elemental cri de coeur."[35] Another scream for attention, perhaps, but it was also an iteration of Molina's earlier declaration to push herself to extremes:

> Above all else, an expression of freedom; when people go to the theater, they should be ready for anything, because each moment, I have something different to say. I don't want to fall into the trap of trying to please the critics or anyone else; I do what I do because it's what I really want, and I'm true to myself; that's how I see it: freedom and expression, educating audiences to understand that when they go to see me, there might be something they don't like…[36]

Her defiance of both social and artistic convention was rare in flamenco because it flaunts the very bonds valued in the Gitano community, but it is becoming more the norm among young professionals trying to distinguish themselves, as if flamenco were participating in the belated audacity of La Movida Madrileña with a postmodern twist. In *Caída del Cielo*, she embodies multiple images of Woman: "The first [part] was to be refined, very white, very beautiful and totally perfect. The second was to be a total contrast to that: dirtier and darker, perhaps also containing something of the forbidden."[37] Dressed in an all-white gown with a frothy bata de cola, Molina, again barefoot, traverses the stage, eyes closed, trance-like, with bridal virginity as she flips the long tail. She sinks down onto the floor into the ruffles as if they were sea foam, and, from the floor, kicks them up into frothy waves like a mermaid. Maintaining the sea imagery, she arises from the foam, sloughing off the gown and emerging as Botticelli's Venus. Next, she does not desecrate the beauty of this image but juxtaposes it with the "dirty" body, reappearing in a plastic skirt dipped in a menstrual ink. Dragging it across the floor, she leaves a muddy, bloody trail until one of her musicians kneels to wash her feet.

In another sequence, her musicians nibble potato chips without offering her any. She then stuffs a bag of chips in the crotch of her bondage leather harness and eats while dancing with exaggerated masculinity. She also dresses as a torero with heavy-duty kneepads, not only to spin on one knee like the famous male dancers but to leap and fall on them, and then twist upside down like a hip-hop dancer. The work engages rather superficially with gendered images, as did Galván's *Fla.Co.Men*, but Molina also shows she will fearlessly dance any role. One portrayal does not negate the others but adds to the multiple dimensions of "artist as woman."

Two years earlier, she had created an ambitious tanztheater production, *Bosque Ardora* (2014, *Forest of Ardor*), in which she went beyond her solo work to create a theatrical framework to contextualize diverse scenarios. As the historical context of *Lo Real* encompassed the idiosyncratic elements in Galván's choreography, giving them a broader social meaning, *Bosque Ardora* rooted Molina's exploration of sexual power play in the realms of mythological and biological nature, beyond the superficial social codes mocked in *Caído*.

The theatrical forest has always been the site of social and gender reversals, therianthropy (human-animal transformations), providing metaphors for mystical powers and unconscious desires. Molina's stage forest, created by a semicircle of potted trees, is a place of danger, freedom, mystery and revelation. The piece starts with a film clip of Molina riding on horseback through a forest until she is suddenly thrown into a lake. She then emerges onstage wearing a mask representing the Greek mythological Teumessian Fox, which could not be caught but was pursued by a dog that would not give up, thereby presenting an insolvable paradox. She removes the mask revealing her makeup—the Japanese exaggerated eyebrows, *hikimayu*, and a sumo-inspired topknot hairstyle—suggesting *Kitsune*, the female shape-shifting fox spirit. Molina initially mimics animal movements with her hands, but as soon as she strikes the floor, not only the artificial sound of the shoes ruptures any pretense of being natural, but also the real sparks that fly out render realistic representation irrelevant. Instead, the forest is a bizarre revisitation of the Garden of Eden, in which she and two male dancers (Eduardo Guerrero and Fernando Jiménez) exchange a range of sexually charged interactions. Clad in animal-skin-like brown velvet and knee-high boots, they dance in precise unison and then break away abruptly. Twitching with rapid-fire body isolations, they are like Hieronymus Bosch-inspired creatures, never quite human or animal.

As in her other works, changes of costume signal changes in concept and persona. While dressed in animal-skin, Molina dominates her male partners, but once she reappears in a man's shirt, tie and yellow stiletto heels, their relationships become more complicated. She teases them like a contemporary temptress, but then they seem to get the better of her, grabbing her topknot and swinging her around. Molina employs some of the same lifts and contemporary dance configurations in *Oro Viejo*, but without any romantic illusions and, instead, affecting a raw power struggle. Exchanging roles of attraction and repulsion, domination and submission, the dancers transform into stylized mating birds and insects that at first suggest animist rites but then dissolve into comical mimicry.

Exploring desire in a quasi-environmental-parable-cum-fertility-ritual, *Bosque Ardora* meanders through the dark woods of myth and dream. Unlike Galván's appropriation of Dadaist absurdism to express paradox, Molina conjures a Salvador Daliesque forest of the subconscious, rife with surprising intrusions. A pair of twin-like trombonists stroll around the stage, their gleaming instruments not only adding visually to the surreal atmosphere, but their long lingering notes help to effect the incongruous transitions. The lines between male-female and human-animal are intentionally blurred and crisscrossed without narrative logic. This tanztheater takes place in an ultimately modern vision of a primeval dreamscape in which the imagistic scenarios are intensely performed and then dissipated, leaving the audience to ponder their consequence.

In the penultimate scene, Molinae merged like a nymph in a green gown with her hair loose to dance a solo *soleares*, the mother of *cante jondo* and the rhythm of solitude. It was an abrupt insertion of "traditional" flamenco in the middle of a bizarrely symbolic journey. No longer Artemis, goddess of the hunt, or the contemporary vamp and huntress of men, Molina danced like a frantic spirit of the woods—distressed, anguished and on the verge of extinction. She seemed to be expressing her undisguised persona while the guitarist strummed the most conventional soleares accompaniment. After the nymph disappeared off stage, one of the male dancers concealed in a wooly white costume lumbered toward the audience.[38] When she suddenly dashed across in front of him, a shot rang out, a blinding light flashed, and then all went dark and silent.

Although the whole piece was grounded in flamenco rhythms, only the soleares garnered spontaneous applause, and several critics of the London performance remarked on its crucial difference from the rest of the choreography as raw emotional virtuoso dancing.[39] What marked it as "traditional" is that it was a solo responding directly to the music, not tightly choreographed with other dancers, allowing for the music's embodied emotion to be communicated directly from the dancer to the spectator. This triangle of response and reception rendered it familiar regardless of whatever other interpretation Molina wished to bestow on it.

Spanish Avant-Garde Tanztheater

In *Lo Real* and *Bosque Ardora*, Galván and Molina go to dark places—both physical and psychological—apt territory for the *sombra* or shadow side of flamenco that cries out against communal and individual oppression. While Galván and Molina "out" flamenco onto the contemporary stage, they are also "outing" their own creative personae to be free agents and integral members of the contemporary international flow of ideas in art. Flamenco was locked in a past in which the present was overshadowed by a legendary golden age that could never be surpassed on its own grounds, that of reprising eternal and universal emotions through a relationship with the music. Galván and Molina expose what was repressed by the stylized nineteenth-century costumes, the mask of defiance, the self-absorption, and the furious foot-stamping that stops abruptly at the cliff of silence. Flamenco moves people by its cathartic letting loose of those dark emotions and then re-sublimating them; its power derives from the play of repression and release. By subjecting flamenco to the grotesque and satirical, deforming its previous norms, they resurrect the anarchic spirit of exiled Cubist and Dadaist artists, and reflect twentieth-century Spain's spasms between republicanism and totalitarianism, akin to the subversive visions of Picasso, Dalí and Almodóvar. As examples of twenty-first-century tanztheater, Galván's *Lo Real* and Molina's *Bosque Ardora* render flamenco as a sophisticated medium that expresses a postmodern aesthetic, defined by embracing the often contradictory layers of meaning, being confrontational and controversial, challenging the boundaries of taste, mixing different artistic and popular styles and media, consciously and self-consciously borrowing from, or ironically commenting on, a range of styles from the past.[40]

On one hand, the two vanguardistas pick apart the flamenco legacy and layer it with ideas and images from other cultures, and on the other, they look to flamenco iconoclasts in the past for inspiration. They could be said to be simultaneously entangling a more distant past and disentangling from a recent one in flamenco history. Discerning spectators note that what distinguishes them from other dancers striving to be cutting-edge by more gratuitous means is the relentless way they push themselves to break through their own limitations. The intense self-consciousness with which they journey into new territory also differs from experiments in the past because they are keenly aware of how flamenco is perceived from the outside, and they want to subvert that perception rather than play to it. They place their bodies in the subject position rather than submerging it into the emotion and culture of the dance.

By disconnecting flamenco from its folkloric conventions, obscuring its musical cues and replacing them with visual symbols, however, Galván and Molina might be inadvertently diminishing flamenco's particular emotional power in exchange for expanding its intellectual range. American cantaora Judith Gelman Myers upon seeing Galván's *La Curva* felt he was not searching for flamenco's essence but attacking its core, saying, "His contempt for the form is clear. What isn't clear is what lies beyond his contempt."[41] Gomez, however, proposes that, like other dancers, Galván and Molina

> are able to walk the tightrope between tradition and novelty by means of their persona or flamenco personality, as it is manifested through their purpose, presence, and style. What becomes apparent is that the persona in flamenco acts as a mediator (one of many) between that which is considered to be authentic flamenco and that which is not.[42]

It is by digging into the past and bringing to light the suffering of individuals and communities, and interweaving the protest of key predecessors into their own that the two vanguardistas keep their balance on that tightrope and do not fall into specious novelty. Their tanztheater productions resonate with the fierce resistance of Mario Maya and La Chana as well as those first heady encounters between Spanish dance, the Parisian avant-garde, and New York modern dance, newly adapted to the twenty-first-century nondramatic idiom.

Notes

1 Judith Mackrell, "Israel Galván: FLA.CO.MEN Review – 'It's an Evening that Screams Avant-garde!'" *Guardian*, 17 February 2017, https://www.theguardian.com/stage/2017/feb/17/israel-galvan-flacomen-review-sadlers-wells-london-flamenco-reinventions-show.
2 John C. Moore, "Purity and Commercialization: The View from Two Working Artists, Pericón de Cádiz and Chato de la Isla," in *Flamenco on the Global Stage: Historical, Critical and Theoretical Perspectives*, ed. K. Meira Goldberg, Ninotchka Devorah Bennahum and Michelle Heffner Hayes (Jefferson, NC: McFarland & Company, 2015), 167.
3 Estela Zatania, "XV Bienal de Flamenco. 'Oro viejo.' Compañía de Rocío Molina," *DeFlamenco*, 10 October 2008, https://www.deflamenco.com/revista/resenas-actuaciones/xv-bienal-de-flamenco-oro-viejo-compania-de-rocio-molina-1.html.
4 Theresa Goldbach, "Fascism, Flamenco, and Ballet Español: Nacionalflamenquismo" (master's thesis, University of New Mexico, 2014), 38, https://digitalrepository.unm.edu/thea_etds/9/.
5 Ninotchka Devorah Bennahum, *Antonia Mercé "La Argentina": Flamenco and the Spanish Avant Garde* (Hanover, NH: Wesleyan University Press, 2000), 3–4.
6 Goldbach, "Nacionalflamenquismo," 45.
7 Elizabeth M. Drake-Boyt, "Dance as a Project of the Early Modern Avant-Garde" (PhD diss., Florida State University, 2005), 2.
8 Ibid., 10.
9 Roland Langer, "Compulsion and Restraint, Love and Angst: The Post-war German Expressionism of Pina Bausch and Her Wuppertal Dance Theater," trans. Richard Sikes, *Dance Magazine* 58, no. 6 (June 1984): 46.
10 Illeana Gomez, "La Nueva Escuela de la Danza Flamenca: Postmodern Shifts in Flamenco Dance" (master's thesis, University of New Mexico, 2010), 18.

11 Tashiro Mimi, "Pina Bausch: Life and Works," Stanford Presidential Lectures (1999), *archive.org*, accessed 25 February 2022, https://web.archive.org/web/20201102085425/http://prelectur.stanford.edu:80/lecturers/bausch/life.html. My italics.
12 Carlos Saura included Maya's martinete in his film *Flamenco* (1995); see "Ay! Musical Hondo Pt 2 Mario Maya Carmen Mora," posted by Albatross35, 13 February 2007, YouTube video, 8:23, https://www.youtube.com/watch?v=PhkEZrY38Do.
13 Mercedes Albi, "Historia del Bailaor Félix Fernández, El Loco," *Albi Danza*, 13 April 2016, https://www.albidanza.com/single-post/2016/04/13/Historia-del-bailaor-Félix-Fernández-El-Loco.
14 Margot Molina, "La Deliciosa Locura de Israel Galván," *El País*, 24 September 1998, https://elpais.com/diario/1998/09/24/andalucia/906589351_850215.html. My translation.
15 Albi, "Historia del Bailaor."
16 Gomez, "La Nueva Escuela," 28.
17 Pedro G. Romero, "Solo: Revolution without Music," *archive.org*, accessed 25 February 2022, https://web.archive.org/web/20160301135607/http://www.anegro.net/english/index.php/israel-galvan/solo.
18 Galván's *Edad de Oro* (2005), *Solo* (2007), *La Curva* (2010) and *Seguiriyas 1938* (2010) were inspired by Vicente Escudero.
19 José Luis Navarro, *Vicente Escudero: Un Bailaor Cubista* (Sevilla: Libros con Duende, 2013), 46.
20 Israel Galván, "La Curva," *archive.org*, accessed 25 February 2022, https://web.archive.org/web/20160508112146/http://www.anegro.net/english/index.php/israel-galvan/la-curva.
21 Ibid.
22 Estela Zatania, "Festival Flamenco Nimes 2012. Israel Galván 'La Curva,'" *DeFlamenco*, 20 January 2012, https://www.deflamenco.com/revista/resenas-actuaciones/festival-flamenco-nimes-2012-israel-galvan-la-curva1-1.html. My translation.
23 Israel Galván, "Flamenco Firebrand Israel Galván: 'I Was Probably Dancing inside the Womb,'" interview by Judith Mackrell, *Guardian*, 12 July 2015, https://www.theguardian.com/stage/2015/jul/12/israel-galvan-lo-real-dance-interview-edinburgh-festival.
24 "With the full collaboration of Spanish Nationalists, Florián Rey and Benito Perojo made five films in Nazi Germany's UFA studios between 1937 and 1939: *Carmen, la de Triana*, *El barbero de Sevilla*, *Suspiros de España*, *La canción de Aixa*, and *Mariquilla Terremoto*." See Eva Woods Peiró, *White Gypsies: Race and Stardom in Spanish Musical Films* (Minneapolis, MN: University of Minnesota Press, 2012), 185.
25 *Tiefland* (*The Lowlands*) was based on the 1896 Catalan play *Terra Baixa* by Àngel Guimerà and made into an opera by Eugen d'Albert (1903), with libretto in German by Rudolph Lothar.
26 Ángeles Castellano, "El Bailaor de la Muerte," *El País*, 29 November 2012, https://elpais.com/cultura/2012/11/28/actualidad/1354116563_812474.html.
27 Hanna Weibye, "Lo Real, Israel Galván, Edinburgh Festival Theatre," *Arts Desk*, 20 August 2015, https://theartsdesk.com/dance/lo-real-israel-galván-edinburgh-festival-theatre.
28 Roger Salas, "Israel Galván: Un baile personal, un estilo diferente," *El Pais*, 6 December 2012, https://elpais.com/cultura/2012/12/05/actualidad/1354736394_001698.html.
29 Patrícia Soley-Beltran, "The Invincible Dancer," *El País*, 17 November 2017, https://english.elpais.com/elpais/2017/11/14/inenglish/1510656865_902610.html. My italics.

30 Belén Maya, one of the first women to make flamenco express sentiments outside of its traditional passions, said, "You can only express two or three ideas, especially as women. You can't talk about things like loneliness, violence, fear, vulnerability. . . not without straying from the realm of the feminine dance. Little by little, women are changing these things." See Michelle Heffner Hayes, *Flamenco: Conflicting Histories of the Dance* (Jefferson, NC: McFarland & Company, 2009), 171.

31 Ibid., 180.

32 Rocío Molina, "Indomitable," interview by Susanne Zellinger, trans. Joel Scott, *archive.org*, accessed 25 February 2022, https://web.archive.org/web/20201020193253/http://magazinimaugust.de/2017/01/05/rocio-molina-indomitable/.

33 Ibid.

34 Laura Cappelle, "Flamenco with an Individual Stamp," *Financial Times*, 11 October 2017, https://www.ft.com/content/00d46d7c-a828-11e7-ab66-21cc87a2edde.

35 Luke Jennings, "Rocío Molina: Fallen from Heaven Review – A Feminist Flamenco Scream," *Guardian*, 15 October 2017, https://www.theguardian.com/stage/2017/oct/15/rocio-molina-fallen-from-heaven-barbican-review.

36 Rocío Molina, "Interview with Rocío Molina. Flamenco Dancer," interview by Sonia Martínez Pariente, *DeFlamenco*, 4 January 2008, https://www.deflamenco.com/revista/entrevistas/interview-with-rocio-molina-flamenco-dancer-1.html.

37 Rocío Molina, "Indomitable."

38 The white shaggy costume remained hanging at the back of the stage throughout the piece. It suggested both an animist deity and a hunter's camouflage.

39 See Jenny Gilbert, "Bosque Ardora, Rocío Molina, Barbican," *Arts Desk*, 17 October 2014, https://theartsdesk.com/node/74122/view; Zo Anderson, "Rocío Molina, Barbican Theatre, Review: The Flamenco Goddess Is Magnificently Weird," *Independent*, 17 October 2014, https://www.independent.co.uk/arts-entertainment/theatre-dance/reviews/roc-o-molina-barbican-theatre-review-flamenco-goddess-roc-o-molina-is-magnificently-weird-9801850.html; Graham Watts, "Review: Rocío Molina – Bosque Ardora – Barbican Theatre," *London Dance*, 17 October 2014, http://londondance.com/articles/reviews/rocio-molina-bosque-ardora-barbican-theatre-3/.

40 See "Art Term: Postmodernism," *Tate*, accessed 18 January 2022, http://www.tate.org.uk/art/art-terms/p/postmodernism.

41 Judith Gelman Myers, "Reviews: New York Flamenco Festival 2014," *earthwize*, 26 April 2015, http://www.earthwize.org/jgm/pdf/flamenco/Generations.pdf.

42 Gomez, "La Nueva Escuela," 24.

Bibliography

Albi, Mercedes. "Historia del bailaor Félix Fernández, El Loco" ["The History of the Dancer Félix Fernández, The Madman"]. *Albi Danza*, 13 April 2016. https://www.albidanza.com/single-post/2016/04/13/Historia-del-bailaor-F%C3%A9lix-Fern%C3%A1ndez-El-Loco.

Anderson, Zo. "Rocío Molina, Barbican Theatre, Review: The Flamenco Goddess Is Magnificently Weird." *Independent*, 17 October 2014. https://www.independent.co.uk/arts-entertainment/theatre-dance/reviews/roc-o-molina-barbican-theatre-review-flamenco-goddess-roc-o-molina-is-magnificently-weird-9801850.html.

"Ay! Musical Hondo Pt 2 Mario Maya Carmen Mora." Posted by Albatross35. 13 February 2007. YouTube video, 8:23. https://www.youtube.com/watch?v=PhkEZrY38Do.

Bennahum, Ninotchka Devorah. *Antonia Mercé "La Argentina": Flamenco and the Spanish Avant Garde*. Hanover, NH: Wesleyan University Press, 2000.

Cappelle, Laura. "Flamenco with an Individual Stamp." *Financial Times*, 11 October 2017. https://www.ft.com/content/00d46d7c-a828-11e7-ab66-21cc87a2edde.

Castellano, Ángeles. "El Bailaor de la Muerte" ["The Dancer of Death"]. *El País*, 29 November 2012. https://elpais.com/cultura/2012/11/28/actualidad/1354116563_812474.html.

Drake-Boyt, Elizabeth M. "Dance as a Project of the Early Modern Avant-Garde." PhD diss., Florida State University, 2005.

Galván, Israel. "Flamenco Firebrand Israel Galván: 'I Was Probably Dancing inside the Womb.'" Interview by Judith Mackrell. *Guardian*, 12 July 2015. https://www.theguardian.com/stage/2015/jul/12/israel-galvan-lo-real-dance-interview-edinburgh-festival.

———. "La Curva" ["The Curve"]. *archive.org*, accessed 25 February 2022. https://web.archive.org/web/20160508112146/http://www.anegro.net/english/index.php/israel-galvan/la-curva.

Gilbert, Jenny. "Bosque Ardora, Rocío Molina, Barbican." *Arts Desk*, 17 October 2014. https://theartsdesk.com/node/74122/view.

Goldbach, Theresa. "Fascism, Flamenco, and Ballet Español: Nacionalflamenquismo." Master's thesis, University of New Mexico, 2014. https://digitalrepository.unm.edu/thea_etds/9/.

Gomez, Illeana. "La Nueva Escuela de la Danza Flamenca: Postmodern Shifts in Flamenco Dance." Master's thesis, University of New Mexico, 2010.

Heffner Hayes, Michelle. *Flamenco: Conflicting Histories of the Dance*. Jefferson, NC: McFarland & Company, 2009.

Jennings, Luke. "Rocío Molina: Fallen from Heaven Review – A Feminist Flamenco Scream." *Guardian*, 15 October 2017. https://www.theguardian.com/stage/2017/oct/15/rocio-molina-fallen-from-heaven-barbican-review.

Langer, Roland. "Compulsion and Restraint, Love and Angst: The Post-war German Expressionism of Pina Bausch and Her Wuppertal Dance Theater." Translated by Richard Sikes. *Dance Magazine* 58, no. 6 (June 1984): 46–48.

Looseleaf, Victoria. "Modern vs. Contemporary." *Dance Magazine*, 1 December 2012. https://www.dancemagazine.com/modern_vs_contemporary-2306900829.html.

Mackrell, Judith. "Israel Galván: FLA.CO.MEN Review – 'It's an Evening that Screams Avant-garde!'" *Guardian*, 17 February 2017. https://www.theguardian.com/stage/2017/feb/17/israel-galvan-flacomen-review-sadlers-wells-london-flamenco-reinventions-show.

Molina, Margot. "La Deliciosa Locura de Israel Galván" ["The Delectable Madness of Israel Galván"]. *El País*, 24 September 1998. https://elpais.com/diario/1998/09/24/andalucia/906589351_850215.html.

Moore, John, C. "Purity and Commercialization: The View from Two Working Artists, Pericón de Cádiz and Chato de la Isla." In *Flamenco on the Global Stage: Historical, Critical and Theoretical Perspectives*, edited by K. Meira Goldberg, Ninotchka Devorah Bennahum and Michelle Heffner Hayes, 166–77. Jefferson, NC: McFarland & Company, 2015.

Myers, Judith Gelman. "Reviews: New York Flamenco Festival 2014." *earthwize*, 26 April 2015. http://www.earthwize.org/jgm/pdf/flamenco/Generations.pdf.

Molina, Rocío. "Indomitable." Interview by Susanne Zellinger. Translated by Joel Scott. *Magazin im August*, 5 January 2017. http://magazinimaugust.de/2017/01/05/rocío-molina-indomitable/.

———. "Interview with Rocío Molina. Flamenco Dancer." By Sonia Martínez Pariente. *DeFlamenco*, 4 January 2008. https://www.deflamenco.com/revista/entrevistas/interview-with-rocio-molina-flamenco-dancer-1.html.

Navarro, José Luis. *Vicente Escudero: Un bailaor cubista*. Sevilla: Libros con Duende, 2013.

Peiró, Eva Woods. *White Gypsies: Race and Stardom in Spanish Musical Films*. Minneapolis, MN: University of Minnesota Press, 2012.

Romero, Pedro G. "Solo: Revolution without Music." *archive.org*, accessed 25 February 2022. https://web.archive.org/web/20160301135607/http://www.anegro.net/english/index.php/israel-galvan/solo.

Salas, Roger. "Israel Galván: Un baile personal, un estilo diferente" ["Israel Galván: A Personal Dance, a Different Style"]. *El País*, 6 December 2012. https://elpais.com/cultura/2012/12/05/actualidad/1354736394_001698.html.

Soley-Beltran, Patrícia. "The Invincible Dancer." *El País*, 17 November 2017. https://english.elpais.com/elpais/2017/11/14/inenglish/1510656865_902610.html

Tashiro Mimi. "Pina Bausch: Life and Works." Stanford Presidential Lectures (1999). *archive.org*, accessed 25 February 2022. https://web.archive.org/web/20201102085425/http://prelectur.stanford.edu:80/lecturers/bausch/life.html.

Watts, Graham. "Review: Rocío Molina – Bosque Ardora – Barbican Theatre." *London Dance*, 17 October 2014. http://londondance.com/articles/reviews/rocio-molina-bosque-ardora-barbican-theatre-3/.

Weibye, Hanna. "Lo Real, Israel Galván, Edinburgh Festival Theatre." *Arts Desk*, 20 August 2015. https://theartsdesk.com/dance/lo-real-israel-galv%C3%A1n-edinburgh-festival-theatre.

Zatania, Estela. "Festival Flamenco Nimes 2012. Israel Galván 'La Curva'" ["Nimes Flamenco Festival 2012. Israel Galvan 'The Curve'"]. *DeFlamenco*, 20 January 2012. https://www.deflamenco.com/revista/resenas-actuaciones/festival-flamenco-nimes-2012-israel-galvan-la-curva1-1.html.

———. "XV Bienal de Flamenco, 'Oro viejo,' Compañía de Rocío Molina" ["The Golden Age"]. *DeFlamenco*, 10 October 2008. https://www.deflamenco.com/revista/resenas-actuaciones/xv-bienal-de-flamenco-oro-viejo-compania-de-rocio-molina-1.html.

PART V
National Theater Histories—Entanglements and Disentanglements

9
THE INTERWOVEN PERFORMANCE CULTURE OF ALGERIA

Marvin Carlson

Despite repeated efforts to "stabilize," "purify" or in various ways "essentialize" performance traditions around the world, the continual interweaving of old and new as well as local and foreign practices is found in all such traditions. In certain areas of the world, however, patterns of trade, migration, conflict and conquest have resulted in particularly dense and complex patterns of mutual influence: the Middle East, where materials, bodies and cultural customs from Asia, Europe and Africa have mingled since the beginning of civilization, is a central example of such a region. Another lies at the other end of the Mediterranean, where the great land masses of Europe and Africa come so close to each other that the opposite coast can be seen. The combination of this proximity of continents to the north and south and to the great ocean areas of travel, trading and conflict—the Mediterranean to the east and the Atlantic to the west—makes this area another site of particularly dense and complex cultural mixing. As Algerian author and activist Hicham Yezza observed in 2013, "Anyone with a passing knowledge of Algerian—and, indeed, Maghreb—history knows it is a land of linguistic, ethnic and cultural hybridity."[1]

Although this deeply rooted hybridity is widely recognized among anthropologists and cultural historians who have studied this region, the comparatively few studies of its theater and performance culture remain, on the whole, organized according to the conventional structuring principle of concentrating on what is seen as a single, basically united theatrical culture. This is especially true of Algeria because of its uniquely close connections with France. The few extended studies of Algerian theater are written in French, mostly by Algerians whose concern is primarily tracing the rise of a theater separate from the French, and so the interweaving of these cultures is downplayed or ignored completely. Typical is the leading text in the field, *Le théâtre algérien* by the Algerian dramatist and man of the theater, Bouziane Ben Achour, which bears the telling epigraph concerning the Algerian makers of theater:

> They were imitators by necessity.
> They became creators by conviction.
> Their posterity is our present.[2]

Scholars of French theater history traditionally ignore francophone theater outside France completely, and students of francophone theater have been concerned only with Canada, the Caribbean and sub-Saharan Africa. Typical is the most recent and comprehensive book in this field, *New Francophone African and Caribbean Theatres* by John Conteh-Morgan and Dominic Thomas, published in 2010. Despite its title, the book mentions Algeria only twice in passing, neither time saying anything about its theater, even though the second mention rather surprisingly notes that Algeria is "the longest French-colonized territory in Africa."[3] Interest in Berber theater and performance, the oldest recorded performance tradition of Algeria, has only recently developed, and due to its emphasis on cultural identity, its scholarship has so far rejected any discussion of interweaving whatsoever. Indeed, a recent study of the field asserts that "in its essence, the Amazigh discourse relies on a negation of the process of 'métissage' [literally "weaving"] that began in the seventh century between local populations and waves of migrants from the Gulf."[4]

Thus, despite the centuries-long mixing of cultures in this area, Algerian theater has been studied, if studied at all, only within particular traditions such as Arab or Berber, and largely as an anti-interweaving narrative delineating their struggle to separate themselves from external influence. Despite the cultural mixing that has been a central feature of this area since classical times, no theater historian in France or in Algeria has explored the effects upon theater and performance practice of this mixing in the way that Khalid Amine and his students have done for Morocco, which has a similar but different history of cultural interweaving.[5] Given the cultural density shared by all of the modern states in this area—Spain (and particularly Andalusia in the south), and the Arab states collectively known as the Maghreb (Morocco, Tunisia and Algeria)—clearly important perspectives of its performance history are hidden when the dynamics of interweaving are denied or ignored. Some preliminary work in this area was undertaken in the Algerian sections of the only book so far to appear in English on the history of theater in the Maghreb, Amine and Carlson's *The Theatres of Morocco, Algeria and Tunisia* (2011). The present chapter may be seen as a further extension of the analysis of Algerian theater in that book, an analysis based not on tracing individual, separate dramatic traditions but on how these traditions have affected each other to create ever new and changing patterns of performance.

Centuries of Invasion, Occupation and Cultural Mixing

The earliest known inhabitants of this area are called "Berbers" by the Romans and the "Amazigh" (plural: "Imazighen") in their own language, called Tamazight. They have been in this area since Neolithic times and are first mentioned in Egyptian records around 3000 BCE. Only in modern times, as a part of the postcolonial search for indigenous, "native" cultural expressions around the world, has there arisen in the Maghreb a significant search for a championing of Amazigh culture, its language and its performance. However, the history of the region from the beginning is marked by Amazigh resistance to various colonizing powers—first the Phoenicians, then the Romans, then the Vandals, the rulers of distant Byzantium, then the Umayyad Arabs, then the Ottomans, and the occupying Europeans—and, one might argue, the independent states of the twentieth century, within which Amazigh culture still remains a distinct unassimilated presence.

Although each of these new invasions added another layer of cultural practice to the complex mixture of activity along the North African coast, their geographic impact was similar. Most came from the sea and established outposts of their own culture along the coasts in cities and fortified enclaves, where their practices blended with those left from previous invaders. The Amazigh peoples, driven into the mountains and deserts to the south, remained always an only partially assimilated group, negotiating ever-changing conflicts, compromises and cultural exchanges across a constantly shifting and highly porous border with the successive dominant forces in the north. In the manner of subaltern cultures everywhere, some ambitious Amazigh adopted enough of these dominant cultures to move into them, occasionally with notable success—as can be seen in such Romanized Imazighen as Terence and Augustine[6]—but over the centuries, more subtle cultural flows naturally operated between these contiguous and, to some degree, interwoven communities. Thus, from the beginning, Amazigh terms, customs and physical products began to make their way into each occupying culture, from the Phoenicians and Romans onward, while elements of those cultures, sometimes out of self-interest and sometimes by force, made their way into the subaltern culture.[7]

In addition to this constant interpenetration of cultural materials between the occupiers and the occupied, the process was made more complex by the already existing hybridity on either side. The Phoenicians and the Romans both came to North Africa from far to the east, already essentially multi-ethnic empires. The Amazigh were comparably a far smaller and less diverse people, but as time passed, new cultural elements entered their world, not only directly from occupying powers but indirectly through non-Roman and non-Phoenician elements rejected by those societies who found refuge among the Amazigh. Particularly significant during the Roman occupation were the Christians and Jews, both subject to waves of persecution. Many sought refuge among the more hospitable Amazigh, bringing new cultural and ritual practices with them, and, somewhat ironically, they were eventually followed by Roman refugees as well, fleeing the invading Vandals from the north.[8] Throughout their century-long reign in North Africa, the Vandals were occupied in conflict with Rome, in a struggle that ranged over much of the Mediterranean. When they were finally defeated in 534, the Western Roman Empire, exhausted by its wars with the northern tribes, had ended, accepting a Germanic barbarian as its ruler, and the new rulers of this region came from Byzantium, the surviving eastern branch of the former Roman Empire, with very different customs reflecting its eastern orientation. Many of the Vandal inhabitants of the Maghreb, like those disposed by their own rule, fled the invaders and were assimilated into the already multifaced Amazigh kingdoms, added to the complexity of that welcoming culture.

The Byzantines, like the Vandals, enjoyed only a bit more than a century in control of this turbulent region. A major new actor appeared on the world stage with the rise and rapid territorial expansion of Islam. In 647, within 30 years of the death of Mohammed, Islamic armies were advancing into the Maghreb and, although bitterly resisted for the rest of the century by the combined forces of Imazighen and Byzantines, had established control of much of the region by the opening of the next century. From that time onward, the area known as modern Algeria (whose current boundaries were set by the French in 1830) has been a predominantly Muslim country, although it was occupied by the French between 1830 and 1956 and divided into departments that nominally made it a part of the French state, an attempt at assimilation that was never attempted in Tunisia or Morocco.

The gradual triumph of Islam in this area did not in any significant measure decrease the heterogeneity of its culture, but more accurately added a major new element to the already many-faceted cultural heritage of this much-contested area. Moreover, Islam itself was divided into competing communities of belief. The major split between Shias and Sunnis, which still profoundly divides the Islamic world, was in fact anticipated by the appearance of the first Islamic sect, the fundamentalist Kharijites.[9] Each of these groups left their mark in Algeria; indeed, a moderate branch of the Kharijites established, in the eighth century, the Rustamid dynasty, which ruled over most of Algeria for over a century, and which for the first time offered this region a government created by the native Amazigh. Fortunately for the processes of cultural interweaving, the Rustamids followed the general practice of their tribal ancestors rather than the restrictive Kharijites, and the state "developed a cosmopolitan reputation in which Christians, non-Kharijite Muslims, and adherents of different sects of Kharijism" lived and interacted in harmony.[10]

During the following centuries, the area continued to be ruled by a variety of Islamic powers, some from outside and some rooted in the Amazigh population. The most significant of these was the last, the Ottoman occupation, which lasted from 1516 to 1830 and extended along the coast of Algeria, north of the Atlas Mountains. Although the Ottomans at first attempted to impose significant elements of their culture upon their vassal state, making Turkish the official language and excluding Arabs and Amazigh from governmental posts, the center of their empire was far-off Constantinople, and despite their extended presence in Algeria, the Ottoman element became at last only another, though important, thread in the interwoven texture of Algerian culture.

Various types of folk and ritual performance, especially in connection with season celebrations, go far back in the cultural practices of this region, as they do throughout the world. Saint Augustine, in addition to his negative comments on the official Roman theater, mentions such folk entertainments as ritual combats taking place in the Algeria of his time, and one can still today find villages there with the descendants of such traditional performances. One of the best known of these is the Festival of Sbeiba, a ritual battle and reconciliation held annually in the village of Djanet. It is claimed to go back centuries, certainly to the pre-colonial era, and in any case, it has clearly taken on elements of different cultural traditions. Legend places its origin in the celebration of the victory of Moses over the armies of the Pharaoh, but its content suggests it has grown out of a half-remembered struggle between two local tribes. Whatever its origin, however, it has now been assimilated into Islamic practice, celebrated on Ashura, the high holy day marking the martyrdom of Hussein, and introduced by prayers to Allah.[11] Long before Western theater in the modern form was introduced to this region, ritual performances—pagan, Islamic and blended—were common, as were oratorical performances, orature being an important feature of both Islamic practice and that of the pre-Islamic peoples of this area. The tradition of public and private storytelling was well established in the Maghreb before the coming of Islam, and although the centrality of the Qur'an gave written expression a new importance, the faith was also spread by Islamic storytellers, in forms like the popular *qissa*. Historians of popular narrative in this region have argued that the early Islamic qissa drew upon the older storytelling tradition for such embellishments as song, mimicry and accessories to develop into the traditional *meddah*,[12] the equivalent in much of the Ottoman Empire and, especially, in the Maghreb of the Middle Eastern *hakawati*. The meddah, under the continuing influence of popular entertainments, came to include more secular than religious material. Particularly popular in Algeria was the *nadira*, devoted to the antics of rogue and trickster figures found in much of the world's folk literature. The central such figure was the iconoclastic Djeha, who makes fun of whoever is in authority, a favorite of the Amazigh storytellers and, as we shall see, an important bridge between traditional folk performance and the later Western-style literary theater.[13]

Various traditional folk entertainments have been recorded, not by performance scholars but by anthropologists and orientalists,[14] at least one of which was introduced to the region during the Ottoman period. Shadow puppetry has been a popular folk entertainment in Algeria since the sixteenth century, and not only its physical form but its Arabic name clearly indicate its Turkish origins. In Algeria, this form is known as *Al-Quaraaqoz*, clearly closely related to the Turkish Karagöz, found throughout the Ottoman Empire. Although the Algerian form retained the major character, who in fact had much in common with the popular folk figure Djeha, his traditional, and much more Turkish, antagonist Hacivad disappeared, and was replaced by a more Algerian upper-class figure, Laala Sunbaya, and her servant. The subversive quality of the texts, sexual, political and social, was retained but, in Algeria, turned to local concerns—especially to anti-colonial ones during the French occupation, whose authorities attempted in vain to outlaw the form.

The French colonizers, replacing the Ottomans in 1830, made a far greater effort than had the Ottomans to assimilate Algeria, eventually making it officially a part of the French nation, a status awarded to no other colony. Over the years of French occupation, which lasted until Algerian Independence in 1962, French policy varied from high tolerance for the preexisting cultural practices of the African state to attempts to remodel its culture into a French one. Whatever the strategy, however, the dynamics of cultural interweaving, which had operated for centuries, continued to characterize the evolving relationship between Algeria and its new occupiers. A clear and striking example of this comes from 1847, in the opening years of the French occupation. In that year was published, in Algiers, the first known modern play written in Arabic, a work only discovered in the 1990s by Dr. Philip Sadgrove of the University of Manchester.[15] This curious work, *Nuzahat al-Mushtaq wa-Ghussat al-Ush-shaq fi Madinat Tiryaq l-Iraq* (The Pleasure Trip of the Enamored and the Agony of Lovers in the City of Tiryaq in Iraq), reflected Algerian interweaving on every level. Its author, Abraham Daninos, was an Arabic-speaking Sephardic Jew who served as a professional translator for the occupying French. Jewish, as we have noted, had been a significant part of the Algerian cultural mix since the first century, and their numbers had greatly increased in the fifteenth and sixteenth centuries when they were driven from Spain and Portugal. This experiment attracted the attention of literary critics in both France and Germany, one of whom accurately characterized it as an "Afro-European hybrid."[16]

Daninos was himself a living example of cultural and linguistic interweaving. Although a professional translator of French and Arabic, his own native language was Ladino, descended from Old Spanish and spoken by Sephardic Jews in Spain before their expulsion to Algeria and elsewhere (along with Muslims) in 1492. All languages are interwoven with other languages, but Ladino's history of such interweaving is particularly complex. Already in

Spain it incorporates elements of most of the other Iberian languages, including Galician, Catalan and Portuguese, as well as elements of Hebrew, Aramaic and Arabic. In Africa, this latter influence increased, and Ottoman Turkish added importantly to the mix.

Daninos's play ingeniously wove together elements from several cultures. In structure, it resembled a traditional European drama, with prologue, cast of characters, stage directions, scenes and a story advanced through dialogue. The prologue, however, was delivered by a semi-religious orator who seemed to come, as did the theme and arrangement of incidents, from the Islamic storytelling tradition and the Ottoman shadow theater, although he used, as these did not, the elevated literary dialect *fusha*, close to the language of the Qur'an but far from the *darja* dialect, which Algerians spoke in everyday life. The work contains direct quotations from familiar Islamic folk sources, especially *The Thousand and One Nights* and a thirteenth-century Arabic compendium of stories, *The Revelation of Secrets*.[17] Even so, its unfamiliar European structure and elevated language limited its potential audience to a small, urban, international community, and it apparently remained an isolated experiment.

Similar Arabic attempts at Western-style theater appeared soon after in Syria and Egypt, however, and were brought to the Maghreb at the beginning of the twentieth century. The first significant such tour to Algiers was in 1908 by the company of Sulayman Al-Qardahi, who is generally credited with introducing Western theater to both Algeria and Tunisia. His opening production there was his signature piece, *Salah El-Din Al-Ayoubi* (Saladin) by the Lebanese playwright Najib Al-Haddad, created in 1898 and first performed by Al-Qardahi that year. The play became a great favorite in Algeria, at least among the literate, educated, urban audiences, as it did throughout the Arab world in the early twentieth century, where its heroic presentation of Saladin, one of the great political and military figures of Islamic history, provided Arab-Islamic states with a sense of a shared past and shared destiny, challenged at present by a new form of the Crusades in the form of European colonialism.

So widely and frequently was this play produced and so closely associated with the ideal of Arab nationalism, that one may lose sight of the fact that, like most cultural products, it was derived from a variety of somewhat incongruous sources. Saladin himself, probably the most celebrated warrior in the Arab pantheon, was in fact not Arab, but Kurdish, born in what is today Iraq. More directly relevant to the patriotic sentiments aroused by the piece in the colonial era, its primary source was the 1825 historical novel, *The Talisman*, by the British author, Sir Walter Scott, whose historical romances provided inspiration for a whole generation of dramatists, both Arab and European. *Taratu el arab* (The Revenge of the Arabs), another widely produced Al-Haddad celebration of Arab-Islamic history, was drawn from *Les Aventures du dernier Abencérage* (1826, *The Adventures of the Last Abencerrage*), a sentimental portrayal by the French Romantic Chateaubriand of the loss of Granada. In addition to their European sources, of course, both dramas very much adapted the general structure of romantic historical drama, itself drawing heavily upon Shakespeare. Similar dramatic works, based on Arab history and written in literary Arabic but structured in a European style, dominated the Algerian stage in the early years of the century, and provided an Arab variation on the dramatic construction of national history, long a central concern in the European theater. In Algeria, however, these works, though increasingly common, remained limited in appeal to Europeanized audiences who were not disturbed by their narrative style or their use of the literary language, fusha. A more general public still remained to be attracted.

The Development of a Popular Theater

The production which marked the beginning of a modern popular theater in Algeria was very different from these historical dramas, and much more reflective of both popular taste and the country's hybrid performance culture. This was the enormously successful *Djeha*, coauthored by Ali Sellali, who wrote under the name Allalou, and the popular actor Brahim Dahmoune. Arlette Roth, one of the first historians of the Algerian theater, writes that *Djeha* owed its great success to its "triple innovation: in genre, theme, and language. The first plays presented in Algeria were in literary Arabic and concerned social themes and noble subjects such as patriotism. *Djeha* was a gross farce in Arab dialect."[18] This somewhat condescending appraisal does not note that *Djeha* drew upon a rich multicultural performance background with wide appeal to its potential audience. Djeha himself, as we have already encountered, was long established as a familiar iconoclastic trickster figure in the folk tradition. Coauthor Dahmoune did not in fact play the title role but rather his overbearing and manipulative wife Hila, a figure clearly related to Karagöz's shrewish wife Aglaia. Alloula had been presenting short folk farces based on these characters for several years before *Djeha*, but here, for the first time, they developed this material into a full-length play in the European style, with three acts and seven scenes. Its plot skillfully wove together material from a variety of cultural sources. Djeha and his wife were developed in a plot which drew heavily upon Molière's *Le Malade imaginaire* (1673, *The Imaginary Invalid*) and *Le Médecin malgré lui* (1666, *The Doctor in Spite of Himself*), a medieval French folktale, *Le Vilain mire* (*The Peasant Doctor*), and themes and characters from that central Arab-Islamic source, *The Thousand and One Nights*.

Similar blended entertainments dominated the Algerian stage for the next decade, first in the work of Allalou and Dahmoune and then in that of Rachid Ksentini, who, like his model Molière, combined the skills of actor, author and director. Although Ksentini was the most popular Algerian dramatist of the 1930s, he, like Algerian theater artists in general, was engaged in a constant struggle with the French authorities. His satiric pictures of contemporary life were often banned as critical of the colonial situation, and drawing upon the critical tradition of Molière was equally dangerous. This situation changed sharply in 1940 with the fall of France and the establishment of the Vichy government, now in control of Algeria. Patriotic themes were now seen not as directed against the French but against the Nazis, the new threat to liberty, and Molière translations and adaptations were now strongly encouraged as a celebration of the French patrimony. As a result, Algerian theaters alone in the Maghreb continued to function throughout the war. The leading new Algerian author of the period was Mohammed Touri, who produced Molière adaptations but specialized in original works, clearly inspired by Ksentini, in which he developed a signature character who appeared with various names but was noted for never smiling, gaining Touri the name "the Algerian Buster Keaton."[19] Another popular author/actor of the period was Rouiched (real name: Ahmed Ayad), who also, like Touri and Ksentini, created a new rogue/trickster figure in the Djeha tradition. Rouiched's Hassan Djeha, however, was very much a figure of his times, who converted to the revolutionary cause and was imprisoned and tortured by the colonial authorities. We may see a certain parallel to the dynamics which converted the wily traditional trickster Figaro into a proto-revolutionary in Beaumarchais's *The Marriage of Figaro*. So effectively did Rouiched blend the figure from popular folk culture with the revolutionary cause that his work led Che Guevara, who visited the Algerian National Theatre in the mid-1960s, to comment, "I beheld the revolutionary theatre itself in the land of Algeria."[20]

Many in North Africa hoped that the widespread support for the Allied cause would build sympathy among the winning powers for independence, which in fact was attained by Morocco and Tunisia in 1956. The French were far more determined to hold onto Algeria, officially a part of France itself, and independence was gained by that country only after five more years of bitter struggle, widespread violence and great bloodshed. The most significant Algerian theater was closely tied to this struggle, and an important part of it was created by dissident figures in the prisons or in exile. With the declaration of independence in July of 1962, theater artists in the new country faced the common post-colonial problem of creating a suitable new theater for the new order. A key figure in this project was the prominent director and dramatist Mustapha Kateb, who had directed Algeria's most important theater in exile in Tunis during the war for independence. Of almost equal importance was the actor, director and dramatist Abdelkader Ould Abderrahmane, known as Abderrahmane Kaki, whose stage name was Kaki. He had also directed an Algerian theater in exile during the war, in Lyon, but not surprisingly, this French-based operation was less political and revolutionary than that of Kateb's in Tunis and stressed an international repertoire and experimental production practices.

These two became the leading figures in the debate over the future course of the new Algerian theater. Both accepted the general belief that this new theater must be "decolonized," but they disagreed sharply over the means. Interestingly both advocated the renewal of the theater by interweaving new material into it, but in the source of that material, they strongly diverged. Rather surprisingly, Kateb advocated moving in the direction Kaki had pursued in Lyon—that is, enriching the Algerian theater by infusing it with inspiration for a broad international repertoire—while Kaki, who might have been expected to agree strongly with this direction, in fact strongly opposed it. The new Algerian theater, he argued, should draw inspiration not from external but from internal sources, from Algerian performance practices of earlier periods, an approach he characterized as heritage theater.[21]

Both approaches were in fact clearly to be seen in Algerian productions of subsequent years, resulting in a theater which both reflected recent European trends and revived and reworked traditional material. Kaki's interest in weaving back into current performance styles and techniques from the Algerian past was particularly significant. This practice, to which in the 1960s he gave the name "festival" or "carnivalesque" theater, was first clearly demonstrated in his 1966 *El Guerrab wa Essalhine* (The Water-Bearer and the Holy Men). Here Kaki utilized, for the first time in modern Maghreb theater, two major elements of traditional performance in that region—the *gouwâl*, or storyteller, and the circular arrangement and involvement of the audience known as the *halqa*. The originality and influence of this work convinced a jury of Algerian critics in 1999 to name it the most important drama produced in that country since the Independence.[22] Kaki's strategy of reworking elements of Maghreb popular culture clearly influenced the leading dramatists of the next generation—Kateb Yacine (the cousin of Mustapha Kateb), Abdelkader Alloula and Slimane Benaïssa—although each developed this strategy in a different way. As the Algerian theater historian Ahmed Cheniki explains, "Kateb Yacine recreated and reinvested the legendary character of Djeha with new meanings. Abdelkader Alloula transformed the structure of the gouwâland of the halqa. Slimane Benaïssa undertook a plunge into ordinary language."[23]

Yacine's Contribution to an Interwoven Theater in Algeria

Of these three, Kateb Yacine most clearly embodies, as an individual and as an artist, the cultural interweaving in Algeria, which is the focus of this chapter. He was in fact the first dramatist to consciously reflect in his work the three basic languages and cultures of Algeria—French, Amazigh and Arabic. He was born Yacine Kateb in Constantine, an ancient city in northeastern Algeria, to a family of Amazigh descent but, like most cosmopolitan Algerians, was equally at home in French or Arabic culture. Yacine spent most of the 1960s in Paris, where, finding his teachers generally placed his last name first, he adopted Kateb Yacine as his pen name. Here he published a series of plays set in Algeria and dealing with the war for independence. The third of these, *Poudre d'intelligence* (Intelligence Powder), was Yacine's first comic work and his first to significantly employ the character Nuage de Fumée (Puff of Smoke), clearly and consciously a reincarnation of the familiar folk hero Djeha, but like Rouiched's Hassan, recruited into the 1950s revolution against colonial rule. The play was premiered in a small experimental theater in Paris, L'Epée de Bois, in 1967 and first presented in Algiers two years later. Much of the play follows the age-old pattern of such works, showing the wily Nuage playing tricks on the gullible authority figure of the Sultan, such as convincing him that his donkey produces gold instead of dung. Late in the play, however, Nuage's plots take a more serious and contemporary turn when he encounters Ali, the son of Nedjma, a semi-mythic figure who represents tortured Algeria in several of Yacine's previous works. Working together for the liberation of Algeria, the two abduct the Crown Prince, who is then killed in a botched rescue attempt by the Sultan's cavaliers.

When the play was first presented in Algeria, it was indifferently received, but this was surely due, at least in part, to the fact that it was translated from French into classical Arabic, a choice distinctly unsuited to this Djeha-based character and that popular tradition. A rather happier reception greeted Yacine's *L'Homme aux sandals de caoutchouc* (The Man in Rubber Sandals), inspired by the struggles of Ho Chi Minh in Vietnam, which Yacine saw in many ways parallel to the anti-colonialist struggle in Algeria. The play, originally written in a rare mixture of French, classical Arabic and Amazigh, was translated into colloquial Arabic and directed at the Algerian National Theatre in 1968 by fellow dramatist Slimane Benaïssa, who subsequently became primarily known for his translations and direction of Yacine's work.

Although the play was not a major success, its appearance at the National Theatre significantly increased Yacine's reputation at home, and a growing desire to connect with his Algerian roots and especially with a popular audience led him to return to Algeria and to a career with a new populist orientation. Finding the National Theatre too conservative, Yacine allied himself briefly with a much more politically sympathetic group, the Théâtre de la Mer, founded in the revolutionary year 1968 by Kadour Naimi under the inspiration of the Living Theatre, with whose work he had become familiar as a student in France. In the Living Theatre, Naimi found inspiration for such devices as improvisation, collective creation, including even the audience, and a devotion to performing in unconventional areas and to lower-class audiences outside the traditional world of theater. In the manifesto of the theater, Naimi called for "a popular theater, directed toward Algerian realities," created for "those citizens who do not know or do not like the state theatre companies'—factory and farm workers, students, and intellectuals—interest in non-conventional theatre." In such innovations, Naimi found close parallels to the traditional folk performance of North Africa, the halqa, both in its physical arrangement and in its freedom from established literary texts. In terms of interweaving, however, Naimi went far beyond the utilization of popular forms from the native tradition, but very much in the eclectic style of international performance of the 1960s claimed inspiration also from Western experimental and classic practices, the Living Theatre, Greek and medieval performance, the theaters of Vietnam, China and Bali, and Griot performance from sub-Saharan Africa.[24]

These concerns accorded closely with those of Yacine's and clearly left their mark on his subsequent work, although his association with Naimi in fact lasted only one season, since Naimi, with a Living Theatre distrust of institutions, found Yacine too willing to work with the theater establishment in Algeria. In fact, however, after their separation, Yacine formed a new organization, the Action culturelle des travailleurs (ACT; the Workers Cultural Action), which ultimately better fulfilled the theatrical and political vision of Naimi. It was established in Bab El Oued, a strongly working-class section of Algiers, where it built a populist audience larger than any in Algeria, or for that matter, in the developing world—the "third world"[25]—and expanded its influence by enormously successful tours of new work by Yacine and the company, first through Algeria, then to France, where they performed primarily for Algerian immigrants in the Renault factory and others, attracting a total audience of more than 70,000 during their five-month tour. Back in Algeria, they continued to tour for another five years, attracting sometimes as many as 10,000 people to a single performance.[26]

Aside from its political significance, Yacine's theater provides a particularly important modern example of the dynamics of theatrical interweaving in Algeria that is the focus of this chapter. Its highly successful performance style was developed by a distinct and, for the most part, quite conscious putting together of elements for traditional and contemporary performance, as well as Algerian and Western sources. In terms of staging, this meant extensive use of outdoor improvised spaces, employing the traditional Algerian halqa which had also been favored by Naimi. Traditional halqa performance included a good deal of improvisation, which Yacine blended with the new European interest in collective creation to create a new dynamic style of interactive theater, able to adapt quickly to changing political conditions.

One of the most distinctive features of Yacine's theater, however, was not the frequent use of the halqa, which equally attracted a number of his contemporaries, but his interest not only in indigenous performance practice but indigenous language, particularly the Tamazight of his own ancestors. Yacine came to believe that an effective Algerian theater, whatever its physical structure, needed to reflect the linguistic mixture of the Algerian people, whose daily life utilized Arabic, French and Tamazight. This would allow the theater to break out of what Yacine called its two traditional linguistic "ghettos,"

Arabic-Muslim and French.²⁷ A recent biography of Yacine has suggested that he "often appears to be going back in time, moving from French to Algerian Arabic, to Berber, as if stripping away layer after layer of oppressive culture."²⁸ Actually, this image is based on any early assumption of post-colonial thought, that a simple removal of colonial practice would allow unmediated access to pre-colonial culture. It was soon widely recognized, however, that the actual process worked in an almost opposite way, as Friedrich Schiller long ago recognized in his celebrated essay on naive and sentimental poetry.²⁹ The modern poet, seeking to recreate the poetic vision of another lost and presumably purer era, can never do so because of the self-consciousness that the intervening time has imposed. Similarly, the post-colonial author, wishing to return to earlier and presumably purer pre-colonial forms of expression, inevitably does so through the colonial experience. Instead of stripping away layers of "oppressive culture," he in fact adds yet another layer, or more accurately, another element to an already complex blend. The process is inevitably one of ever more interpenetrating fusion, not reduction and separation.

The result, though drawing upon a variety of different elements, can produce a quite new manifestation, as is certainly the case with the work of Yacine. Nowhere is this clearer than in how and why he revolutionized the traditional Djeha figure. From its very beginnings, Yacine's ACT theater took this traditional figure as central to its work, and all of Yacine's plays from 1972 onward reflect this. Yacine's biographer, Kamal Salhi, suggests that

> [W]ith the figure of Djeha, culture ceases to be normative act and becomes performance. With a serious eloquence and ill at ease in his western and berber/bedouin dress, Djeha is a symbol for laughter. There is as much movement as speech. The people's language is revived and is vulgarised. With the establishment of Djeha as an artistic influence on the troupe's performing mode, a new cultural group consciousness has appeared.³⁰

This final comment points to a critical way in which Yacine's use of this traditional figure differed from that of other post-colonial Algerian dramatists. While all utilized Djeha's role as an outsider, a renegade and a satiric observer of his surrounding culture, dramatists like Alloula and Benaïssa followed those like Kaki and Ksentini in depicting their Djeha figures as solitary figures, while Yacine, in keeping with his interest in collectivity, both as a political and an artistic goal, insisted that central to ACT training was the development of each actor to assume the Djeha role. The character thus became a part of whatever role they performed. Instead of informing a single figure with a particularly close relationship to a popular audience, the Djeha spirit was absorbed by the entire company in an attempt to create such a relationship. The use of the halqa was closely tied to this, but one may also see related concerns in the work and political theory of Western experimental artists that Yacine admired, such as Brecht, the Living Theatre and the French developers of collective creations. Here, once again, a new approach was developed through the interweaving of native and foreign performance practice.

Obviously, the interest of a major dramatist like Yacine in the Amazigh language gave a stimulus never before felt to the development of actual Western-style drama in that language. Although the Amazigh for centuries had both absorbed and opposed the successive waves of conquerors and occupiers that moved into their lands, and though they had inevitably felt the cultural effects of these interactions, there had never been, before the late twentieth century, any effort to create an Amazigh version of Western-style theater. Like any cultural group, the Amazigh had a rich performance tradition, which included storytelling, dances, ritual performances of many types, and even simple folk farces, but unlike even their Arab neighbors, they remained impervious to the incursion of Western-style theater.

The success of Yacine and his championship of Amazigh culture and language abruptly changed this. Yacine's first major drama, *Mohammed, prends ta valise* (Mohammed, Take Up Your Suitcase), already partly in Tamazight, was the first play translated entirely into Kabyle, the major Amazigh language of Algeria.[31] It was first staged by a school group in 1973 and was presented, over the objections of the school authorities, at the Carthage Festival that year. The school was located in the city of Tizi Ouzou, a center for Amazigh culture and resistance to the Arabization and Islamization tendencies of the central government. The other center for this new Amazigh interest in Western drama was Paris, where a student organization, the Groupe d'études berberes (Berber Studies Group) led by Mohya Abdeall began, in the early 1970s, to translate and stage works by authors like Sartre and Brecht. Their first production was the Kabyle version of Yacine's *Mohammed*.

They presented their work at Peter Brook's Bouffes du Nord theater and to other Paris stages in areas with a significant Amazigh population, but not in Algeria, where an increasing official encouragement of Arabization led to protests by and increasing suppression of the Amazigh minority. In 1979, the fledgling Amazigh theater in Tizi Ouzou was closed and all Amazigh productions banned. Ironically, the use of Western theater practice, encouraged by the French during the colonial period, became, after independence, a threat. In both cases, however, its combination with the workings of an already existing culture created something quite new and different.

The Spread of Theater During the 1980s and Early 1990s

Although Algeria suffered a bloody civil war between the government and Islamists during the early 1990s, the Amazigh theater gradually revived. Tizi Ouzou, its theater now named for Kateb Yacine, remained the center of such activity and, in 1993, during the darkest days of the war, launched the first national festival of Amazigh theater. This festival has continued and inspired others in Algeria and in Morocco. Fouzia Aït El-Hadj, an important playwright and director, assumed leadership of the theater in 2006 and brought it to new prominence. One of her most successful pieces was an Amazigh version, in 2008, of one of the popular new solo performance pieces, *Fatma*, by Mohamed Benguettaf. As in the United States, an important part of modern solo performance in Algeria was concerned with the position of women although, of course, focusing upon local conditions. The production was moved, without a change of language, to the National Theatre in Algiers, where it enjoyed a major success, proving the viability of multiple language works at the nation's central theater, long a stronghold of European-style theater presented in Arabic.

The other leading Algerian director of the 1970s and 1980s, Abdelkader Alloula, did not share Yacine's background connections to or cultural interest in the Amazigh, but his interests otherwise were closely allied. Like Yacine, he had a strong commitment to the neglected rural and working populations and, like Yacine, was based, not at the National Theatre but in his own regional theater, in Oran, where he could more easily explore his own experimentation. Like Yacine, and many leading Algerian experimental directors of this time, he was much interested both politically and aesthetically in the new European vogue of collective creations and, in this way, created such works as *Homk Salim* (1972, *Salim's Madness*) and *El Maida* (1973, *The Table*). Like Yacine, however, and unlike many other young directors of this period, Alloula did not simply follow the patterns of such European champions of this form as Ariane Mnouchkine in Paris, but developed instead a sophisticated blending of contemporary European experimentation and Algerian performance traditions. Although both of these works were developed collectively by Alloula's company, the first departed sharply from European practice by presenting only a single character, played by Alloula himself. The second used the entire company but essentially as a chorus, supporting Alloula. This radical change to the normal European utilization of this approach Alloula described as a conscious effort to blend it with native performance traditions, in this case the traditional storyteller, the gouwâl. From 1972 onward, the gouwâl appeared as a central figure in every play Alloula created. He remarked on his discovery and use of this figure in an interview in 1982: "Traditionally, this is a single, solitary person who tells a story making use of mimicry, gestures, and intonation. This allows us to reconnect with a type of theatrical activity interrupted by colonization. From now on, we can think of a type of theatre that our people need, and this is a very important thing."[32] Alloula's emphasis on the tradition of the Algerian storyteller inevitably led him to the type of staging closely associated with the form of staging known as the halqa. Alloula saw both of these practices as contributing to a new and more complex theater experience that would be both more universal than any of its elements and yet more closely tied to the community's lived experience. As he explained in a 1985 interview conducted at the Oran theater,

> The more I reflect on this, the more I observe that "storyteller" in the halqa, and the more, in this way, I rediscover the art of the theater. It may be that these expressions are less rich, but still the theater is there. And, unfortunately, we have been practicing a type of theater which, in my opinion, is inadequate for presenting the characteristics of our popular culture and of the way we live out our culture. My goal is to make my contribution to the creation of an Algerian theater which can display its own characteristics and in turn provide new elements for the universal theater. We presently practice a theater which is not ours, or which is not yet ours. It is not a question of becoming narrow; it is a question of putting forward and of developing theatrical forms which draw upon elevated tonalities and yet, at the same time, are tied to our lived experience, to our culture.[33]

Alloula's best-known work is a loosely connected trilogy concerning the common people of Algeria, which in his final interview, just a month before his death in 1990, he characterized as part of an evolving experiment in what he called the modern halqa theater.[34] The first play of this trilogy, appropriately named *Al-Agouwâl* (1980, The Storyteller), consists only of five stories performed by this figure, the gouwâl, in the traditional manner. The French critic H. M. Kahina, in a 2004 tribute to Alloula, wittily tied together this work with the following two in the trilogy, *El-Ajwad* (1984, The Generous Ones) and *El-Litham* (1989, The Veil): "'The sayings' of the *gouwâls* are presented in *halqas* to audiences composed of 'The Generous or Good' people, who are both the subjects of these stories and their public. These stories are designed to remove 'The Veil' of silence that covers centuries of oppression of these people by colonizers and others."[35]

New Directions

The death of Alloula in 1990 occurred at the beginning of a decade of major civil unrest in Algeria, which took a heavy toll on the theater and its artists. When a more stable situation was established in the new century, most of the leading figures of the last century were gone, but a new generation continued many of their concerns, taken in new directions. One of the most important of these was the rise of solo performance. Introduced in the mid-1980s, the form proved so popular that an Algerian newspaper reported in 1995 that this was "the era of the solo performer," the "most beloved dramatic form" of the time, devoted largely to satiric presentations of contemporary society.[36]

Although the term "solo performance" was almost certainly drawn from the contemporary rise of interest in that form in Europe and the United States—coming in the wake of the rediscovery and theatrical reemployment of the solo storyteller in Algeria by Alloula and others—it seems equally certain that despite the cachet of the international term, this popular form in Algeria inevitably was deeply imbricated in local culture, both political and aesthetic, and as a result, much more distinctly involved in the ongoing interweaving of this culture than was the solo performance in Europe and America, arising from a very different political and theatrical matrix.[37] An indication of the close relationship between the work of Alloula and the new solo performance movement in Algeria is the fact that his theater in Oran (now bearing his name) has been a center for such new work. Among the creations of one of its most popular solo performers, Samir Bouanani, is *Nassine oua salatine* (2003), directly based on the work of Alloula. For his presentation of this role, Bouanani won the award for best actor at the Journées Théâtrales de Carthage (The Carthage Theater Days) in 2003.

Another Western-style theater, constructed in the heart of Amazigh Algeria, is the Kateb Yacine in Tizi Ouzou. By its very existence, as a European proscenium theater in the land of the halqa, this structure attests to the interwoven culture that surrounds it, and it could bear no more appropriate name than that of the first major Algerian author to recognize the importance of all three of the county's major cultural and linguistic traditions and to bring into the cultural conversation the Amazigh, long marginalized by both internal and external forces. In the twenty-first century, the Amazigh, largely due to figures like Yacine, has not only been given new attention as a culture and language in its own right, but, even more important for this chapter, has been acknowledged as a long-time and continuing contributor to the interwoven culture that makes up present-day Algeria. In this development, the Kateb Yacine Theater has appropriately played a major role: in its ongoing programs, in its national and international outreach, and in its annual festival, which continues to explore the expressive possibilities of the multiple linguistic and performative works presented here. As this chapter was being written, in the summer of 2019, Tizi Ouzou completed the latest such event—a month-long festival offering over 20 productions, widely varying in style and language, a number of which toured to other theaters.[38]

Notes

1 Hicham Yezza, "Beyond Arab vs Berber: The Rich Complexities of Algerian Identity Should Be Celebrated, Not Feared," *Open Democracy*, 26 April 2013, https://www.opendemocracy.net/en/north-africa-west-asia/beyond-arab-vs-berber-rich-complexities-of-algerian-identity-should-be-c/.
2 Bouziane Ben Achour, *Le Théâtre algérien: Une histoire d'étapes* (Oran: Dar El Gharb, 2005), 5, my translation.

3 John Conteh-Morgan and Dominic Thomas, *New Francophone African and Caribbean Theatres* (Bloomington, IN: Indiana University Press, 2010), 29.
4 Jay Cleo, "Playing the 'Berber': The Performance of Amazigh Identities in Contemporary Morocco," *The Journal of North African Studies* 21, no. 1 (2016): 72.
5 See, for example, Khalid Amine, "Theatre in the Arab World: A Difficult Birth," *Theatre Research International* 31, no. 2 (2006): 145–62; and Khalid Amine and Marvin Carlson, "*Al-halqa* in Arabic Theatre: An Emerging Site of Hybridity," *Theatre Journal* 60, no. 1 (2008): 71–85.
6 Others included church fathers Tertullian and Cyprian, the novelist Apuleius, the orator Marcus Cornelius Fronto, and the emperors Macrinus and Aemilian.
7 One example for this cultural interweaving since the Roman time is the literary work of Apuleius, a Berber author and philosopher writing in Latin. See, for instance, Benjamin Todd Lee, Ellen Finkelpearl and Luca Graverini, eds., *Apuleius and Africa* (London and New York, NY: Routledge, 2014).
8 See Andrew H. Merrills, *Vandals, Roman and Berbers: New Perspectives on Late Antique North Africa* (Farnham: Ashgate, 2004).
9 See John Joseph Saunders, *A History of Medieval Islam* (London: Routledge and Kegan Paul, 1965), 66–75, 93–99.
10 John P. Entelis, *Algeria: The Revolution Institutionalized* (Boulder, CO: Westview, 1986), 14.
11 See Nabila Amir, "Fête de la Sbeiba: Un ritual et une histoire," *DjaZairess*, 29 December 2009, https://www.djazairess.com/fr/elwatan/147222.
12 See, for example, Youssef Rachid Haddad, *Art du conteur, art de l'acteur* (Louvain-la-Neuve: Cahiers théâtre, 1982), 28–43.
13 Although the iconoclastic trickster is a central figure in world folk literature and Djeha a familiar variation of this figure in the Maghreb, I have found only one researcher who has attempted to place Djeha in the larger international context. This is a young Algerian linguist, Rachid Bekhechi, who, in a fascinating 2014 blog post, lays out a web of Djeha-related folk figures, centered in the Ottoman Empire but ranging from the Maghreb to China. He suggests the figure inspiring the tales may have lived in Asia Minor as early as the tenth century. See Rachid Bekhechi, "Joha: The Fool, The Shrewd and The Sage," *Kameleon* (blog), 12 November 2014, https://blog.racbek.com/joha-the-fool-the-shrewd-and-the-sage.
14 Particularly important was the work of the French orientalist Edmond Doutté, author of *Magie et religion dans l'Afrique du Nord* (Algiers: Adolphe Jourdan, 1908) and the anthropologist Auguste Mouliéras, born in Algeria to French national parents, author of *Les Fourberies de Si Djeh'a: Contes kabyles* (Paris: Ernest Leroux, 1892).
15 See Shmuel Moreh and Philip Sadgrove, *Jewish Contributions to Nineteenth-Century Arabic Theatre* (New York, NY: Oxford University Press, 1996).
16 From a review of current literature in *Zeitschrift der Deutschen Morgenländischen Gesellschaft* (1850), quoted in ibid., 11.
17 See ibid., 22.
18 Arlette Roth, *Le Théâtre algérienne de langue dialectale 1926–1954* (Paris: Maspero, 1967), 22, my translation.
19 Mohamed Ghriss, "Mohamed Touri: Considéré comme l'un des plus illustres comiques de l'histoire de l'Algérie," *El Watan*, 6 May 2017, https://www.elwatan.com/archives/contributions-archives/mohamed-touri-considere-comme-lun-des-plus-illustres-comiques-de-lhistoire-de-lalgerie-2-06-05-2017. My translation.
20 Che Guevara, quoted in Abdallah El Rukaibni, "Algeria," in *The World Encyclopedia of Contemporary Theatre*, vol. 4, *The Arab World*, ed. Don Rubin (London and New York, NY: Routledge, 1999), 53.

21 See Moussa (Youcef) Selmane, "Modern Algerian Theatre: Translations and Critical Analysis of Three Plays by Kateb Yacine, Abdelkader Alloula and Slimane Benaissa" (PhD diss., Leeds: University of Leeds, 1989).
22 See Kamel Bendimered, "Ould Abderrahmane Kaki, Le Pionnier du théâtre 'ihtifali,'" *Djazair*, no. 3 (2003): 30.
23 Ahmed Cheniki, *Le Théâtre en Algérie: histoire et enjeux* (Aix-en-Provence: Edisud, 2002), 22, my translation.
24 The manifesto is reproduced at "THEATRE DE LA MER: compagnie de recherche et de réalisations théâtrales expérimentales," *Kadour Naimi*, accessed 1 July 2021, www.kadour-naimi.com/f-theatre-mer-algerie.htm. My translation.
25 Kamal Salhi, *The Politics and Aesthetics of Kateb Yacine: From Francophone Literature to Popular Theatre in Algeria and Outside* (Lewiston, NY: Edwin Mellen, 1999), 15.
26 See Nadia Tazi, "Kateb Yacine," *L'Autre Journal* (July–August 1985): 17.
27 Kateb Yacine, *Le Poète comme un boxeur: Entretiens 1958–1989*, ed. Gilles Carpentier (Paris: Seuil, 1994), 33.
28 Salhi, *Politics and Aesthetics*, 121.
29 See Friedrich Schiller, *Naive and Sentimental Poetry*, trans. Julius A. Elias (New York, NY: Frederick Ungar, 1967).
30 Kamal Salhi, "Post-Colonial Theatre for Development in Algeria: Kateb Yacine's Early Experience," in *African Theatre for Development: Art for Self-determination*, ed. Kamal Salhi (Bristol: Intellect, 1998), 63.
31 Linguists differ on the precise number and classification of Berber languages and dialects but generally agree on Kabyle as the major Berber language of Algeria and second most important such language in the Maghreb, with about eight million speakers. Most Berber theater to date has appeared in Kabyle.
32 Abdelkader Alloula, interview by Ahmed Cheniki, quoted in Khalid Amine and Marvin Carlson, *The Theatres of Morocco, Algeria and Tunisia: Performance Traditions of the Maghreb* (Basingstoke: Palgrave Macmillan, 2012), 161.
33 Abdelkader Alloula, "La Halqa inedite d'Abdelkader Alloula," interview by Abdelmadjid Kaouah, *Joha* (blog), 13 November 2009, http://wwwjohablogspotcom-kaouah.blogspot.com/2009/11/la-halqa-inedite-dabdelkader-alloula.html. My translation.
34 Abdelkader Alloula, "Du Théâtre-Halqa à la Commedia dell'Arte," interview by Mohammed Kali, in *En mémoire du futur: Pour Abdelkader Alloula* (Paris: Sindbad, Actes Sud, 1997), 175.
35 H. M. Kahina, *La Nouvelle Republique*, 8 March 2004, quoted in Amine and Carlson, *The Theatres of Morocco*, 162–63.
36 Quoted in Bouziane Ben Achour, *Le Théâtre en mouvement: Octobre 88 à ce jour* (Oran: Dar El Gharb, 2002), 148.
37 See Marvin Carlson, *Performance: A Critical Introduction*, 3rd ed. (London and New York, NY: Routledge, 2018), 98–99, 135–38.
38 S. Oularbi, "Théâtre régional Kateb-Yacine de Tizi Ouzou: 26 pièces programmés pour le mois de Ramadhan,"*Reporters*, 8 May 2019, https://www.reporters.dz/theatre-regional-kateb-yacine-de-tizi-ouzou-26-pieces-programmees-pour-le-mois-de-ramadhan/.

Bibliography

Alloula, Abdelkader. "Du Théâtre-Halqa à la Commedia dell'Arte." Interview by Mohammed Kali. In *En mémoire du futur: Pour Abdelkader Alloula*, 175–76. Paris: Sindbad, Actes Sud, 1997.

———. "La halqa inedite d'Abdelkader Alloula." Interview by Abdelmadjid Kaouah. *Joha* (blog), 13 November 2009. http://wwwjohablogspotcom-kaouah.blogspot.com/2009/11/la-halqa-inedite-dabdelkader-alloula.html.

Amine, Khalid. "Theatre in the Arab World: A Difficult Birth." *Theatre Research International* 31, no. 2 (2006): 145–62.

———, and Marvin Carlson. "*Al-halqa* in Arabic Theatre: An Emerging Site of Hybridity." *Theatre Journal* 60, no. 1 (2008): 71–85.

———. *The Theatres of Morocco, Algeria and Tunisia: Performance Traditions of the Maghreb*. Basingstoke: Palgrave Macmillan, 2012.

Amir, Nabila. "Fête de la Sbeiba: Un ritual et une histoire." *DjaZairess*, 29 December 2009. https://www.djazairess.com/fr/elwatan/147222.

Bekhechi, Rachid. "Joha: The Fool, The Shrewd and The Sage." *Kameleon* (blog), 12 November2014. https://blog.racbek.com/joha-the-fool-the-shrewd-and-the-sage.

Ben Achour, Bouziane. *Le Théâtre algérien:Une histoire d'étapes*. Oran: Dar El Gharb, 2005.

———. *Le Théâtre en mouvement: Octobre 88 à ce jour*. Oran: Dar El Gharb, 2002.

Bendimered, Kamel. "Ould Abderrahmane Kaki, Le Pionnier du théâtre 'ihtifali.'" *Djazair*, no. 3 (2003): 30–31.

Carlson, Marvin. *Performance: A Critical Introduction*. 3rd ed. London and New York, NY: Routledge, 2018.

Cheniki, Ahmed. *Le Théâtre en Algérie: histoire et enjeux*. Aix-en-Provence: Edisud, 2002.

Cleo, Jay. "Playing the 'Berber': The Performance of Amazigh Identities in Contemporary Morocco." *The Journal of North African Studies* 21, no. 1 (2016): 68–80.

Conteh-Morgan, John, and Dominic Thomas. *New Francophone African and Caribbean Theatres*. Bloomington, IN: Indiana University Press, 2010.

Doutté, Edmond. *Magie et religion dans l'Afrique du Nord*. Algiers: Adolphe Jourdan, 1908.

El Rukaibni, Abdallah. "Algeria." In *The World Encyclopedia of Contemporary Theatre*, vol. 4, *The Arab World*, edited by Don Rubin. London and New York, NY: Routledge, 1999.

Entelis, John P. *Algeria: The Revolution Institutionalized*. Boulder, CO: Westview, 1986.

Ghriss, Mohamed. "Mohamed Touri: Considéré comme l'un des plus illustres comiques de l'histoire de l'Algérie." *El Watan*, 6 May 2017. https://www.elwatan.com/archives/contributions-archives/mohamed-touri-considere-comme-lun-des-plus-illustres-comiques-de-lhistoire-de-lalgerie-2-06-05-2017.

Haddad, Youssef Rachid. *Art du conteur, Art de l'acteur*. Louvain-la-Neuve: Cahiers théâtre, 1982.

Kahina, H. M. "Tribute to Alloula." *La Nouvelle Republique*, 8 March 2004.

Lee, Benjamin Todd, Ellen Finkelpearl and Luca Graverini, eds. *Apuleius and Africa*. London and New York, NY: Routledge, 2014.

Merrills, Andrew H. *Vandals, Roman and Berbers: New Perspectives on Late Antique North Africa*. Farnham: Ashgate, 2004.

Moreh, Shmuel, and Philip Sadgrove. *Jewish Contributions to Nineteenth-Century Arabic Theatre*. New York, NY: Oxford University Press, 1996.

Mouliéras, Auguste. *Les Fourberies de Si Djeh'a: Contes kabyles*. Paris: Ernest Leroux, 1892.

Naimi, Kadour. "THEATRE DE LA MER: compagnie de recherche et de réalisations théâtrales expérimentales." *Kadour Naimi*. Accessed 1 July 2021. www.kadour-naimi.com/f-theatre-mer-algerie.htm.

Oularbi, S. "Théâtre régional Kateb-Yacine de Tizi Ouzou: 26 pièces programmés pour le mois de Ramadhan." *Reporters*, 8 May 2019. https://www.reporters.dz/theatre-regional-kateb-yacine-de-tizi-ouzou-26-pieces-programmees-pour-le-mois-de-ramadhan/.

Roth, Arlette. *Le Théâtre algérienne de langue dialectale 1926–1954*. Paris: Maspero, 1967.

Salhi, Kamal. "Post-Colonial Theatre for Development in Algeria: Kateb Yacine's Early Experience." In *African Theatre for Development: Art for Self-determination*, edited by Kamal Salhi, 59–80. Bristol: Intellect, 1998.

———. *The Politics and Aesthetics of Kateb Yacine: From Francophone Literature to Popular Theatre in Algeria and Outside*. Lewiston, NY: Edwin Mellen, 1999.

Saunders, John Joseph. *A History of Medieval Islam*. London: Routledge and Kegan Paul, 1965.

Schiller, Friedrich. *Naive and Sentimental Poetry*. Translated by Julius A. Elias. New York, NY: Frederick Ungar, 1967.

Selmane, Moussa (Youcef). "Modern Algerian Theatre: Translations and Critical Analysis of Three Plays by Kateb Yacine, Abdelkader Alloula and Slimane Benaissa." PhD diss., Leeds: University of Leeds, 1989.

Tazi, Nadia. "Kateb Yacine." *L'Autre Journal* (July–August 1985): 6–18.

Yacine, Kateb. *Le Poète comme un boxeur: Entretiens 1958–1989*, edited by Gilles Carpentier. Paris: Seuil, 1994.

Yezza, Hicham. "Beyond Arab vs Berber: The Rich Complexities of Algerian Identity Should Be Celebrated, Not Feared." *Open Democracy*, 26 April 2013. https://www.opendemocracy.net/en/north-africa-west-asia/beyond-arab-vs-berber-rich-complexities-of-algerian-identity-should-be-c/.

10
WRITING HISTORY AS DISENTANGLEMENT

Toward a Historiography of Modern Greek Theater

Platon Mavromoustakos

Following the war of independence of 1821 against Ottoman rule over the geographical area of modern Greece—a rule lasting 400 years, from the demise of Byzantium and the fall of Constantinople in 1453—the need to compose a history for the newly founded Greek state in 1832 involved tackling the problem of a fragmented past. It was thus imperative to create a model that could convincingly incorporate aspects of the past into one inclusive whole. The model proposed by the "father" of modern Greek historiography, Konstantinos Paparrigopoulos[1] was more than well received and acquired the status of the official historical model supporting the new Greek state. This tripartite model, comprised of ancient Greece, Byzantium and the modern Greek state, served as the foundation both for affirming the particularity of modern Greece and for reclaiming a past which, up until then, remained disconnected. Despite the fact that this past was largely unknown to the majority of the citizens of the new nation-state, it was nevertheless a decisive reference point in setting the ground for the war of its independence and in its founding.

In parallel, the intervention of the powerful countries of Western Europe was every bit as decisive a factor in the successful outcome of the war of independence as was the mobilization of the communities of the Greek diaspora in instigating it.[2] These two factors provided a new framework for the construction of the newly emergent nation-state. Under the influence of the European Enlightenment, the Greeks of the diaspora relied heavily on the Greek antiquity for forging a combative national consciousness.[3] A corresponding emphasis will be ascribed to the ancient world by the great Western powers which helped defeat the Ottoman empire. The outcome of the war for independence will be the genesis of the modern Greek state. The emerging nation is thus formed with a specific constitutive intermediacy: "Greece is at the same time a country and a topos in the western imagination, a reality and a myth, a national property and a (western) international claim."⁴ The conditions that precipitated the new and independent nation-state lead us to posit that it was the outcome of a process of heteronomous self-colonization.⁵

It has been variously argued that, since the inception of the Greek nation-state, the dominant historical narrative has been hard put to escape what has been called the "shade of Homer," or, in a related context, the "tyranny of Greece."⁶ According to this line of thought, the ancient Greeks, in a sense, colonized the modern Greeks. Whether this can be considered as a self-colonization, via the effect of Central European Romanticism's transforming the past (imagined as ancestor) into the colonialist of the young state (imagined as descendant) is a parallel and certainly interesting line of inquiry.

In this manner, the foundations are laid for a continuing entanglement of the relations between East and West: the influence of Central Europe meets in the Greek geographical realm with the long-term presence of the Ottoman Empire. This entanglement is reinforced by the fact that the new Greek state continued to expand and shift its borders until the first few years after World War II, assimilating areas which had, for a long time, been under either Western or Ottoman occupation.⁷ This fact has an additional effect. The fluidity of borders is not only geographical but also political and, primarily, cultural. The new Greek state is continuously negotiating its relationship with the present through the entanglement between the West and the Near East. This political negotiation crosses over into a wider, cultural one.⁸

A question arises every time we try to establish a unitary narrative for Greek history. It is a question central to all of the historical approaches that comprise the field of modern Greek studies.⁹ The issue reappears with every attempt at constructing a specialized history of modern Greek culture. The speculations concerning the establishment of a chronology for the history of modern Greek literature are telling in this respect; the question of its temporal beginnings has been and is still a matter of debate among scholars.¹⁰

The issue looms just as large when it comes to the history of modern Greek theater. Here, arguably more than in other specialized histories, the burden of the relationship with the ancient world dominates the present. A parallel case can be made concerning philosophy; in the history of philosophy, there is a strong incentive to look back to antiquity. Likewise, in the West, the origin of the art of the theater in ancient Greece is automatically recalled. Inevitably, harking back to this distant, idealized past, results in legitimate questions while attempting to create a unified historical narrative for modern Greek theater. Here, a major problem of Greek historiography is once again highlighted: What is the relationship of the ancient Greek world to the modern Greek nation-state, and where are the cultural boundaries of modern Greece to be situated? What is the relationship of modern and contemporary Greek theater to ancient drama? How does modern Greek theater refer back to this determinative foundation of European culture and what might this signify for modern Greek identity?

The ideological parameters of the answer are fairly clear: the acceptance or rejection of this continuity has implications for the conditions of the construction of the Greek identity, as does the acceptance or rejection of the historical prototypes that molded the attitudes and behavior of contemporary Greeks. And, although the nineteenth century's tripartite model of historical continuity gives equal weight to ancient Greece, Byzantium and modern Greece, for contemporary Greeks, "the ancients still (stubbornly) maintain their ancient status."[11]

In light of the above, a critical question for a historiography of Greek theater is, How is modern Greek theater connected to the theatrical or performative activities that took place in the many centuries from Hellenistic times to the war of independence, which addressed Greek communities and a Greek-speaking audience prior to the birth of the modern Greek nation-state?

The absence of autonomous theatrical activity during the times of Byzantium and the Ottoman occupation[12] provides yet another lead into Greek antiquity with its renowned theatrical tradition. From the survival of the large-scale Roman spectacles which Byzantium used to assert its imperial powers, to the performative religious rituals that were widely practiced following the spread of orthodox Christianity,[13] both of which precluded the autonomous presence of theater, the juxtaposition with ancient Greek theater always comes out in favor of the latter. The high status of ancient tragedy prevailed over and above all other representational or ritualistic practices.

The first history of the modern Greek theater was published in 1938, less than 80 years after the appearance of the first professional theater companies in the1860s.[14] Although their advent was in the nineteenth century, a few years before the war for independence, they soon fraternized with a more distant past, looking back to the theatrical culture that flourished in the Ionian Islands and Crete from the sixteenth to the eighteenth century—a theatrical culture that owed a great deal to the Venetian rule. This most likely represented a conscious attempt to endow the history of modern Greek theater with a long timeline and an estimable lineage. Moreover, in the publication year of this history, 1938, the country was ruled by a dictatorship whose rhetoric fully endorsed the unbroken continuity of Hellenism from antiquity to the present.[15]

In order to specify the conditions for a historiography of modern Greek theater, certain basic assumptions need to be considered that bear on all national theater histories:

1. Linking the history of the theater with the history of national literature accords with an older general perspective that adopts a text-centered approach to the theatrical event. Primacy is ascribed to the text rather

than the stage event, so that it becomes, inadvertently or otherwise, a regulator in the process of constructing or confirming a national identity.
2. Even when the delineation of a national history of the theater is detached from the history of literature, it contributes to the construction and confirmation of a national image or to the consolidation of a national identity linked to the general (national) history.
3. Linking national theater histories with geography and national borders determines the boundaries of national theater histories.
4. Linking national theater histories with the national language or the dominant local idiom determines the boundaries of national theater histories.
5. Theater history is primarily examined through the theatrical practices of theatrical organizations, whether national, official or any other kind which is commonly accepted as significant, frequently setting aside other expressions or types that are considered minor, marginal or inferior.

Despite the fact that after the collapse of colonialism, some of these assumptions were curtailed or revised to allow for new features of theater histories—for example, to redefine them in the context of the multiculturalism of postcolonial societies—the above assumptions are linked to specific problems in the construction of a history of modern Greek theater.[16] But before approaching the Greek theater history problems, we have to bear in mind some more ideas connected to the writing of any history and admit that theater historians' work is close to that of a general historian.[17] Among them prevail the following three assumptions on specific topics.

1. Rationalization and Imaginary Construction
   The systematic writing of history is no more than an imaginary construction. Historiography creates links between events and information so as to compose a model that ensures a logical continuity in the presentation of the data. In creating the narrative, it is important to assign phenomena to distinct categories, which then leads to the creation of a logical and useful schema for gathering, classifying and rationalizing the available information and data. Delimiting the kinds of evidence that will be incorporated in the historiographical construction and clarifying the terms and aims that define the historiographer's project imply a systematic approach that will allow the sequence of events to be convincing.
2. Classification and Periodization[18]
   A key element in classification—that is, the establishment of distinct categories of phenomena—is placing events into periods that have a predetermined beginning and end, which allows for a stated (useful) compatibility—the creation of a periodization system. Periodization can follow many criteria. Each periodization can be arbitrary insofar as it is determined by the specific intentions for constructing each particular

narrative. It locates and defines tipping points in historical developments—that is, turning points where there is a change in direction. Nevertheless, these points are, as often as not, dictated by the definition of the variations pre-selected by the particular historiographical approach.

3. Synchronization versus Heterochronism

    The various components of a theatrical production (stage action, dramaturgy, audience) do not find the necessary prerequisites for isochronous evolution—that is, they do not always evolve within the same time constraints. This is typical of the nature of theatrical events, and the Greek case is no exception. Even when a convergence of factors succeeds in completing an event or a trend, allowing for new forms to emerge, the old phenomena, currents or phases can persevere for a long period, perhaps even surviving after the newer ones have ended. The coexistence of different phases of its history belongs to the nature of theatrical activity. Even if the starting points of a new phenomenon, which defines the general characteristics of the theatrical activity, are identified, this does not mean that earlier phenomena are extinct. On the contrary, their coexistence and parallel influence on the formation of the sum total of theatrical activity is a permanent characteristic of theatrical life. For example, the century of the lead actor might give way to the century of the director, but by no means does this mean that there will no longer be actor-led troupes or star-centered strategies in ensemble companies that will determine the development of theater as a whole.[19]

    There is an ongoing trying out, assimilation and consolidation of the various trends: their coexistence constitutes a condition for the development of theatrical art. At the same time, the transfer of artistic trends from one locale to another introduces differences and mannerisms which frequently lend local characteristics to these shared trends. The difficulty itself of transplanting and adopting terms and concepts which determine artistic forms, frequently contributes to the formation of specific characteristics.[20]

To the abovementioned points, we should add special problems connected with the dilemmas of writing a modern Greek theater history, as any other "national" theater history:

1. Theater or Drama

    It would probably be naïve to claim that the Greek-language dramaturgy of Crete and the Ionian Islands alone provided the foundations of modern Greek dramaturgy; it would be even more dangerous to say that we owe the style of modern Greek theater to the massively influential actors/performance organizers from the Ionian Islands around the late nineteenth century.[21] "It is one thing to see the interconnectedness of things and quite another to postulate that all aspects of a culture can be traced back to a single key cause of which they are manifestations."²²

When approaching the history of theater, it is reasonable to focus on those plays that have a long history of stage appeal and intertextual presence and do not rely on prominence acquired through reading. In other words, for the historiography of the theater, the choice of the drama to be examined does not depend on its literary value but on its performativity. Rather than promoting a work that belongs to the realm of "high literature" as representative of the history of theater, the work selected is characterized by its suitability for the stage and the frequency of its stage productions.²³ These dramatic texts sometimes invent a new form of identity and introduce a new form of drama. Erika Fischer-Lichte argues that those texts that provided later periods with the opportunity to appropriate them through novel and updated ways of reading them have proven the most appropriate for a detached, historiographical reading.²⁴

To the extent that theater studies are defined as the science of performance, the historiography of theater must regard the performative event as the decisive regulator. This implies a shift of priorities: even when literature is not in a confrontational relationship with stage practices, as drama theory is in the habit of arguing²⁵ it certainly constitutes a secondary feature of the theatrical event, and its position is hierarchically inferior to stage action. Moreover, the historiography of theater cannot but recognize the significance of the dramatic production in shaping the development of stage practices, irrespectively of the time/period the historical narrative examines.

2. Representations and Theatrical Techniques

   Historians create representations of the past. Whatever their approach, they try to recreate a true past. This is a principle of historical research. However, the effort to fully and accurately represent events is often at odds with the silences and gaps of the past, especially the further back we go to the depths of the centuries (and not only then—silences and gaps abound in more recent periods too).

   The "idea of representation has two contradictory meanings: Mimesis I: to mirror accurately, to present a truthful, faithful copy; and Mimesis II: to substitute, to offer an alternative version."²⁶ In other words, we are reverting to the fundamental assumption of historiography: the attempt to gather, record and accumulate information that implies an objective view of history is countered by the underlying certainty that history is not what happened but what we deem to have happened.

3. Continuations, Discontinuities, Rifts and Ruptures

   The assertion of the continuity of Greek culture was primarily the undertaking of a dominant ideology, bound with the creation of the modern Greek nation-state. It is currently regarded as dubious and is under justifiable criticism.[27] Undoubtedly, however, the historical trials of modern Greece had a decisive influence on the fate of the theater, which, more than any other type of artistic activity, needs normal social living conditions in order to exist.

It would be fair to say that according to the "Western model," the optimal conditions for the theatrical arts to develop smoothly are the conditions ensured by a democratic system, or, at least, a state that is nominally well governed in terms of freedom of expression, wide and equitable access to culture and smooth social functioning. The transition of the young Greek state from the conditions of the Ottoman Empire to the operating conditions of a Western democracy was a slow and drawn-out sojourn, with many setbacks and interruptions over time. In its 200 years of independence, the periods during which undemocratic political conditions prevailed far surpassed those of democratic governance. Indeed, the safeguarding of all political rights which democracy requires as well as the conditions guaranteeing complete freedom of expression were only achieved and fully secured in the last quarter of the twentieth century—that is, after the collapse of the dictatorship of the Colonels in 1974.

Throughout this period, the timeline of Greek theater is similarly fragmented. For many centuries, dramatic texts, the composition of a text destined for the stage, the stage action, the creators of the stage event, and the facilities that hosted it as well as the participating audience coexisted on an occasional basis, in the context of sporadic, and unrelated, theatrical events. These elements lacked cohesiveness, did not last long and were infrequent. Therefore, they did not achieve the necessary consistency that would foster conditions of more or less uninterrupted growth. It is within this context that the Greek theater history appears as the product of an entanglement which it would take a long while to resolve, as it was only after the mid-nineteenth century that modern Greek theater began to progress relatively smoothly. This distinguishes modern Greek theater from its European counterpart, since the beginnings of its history might be more clearly situated in the years after or shortly before the advent of the modern Greek state.

Theater as a whole was instrumental for the formation of a European identity. The history of European theater and drama captures the convergences that define Western culture. Thus, we identify elements in local theater histories (here, the geographic units of the European countries are considered localities) which either contribute to the formation of a national identity or, else, are imposed so as to construct a national identity and become part of the national narrative of every country of the European continent.[28]

In addition, during the formative years of the Greek national identity, a process of the disentanglement of the Greek theater history also made its appearance. Whether this created a new entanglement is something to further inquire into from the vantage point of the present. It is noteworthy that since the beginning of the twenty-first century, more and more so as the bicentenary of the war for Greek independence comes closer, the majority of approaches to Greek identity through theater productions tend to rekindle this debate.

In Greece, the mission of theater to form a national identity through disentanglement was a priority and a decisive condition for its emergence. The birth of modern Greek theater reflects this mission; the theater's repertory and the choices of its creators are directly related to the conditions of identity formation.[29] Toward that end, ancient Greek drama performances took the lead, followed by themes of local dramaturgy and underpinned by the choices of Greek translators (especially during the nineteenth century).

Looking back over the years from independence to the twenty-first century, there are many examples that confirm this special role of theater. During the period leading up to the struggle for independence, a performance of Sophocles's *Philoctetes*, adapted by Nikolaos Piccolos in 1818 in Odessa, acted as a statement of Greek identity and sought to strengthen the patriotic sentiment of the local Greek community it addressed. Many works with ancient themes played a similar role in the effort to galvanize a national consciousness by recalling the ancient Greek heritage. These were either translations, such as Pietro Metastasio's *L'Olimpiade* by Rigas Velestinlis, with various references to the glorious past and the interconnection of ancient and modern Greece, or original plays, such as Athanasios Christopoulos's *Achilles* or *The Death of Patroclus*, written in the nineteenth century. The later work launched a century-long series of dramas written in modern Greek referring to themes from ancient Greek history. While this was the general trend, there were certain isolated cases of performances and works that highlighted some of the key problems in creating a modern Greek identity.

In 1836, Dimitrios Hadjiaslanis Byzantios wrote *Babylonia*, a comedy depicting how modern Greeks were unable to communicate because of their different linguistic idioms, thus raising the issue of the Greek language as a cohesive factor of national identity. In 1816, *O Exintavelonis*, a translation of Molière's *Miser* by Konstantinos Ikonomou, placed the action among the Greeks of the east and is a vivid illustration of the modern Greek state seesawing between European integration and an attachment to the sensibilities and practices, secular and religious, that prevailed during the 400 years of Ottoman occupation.

In the late nineteenth century, the plethora of light comedies, vaudeville and dramatic romances flooding the stage with subjects inspired by rural life pitted their moral agenda of purity against the Western way of life and Central European influences.

At the dawn of the twentieth century, the mainstream controversy regarding modern Greek language found violent expression with riots organized by students on the occasion of a performance of the *Oresteia*. Presented in a simpler language by the then newly established Royal Theater, it sparked a widespread clash between adherents of *katharevousa* (pure) and *dimotiki* (spoken) Greek.[30]

Similarly, during the Interwar period (1918–1939), drama and the stage incorporated the new demands of the urban society that was emerging, characterized by a strong desire for modernization and for integrating European characteristics into itself. The period immediately after World War II saw an ideological confrontation traceable to the war experience and to the subsequent, traumatic civil war: this was expressed at the repertory level as well as through the performance aesthetics. The performances of ancient drama at the Epidaurus Festival, monopolized until 1974 by the National Theater,[31] and the clash between the latter's aesthetics and that of the Art Theater of Karolos Koun,[32] raised many dilemmas regarding modern Greek identity. Here, we might recall the 1959 cancellation of the performance of Aristophanes's *Birds*, triumphantly performed in 1974 at the inaugural appearance of the Art Theater in Epidaurus, and, also, the 1965 performance of Aeschylus's *Persians*, again by Koun, whose company introduced to the treatment of ancient drama an aesthetic mainly originating in the Middle East. Indeed, Koun's conviction that "the ancient theater has an oriental scent,"[33] was a major determinant in the way he staged ancient Greek texts. Through the 1980s and 1990s, the attempt to renew the approaches to ancient Greek drama is widely connected to the performances of Theodoros Terzopoulos.[34] His stage productions involve using a very elaborate training method, combining elements from a wide range of cultural traditions from both the East and the West, ranging from ritualistic elements from popular traditional dances of northern Greece to elements of Japanese theatrical performances. This turn toward the "other" has been an important moment, forming the basis for new approaches to ancient Greek drama, bringing a very much enlarged perspective to productions and taking a necessary distance from the former, highly charged and nationally acclaimed productions.

More recently, the financial crisis of the second decade of the twenty-first century led to the redefinition of the conditions for creating Greek identity. New perspectives were explored in new productions of the Greek repertory of the nineteenth century, and ideological underpinnings of directing ancient drama were questioned, thus creating conditions for moving past the existing certainties. In particular, international concerns regarding the performance of ancient drama were grafted onto local practices, linking existing forms with Eastern theater techniques; this is a groundbreaking element that disentangles (not without controversy and perhaps not permanently) the modern Greek approach to the classics from their connection to national identity. Behind this issue, there still lies an ideological conflict that bears directly on the political dimension of the identity construction processes. In this most recent period, moreover, the questions raised regarding modern Greek history, its continuity and/or discontinuities concern not only all students of modern Greek history but also a large percentage of Greek citizens.[35]

As mentioned at the beginning of this chapter, the establishment of the national borders of Greece, a process that lasted over a century, began with the foundation of the independent Greek state in 1832 and concluded after World War II, in 1948: the incorporation into the Greek state of areas where there was theatrical activity and, therefore, a local theater history required accepting that local history as part of the history of modern Greek theater. There are significant geographic discontinuities, since the evolution of Greek theater aimed at a Greek-speaking audience in modern times appears geographically fragmented into the following fairly distinct sections:

1. Sixteenth century: possible, although limited, theatrical activity on the Ionian Islands in Italian language (in the Venetian-occupied islands of Corfu and Zakynthos).
2. Seventeenth century: dramaturgy appeared in the cities of Venetian-occupied Crete in the Veneto-Cretan idiom (a mixture of Venetian and the local Greek dialect); likely but not proven stage activity on the island. Amateur-instructional theater activity on the Ionian Islands, Chios, Naxos (which passed in the thirteenth century from Venetian rule to the Ottoman Empire) and within Greek communities in the cities of Asia Minor (Ottoman Empire) in schools operating under the curriculum of the Jesuit order.
3. Eighteenth century: organized, systematic theater life on Corfu, mostly based on the performances of traveling Italian opera companies and similar, although more occasional, activities on the other Ionian Islands.
4. Nineteenth century: performances of plays by emerging Greek authors in cities with large Greek communities outside the Greek geographical area, such as Iași, Odessa and Bucharest as well as Constantinople, Smyrna and Alexandria. After the creation of the Greek nation-state, there was similar theatrical activity in Hermoupolis, on the island of Syros, which became part of the Greek state immediately upon independence. During the nineteenth century, theater life developed in Athens and other cities of the new Greece: Patras, Tripoli, Pyrgos and Volos. The same occurred during that period in Thessaloniki and Chania, in Crete, ceded to Greece in 1881 and 1912, respectively; continued and increased theatrical activity on the Ionian Islands mainly with Italian opera and sporadically Greek plays.

5. Twentieth century: gradually, (almost all) theatrical activity was concentrated in Athens. Attempts at decentralization were made after World War II, especially since the mid-1970s, thanks to initiatives by theater creators as well as the attempt to establish a state policy toward the theater.

This geographic/temporal diaspora raises certain other problems related to the national language. The development of modern Greek was an issue that caused conflicts and divisions and preoccupied Greek society almost until the end of the twentieth century. Evidence regarding the survival and evolution of Greek as an oral language from antiquity until the modern period exists in various theatrical texts and in the dramaturgy of the late Cretan Renaissance of the sixteenth century, as well as in the theater production of the Ionian Islands over the ensuing centuries. Here, the link between the history of literature and the history of theater becomes apparent again.[36] However, while language appears problematic for dating the beginnings of modern Greek literature, for theater, the question hinges on stage practices: the search for evidence of stage action constitutes the defining factor and, thus, the demarcations should perhaps be different. If we have reason to doubt that the beginning of modern Greek literature is to be found in sixteenth-century Crete, then our doubts concerning the history of theater are all the stronger, insofar as no definite evidence of a performative event exists, merely indications and conjectures.

Another issue relates to the systematic participation in certain regions, of Greek audiences in non-Greek-speaking theatrical events. One outstanding example is the Ionian Islands, where it is likely that Antonio Molino performed while in Venetian-occupied Corfu in 1527–28 in the Greek-Italian *greghesco* dialect, and read the Italian-language comedy *La Fianciulla* in 1583. There is also the unconfirmed performance in Italian of Aeschylus's *Persians* on Zakynthos as part of the celebrations for the victory of the Christian armada in the naval Battle of Lepanto in 1571. An important dilemma is presented by the operation of the Teatro di San Giacomo in Corfu, with dozens of opera performances by Italian companies during the eighteenth century; these continued in Corfu and the rest of the Ionian Islands long past the end of Venetian rule in the eighteenth century and even upon the islands' becoming part of the Greek state in 1864. The failure of earlier historians of theater to examine that activity is indicative of the concerns about what exactly should be included in the history of modern Greek theater.[37] Similar issues arise regarding the organized theater life established by the Jewish community in Thessaloniki during the last 30 years of the nineteenth century. Conducted in either French or the local Sephardic dialect based on Judeo-Spanish, it has also received scant interest in modern Greek theater studies.

There are fewer doubts regarding the performances taking place in the Greek communities in Romania during the first decades of the nineteenth century, an effort by the Greeks of the diaspora to rouse Greek consciousness in preparation for the struggle for independence and to help consolidate Greek identity in view of the impending uprising. Performances in Asia Minor and Alexandria, from the late nineteenth century, also contributed to the promotion of Greek identity in a non-Greek geographic environment, although with slightly different intentions. In Alexandria, these were consistent with urban ritual, while in Turkey, they simultaneously contained an irredentist connotation. These were mostly performances of traveling companies and not necessarily local professional activities. The traveling companies' association with the *Megali Idea* (Great Aspiration)[38] until 1922, and the emphasis on ethnic origin through local performances by amateurs or school students in the Greek communities of Asia Minor, frequently concealed a declaration of the cultural superiority of the Greeks.

The problem of professional theatrical organizations and ensembles also arose at the same time. Organized theatrical activity at a professional level had begun appearing in the late nineteenth century, mainly in Athens. Although there had been theatrical activities (directly associated with the struggle for independence) in Greek communities abroad, primarily in the Danubian Principalities, the first professional companies were formed in Athens during the 1860s. This is associated with the intermittence of productions and the lack of any dedicated facilities; the latter only began to be acquired in the final decades of the nineteenth century. During the first years of the twentieth century, we witness the appearance of relatively long-standing companies; this became the standard at the end of the Interwar period, during which the first large theatrical organizations were created, to be fully established after the end of World War II.

Due, then, to the frequently abnormal political conditions, a lag is observed in Greek theatrical development; new ideas and trends, directions, and theater-operating modes that set the standards for the European stage appear in Greece only after a considerable period.

As a result, the effort to align with the European stage was ongoing, but Greek theater was not able to approximate the same rate of development before the end of the twentieth century. This effort to be in line with the Western European stage found expression in two short-lived endeavors from the early twentieth century that came briefly into prominence in the century's first decade: the *Nea Skini* (New Stage), founded by director Constantine Christomanos, operated from 1902 to 1905, and the Royal Theater, founded at the same time, which persisted until 1908. These both failed to introduce the presence of the director in Greek theater practice. The same happened with the transfer of aesthetic trends and the direction of dramatic writing. Although certain important theatrical creators did have an eye for new trends and concerns, overall, the dialogue between the Greek and European theater was carried out with constant time lags. This is associated with the trials of Greek political life and the impact on Greek society of the turbulent events that led to the development of modern-day Greece. The restoration of democracy in 1974 and the country's entry into the European Union in 1981 would ensure the conditions of social stability and economic development until the beginning of the twenty-first century that resulted in the elimination of these problems.

The directing of dramatic writing in the last two decades of the twentieth century shows a significant shift from the internal problems of Greek society toward the more general concerns of European dramaturgy, gradually acquiring characteristics of recent European stage realizations. The position on artistic creation of the post–World War II democratic European states, as expressed in the comprehensiveness of their state policy for theater, appeared in Greece during the final two decades of the twentieth century. This time lapse hinged on complex and not always clearly definable circumstances, including social and political developments, as well as pure contingency or the personal efforts of theater creators at all levels.

Therefore, the historiography of Greek theater, from the first appearances of companies to the first decades after World War II, selects the theatrical expressions considered important or central, with a suitably vague criterion for the selection. In this context, the indifference of modern Greek theater historiography to popular genres such as, for example, the revue or the folk shadow theater is telling. These are genres that developed on the domestic stage: the former was influenced by Spanish, French and even Armenian traveling companies, and the latter was developed by adapting the Turkish Karagöz, with its distant Indian roots, to the Greek environment.

The historical narrative is organized around the primacy of companies and practices that either have state support or rely on their great popularity with large audience groups. Here, the example of the establishment of a national theater provides apt illustration. The foundation of the Royal Theater in the early twentieth century, the construction of the building, its operation in the brief period from 1902 to 1908, its reestablishment in 1931, and its regular operation to this day, its repertoire, and the decisions of its administrations frequently occupy the historiography of the modern Greek theater to a disproportionate extent by comparison to other companies whose activities were crucial to the development of the art of theater.[39]

At the same time, many of the issues related to the beginnings of Greek literature might, to a large extent, determine our definition of the beginnings of Greek dramatic production. For instance, fully including Cretan literary production into the body of modern Greek literature is a large subject requiring broader deliberation, as it raises both controversies and questions. So does the search for theater's beginnings in Cypriot texts. It should be noted that it is sometimes possible to monitor literary currents via domestic dramatic productions, though, generally, it is not sufficient for understanding theatrical phenomena. We are, nevertheless, allowed to search for convergences and divergences. In this sense, there is indeed a field of interaction between literary historiography and theatrical historiography, though one full of ruptures and discontinuities.

The discontinuities, ruptures and specific spatial and temporal determinants of Greek theater reintroduce the question regarding a general delimitation of its history. The prevalent data spatially and temporally limit theater in Greece to a specific section of the broader entity that is the modern Greek theater. It remains for us to determine the limits of the notion of modern Greek theater, taking into consideration the limitations, reservations and concerns expressed thus far.

To this end, it may be necessary to define specific parts of the repertoire as basic criteria for the symbolic stations of the various development periods of the theatrical art. A key element of such a definition is the scope of the performative events or dramatic texts that bear a strong ideological burden in terms of fostering a national identity. These are the texts and performances that contribute to consolidating the idea of national identity or, else, raise concerns that redefine the relationship with national identity. The connection of the dramatic texts with their stage production history is one of the key criteria for their selection.

In Lieu of Conclusion

Methods for the periodization and formulation of the narrative terms and selection of the topics that will constitute the modules tracing the history of modern Greek theater:

1. Regarding the facts of modern Greek theater history through a long-distance view, it is clear that the production history of ancient drama was a decisive factor in the formulation of the image of Greek theater. Ancient Greek drama performances contributed substantially to establishing the boundaries of modern Greek identity in terms of self-awareness, mindset and behavior and, ultimately, to legitimizing the ideological standards that shaped the perceptions of contemporary Greek society. At the forefront of the formulation of Greek theatrical activity, they largely determined the conditions of its development. Certain ancient drama performances stand out, allowing the boundaries to be readily recognizable. Theatrical activity determines the conditions shaping the construction of a national identity and alters the facts either by consolidating assumptions or overturning stereotypical perceptions. They are the guides, the temporal and spatial indicators of the boundaries of the periods in which the historical material is distributed.
2. At the same time and within the boundaries defined by these pivotal ancient drama performances, theater productions from the emerging modern

Greek repertoire shaped the dominant discourse, either by strengthening the established definitions of a national identity or by challenging entrenched perceptions. Naturally, adaptations and translations of the works of the international repertoire also had an important role and place. Simultaneously, foreign-language performances by traveling companies not only gave a new impetus to stage techniques, contributing thus to the development of the art of the theater, but were also crucial points of departure for questioning Greek society. Thus, into this questioning were incorporated other than domestic concerns which contributed to the self-determination of national identity by adding new elements to the construction of its profile.

3. Currently, the historiography of the theater is seriously contemplating the directions it should follow. Theater historians are aware that "it is becoming necessary to work closely with theater theorists to take more into account the theoretical components, value systems and ideological data that influence and shape the interpretations of the historical models of theatrical activity." As for the theorists, "it is now clear that it is important to realize that a large number of accepted generalizations lose their power to the extent that many of the theoretical conclusions can only be accepted for a limited number of theatrical practices, or for specific time periods, for certain cultural units, or for certain specific audience groups."[40]

Theater historians frequently place events in chronological order, constructing an evolutionary model and creating a sequence of data, which are linked through a causal nexus or, even, a linear causality, constructing a relatively convincingly structured narrative with an internal logic. In this venture, and for the benefit of a categorized and clear historiographic approach, certain other elements that coexist and shape the phenomena in question are often lost: discontinuities, ruptures, rifts, inconsistencies, as well as evaluations that question the data, are occluded by a pragmatic, factual approach such as is exemplified in the history of modern Greek theater. This makes it necessary to revisit this history. Each period needs a new approach to the earlier history of the theater and, consequently, revised historiographical methods.

Notes

1 The publication of the famous *History of the Greek Nation* (1860–1874) by Konstantinos Paparrigopoulos (1815–1891) was the official response to all controversies concerning the origins of the modern Greek state.
2 There is ample bibliography on the subject. Among the most recent cases in point, see Roderick Beaton and David Ricks, eds., *The Making of Modern Greece: Nationalism, Romanticism, and the Uses of the Past (1797–1896)* (London and New York,

NY: Routledge, 2009); Kostas Kostis, *History's Spoiled Children: The Formation of the Modern Greek State* (London: Hurst, 2018); and Roderick Beaton, *Greece: Biography of a Modern Nation* (Chicago, IL: University of Chicago Press, 2019).

3 "The ancient Greek world thus became for the modern Greeks doubly revolutionary: it preached freedom and preached it as an ancestral virtue." Dimitris Kyrtatas, "Hi kataktissi tis archaias hellinikis historias apo to neo hellinismo kata to 18o kai 19o aiona me ti diamessolavisi tis Dysis," in *Oi chrisseis tis archaiotitas apo to neo hellinismo*, conference proceedings, the Moraitis Foundation for Literary and Cultural Studies, Athens, 14–15 April 2000 (Athens: Moraitis, 2002), 254. For a more detailed approach, see Nassia Giakovaki, *Evropi meso Elladas: Mia kampi stin evropaïki autosyneidissi* (Athens: Hestia, 2006).

4 Yannis Hamilakis, *The Nation and Its Ruins: Antiquity, Archaeology, and National Imagination in Greece* (New York, NY: Oxford University Press, 2007), 58.

5 Cf. ibid., 20, where the notion is discussed by reference to the articles by Michael Herzfeld, "The Absent Presence: Discourses of Crypto-Colonialism," *South Atlantic Quarterly* 101, no. 4 (2002): 899–926; Dimitris Tziovas, "Hi dytiki fantassiosi tou Hellinikou kai hi anazitissi toy hyperethnikou," in *Ethnos-Kratos-Ethnikismos*, ed. Despo Solomou (Athens: Moraitis, 1995), 339–61; Neni Panourgia, "Colonizing the Ideal: Neoclassical Articulations and European Modernities," *Angelaki* 9, no. 2 (2004): 165–80; and Stathis Gourgouris, *Dream Nation: Enlightenment, Colonization and the Institution of Modern Greece* (Stanford, CA: Stanford University Press, 1996).

6 I am using the titles of David Ricks, *The Shade of Homer: A Study in Modern Greek Poetry* (Cambridge: Cambridge University Press, 1989); and E. M. Butler, *The Tyranny of Greece over Germany: A Study of the Influence Exercised by Greek Art and Poetry over the Great German Writers of the Eighteenth, Nineteenth and Twentieth Centuries* (Boston, MA: Beacon Press, 1958). Suzanne L. Marchand treats the same subject as Butler in *Down from Olympus: Archaeology and Philhellenism in Germany, 1750–1970* (Princeton, NJ: Princeton University Press, 2003). For a further development, cf. Alexander Kitroeff, *Wrestling with the Ancients: Modern Greek Identity and the Olympics* (New York, NY: Greekworks.com Inc., 2004).

7 Significant dates of expansion of the Greek state are: Creation of the modern Greek state, including the Peloponnese and Roumeli (southern part of central Greece) in 1832; the Ionian Islands become part of Greece in 1864, Thessaly in 1881, Macedonia, Crete and the northern Aegean islands in 1913; the area of Western and Eastern Thrace were awarded by the Treaty of Sèvres to Greece in 1920 and lost again in 1922; Western Thrace became part of Greece in 1923; and finally, the islands of the Dodecanese in 1947. See map in Beaton, *Greece*, xxiii.

8 "Nobody's brainchild, an unplanned offspring, it was unavoidably the child of its two parents, Europe and the Ottoman Empire." Ibid., 111.

9 As a case in point, see Paschalis Kitromilides, "The Study of Modern Hellenism as an Academic Challenge," *The Historical Review/La Revue Historique* 16 (2019): 249–54.

10 Cf. Georgios P. Savvides, "Pote, pragmati, arhizeiI neoteri helliniki logotechnia?," in *Origini della letteratura neogreca: Atti del secondo congresso internazionale "Neograeca medii aevi,"* Venice, 7–10 November 1991, ed. Nikolaos M. Panayotakis, vol. 1 (Venice: Greek Institute of Byzantine and Post-Byzantine Studies, 1993), 137–41.

11 Alexis Politis, *Romantika chronia: Ideologies kai nootropies stin Ellada, 1830–1880* (Athens: Mnimon, 2003), 106.

12 An absence which is the direct result of religious imperatives, and which explains the dead years for theater from Roman times to the present. See Walter Puchner, *Greek Theatre between Antiquity and Independence: A History of Reinvention from the Third Century BC to 1830* (Cambridge: Cambridge University Press, 2017), 16–39.

13 Cf. ibid., 52–90.
14 This is the two-volume *History of Modern Greek Theater* by Nikolaos Laskaris, published in 1938. It was preceded by a series of scattered writings by Laskaris some years previously, largely influenced by two earlier works of the historian Constantine N. Sathas, *Historical Essay on the Theater and Music of the Byzantines; i.e., An Introduction to Cretan Theater* and *Cretan Theater, or a Collection of Unpublished and Unknown Dramas*, Venice, 1878 and 1879, respectively.
15 The dictatorship of the Fourth of August 1936, which lasted until the occupation of the country by German troops in 1941, was a nationalist totalitarian regime with obvious influences from fascism and Nazism. The aim of the regime was the "Third Greek Civilization," a continuation of the ancient and the Byzantine civilization, based on the ideas of cultural purity and racial unity.
16 The following are among the main works on the history of modern Greek theater: Yannis Sideris, *Historia tou neou hellinikou theatrou*, vol. 1 (Athens: Ikaros, 1951); vols. 1 (repr.), 2a, 2b and 2c, comp. and ed. Platon Mavromoustakos (Athens: Kastaniotis, 1990, 1999, 2000, 2009); Yannis Sideris, *To archaio theatro sti neohelliniki skini, 1817–1932* (Athens: Ikaros, 1974); in addition, Sideris wrote a brief presentation, published in French and English, titled *The Modern Greek Theater* (1957); another history, by M. Valsa, originally in French, titled *Le Théâtre grec moderne de 1453 à 1900* (Berlin: Akademie-Verlag, 1960) was published also in Greek (1994). The relatively recent creation of theater studies departments in Greek universities (as of 1990) resulted in the enrichment of the relevant Greek literature with many general works or individual studies on specific issues. Thus, for instance, see Dimitris Spathis, "To neohelliniko theatro," in *Ellada-Historia-Politismos*, vol. 10 (Thessaloniki: Malliaris, 1983), 7–67; *Diafotismos kai neohelliniko theatre: Epta meletes* (Thessaloniki: University Studio Press, 1986); Theodore Grammatas, *To helliniko theatro ston 20o aiona: Politismika protypa kai prototypa*, vol. 2 (Athens: Exantas, 2002); Platon Mavromoustakos, *To theatro stin Ellada 1940–2000: Mia episkopissi* (Athens: Kastaniotis, 2005); the works of Thodoros Hadzipantazis, *Apo tou Neilou mechri tou Dounaveos*, vols. A1, A2, B1, B2 (Rethymnon, Crete: Foundation for Research and Technology, Crete University Press, 2002, 2012), covering the nineteenth century and his more recent work *Diagramma historias tou neohellinikou theatrou* (Rethymnon, Crete: Foundation for Research and Technology, Crete University Press, 2014), as well as the extensive oeuvre of Walter Puchner with numerous publications on themes related to the history of Greek theater from the sixteenth to the twentieth century.
17 See the introductory remark in Erika Fischer-Lichte, "Theatre Historiography," chap. 5 in *The Routledge Introduction to Theatre and Performance Studies*, ed. Minou Arjomand and Ramona Mosse (London and New York, NY: Routledge, 2014), 71.
18 See Thomas Postlewait, "The Criteria for Periodization in Theater History," *Theater Journal* 40, no. 3 (1988): 299–318; "The Idea of the 'Political' in our Histories of Theater: Texts, Contexts, Periods, and Problems," *Contemporary Theater Review* 12, no. 3 (2002): 9–33; Charlotte M. Canning and Thomas Postlewait, "Representing the Past: An Introduction on Five Themes," in *Representing the Past: Essays in Performance Historiography*, ed. Charlotte M. Canning and Thomas Postlewait (Iowa City, IA: University of Iowa Press, 2010), 1–34; Savas Patsalidis, "Pro historias: Chartographissi provlimaton kai prooptikon," in *Theatro, koinonia, ethnos: Apo tin "Ameriki" stis Hinomenes Politeies*, vol. 1, *1620–1960* (Thessaloniki: University Studio Press, 2009); Thomas Postlewait and Bruce A. McConachie, eds., *Interpreting the Theatrical Past: Essays in the Historiography of Performance* (Iowa City, IA: University of Iowa Press, 1989).

19 Antonis Glytzouris, *Hi anadyssi kai hi edraiossi tou skinotheti sto neohelliniko theatro* (Rethymnon, Crete: Foundation for Research and Technology, Crete University Press, 2011); Antonis Glytzouris, Konstantina Georgiadi, and Maria Mavrogeni, eds., *Hi proïmi ypodohi tou Realismou kai tou Natouralismou sto helliniko theatro* (Rethymnon, Crete: Foundation for Research and Technology, Institute for Mediterranean Studies, 2016).
20 See Hadzipantazis, *Diagramma*.
21 Spyros A. Evangelatos,"Yparhei 'syneheia' sti neohelliniki theatriki historia? (1590 per.–1990 per.)" in *Proceedings of the First Panhellenic Theatrological Conference: Greek Theater from the 17th to the 20th Century, 17–20 December 1998*, ed. Iosif Vivilakis (Athens: National and Kapodistrian University of Athens, Department of Theater Studies, Ergo Publications, 2001), 33–36; Walter Puchner, "Hi nea eikona tis historias tou neohellinikou theatrou opos diamorfothike apo tis theatrologikes erevnes ton teleftaion 25 chronon," in ibid., 21–33; Thodoros Hadzipantazis, "Theatrologia kai historia," *Ariadne* 5, no. 11 (2005): 327–35.
22 E. H. Gombrich, quoted in Thomas Postlewait, *The Cambridge Introduction to Theater Historiography* (Cambridge: Cambridge University Press, 2009), 186.
23 The background to this reasoning is the old conflict illustrated in the arguments exchanged between the German founder of Theater studies Max Herrmann and the critic Alfred Klaar. See the chapter on the history of theater studies in Erika Fischer-Lichte, *Ästhetik der Performativen* (Frankfurt am Main: Suhrkamp, 2004).
24 See Erika Fischer-Lichte, "Theatre and Identity: Theatre as a Liminal Space," in *History of European Drama*, trans. Jo Riley (London and New York, NY: Routledge, 2002), 1–7.
25 The shift from text to event as argued in Hans-Thies Lehmann, *Postdramatic Theatre*, trans. Karen Jürs-Munby (London and New York, NY: Routledge, 2006).
26 Canning and Postlewait, "Representing the Past," 10, 28n16.
27 This idea of continuity was brought under criticism already form the end of the nineteenth century in Greece. A rather venomous comment of the satiric newspaper *Asmodaios* (1875–1885) provides an eloquent example: "Wishing to restore to life a nation that has disappeared from history as a political entity on account of its former glory is as reasonable as wishing to resuscitate animal species that have ceased to exist long ago and whose traces are buried in the Paleozoic layers of the earth […] and yet, it is this kind of absurd thinking that has taken hold of those of us who seek to found our national existence not on the development of existing elements but on memories of classical antiquity—which, by the way, modern Greeks have a very poor knowledge of, acquired via a second-rate translation by A. R. Rangavis of the Compendium of Goldsmith's *History of Greece*." Emmanuel Rhoides, *Asmodaios*, 22 February 1881.
28 S. E. Wilmer, "Reifying Imagined Communities: Nationalism, Post-Colonialism and Theater Historiography," *Nordic Theater Studies* 12 (1999): 94–133; see also S. E. Wilmer, ed., *Writing & Rewriting: National Theatre Histories* (Iowa City, IA: University of Iowa Press, 2004).
29 On the correlation of the present with the ancient world regarding the reception of theatrical events and the frequent use of the term "revival," see Natascha Siouzouli, "Sakralität und Sakralisierung im Kontext europäischer Theaterfestivals," in *Staging Festivity: Theater und Fest in Europa*, ed. Erika Fischer-Lichte and Matthias Warstat (Tübingen and Basel: A. Francke Verlag, 2009), 89–101; and Platon Mavromoustakos, "Das antike griechische Drama als nationale Frage: Kritiker- und Publikums reaktionen auf moderne Aufführungen," in ibid., 303–16.
30 The quest for and establishment of a unitary Greek language, toward the aim of a national education curriculum, was the arena for one of the most profound clashes within modern Greek society, already in motion before the establishment of the Greek nation. The outlook of modern Greek enlightenment, forged during

the same period as the nation's founding, set the ground for the ascendancy of a scholarly language that drew heavily on ancient Greek forms and syntax. In the last 20 years of the nineteenth century, objections were voiced against these archaisms, and a movement was set in motion demanding that the commonly spoken demotic Greek be the nation's official language. An important episode in this conflict was the performance of the *Oresteia*. Successive legislative acts and amendments, from 1911 to 1982, arrived at a final act establishing the unimpeded use and systematic teaching of demotic Greek. For an extensive relevant bibliography, see the "Portal for the Greek Language," accessed 28 July 2021, http://www.greek-language.gr/greekLang/search/index.html.

31 The National Theater of Greece, which was founded in 1931 and still operates in the center of Athens, is considered today as the most important theater of the country. A first attempt to create a national stage in 1902 did not succeed in establishing a continuous operation and the then Royal Theater ceased its functioning in 1908. The foundation of the National Theater in the 1930s was the outcome of many efforts to establish a consistent, well-run theater life.

32 Karolos Koun (1908–1987) founded the Art Theater in Athens in 1942. Since then, it became one of the pillars of independent theater in Greece, standing in opposition to the National Theater's aesthetics, until Koun's death. Koun developed an interesting investigation of modern Greek acting, basing his ideas on popular culture and treating modern Greece as a crossroads of Middle Eastern and Greek cultural elements. The bibliography on Karolos Koun includes a collection of his rare texts and numerous interviews in several publications. See *The Social Status and Aesthetic Values of Theatro Technis*, a lecture delivered by Karolos Koun and edited by Friends of the Theatro Technis, Athens, 1943, 18–19. This was reprinted with many of his interviews and texts in theater programs under the general title *Karolos Koun: Gia to Theatro* (Athens: Ithaca, 1981) and again a few years later with even more of his interviews, under the title *Kanoume theatre gia tin psychi mas* (Athens: Kastaniotis, 1987). At the beginning of the twenty-first century, two books were published presenting and documenting his work at the Theatro Technis: Platon Mavromoustakos, ed., *Karolos Koun: Oi parastaseis* (Athens: Benaki Museum, 2008), with an introduction to the work of Karolos Koun, a selection of his most significant published texts and a full catalogue of the performances he had directed since the 1930s. The publication was presented as a catalogue of the exhibition held in 2008 in Athens by the Benaki Museum on the occasion of the 110th anniversary of Koun's birth. For a general survey of Koun's work, also in Greek, see Dio Kangelari, ed., *Karolos Koun* (Athens: MIET, 2010).

33 Karolos Koun, "Karolos Koun: The Ancient Theater Has an Oriental Scent," interview by Anna Mihalitsianou, *Ena*, 14 August 1984.

34 Theodoros Terzopoulos created his group Attis in 1986. Since then, he has been one of the most acclaimed theater directors in Greece and worldwide and has introduced major innovations to ways of approaching Greek tragedy. See, among others, Theodoros Terzopoulos, *Theodoros Terzopoulos kai Theatro Attis: Anadromi, Methodos, Scholia*, ed. Eleni Varopoulou and Marianne McDonald, trans. Alexandra Kapsali (Athens: Agra, 2000); Frank M. Raddatz, ed., *Reise mit Dionysos: Das Theater des Theodoros Terzopoulos—Journey with Dionysus: The Theatre of Theodoros Terzopoulos* (Berlin: Theater der Zeit, 2006); Yorgos Sampatakakis, *Geometrontas to chaos: Morfi kai metafysiki sto theatro tou Theodorou Terzopoulou* (Athens: Metaichmio, 2002); Penelope Chadzidimitriou and Theodoros Terzopoulos, *Theodoros Terzopoulos: Apo to prosopiko sto pangosmio* (Thessaloniki: University Studio Press, 2010); Theodoros Terzopoulos, *Hi epistrofi tou Dionysou: Hi methodos tou Theodorou Terzopoulou* (Athens: Attis Theater, 2014); Freddy Decreus, *The Ritual*

Theatre of Theodoros Terzopoulos (London and New York, NY: Routledge, 2019); *Dionysus in Exile: The Theatre of Theodoros Terzopoulos*, with a preface by Erika Fischer-Lichte (Berlin: Theater der Zeit, 2019).

35 Hence the general debate over reforms in school history textbooks, with regard to even the most recent years, a quite heated debate engaging historians, high school teachers, politicians and many Greek citizens, which dominated public dialogue over the years 2012–2013.

36 Cf. Nikolaos M. Panayotakis, ed., *Origini della letteratura neogreca: Atti del secondo congresso internazionale "Neograeca medii aevi,"* Venice, 7–10 November 1991 (Venice: Greek Institute of Byzantine and Post-Byzantine Studies, 1993); and Miltos Pechlivanos, "History (and Narratives) of Literature," *Molyvdokondylopelekitis* 6 (1998–1999): 169–86, translated as "Literaturgeschichte(n)," in *Einführung in die Literaturwissenschaft*, ed. Miltos Pechlivanos, Stefan Rieger, Wolfgang Struck and Michael Weitz (Stuttgart and Weimar: Verlag J. B. Metzler, 1995), 170–81.

37 A discussion whether the Ionian Islands' theater practices should be included in the history of modern Greek theater followed the first edition of Sideris's *History* in 1951 in an exchange of letters in the literary journal *Nea Estia*, between Sideris and Dionysios Romas, an important writer and intellectual from the Ionian Islands, resulting in Sideris's consent that the whole matter should be reconsidered; see Platon Mavromoustakos, "Provlimata kataskevis mias historias tou theatrou," in *Proceedings of the First Panhellenic Theatrological Conference: Greek Theater from the 17th to the 20th Century, 17–20 December 1998*, ed. Iosif Vivilakis (Athens: National and Kapodistrian University of Athens, Department of Theater Studies, Ergo Publications, 2001), 39–47.

38 *Megali Idea* was a political concept expressing the will to "liberate" all geographical areas inhabited by Greek populations since antiquity; it appeared circa 1844 and dominated foreign policy in Greece until the defeat of Greece in the Greco-Turkish war of 1922.

39 For instance, Yannis Sideris's *History* devotes almost two out of its four volumes to the events concerning the creation of the National (Royal) Theater of Greece, and M. Valsa's *Le Théâtre* has practically no references to the Athenian revue, a genre considered as a minor type, having appeared in 1895 and become one of the favorite popular entertainments, and as a sharp satirical critique of political or social issues.

40 Henri Schoenmakers, "Between Reasonless Passion and Passionless Reason: Theater Studies in the Nineties," in *Humanities in the Nineties: A View from the Netherlands*, ed. Erik Zürcher and Ton Langendorff (Amsterdam: Swets & Zeitlinger, 1990), 175–206.

Bibliography

Beaton, Roderick. *Greece: Biography of a Modern Nation*. Chicago, IL: University of Chicago Press, 2019.

———, and David Ricks, eds. *The Making of Modern Greece: Nationalism, Romanticism, and the Uses of the Past (1797–1896)*. London and New York, NY: Routledge, 2009.

Butler, E. M. *The Tyranny of Greece over Germany: A Study of the Influence Exercised by Greek Art and Poetry over the Great German Writers of the Eighteenth, Nineteenth and Twentieth Centuries*. Boston, MA: Beacon Press, 1958.

Canning, Charlotte M., and Thomas Postlewait. "Representing the Past: An Introduction on Five Themes." In *Representing the Past: Essays in Performance Historiography*, edited by Charlotte M. Canning and Thomas Postlewait, 1–34. Iowa City, IA: University of Iowa Press, 2010.

Chadzidimitriou, Penelope, and Theodoros Terzopoulos. *Theodoros Terzopoulos: Apo to prosopiko sto pangosmio* [*Theodoros Terzopoulos: From the Personal to the Universal*]. Thessaloniki: University Studio Press, 2010.

Decreus, Freddy. *The Ritual Theatre of Theodoros Terzopoulos*. London and New York, NY: Routledge, 2019.

Evangelatos, Spyros A. "Yparhei 'syneheia' sti neohelliniki theatriki historia? (1590 per.–1990 per.)" ["Is There 'Continuity' in Modern Greek Theater History? (ca. 1590–ca. 1990)"]. In *Proceedings of the First Panhellenic Theatrological Conference: Greek Theater from the 17th to the 20th Century, 17–20 December 1998*, edited by Iosif Vivilakis, 33–36. Athens: National and Kapodistrian University of Athens, Department of Theater Studies, Ergo Publications, 2001.

Fischer-Lichte, Erika. *Ästhetik der Performativen*. Frankfurt am Main: Suhrkamp, 2004.

———. "Theatre and Identity: Theatre as a Liminal Space." In *History of European Drama*. Translated by Jo Riley, 1–7. London and New York, NY: Routledge, 2002.

———. "Theatre Historiography." Chap. 5 in *The Routledge Introduction to Theatre and Performance Studies*, edited by Minou Arjomand and Ramona Mosse, 71–98. London and New York, NY: Routledge, 2014.

Giakovaki, Nassia. *Evropi meso Elladas: Mia kampi stin evropaïki autosyneidissi* [*Europe via Greece: A Turning Point in European Self-Consciousness, 17th–18th Centuries*]. Athens: Hestia, 2006.

Glytzouris, Antonis. *Hi anadyssi kai hi edraiossi tou skinotheti sto neohelliniko theatro* [*The Rise and Consolidation of the Stage Director in Modern Greek Theater*]. Rethymnon, Crete: Foundation for Research and Technology, Crete University Press, 2011.

———, Konstantina Georgiadi and Maria Mavrogeni, eds. *Hi proïmi ypodohi tou Realismou kai tou Natouralismou sto helliniko theatro* [*The Early Reception of Realism and Naturalism in Greek Theater*]. Rethymnon, Crete: Foundation for Research and Technology, Institute for Mediterranean Studies, 2016.

Gourgouris, Stathis. *Dream Nation: Enlightenment, Colonization and the Institution of Modern Greece*. Stanford, CA: Stanford University Press, 1996.

Grammatas, Theodore. *To helliniko theatro ston 20o aiona: Politismika protypa kai prototypa* [*Greek Theater in the 20th Century: Cultural Norms and Prototypes*]. Vol. 2. Athens: Exantas, 2002.

Hadzipantazis, Theodoros. *Apo tou Neilou mechri tou Dounaveos* [*From the Nile to the Danube*], vols. A1, A2, B1, B2. Rethymnon, Crete: Foundation for Research and Technology, Crete University Press, 2002, 2012.

———. *Diagramma historias tou neohellinikou theatrou* [*Diagram of the History of Greek Theater*]. Rethymnon, Crete: Foundation for Research and Technology, Crete University Press, 2014.

———. "Theatrologia kai historia" ["Theatrology and History"]. *Ariadne* 5, no. 11 (2005): 327–35.

Hamilakis, Yannis. *The Nation and Its Ruins: Antiquity, Archaeology, and National Imagination in Greece*. New York, NY: Oxford University Press, 2007.

Herzfeld, Michael. "The Absent Presence: Discourses of Crypto-Colonialism." *South Atlantic Quarterly* 101, no. 4 (2002): 899–926.

Kangelari, Dio, ed. *Karolos Koun*. Athens: MIET, 2010.

Kitroeff, Alexander. *Wrestling with the Ancients: Modern Greek Identity and the Olympics*. New York, NY: Greekworks.com Inc., 2004.

Kitromilides, Paschalis. "The Study of Modern Hellenism as an Academic Challenge." *The Historical Review/La Revue Historique* 16 (2019): 249–54.

Kostis, Kostas. *History's Spoiled Children: The Formation of the Modern Greek State*. London: Hurst, 2018.
Koun, Karolos. "Karolos Koun: The Ancient Theater Has an Oriental Scent." Interview by Anna Mihalitsianou. *Ena*, 14 August 1984.
Karolos Koun: Gia to Theatro [*Karolos Koun: On Theatre*]. Athens: Ithaca, 1981.
———. *Kanoume theatre gia tin psychi mas* [*Making Theater for Our Soul*]. Athens: Kastaniotis, 1987.
Kyrtatas, Dimitris. "Hi kataktissi tis archaias hellinikis historias apo to neo hellinismo kata to 18o kai 19o aiona me ti diamessolavisi tis Dysis" ["The Conquest of Ancient Greek History by Modern Hellenism in the 18th and 19th Centuries, with the Mediation of the West." In *Oi chrisseis tis archaiotitas apo to neo hellinismo* [*The Uses of Antiquity by Modern Hellenism*], conference proceedings, the Moraitis Foundation for Literary and Cultural Studies, Athens, 14–15 April 2000, 251–66. Athens: Moraitis, 2002.
Lehmann, Hans-Thies. *Postdramatic Theatre*. Translated by Karen Jürs-Munby. London and New York, NY: Routledge, 2006.
Marchand, Suzanne L. *Down from Olympus: Archaeology and Philhellenism in Germany, 1750–1970*. Princeton, NJ: Princeton University Press, 2003.
Mavromoustakos, Platon. "Das antike griechische Drama als nationale Frage: Kritiker-und Publikums reaktionen auf moderne Aufführungen" [The Ancient Greek Theater as a National Issue: Critics' and Publics' Reactions to Modern Stage Productions]. In *Staging Festivity: Theater und Fest in Europa* [*Staging Festivity: Theater and Festival in Europe*], edited by Erika Fischer-Lichte and Matthias Warstat, 303–16. Tübingen and Basel: A. Francke Verlag, 2009.
———. "Provlimata kataskevis mias historias tou theatrou" ["Problems of Constructing a History of the Theater." In *Proceedings of the First Panhellenic Theatrological Conference: Greek Theater from the 17th to the 20th Century, 17–20 December 1998*, edited by Iosif Vivilakis, 39–47. Athens: National and Kapodistrian University of Athens, Department of Theater Studies, Ergo Publications, 2001.
———. *To theatro stin Ellada 1940–2000: Mia episkopissi* [*Theater in Greece 1940–2000: A Survey*]. Athens: Kastaniotis, 2005.
———., ed., *Karolos Koun: Oi parastaseis* [*Karolos Koun: The Performances*]. Athens: Benaki Museum, 2008.
Panayotakis, Nikolaos M., ed. *Origini della letteratura neogreca: Atti del secondo congresso internazionale "Neograeca medii aevi"* [*Origins of Neo-Hellenic Literature: Proceedings of the Second International Conference "Neograeca Medii Aevi"*], Venice, 7–10 November 1991. Venice: Greek Institute of Byzantine and Post-Byzantine Studies, 1993.
Panourgia, Neni. "Colonizing the Ideal: Neoclassical Articulations and European Modernities." *Angelaki* 9, no. 2 (2004): 165–80.
Patsalidis, Savas. "Pro historias: Chartographissi provlimaton kai prooptikon" ["Before History: Mapping Problems and Perspectives"]. In *Theatro, koinonia, ethnos: Apo tin "Ameriki" stis Hinomenes Politeies* [*Theater, Society, Nation: From "America" to the United States*]. Vol. 1, *1620–1960*. Thessaloniki: University Studio Press, 2009.
Pechlivanos, Miltos. "History (and Narratives) of Literature." *Molyvdokondylopelekitis* 6 (1998–1999): 169–86.
———. "Literaturgeschichte(n)" [Literary Histor(y/ies)]. In *Einführung in die Literaturwissenschaft* [*Introduction to Literary Studies*], edited by Miltos Pechlivanos, Stefan Rieger, Wolfgang Struck and Michael Weitz, 170–81. Stuttgart and Weimar: Verlag J. B. Metzler, 1995.

Politis, Alexis. *Romantika chronia: Ideologies kai nootropies stin Ellada, 1830–1880* [*Romantic Years: Ideologies and Attitudes in Greece, 1830–1880*]. Athens: Mnimon, 2003.

Postlewait, Thomas. *The Cambridge Introduction to Theater Historiography*. Cambridge: Cambridge University Press, 2009.

———. "The Criteria for Periodization in Theater History." *Theater Journal* 40, no. 3 (1988): 299–318.

———. "The Idea of the 'Political' in our Histories of Theater: Texts, Contexts, Periods, and Problems." *Contemporary Theater Review* 12, no. 3 (2002): 9–33.

———, and Bruce A. McConachie, eds. *Interpreting the Theatrical Past: Essays in the Historiography of Performance*. Iowa City, IA: University of Iowa Press, 1989.

Puchner, Walter. *Greek Theatre between Antiquity and Independence: A History of Reinvention from the Third Century BC to 1830*. Cambridge: Cambridge University Press, 2017.

———. "Hi nea eikona tis historias tou neohellinikou theatrou opos diamorfothike apo tis theatrologikes erevnes ton teleftaion 25 chronon" ["The New Image of the History of Modern Greek Theater, as It Was Shaped by the Theatrological Research of the Past 25 Years"]. In *Proceedings of the First Panhellenic Theatrological Conference: Greek Theater from the 17th to the 20th Century, 17–20 December 1998*, edited by Iosif Vivilakis, 21–33. Athens: National and Kapodistrian University of Athens, Department of Theater Studies, Ergo Publications, 2001.

Raddatz, Frank M., ed. *Reise mit Dionysos: Das Theater des Theodoros Terzopoulos— Journey with Dionysus: The Theatre of Theodoros Terzopoulos*. Berlin: Theater der Zeit, 2006.

Ricks, David. *The Shade of Homer: A Study in Modern Greek Poetry*. Cambridge: Cambridge University Press, 1989.

Sampatakakis, Yorgos. *Geometrontas to chaos: Morfi kai metafyssiki sto theatro tou Theodorou Terzopoulou* [*The Geometry of Chaos: Form and Metaphysics in the Theater of Theodoros Terzopoulos*]. Athens: Metaichmio, 2002.

Sathas, Constantine N. *Historikon Dokimion peri tou theatrou kai tis mousikis ton Vyzantinon, hitoi eisagogi eis to Kritikon Theatron* [*Historical Essay on the Theater and Music of the Byzantines; i.e., An Introduction to Cretan Theater*]. Venice, 1878.

———. *Kritikon Theatron hi syllogi anekdoton kai agnoston dramaton* [*Cretan Theater, or a Collection of Unpublished and Unknown Dramas*]. Venice, 1879.

Savvides, P. Georgios. "Pote, pragmati, arhizei I neoteri helliniki logotechnia?" ["When, Indeed, Does Modern Greek Literature Begin?"]. In *Origini della letteratura neogreca: Atti del secondo congresso internazionale "Neograeca medii aevi"* [*Proceedings of the Second International Conference "Neograeca Medii Aevi"*], Venice, 7–10 November 1991, edited by Nikolaos M. Panayotakis, vol. 1, 137–41. Venice: Greek Institute of Byzantine and Post-Byzantine Studies, 1993.

Schoenmakers, Henri. "Between Reasonless Passion and Passionless Reason: Theater Studies in the Nineties." In *Humanities in the Nineties: A View from the Netherlands*, edited by Erik Zürcher and Ton Langendorff, 175–206. Amsterdam: Swets & Zeitlinger, 1990.

Sideris, Yannis. *To archaio theatro sti neohelliniki skini, 1817–1932* [*Ancient Greek Theater on the Modern Greek Stage, 1817–1932*]. Athens: Ikaros, 1974.

———. *Historia tou neou hellinikou theatrou* [*History of Modern Greek Theater*], vol. 1. Athens: Ikaros, 1951. Vols. 1 (repr.), 2a, 2b and 2c, compiled and edited by Platon Mavromoustakos. Athens: Kastaniotis, 1990, 1999, 2000, 2009.

Siouzouli, Natascha. "Sakralität und Sakralisierung im Kontext europäischer Theaterfestivals" ["Sacredness and Sacralization in the Context of European Theater Festivals"]. In *Staging Festivity: Theater und Fest in Europa* [*Theater and Festival in Europe*], edited by Erika Fischer-Lichte and Matthias Warstat, 89–101. Tübingen and Basel: A. Francke Verlag, 2009.

Spathis, Dimitris. *Diafotismos kai neohelliniko theatre: Epta meletes* [*The Enlightenment and Modern Greek Theater*]. Thessaloniki: University Studio Press, 1986.

———. "To neohelliniko theatro" ["Modern Greek Theater"]. In *Ellada-Historia-Politismos* [*Greece-History-Culture*], vol. 10, 7–67. Thessaloniki: Malliaris, 1983.

Terzopoulos, Theodoros. *Hi epistrofi tou Dionysou: Hi methodos tou Theodorou Terzopoulou* [*The Return of Dionysus: The Method of Theodoros Terzopoulos*]. Athens: Attis Theater, 2014.

———. *Theodoros Terzopoulos kai Theatro Attis: Anadromi, Methodos, Scholia* [*Theodoros Terzopoulos and the Attis Theatre: History, Methodology and Comments*]. Edited by Eleni Varopoulou and Marianne McDonald. Translated by Alexandra Kapsalis. Athens: Agra, 2000.

Theater der Zeit Verlag, ed. *Dionysus in Exile: The Theatre of Theodoros Terzopoulos*. With a preface by Erika Fischer-Lichte. Berlin: Theater der Zeit, 2019.

Tziovas, Dimitris. "Hi dytiki fantassiosi tou Hellinikou kai hi anazitissi toy hyper-ethnikou" ["The Western Fantasy of Hellenism and the Search for the Supra-National"]. In *Ethnos-Kratos-Ethnikismos* [*Nation-State-Nationalism*], edited by Despo Solomou, 339–61. Athens: Moraitis, 1995.

Valsa, M. *Le Théâtre grec moderne de 1453 à 1900* [*Modern Greek Theater from 1453 to 1900*]. Berlin: Akademie-Verlag, 1960.

Wilmer, S. E. "Reifying Imagined Communities: Nationalism, Post-Colonialism and Theater Historiography." *Nordic Theater Studies* 12 (1999): 94–133.

———, ed. *Writing & Rewriting: National Theatre Histories*. Iowa City, IA: University of Iowa Press, 2004.

CODA: THE WHIRLIGIG OF TECH

Theater as Media Archaeology

W. B. Worthen

It has become commonplace to describe contemporary theater as "intermedial," suggesting that the incorporation of electronic, digital media to the analog sphere of stage performance defines a critical conceptual addition to the practice of theater. And yet, the technicity of theater has always been decisively intermedial, absorbing ambient media (social behavior, gesture, clothing, painting, sound, illumination, narrative) and both *representing* them, and representing *through* them, in its own distinctive spatial, haptic and social conventions: acting, costume and design.[1] This intermediality also indexes the challenges to identifying a single medial identity to theater; indeed, theater's penchant to *remediate* historical theater technologies challenges the notion of theater as a single perdurable medium, of *theater* as *one*.[2] Think of the 1585 staging of *Oedipus the King* in the Teatro Olimpico, the remediation of the Stuart masque in *The Tempest*, William Poel's experiments at the turn of the twentieth century, and various projects at reconstructed Elizabethan theaters throughout the twentieth and twenty-first centuries. Much as the 1623 Folio of Shakespeare's plays on a laptop screen is, in being remediated, no longer a book, gaining and losing functionalities, earlier performance systems—gaining and losing functionalities—can be remediated to the modern theater precisely because they are now something other than contemporary theater, participating in social and aesthetic genres that can be remediated to the stage precisely because *this* medium is not *that* one.

The evolving intermediality of theater is also visible in both theoretical and pragmatic terms, as much in Samuel Weber's swerve away from *theater* to *theatricality as medium* as in Eric Bentley's well-worn description of the "theatrical situation"—"A impersonates B while C looks on."[3] Are A, B and C assumed to be human beings? puppets? robots? objects? Is B understood as a character

DOI: 10.4324/9781003353461-17

or as a role, as a represented person or as a set of directions, and what do those directions look like? What does "impersonates" mean in this context? Does it matter whether that activity is inflected by the mid-1950s Method or mid-1960s epic theatricality? Does it matter that A, B and C share common geotemporal coordinates? Whether A is a serf, or C is Louis XIV? Was a hired man A impersonating the same B that, say, a shareholder like Burbage or Shakespeare was? Are technicians also A? The slightest pressure on A, B or C, that is, underlines the difficulty of seeing theater as a single medium, as at any geopolitical site of enunciation, the *longue durée* of theater practice articulates medial change, built into the structures of theatrical space, dramatic genres, and performance practices, including the practices of the audience.

Remediating theater complicates the notion of theater as a single performance medium. Here, I want to consider a striking performance—the Wooster Group *Hamlet*—as doing a specific kind of medial inquiry. While this landmark production has received incisive critical attention—notably for its redeployment of conceptions of theatrical experiment, its vision of performance historiography as remains, and its figuration of textuality in a vividly intermedial space— it also surges with a decisively *archaeological* impulse.[4] Indeed, the Wooster Group *Hamlet* prolongs the theoretical and methodological interests of a field that might be expected to locate the intersection between theater and the post-theatrical performance media it now often mediates: media archaeology. Media archaeology usefully engages the materiality of (mainly) communications media through the analysis of the technological alternatives and avatars that remain behind, some of which, like the typewriter, still operate, if just barely, on a contemporary horizon.[5] But rather than taking medial development as a smoothly progressive narrative of technological succession, media archaeology attends to the intersection of the material, the social and the ideological, in part by examining the "zombie-media: living deads [sic], that found an afterlife in new contexts, new hands, new screens and machines."[6] Not merely about inspecting dead media as the juncture of alternative futures, media archaeology is preoccupied with Siegfried Zielinski's "anarchaeology" and Wolfgang Ernst's "epistemological reverse-engineering," a process of "alienating," so to speak, the interaction of technologies to undo a narrative naturalizing the inevitability of their present-tense formation, both their material configuration and their assumed social uses and purposes.[7] As Ernst puts it, the "discipline of media archaeology is concerned with the technological foundations of discursive and cultural practices."[8]

Thomas Elsaesser's magisterial *Film History as Media Archaeology* undertakes this project with revealing reference to cinema. For Elsaesser, the volatility of "rapid media change" can be captured by attending to technological interaction: film cannot be derived from the magic lantern alone but is part of a "visual culture that include[s] the stereoscope and the phantasmagoria, neither of which could be straightforwardly appropriated as a 'precursor' of cinema."

Not only have the histories of "the telegraph, the radio, the gramophone, and the telephone" been "much more intertwined with that of cinema" than is often recognized, but conceived in the spatializing terms of archaeology rather than the linearity of progressive narrative, the instruments dramatize a dynamic intertechnological evolution.[9] Take the film projector:

> In its very dispositif—made up of mechanisms that are reverse-engineered or adapted from the magic lantern, the sewing machine, and even the machine gun—the film projector (as indeed the cinematograph) is a bricolage assemblage of very different but nonetheless distinct and related technologies. Apart from focusing light, they are concerned with transmission and transport, with conversion and interaction: grips and sprockets, eccentric disks like the Maltese cross, springs, and pick-up mechanisms. In its outer appearance and inner workings, the film projector has retained an identical shape and construction for more than 100 years, long after the technologies to which it owed its existence had been modified or altogether replaced.[10]

The instruments articulate film's—the technological and the aesthetic medium's—development as an ongoing site of material and ideological interaction and appropriation. As Jussi Parikka suggests, technology and the arts "work in a co-determining network of historical relations where aesthetics is also tightly interwoven with science and technology," an interactivity as characteristic of theater as it is of technologies of recorded performance.[11]

If "technology [is] an active agent in the ontological and epistemological sense," it is also an agent in the medial sense, defining what any medium—even the intermediating multimediality of theater—is conceived to be, to do, and to be able to do as an activity and as a structure of materialized representation.[12] Perhaps not surprisingly, for Elsaesser, the purview of media archaeology is "cinema, television, Internet," extended to "the telephone, radar, the computer, and all the other technologies said to be driving these media toward convergence." While this rhetoric of inclusion is inclined to "take digital media" as the means to reconsider the "horizons and boundaries" of history, *theater* as a distinctive technicity tends to be situated outside or behind this convergence. So while "[n]o medium replaces another or simply supersedes the previous one," theater—even the houses participating in "the sheer 'diversity' of nineteenth-century visual culture"—is largely absent from the archaeologizing gaze and, so, from the disciplines explored by media archaeology: "cinema studies, film history, media studies, media theory and art history."[13]

The absence—I am tempted to say the constitutive absence—of theater is pervasive in media archaeology. Theater is not mentioned among the "user types" and "types of sources" listed in Andreas Fickers and Annie van den Oever's comprehensive chart of experimental media archaeology practices:

various genres of literature and film, radio plays and television series, advertising, various forms of technical manuals and literature, videos, installations, and software, and "reenactments." Nor is it found among the illuminating series of articles in the *Routledge Companion to Media Technology and Obsolescence*, which features lucid pieces on the index card, the slide rule, the punched card, the typewriter, the overhead projector, nitrate film, the cathode-ray tube, remote control devices, vinyl records, Kodachrome and Polaroid film, the videocassette, floppy disks, CDs, DVDs, and so on, but avoids, say, the limelight, footlights, the star trap, the theater curtain, let alone embodied technologies like the teapot stance or the "Broadway voice."[14] What makes this absence suggestive is that media archaeology theorists nonetheless call for a methodological and pedagogical practice oddly resonant with the "theory and practice" rhetoric of theater studies and performance studies as professional disciplines. Even while performance studies refined and resisted dramatic theater as a defining critical paradigm and as a defining methodology in the 1980s, many of its research concerns are now inseparable from the disciplinary attitudes of theater studies. The older version of this paradigm was the theater "scholar/practitioner," but this juncture is reified today in the work of performer-scholars, in the ongoing development of canons of "practice-as-research" and "performance research," and in renewed interest in the consequences of "performative writing" as a mode of scholarly production.[15] Yet, while theater is largely absent from the purview of media archaeology, this methodological fusion—the attention to material means of critical reperformance as well as to its implication in critical practice—provides a significant disciplinary foundation, as when Wanda Strauven proposes "to think of media archaeology as a laboratory for history writing and theory making, by engaging with various hands-on media-archaeological methods, such as creative hacking, non-narrative modes of presentation, media bricolage and play"; "*doing* media archaeology" emerges as "a method of trial and error, of hands-on exercises, of creative thinking."[16]

In its distracted, somewhat occluded emphasis on the performative dimension of technology, then, media archaeology does not so much eschew the unmentionable discipline of theater and performance studies as it replicates its methodology. The notion of studio work as part of an informed methodological critique is one aspect of this convergence, as is an unwitting sensitivity to an unusually influential methodological paradigm, Richard Schechner's "restored behavior."[17] Strauven's account of watching television—that is, watching a cathode ray tube screen—resonates precisely with Schechner's sense of performance articulating the past in the incommensurable movements of present behavior.

> For instance, when we are put in front of an early black-and-white cathode ray tube in a living room that looks like a living room of the

1960s, we will watch it with our (altered) knowledge of colour TV, flat TV, internet TV, etc. That is to say, we will be re-sensitized as twenty-first-century TV viewers.[18]

Restored behavior does not restore history but encodes past activity in/as the landscape of present behavior, and Strauven's sense of the complexity of cathode ray tube spectating rubs shoulders directly with the conceptual challenges of spectatorship at venues defining one main stream of contemporary theatrical innovation, *reperformance*: Shakespeare's Globe and the Sam Wanamaker Playhouse in London, the American Shakespeare Center's Blackfriars Playhouse in Virginia, and reperformances like the Wooster Group *Poor Theater* and *Hamlet*. As Ernst suggests, reperforming old media instruments requires "the concept of an operative media *theatre*, with its core theoretical assumption being that a technological artefact is in its medium state only when it *dramatically* unfolds in signal transmission, recording, and replay, and in operative symbol processing."[19] Indeed, we might think that the Wooster Group's experimental remediating and reperformance of film and video—recently taking shape in the 2019 *Since I Can Remember*, which both remasters and reenacts photos, videos and props from their 1978 production of Spalding Gray's *Nayatt School*—precisely responds to this principle of reanimation, which Mark Goodall characterizes as the archaeological remediation of the analog, where sound (all that audible, crackling interference) or video provides a "hauntological" signature and "symbol of postmodern experience."[20]

This interface between "media" and the medialities of theater is troubled, though, by Jussi Parikka and Rebecca Schneider in a recent dialogue that complicates without quite resolving the erasure of theater as an object of media archaeology. In "Remain(s) Scattered," Parikka notes that media archaeology is "one term for the broad field where remains remain at the forefront"; while theater is not mentioned here, it nonetheless abrades the smooth "urgency of the supposedly new with the multiple other times that still persist," times always recorded in its physical structure and representational practices: "the time of the old, the obsolete, the fading, the slowly emerging, the parallel, the returning, the deep time, the time that is not reducible to a linear history."[21] Theater architecture sediments technologies, their temporalities, and the socialities that sustained them: an elderly Broadway theater like the Lyceum (built 1903) houses technologies originating in the eighteenth century (the steel fire curtain) alongside digital equipment from the current millennium, all sustained within an early twentieth-century infrastructure redolent of its period's notions of art, class and propriety, and subjected to practices (acting, design, directing) that at once evoke historical precedents and are constantly changing as well.

But while Parikka offers a suggestive sense that the "performative dimension" of media archaeology "offers a dynamic way to understand the archival and move beyond oppositions of live and documented, live and recorded, to the productive liveness of the archival as an embodied situation," he also provides a striking counter image of the scene of theater in media archaeology: Ernst's account of the founding of the Media Archaeological Fundus at Humboldt University in Berlin.[22] According to Ernst, when Media Studies was established at Humboldt, "it replaced former Theatre Studies," taking over its distinctive spaces as well: "All of the sudden, spaces like the student practicing stage and its relating fund of objects for rehearsal were empty. This was the ideal moment for the Berlin school of media studies (insisting on the materialities of communication and epistemic technologies) to claim such rooms under new auspices," in which the stage became "'the Media Theatre where technical devices themselves become the *protagonist*, and the fundus became the space for a collection of requisites of a new kind: media archaeological artifacts.'"[23]

Geography, in the academic landscape as elsewhere, figures power, and Ernst's narrative of the occupation of "empty" space urges us to accept the transfer of power as a simple transfer among media, as Parikka suggests: the "legacy in performance and theater was transferred and transposed into a different sort of relationality, which was also tied to certain spatial practices involving objects."[24] Perhaps. But what seems more visible is that theatrical terrain—a studio space used for medium-specific practices of training and rehearsal—is rewritten through a striking act of medial reterritorialization, in which the social and material practices of theater are evacuated, replaced by alternative objects and alternate ways of doing, justified by the assertion that they represent a more significant, legitimating agenda as "materialities of communication and epistemic technologies." That is, despite Ernst's sense that the function of media archaeology is "not the negation of the historical disciplines but the necessary complementary perspective on what constitutes culture," theater seems to occupy its usual, precarious place among these disciplines.[25] These transformed media spaces appropriate the methodological emphasis on the *doing* characteristic of theater and performance studies (Ernst describes the technological media as "meant to be the main actors"). Parikka, on the other hand, suggests that media studies' "hands-on approaches, methodologies of tinkering and collective 'doing it together' spirit"[26] appropriately displace to erase similarly inflected practices, the hands-on tinkering and collective training and *doing* of theater training and rehearsal and the space required to engage them.[27] Parikka calls for a more urgent recognition of the performative dimension of media archaeology, but that performativity is visualized here precisely as the conquest and dispersal of theater as a consequential practice.

Rebecca Schneider's "Slough Media" more carefully positions theater among the objects of media archaeology, alongside photography, film, video, digital arts, and other "gestic techniques of the body" as exemplary of the "play-replay nature of media."[28] Schneider understands the function of media as entwined with the human body: "bodies are the extension machines for media, and obsolescence is the mode of that extension." The "scandal of the obsolete is precisely that it is not": as the repurposing of theater space at Humboldt witnesses, the theater is always fading into pastness, irrelevance, and yet it scandalously remains, and remains in a way that works to remind new media of their persistent implication in obsolescence, perhaps most emphatically when they are represented on the stage. It may be that "there is little on this earth more outmoded than the live theater," but theater's mediality consists in an ongoing process of technological appropriation and remediation that is, like *gesture*, one of its constituent media, both "emergent and obsolescent simultaneously."[29] From *The Frogs* to *Hamlet* to *Trelawny of the "Wells"* to *Six Characters in Search of an Author* to *The Dresser* to *Venus*, plays about the theater often represent *theater* as outmoded, past, out of sync with the behavioral conventions of the framing world, reproducing in historical terms the syncopation within the present—since it is "always either behind or ahead of the play, at which you are looking and to which you are listening," your "emotion as a member of the audience is never going on at the same time as the action of the play"—that Gertrude Stein thought constitutive of dramatic performance.[30] What theater instantiates is the archaeological itself: any performance today, in any theater, however new, is built on technologies that not only owe their origins to previous instantiations but that depend on the deep time of a handmade aesthetic: the pins in the costume shop, the practices of rehearsal and acting, the social relations reified in auditorium design, and so on. Theater, that is, instantiates the "retro-futuristic element" of media archaeology, which recursively "hints at a non-linear relation between past and present media technologies, a short-circuiting of media tempor(e)alities which escapes traditional, narrative history of technology."[31]

Theater is an art of decaying, dying before our eyes while it simultaneously projects its future, and it is precisely this medial interface that preoccupies the Wooster Group, where the theater, rather than being excluded from media archaeology, becomes the site and the instrument of an archaeologically inflected interrogation of the interwoven character of performance mediation. The Wooster Group assertively locates the medial in the mediated, its stage in a sense exhuming the implication of the old Humboldt theater in the new media stage, a platform for the interaction of "communication and epistemic materialities": television monitors in the 1970s and 1980s, digital monitors large and small now, projection screens, and "live" (which is not to say unmediated) forms of performance, narration, storytelling and acting. The Wooster Group *Hamlet* provides a striking instance of this paradigm in its well-known interplay between film (actually, the digital remediation of several films, the *Hamlet*s directed by John Gielgud in 1964, by Kenneth Branagh in 1996, and by Michael Almereyda in 2000) and theater, in which the space of performance hosts a medial encounter.[32] In *Hamlet*, the Wooster Group actors perform by physically, gesturally, spatially and vocally reproducing an edited projection of the 1964 Theatrofilm by Electronovision film of the Broadway stage production of *Hamlet* directed by John Gielgud and starring Richard Burton. The digitized film is live-edited during the performance and projected upstage of the actors; they see it on inward-facing monitors and strive visibly to reproduce the screen actors' movements and tonalities in their live performances, as the film's video and audio channels are repeatedly distorted. While this production has been widely engaged for its interrogation of the terms of contemporary Shakespeare performance, its signal work has perhaps less to do with Shakespeare than with the encounter between performance media: the book, film, digitally mediated film, and theater.

As archaeology, the Wooster Group *Hamlet* offers a corrective to media archaeology from a medial site decisively absent from that field—theater—in part by remediating three film avatars that each dramatizes a distinctive ideology of Shakespeare performance. In 1964, the Theatrofilm by Electronovision *Hamlet* promised an extraordinary technical and social innovation that immediately died in the United States, though it had a brief life as the *T.A.M.I. Show*: mediating the experience of "live" Broadway theater by showing a filmed stage production simultaneously in nearly a thousand movie theaters.[33] The citation of the 2000 Almereyda *Hamlet* recalls that film's remediation of Pixelvision, the toy video camera that Ethan Hawke wields throughout the film, a device that failed to sell for the Fisher-Price toy company but that had an extensive zombie life for video artists like Michael Almereyda and for his *Hamlet* too.[34] Almereyda's *Hamlet* also marks the transition between analog and digital means of recording performance, most visibly in the scene in which Hamlet digitizes analog video for his film-within-the-film *Mousetrap*. Branagh's 1996 film, in its effort to be a "full text" *Hamlet*—an effort well after the watershed efforts of Shakespeare editorial studies to disimbricate the authority of conflated editions—articulates another intermediation, here between notions of live/recorded performance and the (ideal) identity of the Shakespearean script.[35]

The Wooster Group production proposes a medial inquiry that traces a temporal dislocation. First, it uses a still-present, always obsolescent practice—theater—to examine successive, post-theatrical technologies of performance. Digital recording and its projection—edited *Hamlet*s projected on a screen upstage but also visible on monitors both facing into the stage and facing the audience—provide both the object of investigation and the instrument to consider a nearly-instantly-obsolete-technology: the multicamera capture of a live Broadway performance as film, so that "liveness" could be reiterated when the film was to be shown more or less simultaneously in mid-1960s movie theaters. Taking an almost apocalyptic practice in hand, perhaps anticipating Anne Washburn's 2013 fantasy of a theatrical reperformance of *The Simpsons* in an electricity-less future, *Hamlet* stages a *past* technology (theater) to engage a *present* technology (digital film/projection), in order to reanimate an almost-instantly *dead* technology (Theatrofilm by Electronovision) that had expired 40 years earlier: the obsolescent stage reanimates a technology buried in the shallow grave of the theater's much deeper pastness.[36]

Like all theater, the Wooster Group *Hamlet* has evolved over time, and the terms of this restoration are now discussed by Scott Shepherd ("Hamlet") at the opening of the performance captured on video at the Edinburgh Festival in August 2013 (this introduction was not part of the performances I saw in New York in 2007). Shepherd notes several elements of the production, describing in particular how the company's replaying of the 1964 Gielgud/Burton Theatrofilm *Hamlet* offers a "reverse Theatrofilm."[37] He also describes how the film (though the digital remediation is not mentioned) has been edited (it is, or was, also live-edited during the performance). Using a laptop to project Gielgud's *Hamlet* in the window of a digital editing suite on the upstage screen, Shepherd demonstrates how to cut pauses within some lines and add them to the ends of others, an audio-editing that shuffles the video track, making the actors' onscreen movements jumpy, a stuttering movement simulated by the Wooster performers. More suggestively, Shepherd notes that, on many occasions, the film's actors are edited out of the picture, seeming to fade from view, "so that you have some chance of paying attention to the actors onstage."

Shepherd's comment on the erasure of actors from the screen points to one dimension of the theater's archaeological work with the film. If theater is always obsolescent, and always—both in its controversial ontology of disappearance and the persistent feeling (echoed from Aristophanes onward) of its pastness—*about* obsolescence, film is about absence constituting the feeling of presence, the image of (in this case, many now-dead) actors brought into living time.[38] The force of this illusion is medium specific: the visual scale of cinema—the dark house, the public privacy, the enormous screen—renders an intimacy to that experience that differs from the analytical potential of film on the small screen, set amid the clutter of a desk or living room, where "rewinding" is, so to speak, always an option, and that also departs from the theater's spatial and temporal thematics of distance. But onstage, the digitized film underlines the fact that the actors *can* be erased *because* they are not present, no longer even present as the projection of light through celluloid: they are a function of code, capable of being rewritten, repurposed within the intermedial relations of the modern stage. Taking the edited, jumpy, vanishing film as its script, the Wooster Group both redramatizes it—Burton's speaking often sounds stentorian, rhetorical, *theatrical* next to Shepherd's—and locates its work within the space of theatrical performance, a space in which a range of socialized media (behavioral conventions, gesture, vocal tone, movement, clothing) are represented and intermediated in and as theater.

This point is theatricalized not only when Scott Shepherd turns out to the booth during act 2, scene 2 and orders the technicians to "skip to the book"—that is, to the satire on old men that he uses to goad Polonius—but also when the materiality of theater critically reconceptualizes the notion of "restoring" film through performance. In act 4, scene 7, for example, the scene in which Claudius winds Laertes into his vengeful plot to poison Hamlet in the duel, the Burton film plays upstage as the Wooster actors perform downstage.[39] Here, though, "Hamlet" remains onstage, as Shepherd is recruited to move the wheeled table back and forth, one of the Wooster tactics for reproducing the camera angles in the matériel of the performance and, so, marking just how active the camera is in suturing the spectator into a changing set of mediated relations to the dramatic action. Of course, "Hamlet" is not present in Shakespeare's scene; he's on his way to kill or be killed in England. And yet, while Shepherd moves the table and watches the scene, Hamlet watches, too, through him, seeing a scene that Shakespeare's character cannot know but that the audience sees "him" observing. While film is, or was, typically understood to "improve" the theater's technological inability to reproduce the "real" accurately, here film is both reproduced and observed by the theater, its lamination of character to actor set apart from the theater's complex, critically suggestive, always alienated simultaneity of virtual identities. As a film designed to remediate the performance of *Hamlet* and also the experience of Broadway theater, the Theatrofilm *Hamlet* provides one archaeological mode for the Wooster Group, in a performance that at once memorializes and rewrites as live a production that attempted to mediate the live into the aesthetic and social structure of cinema.

The Wooster Group's critical remaking of film is enlarged by its interweaving of other *Hamlet* films in the production, and by how they are used. At several points in the action, the upstage screen goes blue, an irritating beeping is heard, and the word "Unrendered" appears in white; on several occasions, "Unrendered" marks the replacement of Gielgud's film with another, either the Branagh or the Almereyda *Hamlet*, and provides the opportunity for an alternative situation of the mediatized on the theatrical platform. In Polonius's scene with Ophelia and Laertes (act 1, scene 3), once Hume Cronyn's Polonius appears onscreen, "Unrendered" appears, and then Gielgud's film is replaced by Almereyda's, with Bill Murray playing Polonius. The video of this scene is visible only intermittently, though the audio track is audible, and the actors reproduce it (to my recollection, more of the video was used in earlier performances than remains in the performance captured on the DVD). While the theatrical remediation of Theatrofilm marks one temporal dynamic of the Wooster production, the encounter with Almereyda's tech-forward 2000 film marks another. Almereyda's *Hamlet*, set in New York City, locates the action in a densely media- and technology-rich environment. Not only does Ethan Hawke's Hamlet film himself and others throughout the film with the

Pixelvision camera, but the film's visual field is rife with surveillance cameras, televisions (in stores, apartments, cars), other forms of photography (Ophelia is a Polaroid artist), faxes, a cellphone; Hamlet's "To be, or not to be" is voiced over as he buys videos in a Blockbuster, videos that will be edited into his film-within-a-film, while *The Crow: City of Angels* runs on monitors in the background.[40]

While the Wooster Group remakes, repurposes and remediates Theatrofilm as theater, but Almereyda's film archives a different moment, not the remaking of theater as film but the moment when performance stood on the cusp between analog and digital, symbolized both by Hamlet's Pixelvision screen (its glimmering shadows the result of recording video on readily accessible audiocassettes, run at high speed) and by Hamlet's film, visibly marking its status within Almereyda's by using the same title designs. Hamlet is shown at his computer monitor laboriously digitizing the videotapes he has rented and editing the files into his *Mousetrap*, a stunning pastiche of pornography, Shakespeare silent films, and a brief slice of the famous Moscow State Jewish Theater actor Solomon Mikhoels performing as King Lear. Remediating the Theatrofilm *Hamlet* as theater marks the inaccessibility of theater to film, recontaining, distributing and erasing the original as a way to confirm the work of theater. Remediating the Almereyda *Hamlet* marks a different interface, the contemporary interplay between analog and digital modes of performance and of recording performance. Hawke's/Hamlet's *Mousetrap* is an editorial act, demonstrating the power of the archive to be sampled and recombined—that is, once its contents have been rewritten as binary code. Hawke here does to Mikhoels what the Wooster Group does to Burton, sampling his performance for alternative purposes, through the intervention of digital means.

All acts of editing are digital, even when the instruments and objects are analog. Film editing means choosing between alternatives, making an either/or binary decision: splicing this take (1/positive) while cancelling that one (0/negative). Indeed, it is precisely the digital dimension of textual editing that is so challenging—is Hamlet's flesh "grieved and sallied" (Q1), "sallied" (Q2) or "solid" (F)?—and that is "resolved" differently in different media. Print uses (well, it may use) the footnote or editorial apparatus; digital books use a hyperlink. Acting is often considered by literary scholars as "digital" in this respect: in this view, an actor has to choose one "interpretation" of a word or a line, inflect it toward one exclusive meaning (as though Hamlet were either mad for love *or* vengeful), while readers can hold several meanings, analog in their continuity, alive in the mind simultaneously.[41] But the Wooster Group actors' embodied confrontation of digitized voice and image realizes the fiction of such a "choice": the stage voice situates any utterance in analog tonalities, a continuum of inflection that is suggestive, meaningful, but not conceivable in binary terms. Hawke's Hamlet edits, but in revoicing Hamlet, Ophelia and Claudius, Scott Shepherd, Kate Valk and Ari Fliakos neither precisely replicate nor offer a precise alternative to the inflections, gestures and movements they reanimate. The film "text" and its live reperformance are like and unlike in precisely the way theatrical embodiment is at once like and unlike, recodes and exceeds, both the script and the "real" encoded in the theater's appropriation of social conventions of speech, movement and gesture.

In some ways, the most suggestive moment of media archaeology in the Wooster Group *Hamlet* is the arrival of the Players in Elsinore (act 2, scene 2); at first reperformed by the Wooster actors (Kate Valk, as the Player, bringing forward a book to prompt Hamlet's memory), they disappear from the screen more or less at Hamlet's performance of the "rugged Pyrrhus" lines. In this elaborate scene, the projection screen goes dark and a software window opens framing an alternate film: the Player scene, featuring Charlton Heston, from the Branagh *Hamlet*. Shepherd gestures, pointing to direct the cursor to enlarge the window until Heston fills the projection screen. Rather than fully replaying this scene, the Wooster Group cast largely watch it, at least they watch the Player's speech, because there is no actor playing the Player (Valk is changing costume). Here, the cinematic edges into the authority of live performance, a cinematic rhetoric emphasized as Branagh renders the diegesis of the Player's narration onscreen: as the Player speaks, the screen fills with John Gielgud/Priam staggering and then in closeup weakly defending himself against Pyrrhus's oncoming blow, and then Judy Dench/Hecuba wails her "bisson rheum" (Valk, costumed like Dench, is guided forward by Shepherd/Hamlet, reperforming Dench's silent lamentation in "closeup," that is, downstage). The Player speaks, so to speak, directly from the film, on the stage and to the auditorium: the Wooster performers reenact *what* he narrates but not his performance of narration.

The Wooster Group takes an allegorical engagement with Branagh's film, mediating the unspoken notion of performance's fidelity to the text of the play. Branagh's film fills in what the Wooster Group leaves unrendered: Heston's Player (who is, it might be said, terrific), unreenacted, occupies the sphere of "live" performance.[42] Branagh's urgently unabridged *Hamlet*—a "full text" version, "what some critics have referred to as the 'eternity' version," he suggests—ran over four hours and was, like Hamlet, slightly "out of joint" with its time. For while Shakespeare editorial scholarship of the previous decade had been arguing for the material independence of various editions of Shakespeare's plays ("arguments will always rage about exactly what constitutes a 'full text," Branagh notes), even to the extent of publishing three versions of *King Lear* in student complete-works editions, Branagh offered a conflated-text *Hamlet*, eschewing the cuts (no Fortinbras in Olivier's film, nor in Almereyda's) that often help to bring a film into the two hours' traffic of the cinema.[43]

Branagh's "full text" film is hardly a version of "fidelity," though, but claims the analogizing fidelity often asserted as the theater's obligation to the play.

Its Regency setting and costumes, for instance, might be taken as a rhetorical instrument materializing a legible class and gendered social hierarchy and, so, making the "historical" formalities of early-modern social behavior visible in the more familiar register of that ubiquitous screenwriter of romantic historical films, Jane Austen. Branagh's "full text" fidelity precisely articulates the conventions of film, conventions nowhere more palpable than the decision to do something dramatically uninteresting—though, as the multilocation spatiality of the early modern stage suggests, perhaps not technologically unavailable—to Shakespeare, and so unimaginable as part of "Shakespeare's play": staging the Player's narrative, Priam and Hecuba, during his speech. As Branagh puts it, "my film-maker's instincts made me long [...] to allow audiences [...] to be transported, as Hamlet is in his mind's eye, back to Troy and see Priam and Hecuba."[44]

Allowing the Player, Branagh's Player, Charlton Heston, to speak for himself, unremediated, the Wooster Group allows a moment of the film's asserted transparency to the text to remain in its performance, the assertion that the medium of performance, film in the theater, shows the play as it is, "full." The production stages its medial others—the realism of film, the authority of the text—as a way to invoke and hollow out this rhetoric, allowing it to remain visibly contradicted by a performance asserting the theater's implication in an impossible reiterativity. Staging film, the Wooster Group *Hamlet* makes its most decisive recognition: the stage always represents the media it uses, absorbing and recoding them to purposes that are—like theatrical technologies and tastes—necessarily, sometimes brilliantly, refunctioned as theater.

Perhaps recalling the old instruments in the Humboldt Media Fundus, the Wooster Group here operates its medial others, technological practices that historically succeeded theater but that, in the whirligig of tech, are remediated within the evolving, densely intermedial practices of the stage. Theater represents the media it repurposes. Sometimes—as, perhaps, is the case with Shepherd's more-or-less illegible costume as Hamlet, a loose collarless (doublet-like?) shirt, boots and a long culotte skirt—that remediation remains relatively opaque, not-yet-interpretable, unlike Burton's bad-boy, basic, black V-neck sweater, slacks and shoes in 1964. But much as theater remediates clothing as costume, social behavior as conventionalized gesture and movement, architecture as signifying design, the Wooster Group stage retools digital film within the assertive "liveness" of theater, a "liveness" it precisely stages, as all "liveness" is today, in conversation with mediated representation, as distinguishable from, yet culturally bound to, the reiterative performativity of other practices of mediated reenactment.

In its dialogue with the editorial consequences of digitization, the Wooster Group *Hamlet* triangulates a critical inquiry into the conditions of performance, including Shakespeare performance, at a moment in which film—long regarded as itself a kind of text, as a more productive object for scholarly critique than theater because it is (now) so easily produced as an object of *reading:* stopped, detemporalized, analyzed, cited—is not merely replayed but remediated and reperformed. Each of the films interwoven into the Wooster Group *Hamlet* occupies a distinctive medial interface. The Theatrofilm *Hamlet* claims to reproduce the social and aesthetic experience of Broadway liveness in the cinema. Almereyda foregrounds the slippage between analog and digital as the contour of Hamlet's, and the audience's, experience of action. And Branagh articulates the dependence of a performance's "fidelity" to the dramatic work on the rhetorical power of the medium's performative conventions: the medium produces "fidelity" in the infrastructure of its rhetoric. The Wooster Group's post-digital stage produces these medial interrogations as the instruments of its performance: the theater provides the means through which each of these conceptions of mediated reproduction is analyzed, situated and situated within/as theater.

In reembodying the films, this *Hamlet* materializes a crucial, Foucault-via-Beckett question as essential to theater: "What does it matter who is speaking?"[45] The answer here is sedimented, requiring an archaeological attention: Shakespeare and Burton and Hawke and Branagh and Shepherd and Hamlet—to say nothing of Gielgud and Almereyda and Branagh-as-director and Elizabeth LeCompte, the technicians in the booth, the stage hands, the screens and monitors—all simultaneously, undecidably, interactively speak, and speak in ways that mark the critical intermediality of theatrical performance, the "*dis*continuity of the media-artefactual message" systems it gathers, a discontinuity otherwise associated with digital mediation.[46] Indeed, remediating and so reanimating three films as theater, *Hamlet* resituates them within an alternative, *theatrical*, productive practice, one that dramatizes the interface between media archaeology and theater historiography. They function here as scenography, as script, and as part of a technological and media history that the production interrogates through the means of contemporary theater, particularly *reperformance*. Film, remediated as edited and, so, performable digital files, is functioned within the analog relations of theater. Rather than a historical account of film and stage *Hamlets*, or a mere act of historical citation (Branagh's Olivier-blonde dye job in his *Hamlet*), the Wooster Group production dramatizes the temporal and technological interweaving characteristic of an archaeological impulse: zombie media are repurposed by a living (if obsolescent) medium to open an interactive understanding of medial relations alternative to the "succession" narrative (theater to film to television to digital). Rather than an act of historical recovery, the archaeological impulse here stages past material to reorder the medial present, and perhaps the future as well.

Indeed, Ernst's well-placed confidence that "technological media can be restored to self-active statements" dramatizing the "more-than-human or even non-human agencies of artefacts" precisely recalls the ubiquitous agency of objects (Nora's letter-box, Hamlet's book, perhaps even Philoctetes's foot) in theater. Replaying successive performance media, the Wooster Group witnesses not only the agency of film on and in theater but also suggests how technical objects, when reanimated, reenact their technical protocols, what Ernst privileges as "their own inherent techno-logics," in an alternative environment that restructures the meaning and purposes of those logics through the means of reperformance. For while Ernst privileges the "self-active" nature of technological objects, which propose a "time-critical difference from the traditional cultural archaeological artefact" relying on the "reconstruction of its performance by humans," this effort to phrase an autonomous technological history remains in covert dialogue with the scene of its performance, the stage on which it reperforms.[47] Replaying zombie tech, whether a CRT or Theatrofilm, dramatizes the signifying force interwoven in the performative logic of the scene and practice of restoration. In its encounter between reciprocating obsolescences, the Wooster Group *Hamlet* witnesses the symbolic necessity of the archaeological appropriation of the Humboldt theater: staging old media, it seems, requires the mediation of the old theater after all.

Notes

1 See, for instance, Sarah Bay-Cheng, Chiel Kattenbelt, Andy Lavender and Robin Nelson, eds., *Mapping Intermediality in Performance* (Amsterdam: Amsterdam University Press, 2010); and Freda Chapple and Chiel Kattenbelt, eds., *Intermediality in Theatre and Performance* (Amsterdam: Rodopi, 2006). To be clear, then, I am not seeing "multimedia theater" or "intermedial theater" as distinct from theater, or as occupying a distinctive place on the theatrical horizon.
2 Jay David Bolter and Richard Grusin, *Remediation: Understanding New Media* (Cambridge, MA: MIT Press, 1999).
3 See Samuel Weber, *Theatricality as Medium* (New York, NY: Fordham University Press, 2004), as well as my critique of it in "Introduction: Theatre, Media, Technology," chap. 1 in *Shakespeare, Technicity, Theatre* (Cambridge: Cambridge University Press, 2019); and Eric Bentley, *The Life of the Drama* (New York, NY: Atheneum, 1964), 150.
4 On experiment, see Thomas Cartelli, "Channeling the Ghosts: The Wooster Group's Remediation of the 1964 Electronovision *Hamlet*," chap. 6 in *Reenacting Shakespeare in the Shakespeare Aftermath: The Intermedial Turn and Turn to Embodiment* (London: Palgrave Macmillan, 2019); on remains, see Rebecca Schneider, *Performing Remains: Art and War in Times of Theatrical Reenactment* (London: Routledge, 2011); on textuality and intermediality, see W. B. Worthen, *Drama: Between Poetry and Performance* (Oxford: Wiley-Blackwell, 2010), 123–38.
5 See Richard Polt, "The Life, Death, and Rebirth of the Typewriter," in *The Routledge Companion to Media Technology and Obsolescence*, ed. Mark J. P. Wolf (New York, NY: Routledge, 2019), 60–73.
6 Jussi Parikka, *What Is Media Archaeology?* (Cambridge: Polity Press, 2012), 3.
7 Wolfgang Ernst, quoted in Thomas Elsaesser, *Film History as Media Archaeology: Tracking Digital Cinema* (Amsterdam: Amsterdam University Press, 2016), 42.
8 Wolfgang Ernst, quoted in Nikita Braguinski, "Media Archaeological Fundus," *Sound & Science: Digital Histories*, accessed 1 February 2022, https://soundandscience.de/contributor-essays/media-archaeological-fundus.

9 Elsaesser, *Film History*, 52, 24, 25.
10 Ibid., 305.
11 Parikka, *Media Archaeology*, 69.
12 Jussi Parikka, *A Geology of Media* (Minneapolis, MN: University of Minnesota Press, 2015), 1.
13 Elsaesser, *Film History*, 81, 73, 87, 86, 352. Elsaesser does mention "the 'materiality' of clunky eighteenth-century stage machinery or the elaborate illusionism of a Pepper's Ghost phantasmagoria" as alternatives to "the effortless creation of such three-dimensional 'special effects' in computer graphics virtual space," noting the "imminent disappearance into homogeneity and conformism" of "the sheer 'diversity' of nineteenth-century visual culture"; *Film History*, 86.
14 Andreas Fickers and Annie van den Oever, "Doing Experimental Media Archaeology: Epistemological and Methodological Reflections on Experiments with Historical Objects of Media Technologies," in *New Media Archaeologies*, ed. Ben Roberts and Mark Goodall (Amsterdam: Amsterdam University Press, 2019), 50.
15 On practice-as-research in Shakespeare studies, see Sarah Dustagheer, Oliver Jones and Eleanor Rycroft, "(Re)constructed Spaces for Early Modern Drama: Research in Practice," *Shakespeare Bulletin* 35, no. 2 (Summer 2017): 173–85; Stephen Purcell, "Practice-as-Research and Original Practices," *Shakespeare Bulletin* 35, no. 3 (Fall 2017): 425–43; and the essays collected in Shannon Rose Riley and Lynette Hunter, eds., *Mapping Landscapes for Performance as Research: Scholarly Acts and Creative Cartographies* (London: Palgrave Macmillan, 2009).
16 Wanda Strauven, "Media Archaeology as Laboratory for History Writing and Theory Making," in *New Media Archaeologies*, ed. Ben Roberts and Mark Goodall (Amsterdam: Amsterdam University Press, 2019), 23, 24, italics in the original. See also Matt Ratto, "Critical Making: Conceptual and Material Studies in Technology and Social Life," *The Information Society* 27, no. 4 (2011): 252–60, DOI: 10.1080-/01972243.2011.583819.
17 Richard Schechner, "Collective Reflexivity: Restoration of Behavior," in *A Crack in the Mirror: Reflexive Perspectives in Anthropology*, ed. Jay Ruby (Philadelphia: University of Pennsylvania Press, 1982), 51.
18 Strauven, "Media Archaeology," 26–27.
19 Wolfgang Ernst, "Media Archaeology-As-Such: Occasional Thoughts on (Més-) alliances with Archaeologies Proper," *Journal of Contemporary Archaeology* 2, no. 1 (2015): 19, my italics.
20 Mark Goodall, "The Ghosts of Media Archaeology," in *New Media Archaeologies*, ed. Ben Roberts and Mark Goodall (Amsterdam: Amsterdam University Press, 2019), 79.
21 Jussi Parikka, "Remain(s) Scattered," in *Remain*, by Iona B. Jucan, Jussi Parikka and Rebecca Schneider (Minneapolis, MN: University of Minnesota Press, 2019), 10.
22 Ibid., 27.
23 Wolfgang Ernst, quoted in ibid., 17–18, my italics; it is perhaps worth recalling that in Athenian theater, "protagonist" referred to the "first actor," not the main character.
24 Ibid., 18. As Braguinski notes, "The collection's open attitude is also reflected in the *Fundus* element of its name, which in German denotes a repository for a theater's props and sets—a fitting label for this Humboldt University collection, as it emphasizes the aspect of active experimentation." Braguinski, "Media Archaeological Fundus."
25 Ernst, "Media Archaeology," 18.
26 Parikka, "Remain(s)," 21.
27 Wolfgang Ernst, quoted in Trevor Owens, "Archives, Materiality and the 'Agency of the Machine': An Interview with Wolfgang Ernst," *Signal* (blog), *Library of Congress* 8 February 2013, https://blogs.loc.gov/thesignal/2013/02/archives-

materiality-and-agency-of-the-machine-an-interview-with-wolfgang-ernst; Owens's piece has several photographs of the Media Archaeological Fundus and its associated Signal Lab; see also "Media Archaeological Fundus," *musikundmedien. hu-berlin*, accessed 19 July 2022, https://www.musikundmedien.hu-berlin.de/de/medienwissenschaft/medientheorien/fundus/media-archaeological-fundus.
28 Rebecca Schneider, "Slough Media," in *Remain*, by Iona B. Jucan, Jussi Parikka and Rebecca Schneider (Minneapolis, MN: University of Minnesota Press, 2019), 51.
29 Ibid., 58, 71, 72, 68.
30 Gertrude Stein, "Plays," in *Last Operas and Plays*, ed. Carl van Vechten (Baltimore: Johns Hopkins University Press, 1995), xxix.
31 Ernst, quoted in Owens, "Archives."
32 John Gielgud, dir., *Hamlet* (1964; Los Angeles, CA: Image Entertainment, 1999), DVD; Kenneth Branagh, dir., *Hamlet* (1996; Burbank, CA: Warner Home Video, 2007), DVD; Michael Almereyda, dir., *Hamlet* (2000; Los Angeles, CA: Miramax, 2000), DVD.
33 On Electronovision, see Worthen, *Between Poetry and Performance*, 127–30; the film was to be shown in 976 movie theaters in the United States on 23 and 24 September 1964. See also Cartelli, *Reenacting*, 187–92. Electronovision was also used to broadcast the *T.A.M.I. Show*, the Teenage Awards Music International broadcast of 1965.
34 On Pixelvision, see Peter Donaldson, "Hamlet among the Pixelvisionaries: Video Art, Authenticity, and 'Wisdom' in Michael Almereyda's *Hamlet*," in *A Concise Companion to Shakespeare on Screen*, ed. Diana Henderson (Oxford: Wiley-Blackwell, 2006), 216–37; and W. B. Worthen, *Shakespeare Performance Studies* (Cambridge: Cambridge University Press, 2014), 156.
35 Kenneth Branagh, "Introduction," in *Hamlet by William Shakespeare: Screenplay, Introduction and Film Diary* (New York, NY: W. W. Norton, 1996), xiv.
36 Anne Washburn, *Mr. Burns: A Post-Electric Play* (New York, NY: TCG, 2017); the play was produced in New York at Playwrights Horizons in 2013.
37 The Wooster Group, *Hamlet* (New York, NY: The Wooster Group, 2015), DVD.
38 See Peggy Phelan, *Unmarked: The Politics of Performance* (London: Routledge, 1993), 148 passim.
39 In identifying scenes, I refer to William Shakespeare, *Hamlet*, ed. Harold Jenkins (1982; repr., London: Thomas Nelson for Arden Shakespeare, 1997), a "conflated" edition based on Q2 and, so, more closely resembling the texts used as the basis of the films and the Wooster Group *Hamlet*.
40 I have discussed the role of digital media in this film extensively in "Fond Records: Remembering Theatre in the Digital Age," in *Shakespeare, Memory and Performance*, ed. Peter Holland (Cambridge: Cambridge University Press, 2006), 281–304, and in *Shakespeare Performance Studies*, 172–95.
41 The strongest phrasing of this argument is made by Harry Berger, Jr., *Imaginary Audition: Shakespeare on Stage and Page* (Berkeley, CA: University of California Press, 1989).
42 On the notion of recorded forms of media performing "live" for their audiences, see Philip Auslander, "Digital Liveness: A Historico-Philosophical Perspective," *PAJ: A Journal of Performance and Art* 34, no. 3 (September 2012): 3–11.
43 Branagh, "Introduction," xiv.
44 Ibid.
45 Foucault cites Samuel Beckett's "What does it matter who is speaking?"; Michel Foucault, "What Is an Author," in *The Foucault Reader*, ed. Paul Rabinow (New York, NY: Pantheon, 1984), 101. Beckett's original text, from "Texts for Nothing," appears in his own English translation as "What matter who's speaking?"; Samuel Beckett, *Stories and Texts for Nothing* (New York, NY: Grove, 1967), 85.

46 Ernst, "Media Archaeology," 17.
47 Ibid., 17, 20.

Bibliography

Almereyda, Michael, dir. *Hamlet*. 2000. Los Angeles, CA: Miramax, 2000. DVD.
Auslander, Philip. "Digital Liveness: A Historico-Philosophical Perspective." *PAJ: A Journal of Performance and Art* 34, no. 3 (September 2012): 3–11.
Bay-Cheng, Sarah, Chiel Kattenbelt, Andy Lavender and Robin Nelson, eds. *Mapping Intermediality in Performance*. Amsterdam: Amsterdam University Press, 2010.
Beckett, Samuel. *Stories and Texts for Nothing*. New York, NY: Grove Press, 1967.
Bentley, Eric. *The Life of the Drama*. New York, NY: Atheneum, 1964.
Berger, Harry, Jr. *Imaginary Audition: Shakespeare on Stage and Page*. Berkeley, CA: University of California Press, 1989.
Bolter, Jay David, and Richard Grusin. *Remediation: Understanding New Media*. Cambridge, MA: MIT Press, 1999.
Braguinski, Nikita. "Media Archaeological Fundus." *Sound & Science: Digital Histories*. Accessed 1 February 2022. https://soundandscience.de/contributor-essays/media-archaeological-fundus.
Branagh, Kenneth, dir. *Hamlet*. 1996. Burbank, CA: Warner Home Video, 2007. DVD.
Branagh, Kenneth. "Introduction." In *Hamlet by William Shakespeare: Screenplay, Introduction and Film Diary*, xi–xix. New York, NY: W. W. Norton, 1996.
Cartelli, Thomas. *Reenacting Shakespeare in the Shakespeare Aftermath: The Intermedial Turn and Turn to Embodiment*. London: Palgrave Macmillan, 2019.
Chapple, Freda, and Chiel Kattenbelt, eds. *Intermediality in Theatre and Performance*. Amsterdam: Rodopi, 2006.
Donaldson, Peter. "Hamlet among the Pixelvisionaries: Video Art, Authenticity, and 'Wisdom' in Michael Almereyda's *Hamlet*." In *A Concise Companion to Shakespeare on Screen*, edited by Diana E. Henderson, 216–37. Oxford: Wiley-Blackwell, 2006.
Dustagheer, Sarah, Oliver Jones and Eleanor Rycroft. "(Re)constructed Spaces for Early Modern Drama: Research in Practice." *Shakespeare Bulletin* 35, no. 2 (Summer 2017): 173–85.
Elsaesser, Thomas. *Film History as Media Archaeology: Tracking Digital Cinema*. Amsterdam: Amsterdam University Press, 2016.
Ernst, Wolfgang. "Media Archaeology-As-Such: Occasional Thoughts on (Més-)alliances with Archaeologies Proper." *Journal of Contemporary Archaeology* 2, no. 1 (2015): 15–23.
Fickers, Andreas, and Annie van den Oever. "Doing Experimental Media Archaeology: Epistemological and Methodological Reflections on Experiments with Historical Objects of Media Technologies." In *New Media Archaeologies*, edited by Ben Roberts and Mark Goodall, 45–68. Amsterdam: Amsterdam University Press, 2019.
Foucault, Michel. "What Is an Author?" *The Foucault Reader*, edited by Paul Rabinow, 101–20. New York, NY: Pantheon, 1984.
Gielgud, John, dir. *Hamlet*. 1964. Los Angeles, CA: Image Entertainment, 1999. DVD.
Goodall, Mark. "The Ghosts of Media Archaeology." In *New Media Archaeologies*, edited by Ben Roberts and Mark Goodall, 69–82. Amsterdam: Amsterdam University Press, 2019.

musikundmedien.hu-berlin. "Media Archaeological Fundus." Accessed 19 July 2022, https://www.musikundmedien.hu-berlin.de/de/medienwissenschaft/medientheorien/fundus/media-archaeological-fundus.

Owens, Trevor. "Archives, Materiality and the 'Agency of the Machine': An Interview with Wolfgang Ernst." *Signal* (blog). *Library of Congress*, 8 February 2013. https://blogs.loc.gov/thesignal/2013/02/archives-materiality-and-agency-of-the-machine-an-interview-with-wolfgang-ernst.

Parikka, Jussi. "Remain(s) Scattered." In *Remain*, by Ioana B. Jucan, Jussi Parikka, and Rebecca Schneider, 1–47. Minneapolis, MN: University of Minnesota Press, 2019.

———. *A Geology of Media*. Minneapolis, MN: University of Minnesota Press, 2015.

———. *What Is Media Archaeology?* Cambridge: Polity Press, 2012.

Phelan, Peggy. *Unmarked: The Politics of Performance*. London: Routledge, 1993.

Piccini, Angela. "The Cube: A Cinema Archaeology." In *New Media Archaeologies*, edited by Ben Roberts and Mark Goodall, 177–203. Amsterdam: Amsterdam University Press, 2019.

Polt, Richard. "The Life, Death, and Rebirth of the Typewriter." In *The Routledge Companion to Media Technology and Obsolescence*, edited by Mark J. P. Wolf, 60–73. New York, NY: Routledge, 2019.

Purcell, Stephen. "Practice-as-Research and Original Practices." *Shakespeare Bulletin* 35, no. 3 (Fall 2017): 425–43.

Ratto, Matt. "Critical Making: Conceptual and Material Studies in Technology and Social Life." *The Information Society* 27, no. 4 (2011): 252–60. DOI: 10.1080-/01972243.2011.583819.

Riley, Shannon Rose, and Lynette Hunter, eds. *Mapping Landscapes for Performance as Research: Scholarly Acts and Creative Cartographies*. London: Palgrave Macmillan, 2009.

Schechner, Richard. "Collective Reflexivity: Restoration of Behavior." In *A Crack in the Mirror: Reflexive Perspectives in Anthropology*, edited by Jay Ruby, 39–81. Philadelphia, PA: University of Pennsylvania Press, 1982.

Schneider, Rebecca. "Slough Media." In *Remain*, by Ioana Jucan, Jussi Parikka and Rebecca Schneider, 49–107. Minneapolis, MN: University of Minnesota Press, 2019.

———. *Performing Remains: Art and War in Times of Theatrical Reenactment*. London: Routledge, 2011.

Shakespeare, William. *Hamlet*. Edited by Harold Jenkins. 1982. Reprint, Walton-on-Thames: Thomas Nelson for Arden Shakespeare, 1997.

Stein, Gertrude. "Plays." In *Last Operas and Plays*, edited by Carl van Vechten, xxix–lii. Baltimore, MD: Johns Hopkins University Press, 1995.

Strauven, Wanda. "Media Archaeology as Laboratory for History Writing and Theory Making." In *New Media Archaeologies*, edited by Ben Roberts and Mark Goodall, 23–43. Amsterdam: Amsterdam University Press, 2019.

Washburn, Anne. *Mr. Burns: A Post-Electric Play*. New York, NY: TCG, 2017.

Weber, Samuel. *Theatricality as Medium*. New York, NY: Fordham University Press, 2004.

Wooster Group. *Hamlet*. 2007. Wooster Group, 2015. DVD.

Worthen, W. B. "Fond Records: Remembering Theatre in the Digital Age." In *Shakespeare, Memory and Performance*, edited by Peter Holland, 281–304. Cambridge: Cambridge University Press, 2006.

———. *Drama: Between Poetry and Performance.* Oxford: Wiley-Blackwell, 2010.

———. *Shakespeare Performance Studies.* Cambridge: Cambridge University Press, 2014.

———. *Shakespeare, Technicity, Theatre.* Cambridge: Cambridge University Press, 2019.

INDEX

Note: Page references with "n" denote endnotes.

Abdeall, Mohya 226
Abrahamic religions 181
Achilles (Christopoulos) 241
acting 178–181
Action culturelle des travailleurs (ACT) 224–225
activism 43, 52
adaptations 63, 149, 154, 159, 221, 248
aesthetics 67, 140, 180; avant-garde 69; colonized 89; Euro-American 181; modern 128; and technology 260
affective nationalism 50
Afronauts (Bodomo) 40, 47, 49, 50–51, 53
The Afterlife of Reproductive Slavery (Weinbaum) 41, 51–52
Aguilar, Gaspar 21
Ailey, Alvin 196
Akomfrah, John 80, 81–82, 88
Al-Agouwâl (Alloula) 228
Algeria 218; cultural mixing 215–220; interwoven performance culture of 26, 213–229; invasion of 215–220; liberation of 223; new directions 228–229; occupation of 215–220; popular theater, development of 220–222; theater during 1980s 226–228; theater during early 1990s 226–228; Yacine and interwoven theater 222–226
Algerian National Theatre 221, 223
Al-Haddad, Najib 219

Al-Ḥakawātī 62
Al-Ḥalqa 62, 74n47
Al-Kacem El-Gour, Abu 68
Al-Khozai, Mohammed 64
Alloula, Abdelkader 220, 222, 225, 227–228
Al-Mamūn 62
Almodóvar, Pedro 193
Al-Qardahi, Sulayman 219
Al-Quaraaqoz 218
Al-Rai, Ali 62–63
alternative theater 59, 70, 267, 271–272
Alter-Politics (Hage) 49
Amaya, Carmen 200
Amazigh 214–217; culture 215, 222; kingdoms 216; language 226; storytellers 217; theater 226–227
Amsterdam Female Student Association 149
anarchaeology 259
ancestral catastrophe 39
Andersen, Hans Christian 196
Anderson, Benedict 154
Andrade, Oswald de 44
Andreini, Giovanni Battista 4
Ankoku Butoh 107
An-Naqdu al-Muzdawij (Double Critique) (Khatibi) 59
Anthropophagic Manifesto (Andrade) 43–44

appropriation 260, 269; of African content 90; Arabs' 61; archaeological 272; of flamenco 193; native 63; technological 264; without permission 89, 97
Arab nationalism 62, 219
Arab Spring 69
Arab world: double resistance 64–67; entangled theater/performance histories in 58–70; fear of interweaving in 67–69; postcolonial turn 64–67; postcolonial turn in 59
archaeology 59, 69; theater as media 258–272
archives 82; colonial 25, 42, 128–129, 136, 140–141; digitized newspaper 130; historical 41, 113; hospital 43; production 93
Arc/Procession: Develop, Catch Up, Even Surpass (Kentridge) 84
Artaud, Antonin 110–111
Atsumori 177
audience(s): Dutch 149; Europeanized 220; female 133; German 5, 199; Greek-speaking 236, 243–244; informed 192; Japanese 10; lower-class 223; Nahua 17–18; as "other" 180; populist 224; urban 219
authenticity 192
authorship 225–226
avant-garde: aesthetics 69; Arab, critique of modernist regimes 69; art 26; flamenco as protest 194; flamenco's historical dimensions 192–193; Galván and past 196–198; rediscovering roots 195–196; Rocío Molina 200–204; tanztheater 205–206; in twenty-first-century 190–206
Ávila, Gaspar de 21
Aydabi, Yousif 68
Ay! Jondo (Galván) 196
Aziza, Mohammed 64
Aztec Empire 14

Babylonia (Byzantios) 241
backstage 95, 169
Badawi, M. M. 63
Bai Juyi (Po Chü-I) 171
Bardou-Jacquet, Antoine 46
Battersby, John 86
Baudet, Thierry 145
Bausch, Pina 195

Belmonte, Emilio 201
Ben Achour, Bouziane 214
Benaïssa, Slimane 222, 223, 225
Benguettaf, Mohamed 227
Bentley, Eric 258
Berg, Alban 90
Berraondo, Txiki 200
Between Gaia and Ground (Povinelli) 39
Bhabha, Homi 63, 85, 153
Bharucha, Rustom 65
Bini, Dante 115
biocapitalism 51
Black Lives Matter 145
Black Reconstruction (Du Bois) 46
Blaeu, Françoys 151, 155
Blokker, Jan 149
Bodomo, Nuotama Frances 40, 47–51, 53
Borowski, Mateusz 46
Bosque Ardora (Forest of Ardor) 195, 203–204
Bouanani, Samir 229
Braak, Menno ter 148
Bradstreet, John 5
Brazilian culture 44
Brecht, Bertolt 25, 226
British Malaya 128, 141n2
Brockett, Oscar 64
Brooks, Lynn 20
Brown, Robert 5
Buddhism 170, 174
bugaku 3–4, 12; ceremony, dramaturgy of 3
Burton, Richard 265
Butoh 107
Byzantios, Dimitrios Hadjiaslanis 241

Caída del Cielo (Fallen from Heaven) 202
Calderón de la Barca 21
Calvinist ethic of suffering 156–157
Canta Gitano (short film) 199
capitalism 51
Cargill, Thomas 133–134, 136
Carr, Helen 155
Castellanos, Don Ángel Díaz 43, 45
censorship 111, 157
Chakrabarty, Dipesh 40–41, 52, 61
Charles V, Holy Roman Emperor 23
Chatterjee, Partha 154–155
Chauke, Thulani 91
Chekhov, Anton 181–183, 184
Chelkowski, Peter J. 63
Cheniki, Ahmed 222
Cherkaoui, Sidi Larbi 70

Chilembwe, John 91–92, 94
chorus 8–9, 95, 227
Christian Idealism 170
Christianization 22, 24
Christopoulos, Athanasios 241
cinema 118, 259, 271; 'precursor' of 259; visual scale of 266
class and reversibility 174–181
Clover, Joshua 97
Coen, Jan Pieterszoon 145
Cohen, Sande 37
collage 80–81, 83, 86, 88–89, 98
colonial British Singapore: global economic and cultural network 130; theater history of 129
colonial historiographies 25
colonialism 39, 97
coloniality: and knowledge 60; and labor 60; and race 60
(post)colonial theory 64–67
colonized aesthetics 89
Comici Fedeli 4
Comici Gelosi 4
commercial: services 137; venues 192
Commonwealth War Graves Commission 79
communication: direct 134; materiality of 259, 263–264; West African 90
The Conquest of Jerusalem 17, 18–19
Constancy in Faith 24
Conteh-Morgan, John 214
Contesting Performance: Global Sites of Research 61
Contesting Space in Colonial Singapore: Power Relations and the Urban Built Environment (Yeoh) 135
Corpus Christi Day 9
Cortés, Hernán 13–14, 18–19, 20
Cortés, Joaquín 191
costume 176, 184n2, 195, 202, 204–205, 208n38, 258, 270; clothing as 270; Namahage 172; shop 264; white shaggy 208n38
Cretan Renaissance 244
crisis 73n43, 182, 242
criticism 18–19, 90, 134, 147, 198, 240, 251n27
Cuando las Piedras Vuelen (*When Stones Fly*) 202
cultural friction 58
cultural identity 192, 214
cultural mixing 215–220
cut 92, 266

Dahmoune, Brahim 220
dance: anti-modern 195; *bugaku* 3–4; Butoh or *Ankoku Butoh* 107; cosmic court 3; feminine 201, 208n30; Hijikata Tatsumi 106–112; Japanese 9; Pedi stomping 87, 101n41; Spanish 206
Daninos, Abraham 218–219
Das, Santanu 79, 98
Davidson, Justin 85, 88
Davis, Tracy C. 80, 131
The Death of Patroclus (Christopoulos) 241
decolonial approach(es) 42, 58–59, 66, 69–70
deconstruction: decolonial 59; decolonizing 66; and double critique 65; of traditional norm 191
De Japoniorum martyris 12
Derrida, Jacques 111
de Ruyter, Michiel 147
desire and violence 149–151
deviant nationalism 61
de With, Witte 147
Diaghilev, Sergei 196
dialogue 58, 219, 245, 270, 272
director(s) 182, 199–200, 202, 220–221; experimental 227; theater 252n34
discourse 46–51
disentanglement 26; writing history as 234–248
diversity: standards of 69; of world's theater/performance experiences 61, 132
Djeha (Allalou and Dahmoune) 220
documentary theater 46–47
Donnelly, Mark 38, 45
double critique 58–60, 65–67, 70n5
Dower, John 116
drama: Greek 63–64, 238–239, 242; during Interwar period 242; romantic historical 220; spoken 25; Western 63, 226
dramaturge 197, 202
dramaturgy: of *bugaku* ceremony 3; of decolonisation 42
Drei Schwestern (*Three Sisters*) 181, 183, 183
Dudley, Joanna 87
du Perron, Edgar 148
Durán, Diego 6, 15
Dutch East India Company 150
Dutch Golden Age 147

Index **281**

Dutch nationalism 147
Dutch Repertory Company 149

E.A.T. (Experiments in Art and Technology) collective 112, 115
El-Ajwad (Alloula) 228
El-Hadj, Fouzia Aït 227
Elizabeth, Abderhalden Cortés 43
El-Litham (Alloula) 228
El Loco, Félix 196–197, 200
El-Ramly, Lenin 72n22
El sacrificio de Abraham 15
El sacrificio de Isaac 15
Elsaesser, Thomas 259–260
El Sombrero de Tres Picos 196
embodiment 269
enlightenment 170; European 234; Greek 251n30
entangled history 24; coining of 1; defined 2; *vs.* influence 1–2; *vs.* reception 1–2
entangled theater/performance histories: in Arab world 58–70; in Mexico 24
epic 80–81, 87, 259
epistemological reverse-engineering 259
Ermarth, Elizabeth Deeds 51
Ernst, Wolfgang 259, 263
Escudero, Vicente 197–198
ethnofictions 42, 45
Eurocentrism 66
European Enlightenment 234
European imperialism 65
European theater history 25
European Union 193, 246
evangelical performances 15
evangelization 15
exhibition 40, 50, 114, 131, 185n10
experimental metropolis 108, 109, 113, 115, 117

failure: of avant-garde art 69; financial 117; of historians of theater 244; political 153
Falero, Alfonso 171, 177
Fall of Our First Parents 16–17, 18
Fanon, Frantz 64, 65, 88
fantasy of conquest 152–155
Fatma 227
fear of engulfment 152–155
Fedorchenko, Aleksey 46
feminism: Black 41, 46; as social revolutions 193
Feral Atlas (website) 52

Ferdinand II, Holy Roman Emperor 4
Ferdinand VI, King of Spain 43
festival(s): Arab Theatre Festival 67, 73n43; Carthage Festival 226; Edinburgh Festival 266; Epidaurus Festival 242; Festival of Sbeiba 217; Festival Plaza 114; global performance 115; Holland Festival 101n45; Kasuga Wakamiya 167, 186n21; for Quetzalcoátl 15; Salzburg Festival 90; Spanish 21; Sundance Film Festival 40
Fickers, Andreas 260
film: digitized 265–266; documentary 47; film-projection technology 118; promotional 116, 119; sci-fi 47
Film History as Media Archaeology (Elsaesser) 259
fire: insurance 136–137; mitigation 128, 133, 135; prevention 129, 136; protection 139–140; safety 127–128; theater 127–128, 130–131; tragedies 130
Fla.Co.Men (Galván) 190, 203
flamenco 26; historical dimensions 192–193; music 201; as protest 194; scream 190–192
Flamenco (film) 201
"Fly me to the Moon" (exhibition) 40, 50
foreigners and reversibility 171–173
forgetting 25, 106, 108–109, 122
formalism 69
Franco, Francisco 192; death of 193; reactionary cultural policy 193
Furuhata Yuriko 116
fūryū 8–9
Fūshikaden (Zeami) 180

Gagakuryō 4
Galván, Israel 191, 194, 196–198
Gan, Elaine 55n39
Gante, Pedro de 15
Gassner, John 63
Gatlif, Tony 199
Geerke, H. P. 147
Gemeentelijk Theaterbedrijf (Municipal Theater Company) 148
gender: ambiguity 181; divide 200; inequality 194; parity 190; relations 155
Genpei War 174–175
Gerhard, William Paul 131, 135
gesture 6, 50, 91, 145; coded 193; conventionalized 270; story making use of 227

Gielgud, John 265
Gigaku 3, 12
Giraud, Eva Haifa 53
Gitano community 192, 194, 199, 201–202
global designs 59
globalization 59, 67
Global North 73n43, 156
The Go-Between (Huntley) 167
Gomez, Illeana 195
González, Felipe 193
Goodall, Mark 262
Goor, Jur van 149, 161n27
Gray, Spalding 262
Great Big Mirror Dome (film) 116
Great War *see* World War I
Greek identity 236, 241–242, 245, 247
Greek theater 236–240; ancient 236; contemporary 235; historiography of 236, 246; modern (*see* modern Greek theater); timeline of 240
Grønstad, Asbjørn Skarsvåg 88
Groupe d'études berberes (Berber Studies Group) 226
Guernica (painting) 193
Guevara, Che 221

Hadjithomas, Joana 47
Hage, Ghassan 49–50
Hamlet (Shakespeare) 150
Hamlet (Wooster Group) 259, 264–265
Hartman, Saidiya 38
Hayashi Mitsui 121
The Head & the Load (*H&L*) 80; collage used in 83, 88; Davidson on 85; directionality of 84; overview 83; physical staging 87; polyphonic historiography 80–81; production history 90–96
Hegel, Georg Wilhelm Friedrich 51, 60, 170
hegemony: Western 67; of Wilfred Owen's poetry 97
Heidi, Abderhalden Cortés 43
Heike Monogatari (*Tales of the Heike*) 175
Henkel, Karin 181–182, 184
Hidden Figures (Shetterly) 46, 48
Higgins, Scarlet 97
Hijikata Tatsumi 25, 115–118; dance 106–112; performance at Osaka World Exposition 106–109; two presences at the Osaka Exposition 118–121

Hildy, Franklin 64
Hiraga, Sebastian T. 121
Hirohito, Emperor 171
histoire croisée 1; *see also* entangled history
Historia de las Indias (Durán) 14–15
Historia general de las cosas de la Nueva España (Sahagún) 14
histories of interweaving 2, 25
historiography 37; and epistemic coloniality 60; Eurocentric 63; of lost performances 121–123; performance 60–64; polyphonic 80–81; reversibility as 167–184
History and Theory (Journal) 37
History in the Discursive Condition (Ermarth) 51
History of the Theatre (Brockett and Hildy) 64
History Out of Joint (Cohen) 37
history plays 148–149
history whitewashing 48
Ho Chi Minh 223
hone 193
Hudson, David 85
humanism 40
human tragedies 130
Huntley, L. P. 167
hybridity 213, 215

iconoclastic trickster 220, 230n13
iconology 84, 194, 201
identity: cultural 192, 214; Greek 236, 241–242, 245, 247; politics 60
ideology: of Islam 66; of Japanese exceptionalism 171; of Shakespeare performance 265
Ikonomou, Konstantinos 241
images: African 97; gendered 203; mirror 177–178; reshuffled 42; reversed mirror 173; woodblock 185n10
Imagined Communities (Anderson) 154
imitation 62, 64, 69
Immoos, Thomas 12
imperial historiography 129
improvisation 90–92, 192, 197–198, 223–224
Impulso (film) 201
Indian Ocean slave trade 153
Indigenous: artists 52; Japanese thought 170, 173, 187n35; language 224; peoples 14, 16, 89; population 14, 23; theaters 132, 139–140; women 151, 155

Index **283**

influence: described 1; *vs.* entangled history 1–2
intercultural entanglement 86
interculturalism 25, 58, 80, 83, 87, 97
interpretive methodology 157–159
intertextuality 239
interweaving: defined 2; histories of 2; of Japanese and European performance cultures 13
interweaving performance cultures 2–3; and German theater 4; histories of 25; Japanese and European 13; processes of 3
intracultural/intercultural: entanglement 86; paradigm 58, 73n43; performances 25; production 97; theater 73n43
Islam 64, 66

Jamal, Ashraf 86
Jan Pieterszoon Coen (Slauerhoff): interpretive methodology 157–159; production history 148–149
Japan: Chinese performing art forms 3–4; and Christian faith 7; dance forms 10; Korean performing art forms 3–4; missionaries in 6; persecution of Christians in 12; plays in 6–7; US postwar occupation of 116
Japanese exceptionalism 171
Japanese Red Army Faction 117
Jemaa el-Fna 74n46
Jennings, Luke 202
Jesuits 9, 12–13, 16, 24
Jesuit school theaters 13
jo-ha-kyū 3
Jones, Richard 5
Joreige, Khalil Lamia 47
Journal of the Statistical Society of London 136
JP Fuji Group 115
Julius Caesar (Shakespeare) 5

Kabuki 9–12, 167–168, 182–184
Kahina, H. M. 228
Kamachi Mitsuru 9–10
Kan'ami Kiyotsugu 176
Kasuga Wakamiya festival 167
Kateb, Mustapha 221–222
Kempe, William 5
Kentridge, William 25, 80, 83–85, 90, 94–96; *American Theatre Magazine* profile on 93; Jamal on 86; polyphonic historiography 80–81, 97; spasm of history 91
Khatibi, Abdelkébir 59, 65–66, 70n5
Khayāl Al-Zill (shadow play) 62
King Lear (Shakespeare) 5
KIT Royal Tropical Institute in Amsterdam 149
Kocka, Jürgen 1
Kongō Ujimasa 173
Kortenhoef, Pieter 151
Koun, Karolos 242
Kreisler, Fritz 87
Ksentini, Rachid 220–221, 225
Kyd, Thomas 5
Kyōgen 168, 188n49

La Chana (Antonia Santiago Amador) 200–201, 206
La Chana (film) 201
La Curva (Galván) 198, 205
La Fianciulla (film) 244
La Movida Madrileña 193
Landau, Jacob 63
language: French 66; of Manicheism 65
Las Casas, Bartolomé de 6
Lasso, Orlando di 4
Lebanese Rocket Society 47
The Lebanese Rocket Society: A Tribute to Dreamers (Hadjithomas and Joreige) 47
Lees, Lynn Hollen 128
Le Malade imaginaire (Molière) 220
Le Médecin malgré lui (Molière) 220
Les Aventures du dernier Abencérage (Chateaubriand) 219
Le Vilain mire (*The Peasant Doctor*) 220
L'Homme aux sandals de caoutchouc (Yacine) 223
Liberating Histories (Norton and Donnelly) 38, 45
liberation: of Algeria 223; of theater 25
light/lighting 114, 131, 137, 149, 206, 266
Lim Beng Choo 175
Liñan, Manuel 191
literature 38; apologetic 147, 160n13; dramatic 62; Dutch national 147; folk 217, 230n13; high 239; modern Greek 235, 244, 246
Litterae annuae 6
Living Theatre 223–224
logocentrism 71n5–6
L'Olimpiade (Metastasio) 241
Lope de Vega 13, 21

Lorca, Federico García 192–193
Lo Real/Le Réel/The Real (Galván) 195, 198–200
Los primeros mártires de Japón (Lope de Vega) 13

Mackrell, Judith 190
Mahlangu, Nhlanhla 94–96, 98
Mapa Teatro 40, 41–42, 43–45, 52–53
Maqamat 64
Maqoma, Gregory 91, 96
Marker, Chris 117
Marlowe, Christopher 5
Marquerie, Carlos 202
The Marriage of Figaro (Beaumarchais) 221
Marx, Karl 40–41, 170, 185n12
Marx, Peter W. 80
Marxism 65, 170
masks, and reversibility 173–174
Massine, Léonide 196
materialism 170
materialist historiography 170
Maya, Belén 191, 199, 201, 208n30
Maya, Mario 196
Mbembe, Achille 70n3
McClintock, Anne 152
McCoy, Ann 92
media: digitally sourced 26; mixed 38, 43; moving-image 106, 110, 115, 119; popular 191; print 135; scrapbook 113; socialized 266; visual 109
media archaeology: performative dimension of 262–263; retro-futuristic element 264; theater as 258–272
mediality 264
medieval 6, 175, 224
memory: color of 93, 98; public 79, 99n12; theatrical 184; traumatic 183; vocal 122
Mendoza, Antonio de 19
Ment, Eva 149–156
Merchant of Venice (Shakespeare) 5
Merrick, George 89
Metahistory (White) 37
Metastasio, Pietro 241
methods/methodology: collective creation 42; of "double critique" 69; historiographical 167–184; interpretive 157–159; scientific 170
The Methuen Drama Handbook of Theatre History and Historiography 61

Middel, Cristina de 49
Midori Group 115, 118–119
Mignolo, Walter D. 59–60, 63, 65, 66, 71n16
Mikhoels, Solomon 268
Miller, Philip 86
Mimesis: African Soldier (Akomfrah) 80, 82
Mira!/Los Zapatos Rojos (Galván) 196
miscegenation 155
Miser (Molière) 241
Mnouchkine, Ariane 227
Moctezuma II 14
modern Greek theater 234–248; birth of 241; history of 235–237, 250n16
modernism and collage 81
Mohammed, prends ta valise (Yacine) 226
Molière 63, 221, 241
Molina, Rocío 191, 194, 200–204
Molino, Antonio 244
Moonwalkers (Bardou-Jacquet) 46
Moore, John C. 190
More Sweetly Play the Dance (Kentridge) 84
Moryson, Fynes 5
Motolinía, Toribio de 6, 16, 18
Mroué, Rabih 70
multilingualism 65–86, 227
Munslow, Alun 37
Murobushi Kō 109
music: Chinese 3; flamenco 201; kora 87; piano 197; Vietnamese 3
mutual influences 1, 20
Muybridge, Eadweard 110, 112
Mwamba, Matha 48
Myers, Judith Gelman 205

Naimi, Kadour 223–224
Nara period 3
Nasser, Gamal Abdel 69
National Archives of Singapore 127–128
nationalism: affective 50; Arab 62, 219; deviant 61; Dutch 147; Pan-Arab 62, 219; patriotic 147
national theater histories 24–25
naturalism 53, 259
Navarette, Alonso 13
Nayatt School 262
the Netherlands: fantasy of conquest 152–155; fear of engulfment 152–155; interpretive methodology 157–159; rogue heroes 145–148; Specx Affair 151–152; violence and desire 149–151

Index   285

New Francophone African and Caribbean Theatres (Conteh-Morgan and Thomas) 214
newspapers 129–130; nineteenth-century archives 132; Singaporean 131
Nihongi (Chronicles of Japan) 171
Nihonjinron 171
Nikolais, Alwin 196
Nishio Minoru 180, 187n40
Nkoloso, Edward Makuka 48–49
Nō 168, 188n49
Norton, Claire 38, 45, 47
Nōsakusho (Zeami) 180
Nuzahat al-Mushtaq wa-Ghussat al-Ush-shaq fi Madinat Tiryaq l-Iraq (Daninos) 218

Oedipus the King (Sophocles) 258
Oever, Annie van den 260, 273n14
Of Lunatics, or Those Lacking Sanity (Mapa Teatro) 40, 41–42, 44, 46, 52–53
Ohnuki-Tierney, Emiko 171
Okuni (Izumo no Okuni) 10, *11*
Olusoga, David 80, 82
omote 169–170, 173, 178–179, 182, 185n6
orality 98
Origuchi Shinobu 171
Oro Viejo (Molina) 201, 204
orthodox Christianity 236
Osaka World Exposition 106–109; Hijikata Tatsumi performance at 106–109; as performance location 112–118
Othello (Shakespeare) 5
otherness and reversibility 168–171
Ottoman Empire 235, 240
Ottomans 215, 217–218
Overland Mail (Walford) 136
Owen, Wilfred 87, 97

Pagés, María 191, 201
palimpsest 90–96
Pan-Arabism 67
pantomime 3
Paparrigopoulos, Konstantinos 234
Parikka, Jussi 260, 262
past: colonial 40, 145–146, 148, 154; disciplinary 38; fragmented 234; and Galván 196–198; geopolitical 42; imperial 39; performing 51–53
patriarchy 201

pensée-autre (other thinking) 66
Pepsi Corporation 108, 112, 115–116, 120–121
performance cultures 2–4, 13, 106
performance historiography 60–64
performance space 112–118
performative locations 58
perspective: Buddhist 173; explanatory 37; interstitial 63
phenomenology 2–3, 237–238
photography 47, 110–111, 196, 263, 268
Picasso 193
Piccolos, Nikolaos 241
Plaatje, Sol 82
plays: Christian 24; Elizabethan 5; English 5; in Japan 6–7; kabuki 175; martyr 12; mystery 10, 12; radio 261; sacred 6–9, 11
Poel, William 258
poetry 64, 97, 171, 198, 225
politics: of globalization 67; identity 60; of nostalgia 66; of respectability 157
polyphonic historiography 80–81, 97
popular: culture 74n46; entertainments 217
poses 61
postcoloniality 59
Pottasch, Alan 116
Poudre d'intelligence (Yacine) 223
Pour en finir avec le jugement de dieu (Artaud) 110
Povinelli, Elizabeth 39, 45
procession 7–10, 14, 84, 86, 91, 95, 167, 176
proscenium 74n47, 229
protests 26, 84, 117, 145, 194, 206
proverbs 90
Provincializing Europe (Chakrabarty) 40, 41
public: memory 79, 99n12; storytelling 217

Quijano, Aníbal 60
Quinn, Edward 63

race, and coloniality 60
racialization 45
racism 39
rationalism 40
Ravel, Maurice 87
Raz, Jacob 176
realism 270

reception: described 1; *vs.* entangled history 1–2
regulation: building 132; fire insurance 136; theater 128, 138, 140
relativism 121, 156
remembrance 25, 82
restored behavior 261–262
Rethinking History (Journal) 37
retrospectives 117
The Revelation of Secrets 219
reversibility: acting 178–181; and class 174–181; and foreigners 171–173; as historiographical method 167–184; and international performance 181–184; and masks 173–174; and otherness 168–171; performing social roles 174–178
rhetoric: cinematic 269; of inclusion 260; West African 90
rhythm 3, 87, 92, 192, 194, 196–199, 201, 204
ritual 17, 173, 176; folk 171; performances 14–15, 217, 226; religious 167; sacred 94
rogue heroes 145–148
Rolf, Abderhalden Cortés 43
Romeo and Juliet (Shakespeare) 5
Romero, Pedro G. 197
Roth, Arlette 220
Röttger, Kati 42
Routledge Companion to Media Technology and Obsolescence 261
The Routledge Companion to Theatre and Performance Historiography 80
Royal Mining Company 43

Sabela, Bartek 49
Sachs, Edwin Thomas 131
Sackville, Thomas 5
sacrifice 17–18
The Sacrifice of Abraham 17
Sadgrove, Philip 218
safety: ensuring/insuring theater 136–140; imperial aspiration for 135
Sahagún, Bernardino de 6, 14, 17
Saint-Simon, Henri de 194
Sakabe Megumi 168–170
Salah El-Din Al-Ayoubi (Al-Haddad) 219
Salas, Roger 200
Salau, Mohammed Bashir 89
Salhi, Kamal 225
Samudaripen (mass killing) 198–200
Sansour, Larissa 47–48

Santiago Amador, Antonia *see* La Chana
Sarugaku dangi (Zeami) 174
Satia, Priya 39
Satie, Erik 87
Saura, Carlos 195, 201
scenery 137, 139
Schechner, Richard 261
Schiller, Friedrich 225
Schneider, Rebecca 262, 263–264
Schwitters, Kurt 85
Scott, Sir Walter 219
scripts: African 82; of *maqamat* 64; preserved 17; scenography as 271; Shakespearean 265
Second World War 147, 149
Sellali, Ali 220
Serpell, Namwali 49
Shabangu, Mncedisi 88
shadow puppetry 218
Shakespeare, William 5
Shetterly, Margot Lee 46
shōgun 10
Sibisi, Thuthuka 86, 93
Since I Can Remember (Wooster Group) 262
Singapore: colonial modernization agenda in 128; Municipal Ordinance 1887 131; National Archives of 127–128; newspapers 131; theater history of British colonial 129; theater law 132–133
Slauerhoff, Jan Jacob 26, 145–162
slavery 51–52
"Slough Media" (Schneider) 263–264
social roles, performing 174–178
Sohst, Theodore 137–138
soto 169, 174, 182
Soviet Union 48
Space Exodus (Sansour) 47, 50
Spanish Tragedy (Kyd) 5
spectators 4–7, 12–13, 16–18, 87, 97, 119, 198, 201, 205
Specx, Jacques 150, 151
Specx Affair 151–152
stage 186n32; Algerian 220; Arab 61; cavernous 84; European 12, 245–246; practices 244; Spanish 197
Stein, Gertrude 264
Stoler, Laura 129, 136
storytelling 74n46, 226, 264; Islamic 219; private 217; public 217
Straits Fire Insurance Company 137
strategic unweaving 2

Strauven, Wanda 261–262
studio: Asbestos Studio 116, 119, 122; Kyoto film studios 120
Stuyvesant, Peter 147
surrealism 49, 117, 204
The Talisman (Scott) 219
tanztheater 205–206
Taratu el arab (*The Revenge of the Arabs*) 219
tatemae 169
Taylor, Diana 17
technology 260, 265–267; cultural 128; digital 52; film-projection 118; performative dimension of 261
The Tempest (Shakespeare) 258
temple 3–4, 14, 180
Terauchi Naoko 4
Terzopoulos, Theodoros 242
theater law 132–133
The Theatres of Morocco, Algeria and Tunisia (Amine and Carlson) 61, 214
Theories of Surplus Value (Marx) 40
Thomas, Dominic 214
The Thousand and One Nights 219, 220
Tiefland (1954, The Lowlands) 199
Time's Monster (Satia) 39
Titus Andronicus (Shakespeare) 5
Titus the Nobleman of Japan 24
tourism 192
Trachtenbuch (Weiditz) 21, *21, 22, 23*
tragedies: human 130; theater fire 131
translation 1, 5, 58–59, 63–64, 221, 223
Triumphs and Laments: A Project for Rome 84
Tsing, Anna L. 52, 55n39, 58
Turia, Ricardo de 21
Turkish Karagöz 246
Tzara, Tristan 88

uchi 169, 172, 182, 185n6
United States 46, 48, 117, 130–131, 193, 227, 229
universalism 39, 60, 62, 228
ura 169, 173, 178–179, 182, 185n6
Ursonate (Schwitters) 85–86

vanguardistas 191
Velestinlis, Rigas 241
Victoria Theater 138–139
video 52, 84, 261–263, 265–268
violence 149–151

Walford, Cornelius 136
Washburn, Anne 265
Wayang(s) 127, 131, 135–136, 141n1
Weber, Samuel 258
Weheliye, Alexander 45
Weibye, Hanna 200
Weiditz, Christoph 20–21, *21, 22, 23*
Weinbaum, Alys Eve 41, 46, 51–52
Werner, Michael 1
Westernisation 69
What Comes after Entanglement? (Giraud) 53
White, Hayden 37
White Anglo-Saxon Protestant culture 46
whiteness 82
Whyte, Murray 93
Wooster Group 268–269
The World's War (Olusoga) 82
World War I: and colonialism 81–86; people of color in 79; role of Africans in 79–80, 82; role of Indians in 80
World War II 171, 245
Wozzeck (Berg) 90–92
The Wretched of the Earth (Fanon) 64, 68
writing: history as disentanglement 234–248; nonhistorical 39

Yacine, Kateb 222–223, 225, 226
Yeoh, S. A. 135
Yezza, Hicham 213
yin/yang principle 3
Yokomichi Mario 173
Yoshida Teigo 172
Yoshimitsu 176–177, 180
Youssef Najm, Mohamed 62–63
Yunusa, Yusufu 89
Yusa Michiko 180

Zambia 48–49
Zárate, Fernando de 21
Zatania, Estela 198
Zeami Motokiyo 173, 174, 175, 177
Zero Jigen (performance–art group) 116
Zielinski, Siegfried 259
Zimmermann, Bénédicte 1
Zohn, Patricia 92

For Product Safety Concerns and Information please contact our EU
representative GPSR@taylorandfrancis.com
Taylor & Francis Verlag GmbH, Kaufingerstraße 24, 80331 München, Germany

www.ingramcontent.com/pod-product-compliance
Lightning Source LLC
Chambersburg PA
CBHW051351290426
44108CB00015B/1965